Republic of China – Centennial Plate
(Cover Image)

On September 17th 2012, 93 year old retired British Captain Gerald Fitzpatrick made a trip with his wife from Britain to Washington D.C. to give his belated thanks to the family of the late General Liu Fang-Wu, who saved him and over 7,000 British soldiers in the Battle of Yenangyaung in Burma 70 years ago.

Major General Lee Hsien-Sheng, Director General of the Defense Mission of the Taipei Economic and Cultural Representative Office in the U.S.A., presented Captain Fitzpatrick a R.O.C. centennial commemorative plate on behalf of National Defence Minister Kao Hua-Chu to thank Captain Fitzpatrick for his decades worth of efforts in writing books and giving talks to preserve and restore the historical truth, as a witness of the courageous rescue of the British forces by the Chinese Expedtitionary Force.

On April 17th 1942, a large number of British forces were encircled in the oil fields in Yenangyaung, Burma, by the Japanese, who used outflanking tactics to deny the British any chance of escape. The situation was dire, and that was when the regiment Commander of the 113th Regiment of the Chinese Expeditionary Force, Liu Fang-Wu, was summoned to lead his men to an emergency rescue. At nightfall on April 19th, after intense fighting, the Chinese Expeditionary Force completely defeated the Japanese and saved our 7,000 British soldiers and more than 500 British and American journalists, missionaries and their families, who were trapped in desperate conditions. Major General Lee Hsien-Sheng said that there were only about 800 men in the Chinese regiments, and 500 of them were either injured or killed and that the degree of their sacrifice and valor merits historical recognition.

Major General Lee said, he is extremely proud of General Liu Fang-Wu, who was among the 6th class to graduate from the Whampoa

Military Academy. he said that among the generals who fought in the war against Japan, Regiment Commander Liu Fang-Wu, who fought in the Battle of Yenangyaung, is a national hero in the hearts of the Chinese people and that he was happy to witness this part of history being told today. Major General Lee also expressed his deepest gratitude to Captain Fitzpatrick for being responsible to history and restoring it by speaking out for the Chinese military despite the mainstream opinion in Britain. Major General Lee further said Captain Fitzpatrick's outspokenness and sense of gratitude are a reflection of a soldier's pursuit of the values of affection and loyalty.

Ministry of National Defense

★ ★

December 24, 2012

Captain Gerald Fitzpatrick (Rtd)
Royal Army
United Kingdom

Dear CPT Fitzpatrick,

    Firstly, on behalf of Minister Kao Hua-Chu of National Defense and Admiral Lin Jan-Yi, Chief of the General Staff, as well as every member of the Republic of China Armed Forces, I would like to extend our gratitude for your dedication to conserving the rarely known part of WWII history in the Pacific Theater. Without your hard work, the true story of the 1942 Burma Campaign would have diminished in the tide of time.

    We here at the MND, R.O.C., appreciate every opportunity to manifest and maintain the true WWII history of our predecessors. Your masterpieces are undoubtedly solid evidence. We also admire your holding of steadfast stance regardless all the odds you have faced in the past seven decades. We are convinced that the truth of the Battle of Yenangyaung will be forever remembered.

    With all the respect, I wish to have a chance to meeting you here in Taipei in January or February 2013 at your convenience. It is our honor to meet with a veteran like you who have fought with the R.O.C. Armed Forces during WWII and exchange ideas with you. The Point of Contact is COL Chin Chen-Yuan, our defense attaché to United Kingdom,   We wish Mrs. Fitzpatrick and you a Merry Christmas and Happy New Year, and good health and prosperity in the years to come.

                                                                  Sincerely,

                                                                  Lt. Gen. Han Gan-Sen
                                                                  R.O.C. Air Force
                                                                  Deputy Chief of the General Staff for Intelligence

General Liu Fang-Wu.
Courtesy of the family – James H. Liu, Margaret L. Sun, Robert W. Liu and Jenny Tsai

CHINESE SAVE BRITS – in BURMA

(Battle of Yenangyaung)

Patterned General Slim's 'CHINDITS'

Dedicated to the family of General Liu Fang-Wu
Commander of the Chinese Army Expeditionary Force
in Burma 1942

Captain Gerald Fitzpatrick

© G. Fitzpatrick, 2013

Published by Fitzpatrick Publishing

All rights reserved. No part of this book may be reproduced, adapted, stored in a retrieval system or transmitted by any means, electronic, mechanical, photocopying, or otherwise without the prior written permission of the author.

The rights of G. Fitzpatrick to be identified as the author of this work have been asserted in accordance with the Copyright, Designs and Patents Act 1988.

A CIP catalogue record for this book is available from the British Library.

ISBN 978-0-9572783-1-8

Book and cover layout & design by Clare Brayshaw

Prepared and printed by:

York Publishing Services Ltd
64 Hallfield Road
Layerthorpe
York YO31 7ZQ

Tel: 01904 431213

Website: www.yps-publishing.co.uk

CONTENTS

Preface		x
Foreword		xiv
Chapter 1	Get Yourself an Irish Mother	1
Chapter 2	Commissioning	17
Chapter 3	Chicanery and Machinations of War	36
Chapter 4	The Comedy of Lamentable Command	48
Chapter 5	Where is the War?	69
Chapter 6	Now it's War – British Style	77
Chapter 7	Churchill – 'Washed his Hands'	99
Chapter 8	Defunct – Discarded – Disintegrating	111
Chapter 9	Chinese Delight	127
Chapter 10	British Hierarchy Meeting Adversity	133
Chapter 11	Endurance – Swim – Sea Snakes	144
Chapter 12	Wicked Hill to Heaven	172
Chapter 13	A Hard School	192
Chapter 14	The Joys of Ceylon	198
Chapter 15	Delights of Delhi – Settling In	209
Chapter 16	Change of Commanding Officer – Delhi	224
Chapter 17	Farewell to India	242
Chapter 18	Meet Frank Stott – P.O.W. – Rangoon Jail	258
Chapter 19	Montgomery's British Army of the Rhine	276
Chapter 20	30 Corps – with Brian Horrocks	285

Chapter 21	Rhine Army Headquarters – with Brian Horrocks	290
Chapter 22	Decision Time and Skiing	300
Chapter 23	'Manny' Shinwell – The Dregs	306
Chapter 24	Rhine Bridges – Viewing	317
Chapter 25	Mama's Boy	320
Appendices		335
Supplement	"Foresee The Future By Reviewing The Past"	353

ENDORSEMENT
MR J.E. MAJOR B.E.M.

Owston Ferry

I served in Burma throughout the long withdrawal, from December 1941 to May 1942, with the 2nd Battalion, the Kings Own Yorkshire Light Infantry, and never once parted from the regiment.

Four days after arriving on the Indian border at Kohima, having starved and thirsted for many weeks, I was evacuated to Brielly with malaria and dysentery.

I have read the galley proof of the book *No Mandalay No Maymyo (79 Survive)*, by Captain Gerald Fitzpatrick and, not before time, the book records all action as I remember it precisely.

I was proud to be one of those to survive, and am amazed to see revealed subsequently, the influences of the government, particularly the indifference shown to those in command, by the British Prime Minister. Also, the shabby treatment, by the British, of Australia and China, including the excellent Chinese army, the one which relieved us in a desperate situation, was deplorable in the extreme.

I am now aged 84 and throughout my life I have regretted the loss of so many of my good friends and colleagues in this action, undertaken as members of the British armed forces.

J.E. Major, BEM

PREFACE

There's nothing more certain than that any setback or reversal, suffered by the British, through Government error or misjudgement; it will be overlooked; 'as being of no consequence'. The laudable phrase used as the get-out; "The old fashioned British cover up", is synonymous with, "Airbrushed out!" Both axioms are appropriate terminology for my serious active service under several incompetent, much decorated, and applauded Military leaders throughout World War Two.

Of Catholic Irish stock, and from the underprivileged existence of my childhood, I was to meet with success beyond my wildest dreams, serving into my tenth year in the British Army; as a Sapper for the first twelve months, and later, as a Commissioned Infantry Officer.

With good reason, my earlier youthful intent was to join with the very active pre-war, Irish Republican Army. At the age of twenty, in 1939, six weeks after the outbreak of World War Two; on the 17th October 1939, a man named Hitler changed all of that, and I freely volunteered to serve a British King and Country. My specialist employment in engineering would have justified exemption from military service.

Shattered, on day three of my arrival at the Royal Engineers, Brompton Barracks, Chatham. The fact that I could be threatened in this way nullified all future allegiance to; 'anything or anybody, of British Control or Authority'.

Posted to join with a London Territorial unit, which was overseen by a 'poncy' crew of pre-war Territorial Officers, I had my first experience of bigotry, and upper class priggishness. It was as though two distinct levels of existence were the norm.

As a twenty year old, my background comprised of serious Technical College study, followed by five years engineering employment, accomplished alongside respectful senior men of the highest calibre. This was coupled with demanding night school attendance, and achieving National Certificate standard. Success at rugby, swimming, and boxing, had shaped me as a reasonably competent individual.

Winning the London Divisional Swimming Championships, at Chelsea baths, and overcoming the inevitable, boxing champion's challenge, established me as, 'a bit of a something', within the unit.

Months of RE, Field Company training, in mid 1940, embracing the period of the Dunkirk fiasco, signalled the extermination of Allied forces. The defeat and complete annihilation of British forces, in Europe, meant to all and sundry, throughout the world, the war was over, and Britain defeated.

A beaten nation, the French Government capitulated; a large portion of the country becoming known as Vichy France, and embraced within the Axis powers.

Britain was a beaten nation, with its military structure in complete disarray. Battalions, Brigades, and Divisions, were in tatters, with complete frailty in Government, and Military control. The Axis powers, Germany and Italy, with little opposition, could have attacked, walked through, and occupied Britain.

Having British forces, and the nation, contained and secured on the nearby British Isles. Hitler, 'sadly for him', visualised another seemingly easy conquest, withdrew his forces from the Western Front, and turned his attention to Russia, in the east. British Prime Minister, Churchill, the eternal opportunist, exploited Hitler's catastrophic mistake to the full.

Compensating for the loss of numerous officers, killed or captured, at Dunkirk, brought rapid promotion for survivors, and caused a shortage of junior infantry officers.

Successful in my quest for a commission, I was posted to 163 Officer Cadet Training Unit, (formerly The Artist's Rifles), situated at Shorncliff Camp, a short distance from Folkestone. Fearing invasion, in August 1940, we became housed in railway goods wagons, stretched along the Ferry Jetty at Folkestone Harbour.

Twelve months commissioned, and I was posted by the most detestable of COs to; unnamed, "A peace station in a tropical destination". Confined and cocooned, in troopship, and train, with no news of the Eastern war progress, it took three months, 4th December 1941, to 5th March 1942, to reach Rangoon, in Burma. It was here, I met with catastrophe.

Joined with an emaciated and virtually mutilated Battalion, I had no idea of the failings, and frailty, of the recently appointed inept Army Commander, and the subsequent treachery of a British Prime Minister.

Through the doctor son, of a doctor joined with our unit in Burma, and resulting from my first book, 'No Mandalay, No Maymyo': I received startling revelations of events, including the ultimate in perfidious action, carried out by the ineffable, and indifferent, Churchill appointed, Army Commander.

Incidents of an unpalatable nature, committed by British Troops of any kind, are not openly acceptable, or admitted, by the British Government; They are 'Airbrushed Out'. To admit the necessity of such action would mean revealing the reasons, and possible Military shortcomings, in causing such a necessity: I have the satisfaction of ensuring my own experiences, including dispatching disidents and they are not pleasant. British press readily besmirch, and the Government hides behind time! – Let's overlook it?

The spectacular action, undertaken by a Chinese Army Expeditionary Force Regiment, under Chinese Army General, Liu Fang-Wu Command, is given no credence whatsoever by Churchill's chosen Commander, General Alexander. Alexander proves to be disgusting beyond measure in his Memoirs. He belittles, and denies, all action undertaken by the most excellent Chinese Army.

'The Freedom of Information Act' of recent years, reveals the treachery carried out by America, under President Roosevelt. In attempting to 'save his own skin', during the period through which, 'The World', considered Britain moribund. The USA Secretary of State, Cordell Hull was secretly undertaking peace negotiations with the Japanese: (Copy of the shabby conduct of affairs is obtainable from; USA Information Resource Center, London.)

The outstanding recording, and observations, of the same 'Peace Negotiations' are made by the brilliant Japanese Professor, Iguchi Takeo. He refers in his writings; as, "Demystifying Pearl Harbour".

Returning from duties in the East, following a brief rest period, I was posted to the post war ruin that was Germany. The country was devastated; it seemed that nothing had survived the onslaught of the Allies attack. Following brief attachments to minor holding units, and staff duties, I was moved forward to beyond my wildest dreams, and with not one hour of tuition, to hold the uppermost Staff Captain appointment in the British forces; as General Staff Officer, Grade III, (Operations), BAOR: (British Army of the Rhine).

At Headquarters, BAOR, Montgomery was a General disliked by many, and I was pleased to see him depart. I was blessed however to serve twice under his successor, General Brian Horrocks, first at 30 Corps, and later, at Rhine Army.

Unforgettable, I was central to the development of what became known as 'The Cold War', a tepid period, in the Russian/Allies relationship. It was coupled with the run down of the British Army, and general demobilisation of conscript troops. Persistent incidents occurring along inter-zone borders, brought about, firstly, the closing of the autobahn, and later, the rail links to Berlin.

The outcome resulted rapidly, into: 'The Berlin Air Lift'.

Disgusted by the perfunctory visit made by, the British Government, Defence Minister, and his insulting seventeen force commanders; (medic-tanks-signals-etc), followed by an equally off hand performance, by his Governmental, Shadow Defence Minister, I defiantly, 'Pulled a Sting' on the man.

After almost ten years of pure dedication, I was sorry to leave an occupation of absolute joy, as matters were taken out of my hands: It was many years later that I was made aware that, in some underhand British Governmental manner; I was placed, 'On Reserve', for a further ten years. A further Governmental Decree ensured that, because my Army Service terminated at a certain date, I was to receive no pension; Others departing, before and at a later date, did receive pensions.

FOREWORD

Time and tolerance are of great consequence in recording the past. Grubby Generals, and Politicians, along with their acolytes, can hide for only so long. At the age of ninety-three, I have tolerated time, and have no fears in revealing the truth of my long existence. There have been good, and there have been bad times for me to endure. And why should you not appreciate them with me?

Being born is simply moving into the world of acceptance. Whatever is on offer has to be enjoyed, 'that is all there is'. There is no such thing as rich or poor, abundance or famine, and one can live or die pondering. In our mid seventies, and sat in the General Elliott pub, opposite Leeds markets, Bernard, my late, eighteen months junior brother, was the first ever of our family to grade one of our parents; Father! He was unkind in the extreme.

Enduring the direst of the post World War – One depression, throughout the 1920s and 30s, general expectations were limited to; Can you hold your job?

With a highly educated Irish Catholic mother, she sought for better. School holidays at her County Mayo homeland, in the West of Ireland, revealed a wider gird of worldliness.

Sound in physique; at the age of fifteen, I trained with the City of Leeds, Olympic swimming squad, and with stamina above most, my father considering me good enough, and wanted me to take up professional boxing.

As war broke out in September, 1939 at the age of twenty, (on 10th August), I was perfect material for the Royal Engineers. Avoiding a possible, 'Company essential retention order', because of my work standard, I enlisted voluntarily, on 17th October 1939, along with my works colleague. Hopefully, we might both serve together throughout the war?

We were shocked, however, at suffering the vilest and foulest possible deed of overbearing indifference, at Chatham Barracks. David Williams, my chum and I, were parted, and met but once, later in our lives.

In mid 1940, my mantle of 'Mr Nobody' was shed, as the might of the Axis Powers overcame the ill equipped and distraught British Forces, fleeing Europe through the port of Dunkirk. Attempting to replace missing infantry officers, a 'Trawling Officer?' scouring for potential replacements, was released by the War Office. Being one of twelve Sappers, undertaking trade tests at Chatham, and considered 'suitable material', we were made the offer of, 'Selection Testing'.

Tested to the limit, at the Officer Cadet Training Unit, I became one of the thirty per cent successful candidates, and was commissioned on 7th December 1940. Shuffled between three battalion units for twelve months, in England and Ireland, there came the ultimate insult for one who could have willingly deserted, and joined with the Irish Republican Army. With no choice, and by the most obnoxious of Commanding Officers, along with eight other Subalterns, given no designated destination, and with no possibility of obtaining further information, I was posted to; "A battalion situated in a peace station in the tropics". At Gourock, near Glasgow, we boarded SS Strathallan, the luxurious P and O liner, bound for who knows where?

In a convoy of about seventy ships, we set sail on the 4th December 1941, and within three days, had the absolute joy of seeing a notice board message saying, in effect, "The Japanese have bombed the American Navy Base at Hawaii". It meant that after British involvement in war for two years and three months, the Americans were being invited to join in with the struggling British Allies.

In three months of travel by sea and rail, never once was our eventual destination revealed, although we did, after three months, eventually arrive at the Burmese port of Rangoon, to disembark on the 5th March 1942.

It was incomprehensible to imagine the seemingly, dregs of a battalion we joined with, squat in a bomb crater near the village of Hlegu, (approx 30 miles to the east of Rangoon).

Reared in penury, I had no idea of 'Upper Bracket skulduggery', as practiced at higher levels, but I was to learn. 'British-ness' is determined, in that if matters go right, the 'Top Brass' will claim it as their own. If it fails, in adversity, out comes the British 'stiff upper lip', and scowling brow; whoa betide the 'Chief'; I was to experience all of this! Forsaken and discarded by a much vaunted and highly regarded British Prime Minister, busted, blighted, and maligned with Political Chicanery and Inept Commanders, I had to survive!

Throughout the next three years in India, exploiting the system, and being a specialist weapons expert, I assumed the mantle of, 'a loose cannon'. I covered almost every inch; From Srinager in the north, where I sailed in a houseboat, to Ceylon, (Sri Lanka), in the south, where I met with Mountbatten; and from Bombay in the west, to Assam in the east, where I lived in heaven. Opening the doors of the Taj Mahal, in Agra, in order to view it by moonlight, was very special.

Publishing my first book, 'No Mandalay, No Maymyo', in 2001, at the cost of, what I consider to be, a fortune; What a treat! I could never have anticipated the euphoric reaction emanating from the effort, by so many diverse people. As is the way with military men, few of my former colleagues, now departed, or in their late eighties, could adequately relate the deplorable neglect, and indifference suffered, in the enigmatic 1941/42 Burma campaign. They could now, and proudly did so!

The book project was spurred on following vilification I suffered at the malignancy of the 'Observer' newspaper; Editors, Donald Threlfall, and Anthony Howard.

Resulting from his reading my first book and 'out of the blue', the sordid truth emerged. The breakthrough came from a retired professional gentleman; himself the son of a rare doctor; the one joining with our unit in the most bizarre, and unusual of circumstances, in Burma, over sixty-five years beforehand. Prestigious residents of Burma, the doctor's family were central in the pomp and circumstances prevailing amongst colonial governors, and not all of it was pleasurable.

Failure, or reluctance, of British Governmental backup, in any theatre of operation, is seldom allowed to be questioned. The fact that the Republic of China Army Expeditionary Force operation, at Yenangyaung, saved numerous British lives, was cast into obscurity for some reason, by both Alexander, the army commander, and Prime Minister Churchill.

Attempting face-saving expediency, Churchill conveniently conjoined the two distinctly differing periods of the Burma war; (The damned, and humiliating withdrawal, of 1941/42); (And the subsequent success of the trained, equipped, and well provisioned 1943/45 force). The two completely differing campaigns became patronisingly recognised under the one consolidating title;

"THE FORGOTTEN ARMY": -
THEY WERE TWO COMPLETELY SEPARATE
AND DIFFERING CAMPAIGNS

Thank goodness the dear departed friends from my overseas draft; Jimmy Ableson – Bill Riddle – Stuart Renton – Tim Watson. Did not know of Churchill's belittlement;
GOD BLESS THEM

American bombing of Japan, in 1945, caught me out, when on one month of home leave, back in England, from India. The war virtually ceased, and I was diverted to Germany, to join the British Army of the Rhine, and have an absolute ball!

Following a brief period at a holding unit, I was opened out to shear joy. I held a series of General Staff appointments; Starting at Montgomery's BAOR, HQ. My greater privilege was meeting with General Brian Horrocks, at 30 Corps, and later at HQ Rhine Army; Witnessing the start of the Berlin Airlift, and living close to the beginning of the Cold War.

By this time, and with nine years of most testing service behind me, I was a very different animal to the newly commissioned subordinate boy. In my wildest dreams, I could never have envisaged entering the Houses of Parliament, and 'pulling a scam', on that most detestable and vitriolic of parliamentarians; Defence Secretary, 'Manny' Shinwell.

By far! – 'The New Look' ladies, dress remains my greatest memory of that brief and eventful visit to London, to which I was conveyed in a very cold RAF Dakota aircraft.

* * *

DEGENERATES!

Military journals, and magazines, usually welcome and publicise details of books, relevant to actions undertaken within their orbit. In the case of my first book; "No Mandalay, No Maymyo", I met with reluctance in the three main organisations in which I served. Not one commented on my book.

Royal Engineers, (17th October 1939); Having commented on the dastardly action of an Orderly Room Sergeant, the man I met with on my third day at Chatham, the 'Sapper' magazine editor, was surprised to find; "He did not have a reviewer".

Kings Own Yorkshire Light Infantry, (7th December 1940); Avoiding me, and not seeking to hear my story, whilst accepting the publication of distorted reports, contained in leading newspapers, led by The Observer, I was virtually 'blackballed' from the Regimental Officers Club. The Regimental Colonel, a man I never knew, and one who did not know me from Adam, was however coerced by some woman at The Sunday Telegraph, into commenting unfavourably, and patronising. Nothing of my book was mentioned in the Regimental Magazine; "The Bugle!"

Burma Star Association, (5th March 1942), I disembarked Rangoon. The Editorial Committee of the Burma campaign magazine; "Dekho!" saw fit to ignore my first book. Better equipped, and with justification, I now disclose the tragic shortcomings, incompetence and indifference, in overall British Government and Military Command, in the Burma 1941-2 campaign. Unimpeachable detail is contained within this book.

* * *

Expedition Cancelled

Receiving a surprise invitation to visit Burma, (Myanmar), in early 2005, and in the process of preparing a personal itinerary, I was stopped in my tracks.

The Rangoon based representative of my Travel Agent enquired; "Was I the Second Lieutenant who? – Knowing what was coming, I turned to my wife, and said; "The trip's off!"

Dacoits had shot my Corporal, 'Gigger' Lee, as his niece says; "In the bum!" I commanded extermination of the Dacoits.

1

GET YOURSELF AN IRISH MOTHER

Never in a million years could one imagine that a simple kind and sensible act, carried out on an Irish church forecourt, would influence decisions, and dramatic actions I was to make throughout my life. As a lively but much deprived ten-year old, coming from a humble poverty ridden working class background and with no idea where life might take me, I had negligible prospects. However, the fortunes of life were to take me on a surprisingly long and adventurous journey. From my sheltered and inhibited world, I was to have success, far beyond my wildest dreams. The core of my life was shaped, and expanded, in one short episode, when on holiday with my mother, at her childhood Irish homestead.

The enlightening incident followed Sunday Mass, as we stood on the parish communal square outside St Patrick's Church, in Newport, County Mayo. The four of us kids; brother, Bernard, and sisters, Kathleen and Joan, standing beside mother. We saw what appeared to be two whales escaping from a sardine tin. Two members of the Irish Garda, an Inspector and Sergeant, emerged from the small Panda police car. They were huge, a size of men the likes of which we did not normally see back in England.

With hats and jackets suitably adjusted, they made straight towards mother, and ascertained that she was indeed Mrs Eileen Elizabeth Fitzpatrick, and that we were her children. They went on to establish that we were in fact, in the long much overstayed eighth week, of our scheduled two weeks holiday, before seriously declaring the purpose of their visit:

We have an enquiry from the City of Leeds, Education Department:

They want to know. "Are your children receiving an education whilst in Ireland?"

This was a most forbidding approach, as our only visit to the school was to learn that my mother, formerly Eileen Elizabeth O'Grady, had been the star student of the school over all times, although there was never a thought of our attending the school. With new interests, there was so much more to do on the modest farmstead.

As the child I was, this sounded like real trouble. It appeared that our father, who remained back in England, had, in his usual manner, washed his hands of the matter. We were suddenly uplifted, from simple nobodies, to being the centre of attention for the whole parish. Not enjoying the somewhat daunting situation, and in a state of apprehension, I was dreading to see handcuffs appear.

Mother had not been the best of pupils at the local school for no good reason. She made no mention of the humbling existence, or of the indolent, psychological misfit of a father, we had left behind in Leeds. She said proudly; "They're turning the hay, and helping to stack". "They milk the cows and feed the calves". "They're loading turf into creels at the bog, leading the donkeys, and stacking turf by the house". "They help in escorting heifers to Moran's bull". "They've joined with the men in sea fishing". "They dig and prepare vegetables from the allotment". "They gather eggs from the rough layers". "They know how to bake a potato cake". "And we did Reek Sunday last weekend". (We had climbed Croagh Patrick, the 2512 ft holy mountain, on the last Sunday of July). "Is that enough?

With a whimsical glint in his eye; "That is indeed enough!" said the Inspector. "There now sergeant, isn't that great now?" "Isn't that the most wonderful of educations?" "We'll let the people in Leeds know of this". Hardly able to believe my ears; The inspector thanked mother, wished us well for the remainder of the holiday, and went on his way. I had no idea how much this brief, and simple communication was to influence, and have so profound an affect, throughout the remainder of my life.

This was by no means the end of it, as we swam totally un-harnessed in beautiful Clew Bay; ninety year olds still remember my rocking the rowing boat, and climbing the nearby, former Pirate Queen, Granuaile's castle. With no more than a short stick in hand, to apply steerage, we sat back on the haunches, and rode donkeys on the hill behind the house. At one and a half times the size of a normal donkey, Kelly's ass was by far the biggest and fastest of the mounts. Being here was like being in Heaven! It was to be many years before I fully appreciated the value of the inspiring Irish experiences. By then, I was to be in a position of command, and thankfully, able to apply the wisdom and the psychological logic imparted in an Irish churchyard.

From being a fifteen year old apprentice engineer, at the manufacturer of railway carriage locks, I progressed to the highest level of workshop skills, as, 'a tool-room apprentice'. Moving on, to become a design draughtsman in hydraulics, and aiming for a Batchelor of Science degree, my life was interrupted with the long anticipated declaration of war with Germany; on 3rd September 1939; I was aged 20 years, and one month.

Prime Minister Neville Chamberlain declared; "We are now in a state of war with Germany!" This new challenging situation was to over-ride the determined IRA intentions I had nurtured for some time. With the world changing around me, and enjoying a prime physical condition, I knew that I could become a good soldier. The problem was, in escaping the almost inevitable claim being made by my employer; 'for my essential military exemption'; owing to war work.

Following four or five weeks of deliberations with my friend and workmate, David Williams, the two of us decided that we were not going to become 'tied slaves', and remain at the whim of an employer, 'commandeered, and commanded,' on the home front.

War gripped Britain in a manor long anticipated, although the country was greatly under prepared. News-films had been shown over recent years, demonstrating mass rallies of Nazis, held throughout Germany. Nazi youth gatherings, staged at countrywide camps looked inviting, and most impressive; with nothing similar in Britain, we envied them. Ignored by the remainder of Europe, was the awesome and rapid development of Nazi aggression. As little as four years following the 1918 armistice of World War One, Hitler started his rise to power with the infamous Munich Beer Hall Putsch. He succeeded on 8th November 1923. Having overseen the murder of his rival, Ernst Rohm, by the dreaded SS, on 31st January 1933, along with hundreds of other top Nazis, in what became known as 'The Night of the Long Knives'; Hitler became Chancellor of Germany, as early as 30th June 1934.

The signs were there; On 20th February 1938, Mr. Anthony Eden resigned as British Foreign Secretary over; 'The Policy of Appeasement'. Eden foretold coming events, particularly following Adolf Hitler's earlier,15th September 1935 decree, relegating Jews, to 'sub-human-status'. There was no significant or urgent reaction shown to Eden's desperate gesture. On the 9th November 1938, it was 'Kristallnacht' in Germany. This was the night Nazis burned 267 synagogues, destroying thousands of Jewish homes and businesses. The smashing of glass in the windows of shops, and business premises, gave the night its name.

It was not easy to keep tabs on events, but they continued a-pace. Having completely shattered the, 'Four Powers Munich Peace Pact', made between; Britain/France/Germany/and Italy, on 29th September 1938, the split was made. Germany and a little later, Italy, formed the aggressive and powerful, 'Axis Powers'. The belligerence was there to see by all, except the dyed in the wool British Government. Britain and France became the struggling, 'Allied Powers'. Germany, the strong man of Europe, totally ignored the recently made, (23rd August 1939) Peace Pact, with Russia, and furthermore, blatantly ignored the futile Pact between Britain and France, made as recent as 31st March 1939, whereby they pledged support for Poland against German aggression. The fat was truly, in the fire!

The writing had been on the wall for several years, and the man in the street was in no doubt that Germany was mobilising and training for war. Italy's, Il Duce, Benito Mussolini was modelling his indifferent army, on similar lines. War was imminent, and Anthony Eden appears to be the sole Parliamentarian to have reacted.

The long years of slump, and depression, continued to impede America, the country was reeling from the notorious Wall Street Crash of 1929. USA was mainly comprised, and controlled, by Italian, German, and the numerous anti-British Irish immigrants; (They had memories of years long past). The Germans and Italians sympathised with, and supported the Axis Powers. The Irish remembered their Home Country's Potato Famine, seventy years earlier. This delicate situation, with so many hostile immigrants, left America sitting on the fence. However, 'Uncle Sam' sought to profit from the, possible, remote conflict. America badly needed money!

On the 17 October 1939, six weeks after the war declaration, on departing the office, my work colleague, David Williams and I, volunteered for service with the Royal Engineers; Me as Number 1882721, and David 1882722. It was some time before I was made to realise the awesome significance of that single digit, defining seniority. Confident that joining together in this manner, it was not unreasonable to anticipate, or expect, that the two of us would continue serving together throughout the war.

Feeling content with my experience to date, and happy to escape the dull workaday routine, the new-found freedom of life seemed good, particularly with a chum with whom to serve out my army days. However, I was sadly, and bitterly disillusioned, in less than one week of army service. I found my life, and all that I considered justified and honourable beliefs, shattered beyond all measure.

Lists of postings from Chatham RE, Brompton Barracks, were saddening. In all happiness, and contentment, David and I had been there for only three days; with a shortage of uniforms, we remained, still wearing civilian clothing; David was listed to go to Wales, and me, to Chelsea, London.

It was obvious that we had a major problem, and not unreasonably, approached the Orderly Room, where we had words with the Sergeant in charge. It was clearly an easy matter for an ORS to rearrange destinations, in order that we might go together to one station, in the same way, and in the same good faith, that we had joined with; His Imperial Majesty's Armed Forces.

There was venom in it, as the sergeant barked; -

"If you are not out of this office in one minute, you will be in the guardroom, for insolence!"

This rebuke, by a uniformed senior soldier, was the most violent reaction I had ever met with. To deny me a voice, being treated like a heap of shit, I was mortified for the first time in my life. I considered it to be sacrilegious, humiliating, and one problem that I could do nothing to redress; To be criminal, totally unforgivable, and, most certainly, never to be forgotten, or forgiven. Stamped for life, each with a Regimental number, two proud, sensitive, and highly educated twenty-year-olds, were instantly, dehumanized; Now total nonentities, to be treated as chattels, at the whim and fancy of; 'Any man of higher standing, or military rank'.

Having a denigrated time-served, World War-One husband, penalising her into poverty, my mother should have upbraided me for enlisting into a British military force. She had lost her brother, Thomas O'Grady, shot at the door of the family homestead, by Churchill's, 'Rag-Tag and Bobtail', Black and Tan irregulars;

Formed in 1920, an unaffiliated set of unemployed and ex-Public Schoolboy 'Hoo-Ray Henry's, were shooting haphazardly at any moving Irishman, as though shooting wild boar. Lieutenant-Colonel Gerald Smyth, in a speech at Listowel, on 19th June 1920, is reported to have said, -"We are going to have sport now". – "The best house in the locality is to be commandeered, the occupants thrown into the gutter. Let them die there – the more the merrier". – "The more you shoot, the better I will like you" – "You may make mistakes occasionally and innocent persons may be shot, but that cannot be helped, and you are bound to get the right party some time".

Another prominent 'Rabble Force Commander' was General Arthur Percival, whose force accounted for possibly 4,000 Irishmen in the Cork area. He later showed his true colours, surrendering in the most cowardly fashion to the Japanese, at Singapore in 1942. For the remainder of Percival's life, he was 'blackballed' by Churchill, who wanted no reminders of his numerous personal Parliamentary 'hidden' failings, and detrimental interferences.

Never! Ever! Would my mother, this proud lady, have tolerated her son being subjugated, to anyone of the British armed forces, regardless, of rank?

I had not sold my soul to some King, one that I would never meet, for the measly two shillings (2/-) pay per day. I was sick at heart, and wondered, what the Hell kind of an organisation had I joined?

This initial treachery was as nothing, to what was to come at a later stage. I was to be disgusted, and completely disillusioned at the lack of British Parliamentary integrity, and senior military command; to be discarded as trash; Denied ammunition, food, and general provisioning, in the worst of all military turmoil's, by the topmost, and highest regarded, British figurehead.

Oh yes! I now knew for certain that I was Irish, and hurting in a way that I had never previously known. Having been so close to joining with the Irish Republican Army (IRA), I could quite easily have walked out, and joined with them. Maybe I should have done just that! It was the fact that I, of choice, had freely joined with the British Army, and it pulled on my conscience. Freely making the choice, I was reluctantly, going to live with it. I had inner values of my own, and the British Army, and Government, were never going to own me. However, it was a job, with pay.

How could one compare this brutal, and insensitive, British Army Reception treatment, to the merciful understanding, shown in those happy, earlier days, by the Inspector of Irish Garda? It was impossible at this stage, to visualise that before finishing my army service, I would be in a position to contemptuously spoof, and 'sting', a renowned, arrogant, and the most disgusting, and belligerent, British Minister for Defence. I was to do it with great panache.

Having drawn back-credited tradesman pay, totalling a staggering, £9/0/0, nine pounds, and hearing that David Williams was on leave at the same time as I was, we arranged to meet at, 'Whitelock's', the Leeds historic centre bar. Occupying the small alcove between the long bar and the restaurant area, it was a bit of a squeeze, which meant David's girl sitting on his knee. The next part was subtle, and I don't think there was much in the way of hindrance by underwear. The girl was not to be denied, and with no more than, what appeared to be a slight adjustment of her skirt, David and the girl were 'At it!' And it was not only David with a nice smile on his face. It was now mid-day, and David said this was number three already? We parted, David was gone, and throughout the remainder of our lives, (I'm now aged 93), we were never to meet again. I heard that he died some years ago. God bless him! He served!

Disillusioned as I was with my army reception, it did not take long for me to form a 'mind set'; "I will perform my duties to my own high standards, but there will be no question of showing respect, regardless of rank".

With a Yorkshire accent, and joining with 501 Field Company RE, a London Territorial Unit, at King's Road Barracks, Chelsea, things were not made for total comfort. Overcrowded barracks meant many large lush houses were requisitioned, and my 'kip' was a space on the floor, at No 1 Cadogan Square. It was an eight-foot by four-foot portion of parquet flooring in the grand house, formerly the opulent home of legendary aircraft designer, and yachtsman, Sir Tommy Sopwith, and it was fine. The place accommodated possibly forty or fifty Sappers. The modest mix of Scots, Welsh, Midlanders, and Yorkies, reduced the Cockney influence somewhat, and made for a bit of inter-regional rivalry, and competition.

Remaining with only civilian clothing, and provided with one army issue blanket, it amused the pyjama clad Cockneys to find that, 'this man from the North', slept 'bollocko!' I had never before been away on my own, and had no reason to own pyjamas. Many torches attempted to reveal my better features. There were numerous 'sweeties' amongst the London Territorial Army bunch.

When it came to the London Divisional swimming championships, held at Chelsea baths, I managed to beat the long established champion, much to the chagrin of himself, and his mates. This brought a further challenge from a tough looking, Corporal Beer, a long established boxer who was put forward, ostensibly, to sweep the floor with me. To strike a senior rank was a most heinous offence, and Beer was my senior, but, contesting in a remote corner of the barracks, I hardly remember trying before Beer packed in. From now on, I was 'Sapper Somebody!', and in this unit, it mattered. Our southern brothers were not to know that, apart from training with the 1936 City of Leeds Olympic Swimming Squad, I had given many 'exhibitions' of boxing, at clubs and church halls around the Leeds area. We Yorkies were no longer 'patsies', and attitudes changed.

Tunbridge Wells was the first posting of the unit, to be quartered in opulent residential properties, along the exclusive Broadwater Down 'Boulevard'. All houses with lush carved staircases and the best of everything, but not for long. 1939 was a cruel winter, with snow knee deep. The lovely staircases and all available timber became fuel for fires. The Officers, from this London Territorial Army contingent appeared to spend all their time, 'Up in Town', (London), and it was as though we Sappers were left, to engage in our own arrangements for survival.

Clearing snowed-up walkways throughout Tunbridge Wells town enhanced the popularity of the unit, and made us welcome at the most excellent theatre, although we were soon, 'back to basics'. The challenge came from Adjutant, Major Mike Calvert; (He was later number two to Colonel Ord Wingate; 'A Queen! of Chindit fame', and generally became known as, 'Mad Mike'). Whilst on a bridging exercise, the idiot challenged me at swimming, by both stripping off, starkers, and racing across the freezing river and back. I declined, but Calvert did the swim. Having almost frozen stiff in crossing, he made the mistake of getting out on the far bank, completely breathless, he wasn't badly hung, and then had the indignity of having to re-enter the water, in order to recover his clothing. Calvert and I were destined to meet again, in different circumstances at a later date.

Our operational training ground was situated within the Marquise of Granby's palatial estate, at Frant, close by Tunbridge Wells. We did fieldworks, dug trenches, did bridging, and with explosives, carried out demolitions, and from M'Lords private herd, knocked off the occasional deer. It was butchered, packed, and dispatched amongst the ranks, in convenient sized bundles. Nobody really knew how it happened, but the frequent night compass, and map-reading exercises, invariably finished in a pub.

Ashford, in Kent, became a favoured spot for Sapper tourism. In a small convoy of open back trucks, we travelled there at regular intervals, about every three weeks. The purpose of the trip was not disclosed, but never once did we dismount the vehicles. It was an occasion for Officers and NCOs to plough over maps, and for us 'squaddies' to 'baa!' at the shopping ladies, as though a flock of sheep. Whatever became of Ashford? You can't blame me.

Posted back to Chatham, St Mary's Barracks, on the 24th May 1940, I lost all track of 501 Field Company. It was trade-testing time, in order to justify my Specialist Draughtsman pay. I passed Grades Three and Two, and had a time delay requirement imposed before sitting Grade One. This was a most delicate period of the war, and news of any kind became sketchy. Soldiers did not have wireless sets, and National Security helped mask the 'cock-ups', made by Whitehall military Brass Hats, and there were many.

'The Whitehall Wooden Tops', had, for twenty long years, enjoyed the perks of officialdom, and the military fart-arsing around the London scene. They had revelled, and unashamedly reflected on the success of World War-One, and saw no reason for change. Ingestion, and reflections, of past successes, along with the inbred public schoolboy arrogance, saw no end, as they remained blind to the previous six years of supreme German military development. In this short time, Chancellor Hitler had emerged as the power of Europe. With modern mechanisation, and efficient armour, he equipped the splendid Nazi armed forces to the highest degree.

Whilst remaining at Chatham, the German onslaught, or Blitzkrieg, began. The French Maginot Line; (A defence system, designed in 1929, by a French Minister of that name), was considered impenetrable. Along with the French forces, it proved to be of no avail, and collapsed, it was of no hindrance. The assault, by Panzer tanks, and the highly trained, and equipped Nazi forces, was formidable. British troops floundered, as they were left to make the best they could of it, mostly through French sands, near Dunkirk.

An armada of little boats made names for themselves, conveying survivors escaping the onslaught. The resultant chaos amongst British Forces immediately following their return to England was quite unbelievable, they were devastated. The unexpected efficiency and suddenness of the German success, was completely outside all Whitehall contingency plans. The appallingly failed situation, and total lack of Government, and Military control, has never been accepted, it has been conveniently 'airbrushed' out of British history. All is conveniently centred on the dramatic Dunkirk evacuation, as though a success.

Desperate though the European situation remained; little was confirmed to the general public. News was stifled, and the series of confusing rumours became alarming. It took a little time to realise, and appreciate, the British army was knackered. Men now considered 'survivors', were scattered far and wide, dispersed throughout the country; recuperating, mostly in there own homes. There remained no such thing as, 'an effective consolidated British force'. Depleted Regimental Depots were isolated, and of no consequence, there were no Divisional, Brigade, or Battalion structures.

Survivors of the British Military hiatus are graciously honoured, annually!

America, and the rest of the world, viewed the situation in Europe, and all considered Britain a defeated nation. Hitler must, in hindsight, have realised that he could have crossed the English Channel, with ease, and virtually walked through the country. Churchill and his Brass Hats, as ever, claimed credit for the evacuation of British troops, and the stemming of Hitler's assault, but, it was a vital strip of water, that became the true England saviour; It's known as the English Channel.

America continued sitting on the fence, as a country influentially formed, and controlled, by its belligerent, anti-British, immigrant population. President Roosevelt, 'with his hands tied', showed great reluctance to making any committal.

In the Dunkirk evacuation, large numbers of junior British officers were either killed or captured. The considered life expectancy of an infantry officer, in action, was one and a half days. Caught in a desperate situation, and brought about through its own blundering, the British Ministry of Defence got lucky, as thick skins melted.

Fear, and shear desperation, made parliamentarians see some sort of sense. It had always been considered infra-dig to send out a man, recruiting potential officers, and it was the last thing they wanted to do. Officer recruitment, in normal times, was a matter of; 'Whom do you know?' 'Who do you do?' 'And what public school did you attend?' For a poor humble sod like me, there was not a cat in hells chance. But these were not normal times.

In shear desperation, the War Office sent out a batch of officers on what could only be called, 'a trawling mission'; the purpose of which was to find, 'suitable infantry officer material'. Back in Chatham, having passed Grades Three and Two Trade Tests, my pay was now increased from two shillings, to three-shilling and three-pence (3s-3p) per day. Had I taken Grade One, my pay as a Lance Corporal would have been six-shillings and nine-pence (6s-9p) per day, a most generous pay-day at the time, and I would not have sought to go further.

Filling in time between tests, I was seconded onto the Regimental Police. It was here that I met with the most brutal of men. The regular police were all former prison officers, mostly from different prisons throughout the south of England. Each of these brutes was intent on outdoing others in their savagery, and no man was safe when in their care. Officers did not visit, and complaining was useless.

The most futile time-filling exercise, was sandbagging around Rochester Cathedral. A squad of about fifty sappers were marched the two or three miles, all topless, and inspected, immaculate, before departure into the scorching summer sun. The sandbags were fine, but with no sand available, the bags were filled with coal dust from a nearby merchant's stock-yard, and built up around the Cathedral. I would like to have seen the effect of a machine-gun blast on the bags, but the real fun began on our return journey. Women poured out from shopping, to see what looked like African troops, and cheered as we performed, 'the duck-arse strut', through the town.

Appreciating that we might have some form of education, the dozen undertaking trade testing were interviewed by the War Office 'trawling officer'. He stressed the urgent need for replacement Infantry Officers. He gave the format of general duties, most of which I had long since worked out for myself. It was however, when he mentioned the exorbitant pay of eleven-shillings (11s-0d) per day, my ears pricked. I had not the slightest idea of the meaning, or responsibilities, of 'Commissioned Officer' rank. My father had got no further than a Private, and we did not know anybody of Commissioned rank from whom to seek advice, but I knew that this was an opportunity coming out of the blue, and I wanted some of that!

Brought up in the working class slum district in Leeds, life had been hard, but, as kids we did not know this. It was a case of equality, and with everybody, 'stuck in the same boat'. Hardly ever leaving the locality, there were no means whereby we could identify a difference in class standards, it was never a thought, and something we never saw. Now here, and quite out of the blue, was my chance of escape. I had seen so many 'tarts and old farts' in the officer class, and with no idea of the significance, or the awesome situations I was eventually to find myself in, I knew that given the chance, I could compete with them.

It was only on joining the army that I realised the different levels of existence. It was up through the Other Ranks, from Corporal to Sergeant

Major, for one classification. But there was another, almost secretive level, 'The Officer Class'. They had a completely different existence to common soldiery. This upper level appeared to come from select society.

I did not like this hierarchal clique, for whom I had no respect. I considered myself their equal in every way. From what I had seen, I realised that I was by far better an engineer. In fact, the daily function of former Territorial Officers, appeared to be for them to attend the first parade of the day, and then vanish with the words; "Carry on Sergeant!" Not to be seen again until the following day.

Being selected, my name went forward for Commissioning, and the miracle started. My life was in for a complete change, and I had no idea of what I was letting myself into. It was as though moving from being a sheep to being the shepherd, and from some of my former friends, there was considerable hostility, even bitterness. I was reneging on them; 'and moving over to the other side'.

The Commissioning process meant undergoing a series of increasingly high level interviews, with a succession of Colonels, Brigadiers, and Generals. After what seemed a never ending series, the final interview was conducted in a huge hall, with twenty-one invigilating 'big wigs'. All were seated in a widely spaced-out semicircle. They were a mixed bunch; Members of Parliament, seniors from all armed services, academics, and high flying business men.

My turn came to face the music, and I knew that this was the time for, 'make or break'. Answering questions on geography, politics, war, sport and general matters, I felt pretty confident. Eventually, they got around to what I knew to be, the crunch question, and I was ready; "What school did you attend?"

I did not have the 'La-De-Da' backing of such as Charterhouse, Eton or Winchester, but I knew that whatever the school, it had to sound good. It was a gamble in so far as, of the twenty-one inquisitors, I considered that there might be at least five or six Catholics amongst them. I had to play 'My old school tie' ; (although there wasn't one). Presenting my humble school, it had to be seen as impressive, and pleased as I was with my performance to that point, this was the final and vital throw, as I proudly announced; -

"Hunslet, St. Joseph's, Roman Catholic, Boys School".

The happy band of interrogators could have no knowledge of the humble Leeds district, or of the school. They did however know that I had named it with pride, and with a great deal of confidence.

The next twenty-four hours seemed like a lifetime before being called to the office once more. I rejoiced to hear that I was successful, but saddened somewhat to find that one of my close colleagues, a distinguished artist in later days, had failed. He did not know how many degrees there were in a circle.

Gerald at St. Patricks Church, Newport

Gerald at O'Grady Homestead – Spot where mother's brother Thomas O'Grady was shot by 'Black and Tans'

Seven Arch Bridge on road to O'Grady Home, Mulranny, Achill Island

Granuaile Castle Ruin at Clew Bay

2

COMMISSIONING

8th August, Two days before my twenty-first birthday; (10th August 1940), is one of my most significant of days. Posted for four months officer training, to 163 OCTU (Officer Cadet Training Unit); (also known as, The Artist Rifles), situated about four miles west of Folkstone, at Shorncliff Park camp. Issued with a white band to fit around my 'fore and aft' cap, and two strips for the epaulettes, I became dressed and identifiable, as 'an officer cadet'.

The feeling of change was remarkable, with warmth in the reception by Squad Commander, Lieutenant Coombes, an officer of The Rifle Brigade. He appeared as a human being, and different to the Territorial Officers of the Royal Engineers, the ones with whom I had previously had contact. Coombes remained with the squad throughout training sessions, and spoke with all, in a friendly and understandable manner, whilst at the same time, making crystal clear the high standard of requirements. There were no threats, although we were left in no doubt that any aberration, or perceived weakness, meant 'RTU'. Objection, or questioning the decision, was taboo. The words; RTU – "Return to Unit", with the subsequent demeanour, and scoffing, amongst other ranks, would be seen as, 'failure'. Guideline on OCTU failures, as given by Coombes, was between thirty and fifty per cent. Unfortunately, four or five, of our intake of thirty, were RTU within two days of arrival, there was no explanation. It was simply a matter of; "Go!"

After four days, and with some trepidation, I was called before Coombes and thought this to be the call of death; "Fitzpatrick, you are weak on the three-inch mortar and machine gun"; at that, I fully expected the fateful words. He did, however, allow me to speak, and explain; "As a Sapper in the RE, I had never before seen these weapons, but please don't ditch me?" I further requested that if he let me have a copy of the manual, and access to a mortar over the weekend, I would take the squad on Monday morning. He did! And I did! The look on Coombes' face said it all. He appreciated my guts, and I was in! I did not, and would not, let him down.

A former Engineering tool-room trained apprentice, and design draughtsman, I walked through the task, and was complimented for my efforts. The three inch mortar was to become a tremendous friend of mine, and it remained so for the remainder of my service.

Following Dunkirk evacuation fiasco, the British Army remained in turmoil. The Whitehall Brass Hats had Churchill chunter words of defiance. They knew to a man, that England was, 'up the creek without a paddle'. The country was sunk by the long anticipated, and spectacular, German Blitzkrieg throughout Europe. England, and the rest of the world, knew it! Britain was doomed! Well knackered!

Hitler was not a 'Silly Billy'. He had plans of his own. With British forces utterly defeated; in turmoil, completely out of control, lacking command of any kind. To Hitler, the seemingly, rag-tag and bobtail survivors of the Nazi 'Blitz', were cosily settled and contained on a secure island, just twenty-one miles away from German Panzer tanks, and Storm-troopers. Established along the French coast, German 'U' Boats, (submarines), were sinking many thousand tons of Allied shipping daily, and at the same time, scuppering the British Island's struggling contents, civil and military. So! What's the hurry? The dear man had not been mass producing armaments, bomber, and fighter aircraft, for no good reason. He was now about to release them, on a subdued, and defeated nation.

The War Office were determined that we cadets should not miss the first spectacular show of the war, and our three small platoons of trainees, were moved four miles, from Shorncliff training camp, to the occupation of Folkstone Harbour jetty. The new accommodation quarters were established in a line of railway goods wagons, six men to a wagon, all stretched along the dog-legged jetty. A guncotton slab was attached to all wheels of the wagons, and on the ground, lying alongside each, was a primer with electrically connected detonator. The whole lot was ready for instant destruction in the event of the expected attempt at invasion. Movement of Axis forces could be seen, just over twenty miles away, along the coast of France. England was there for the taking.

Incongruous though it might seem, we had little time to consider the precarious situation into which we were now so delicately placed, and with so scant a force. At this point we come to one of those periods 'airbrushed' out of Churchill's, and Britain's, recorded history. In the ninety or so miles, from Folkstone to London, there was not one single co-ordinated military force; No Division, Brigade, or Battalion existed. There were a number of small Royal Air Force bases, all inadequately equipped to resist invasion. With incredulity, we of the small OCTU party knew that a modest German assault on our position, or along any part of the south coast, must result in a resounding Nazi success. The 'Wooden Tops' of Whitehall were still fighting as though engaged in World War-One. The success, and consummate speed of the German onslaught, was far beyond the comprehension of British Military Command.

Having Britain wrapped within his 'U' Boat controlled corral, Hitler had the country at his mercy. The naughty man was about to launch his attacking Luftwaffe bombers, and fighter planes, against selected British townships.

For we most favourably positioned cadets, the show began, as the mighty bombers set about attacking London. With front line seats; firstly, we could hear the distant drone, coming from the East, before seeing the evil flights of aircraft. With the sun behind them, and in set formations, the disciplined squadrons came roaring in.

With forty or fifty aircraft in each flight, Heinkel and Dornier bombers were accompanied by Messerschmitt fighters, and the dread, Stuka dive-bombers. Freely crossing the English Channel, one flight following on the tail of the other, they came with absolute impunity. Folkestone and Dover were vulnerable in the extreme. Witnessing the world's most spectacular air show, it was as though our small force of cadets, on the most exposed piece of English soil, were being totally, and purposefully, ignored. It required little imagination, and we were in no doubt, the two defenceless channel ports, Dover and Folkstone, were earmarked for an Axis invasion, in due course. But who would know when?

The picture began to change rapidly, as Royal Air Force fighter planes joined in the sport, although there appeared to be pitiable few fighters. Seldom could twenty be counted in any one flight, but it was a treat to see them, and to hear the roar of engines, and bursts of gunfire. On the big day, in September, when casualty records were broken, the sky was filled with a mix of RAF fighters, and Nazi bombers; and we watched. It was all that we could do. A new era had begun.

Whatever happened, and however it happened, was not for us to know. There was no Nazi seaborne assault. Hitler, turning his back, ignored England as though putting it in cold storage, to be dealt with at a later date. Nazi hordes were withdrawn from the French coastline, and directed towards the East.

On the 8th April 1940, Panzer tanks and Storm Troopers began invading Norway, and Denmark, and almost immediately, turned to an assault on Russia! Hitler envisaged easy pickings in that direction, as the might of the Russian army had previously struggled in conflict with little Finland for two or three years, and failed.

Possibly, on the strength of Russia's seemingly weak performance, Hitler saw easy pickings. However, he met with a, 'false dawn', and completely misread the Russian potential, along with the treacherous weather his troops were about to encounter. He considered his super-equipped forces would conquer what he considered, a feeble Russia, within weeks; Churchill, and England, could wait, and breathe again!

Churchill's subsequent self eulogizing, and glorification, failed to acknowledge his luck, in this; the most amazing fluke of war. Hitler had, mistakenly, let Churchill, and Britain, off the hook for the time being, and I don't think the lucky Prime Minister ever thanked the man for this merciful act. Hitler's, error of judgement, was the greatest stroke of luck in Churchill's 'chequered' career. One squadron of Panzer tanks could have landed, and conquered Britain, with ease!

We were very puzzled one day, as a British fighter plane crossed in isolation, away from the coast, and out towards the East. The plane gradually descended, some distance out, before dropping into the sea. The timing and circumstances of this unusual action was not immediately recognised. It was later established that Fighter Pilot, Irishman, Paddy

Finucane, knowing that he was mortally wounded, accepted that he had no chance of survival, phoned his flight commander to say, "Goodbye!" The gallant Irishman had chosen to perish in the aircraft he loved to fly.

Churchill declared, what became known as, 'The Battle of Britain', ending on 31st October 1940. The heaviest bombing Blitz, recorded on the recent 21st August. (RAF lost 915 aircraft, the Luftwaffer 1,733, although many claimed this to be an inflated figure; pilots fibbed at times!). The worst of nights came some time later; on 10th May 1941, when one hundred thousand, (100,000), incendiaries, were dropped on London, killing 1400 civilians. Hitler, however, had other targets in mind; like Russia! The air assault on Britain was not all one way, and in retaliation for attacks on London, Berlin was bombed, by a squadron of the RAF, on 26th August 1940.

There was change, and the stages were never clearly set. We move on a bit; Hitler closed down his Western Front, and set to attack what he must, in due course regret. He saw what he considered, 'a feeble Russia', and treacherously breaking the recently signed, 23rd August 1939, Axis/Soviet Peace Pact; conquest looked to be a simple task. Regardless of any pact, the Panzer led assault was previously, and carefully planned, under the code name; "BARBAROSSA", by German General Staff, (This pre-determined code-name for the invasion of Russia, was unearthed in German documentation, found at a much later date).

Having seen Russian forces fail in conflict with little Finland. Hitler was now confident that his Panzer Tank Divisions, and Storm Troopers, would conquer Russia, hopefully, "Before Christmas"? He could not have been more wrong, as he met with determined resistance, and his Panzer tanks became bogged down in a succession of severe Russian winters. Following what turned out to be a long and most arduous campaign, the dead of both sides counted in millions.

With Hitler's about turn completed, away from the Western French coastline, it left the devious British Prime Minister to hold-forth, and claim the changed situation; 'To be his personal masterminded success!' It was about this time that Churchill uttered some of his much publicised sayings. He invented the title; "The Battle of Britain", and stomped on to declare; "This is our finest hour". The predatory British Prime Minister failed to give Hitler credit for taking his forces elsewhere, whilst at the same time, sought the glory he was to revel in, in years to come. It was however, Emma Soames, Churchill's grand-daughter, who some time later let the cat out of the bag, she was aptly reported as saying; *"He enlisted the language of Shakespeare, and sent it to war"*. How right she was! And he did not stop at that, although it was a very different matter when it came to his accepting adversity of any kind; as we see later with his Eastern based Capital ships.

Observing the vanquished situation within Britain, USA President Franklin D Roosevelt was not going to lose out on a chance to profit. The charlatan conducted the first of his underhand acts; He established a covert relationship with the French Marshall; Petain, the Pro-Axis Commander of Vichy France. Vichy was mostly, the southern part of France, established eight days after the fall of Paris, and totally under German control. By his contact, with Petain, FDR was virtually negotiating with both Hitler, and Italy's Mussolini. Exploiting the situation further, it was thought by many, that America was also pumping money out of Britain, and surreptitiously, provisioning the Axis Powers. These were desperate days, and America was seeking its own revival, to recover from the many years of poverty.

In pre-war USA, many years of depression had taken its toll. A Yank would grovel for a crust of bread, and thousands upon thousands ignominiously, queued daily at National Soup Kitchens. The day of the 'Fat Yank' was but a dream; it was to be a long time in coming. Crooner, Bing Crosby's singing of the plaintive song; "Buddy can you spare a dime?" Was most apt; it could almost be considered a hymn.

It was moving time, and we gentle few, 'the Billy Big-heads' of valiant 163 OCTU, having denied the Nazi hoards their Channel crossing, considered ourselves to be; 'The saviours of Folkstone?' Unceremoniously, we were banished, to North Wales, and billeted in the coastal town of Pwthelli. The 'welcome in the hillside', was muted with the rain and cold. There was however, an unexpected attack of 'suddenness' in the billet, shortly after we landed. Almost within hours of our arrival, two nieces of our landlady, Mrs Roberts, visited. They came down from their hillside farm to view Fenton and myself, her two lodgers.

It was as though attending a cattle show, and we were it. The two big busty bints spent little time, and considering us a pair of wimps, went off, back into the hills. Some days later, I was however favoured, and hailed a hero, as the rescuer of Mr Roberts. It was as he returned from town one evening, a little, 'the worse for wear'. I caught up with him, and walked him down the street. He was soaked to the skin, and swore that I had pulled him from the river; and why should I deny?

The undying memory of North Wales is of hills and water. Improvising training, we went through every aspect, in as gruelling a manner as could be put to us. Environmental adjustment proved a most testing process, and one that reduced our squad to little more than fifty per cent of the initial draft. Some even, rejected at the very last minute, as we paraded for results. OCTU Commandant, Major Neal, of the Inniskilling Regiment, made the awards, and received each and every candidate, one by one. The ones rejected in this final parade, left instantly, many of them in tears, and it was hearts in the mouth, for those of us remaining in the queue.

"Fitzpatrick!" "I'm pleased to advise you that you have passed". "You are being posted to your choice of Regiment; The Kings Own Yorkshire Light Infantry. I know that you will make a fine officer". He shook me warmly by the hand, I saluted, and he wished me well. My joy was unbounded, as I replied, "I won't let you down Sir!" And I never did!

7th December 1940. – No 160575, Second Lieutenant, Gerald Fitzpatrick. With a single 'pip' sewn on each epaulette, I was granted seven days leave. For once in my life, I had got one up on my father. He was dumbfounded, I had moved into the world that he detested. Having served in the KOYLI, for nine years before, and then throughout the First World War, he never got beyond the rank of 'Private'. (He was however, mentioned in despatches twice, and denied higher honours; for insubordination).

Being unsure of my acceptance, and potential, along with the fear of failure, I had said nothing of my acceptance into OCTU. My parents were staggered beyond comprehension that I should become a Commissioned Officer, particularly my father, as it was into his former regiment.

There was nothing earth shattering, in the arrival of a new subaltern, into the KOYLI Officers Mess, at the Strensall Depot, near York. The place was like a museum, and the exhibits; senior rank officers, almost all survivors from World War-One. For them, nothing had moved, forward, backwards, or in any direction. I was dumbstruck at this oasis of indifference to the world that I had come to know. It was as though the world had stood still. The protocol was unwritten, and as an example; 'no junior officer spoke to a senior, until he was first spoken to'.

It was most important to remember 'which way to pass the port', on the weekly 'formal' dinner night. No questions asked about 'black market' dealings, and one simply accepted that haunches of beef were readily available, several members being landowners might be the answer. On dinner nights, as many as up to six guests were invited to join and dine with us, and the drinks flowed freely. It was not for a junior to question his observing a senior, walking off with a bottle of whisky. Viciously, in sharing the costs of the night, it made one hell of a dint, in what I considered the princely payment of eleven shillings a day.

I was however fortunate in meeting, Q.M. 'Tiny' Wilson, himself a former 'Ranker'. He remembered my father with whom he had served during the First World War, and virtually, took me under his wing. He saved me money, when selling me the walking-out dress uniform of a former officer, one killed in the earlier campaign, in Norway.

Having been at the Depot only a few days, and having no recognised duties, I had the temerity to request my first meeting with Commanding Officer, Lieut. Col. Henry Wells-Cole. My request for leave over the Christmas period was refused, and he gave me something to do:-

"You'll stay here!" "You'll attend the military ball, at York De Grey Rooms, and you will dance with my daughter!"

Daughter, Troth was a dainty dish, a long way out of my range. She was most attractive, highly educated, and beautifully spoken. We had but one dance, and she obviously found me, 'Naff !' In the circumstances, and for consolation, Tiny and I spent the remainder of the evening concentrating on the assortment of bottles on the table. Yes! I was totally pixilated! The highlight of my stay at Strensall was playing rugby alongside the great, and legendary, Trevor Foster, of Bradford Northern, and England, Rugby League fame. I was so delighted, some time later, to see him play at the Leeds ground, at Headingley. It was in a Test Match. He danced through, scoring two tries, against the formidable Australian Rugby League tourists.

Granted week-end leave the following week, I met with a dilemma. Leaving Leeds in indifferent weather, I found the snow to be knee deep on my arrival at York, and with not a hope of a taxi, or any other aid. As for finding the barracks at Strensall, five or so miles from the station, I had not a clue. Help came! It was the Salvation Army; I was graciously allocated one of their beds on the station platform. This much appreciated act, possibly, saved my career as an officer.

Accompanied by colleague, fellow junior Bobby Fenwick, (I believe he was the son of a bishop), I was sent to Netheravon, Small Arms Training School, to be blessed to undertake, of all things; Training on the three-inch (3") Mortar. How could I be so lucky? By this time, with my testing experience at OCTU, where I had proved myself to Platoon Commander Coombes, I knew more about the weapon, and its operation, than the training school instructors.

Never having previously stayed at a hotel of any kind, I was guided by Fenwick for our overnight stay in London. For one pound, seven shillings and nine pence, (£1/7/9), we stayed at The Cumberland Hotel, Marble Arch. My father's weekly dole money at the time, and with six to feed, was only three pence more than this, at one pound, and eight shillings, (£1/8/0). The Cumberland Hotel charge was a fortune, in my eyes, and I missed taking breakfast. I was under the delusion that it would be served in my room.

No doubt, on hearing of my promotion, the true Irish connection 'kicked in'. My mother's two brothers, Patrick and Dominic, were both doing very nicely for themselves in America, sought to help. Aware of the belittling, back to back, two bedroom cellar-kitchen, house, in which I was reared. They sent mother cash enough to buy a rather nice three bedroom house, one with the luxury of an internal bath and toilet. The house was situated close by an attractive park, in which mother established a vegetable allotment. (I reckon the Yank donation would have been; one thousand Dollars).

It was ironical, and a true godsend, that I, of all people, was fortunate enough to be sent on a three-inch mortar course, following my OCTU introduction to the weapon. I qualified 'Distinguished!' Rather surprisingly, I was delighted when Henry Wells-Cole sent for me to command his Mortar Platoon. He was now commanding the former territorial Battalion, 7th KOYLI, based in Essex, an irregular unit consisting of territorial soldiers, with an intake of conscripts. Henry knew that he was getting a man who knew the job.

I had no idea of the magnificent significance of being a specialist officer, particularly one commanding a three inch mortar platoon. It gave me an immediate independence. I was never to be controlled by a Company Commander. I could not have 'bought' a better job.

Throughout the remainder of my service, I never once took orders from a Company Commander, nor did I have to answer to one. It was magic! In the seven months spent with the 7th Battalion, KOYLI, I truly established myself as a competent young officer. Based at Chalkwell School, at Leigh-on-Sea, in Essex, we used the streets, and I drilled my platoon to perfection. Moved to the countryside, we had the pleasure of ploughing through unpleasant Essex mudflats; exercising in dull offensives, against those imaginary hordes of invading Nazi's.

The only unrestrained hostility and resentment we encountered, came from the oddest, and most unlikely of quarters, where one might expect civility, and even a measure of respect. When housed in the 'luxury' of tented accommodation alongside the greens of Thornton Park Golf Club, we were denied access to all parts of the building, except one requisitioned room, designated; 'The Orderly Office'. So exclusive did they consider themselves, that not one club member would exchange words with any one of our unit. I encountered, the rare, and unpleasantly similar sentiments at a prominent pub, situated in the centre of Hunstanton, where I was unfortunately billeted for a short period. One doesn't forget these niggling bits! It was as though we were pariahs to these inhospitable people. And this, in England!

In August 1941, the battalion was posted to Cheltenham, housed in the old wooden stables at the racecourse. With unaccustomed suddenness, Whitehall Brass Hats came to life, and in a shock decision; the 7th Battalion K.O.Y.L.I. was to be converted, to become a tank unit – '149 RTR'. As a competent mortar officer, Henry Wells-Cole, the dear sweet thing, found me 'not sidelined', but, 'surplus to requirements'. I was transferred to a regular service battalion; 1st Battalion KOYLI, in Northern Ireland, Commander, Lieut. Col. Edward Earnshaw Eden (E.E.E.) Cass.

There was much anecdotal guff about Cass, and he took himself very seriously. A short man, with a handlebar moustache, it was said that he had played rugby for the army. However, I don't know where he was positioned in the earlier, Norway campaign, in which the unit had been involved? He reportedly carried two revolvers, and threatened his men; "If any man attempts to desert, I shall shoot him!" You've got to be at the rear of activities, to observe a deserting man. So, who was leading the battalion? What was made very clear, however, was that Cass had no time for Emergency Commissioned Officers; he considered them, inferior beings.

On arrival at the 1st Battalion, the adjutant had the responsibility of informing each ECO, exactly what was expected of them. A vital part of the instruction being, that at meal times, he must 'not sit facing Cass'. It was as though the regular, and traditional, Cass, could not bear the sight of ECO's, and he never addressed one directly. Majors Terence Leslie Gossage, and Digby Seymour Shuttleworth, two poncey lumps, had pride of place; There was no such thing as a word of welcome to this unit.

I was beginning to appreciate the changes, and the various postings. It was broadening my mind, and I started classifying individuals, particularly my seniors. Many appeared remote, and considered themselves to be on some other planet. Always most reluctant to converse with juniors, they resented criticism. I found that I was respecting ones of my own rank, and file, much better than the cliquish seniors. Proud insular Irishness within me, discarded the bullshit, I was 'ploughing my own furrow', and I was feeling a change of reaction. My fellow juniors came from such diverse backgrounds, and almost without exception, had feelings much as my own towards seniors. The humble background of my early years was now behind me; I was developing greatly in confidence, ready to stand my ground when necessary.

My obsession of instinctively assessing the performance of senior officers stemmed from the arrogance of their assuming superiority, and expecting instant subservience. There was always something missing, and a lot of 'cloak and dagger' atmosphere. Mostly, the 'regular army' seniors came from 'Poncy' Public Schools', with snobbery, associations, and old boys clubs, embedded into their lives. The army was very much an old boys' network, with individuals having to work their way up the ladder to get a chance of the top job. It was a quiet, slow and progressive life, there was not a lot of getting up peoples noses, especially noses belonging to people who also wanted a chance at the same job, and thought it might be their turn.

Maybe my father's old mantra applied; "In spite of their education, and in their dumbness, were incapable of qualifying in professionalism, as accountants, doctors, solicitors, architects, or high level engineers". In order to justify their existence, they then had the choice; either the Church, or the Army?

Taking the Army; superiority, and seniority of rank, was acquired by simply staying there. The longer the time served, the higher the rank, and the assumption that this man is born to be a leader of men. In due course of time, I was to encounter the myth, and see it to be far from the truth. These individuals had not lived alongside what I considered to be, 'proper men', men who worked in the exacting environment of industry, as in an engineering workshop

Whilst these Public School boys were learning Greek, and Latin, I had come from a much harder background. I had spent the last five of my twenty years, from aged fifteen to twenty, pre-war, in serious employment, and had become accustomed to training with competent and exacting men of high calibre, managers and tradesmen of top quality. I had at all times received the most careful coaching and encouragement. Managers and Foremen replicated Officers and NCO's, and I could never, for instance, imagine a Foreman treating me in the inhuman manner in which I had been treated on day three of my service at the RE Depot at Chatham.

The insult was to remain with me forever, and my scepticism of those, in higher rank, above me, unrelenting. I had been the top tool-room apprentice, at a national firm of locksmiths, followed by invitation, to an internationally famous traction-engine manufacturer. Night-school training, further qualified me, to be recruited into the demanding experience of design draughtsmanship in hydraulics. Apart from experience on the workbench, I could expertly operate all machinery; screw-cut on lathes, and operate planers, drills, grinders and presses, shape, and harden various tools in oil or water. It resulted from a period at technical college, and attending a lot of extra night-school.

Having freely deserted him, and his company, to join with H M Forces, the letter of recommendation by the Technical Director of my previous employers, in support of my commissioning, is shown overleaf.

CONTRACTORS TO THE ADMIRALTY, WAR OFFICE, AIR MINISTRY, ALSO COLONIAL AND FOREIGN GOVERNMENTS

TELEGRAMS: "RIVETTER, LEEDS"
TELEPHONES: 75481 & 2 HUNSLET
CODES: 5TH EDITION A.B.C.
BENTLEYS

HENRY BERRY & C⁰. LTD.,

HYDRAULIC ENGINEERING SPECIALISTS,

CONTRACTS SUBJECT TO USUAL STRIKE CLAUSE
LONDON OFFICE:
ABBEY HOUSE, VICTORIA STREET, S.W.1.
GRAMS: "BERRYCO, SOWEST, LONDON."
PHONE: ABBEY 6535.

CROYDON WORKS, HUNSLET,

LEEDS, 5th July, 19 40.
10.

OUR REF. PGC/WR.
YOUR REF.

O. C. "A" Company,
R. E. ~~Signals~~,
St. Mary's Barracks,
Chatham.

Sir,

Re: Fitzpatrick G. Reg.No.1882721.

I am given to understand that Fitzpatrick has applied for a commission in the Royal Engineers and I have been asked to provide a reference.

Fitzpatrick was a student with my Company before the war and joined the services voluntarily; although he could have obtained exemption as we are engaged to full capacity on work of the most urgent National Importance. We set an extremely high standard in our training and if Fitzpatrick had not given every satisfaction in theoretical and practical engineering training he would not have been allowed to continue, this is a condition of our student's agreements.

As a matter of fact he was quite outstanding on the practical training in his workshop practice and his work in the Drawing Office was quite above average.

If you do not know the standing of Henry Berry & Co.Ltd. I might say that the firm was founded as long ago as 1883 and enjoys a reputation of very high standing in the world of heavy engineering, our work is very exacting and highly specialised, particularly in the matter of calculations of designs, which are very varied, it therefore follows that Fitzpatrick's training has naturally resulted in his having attained a standard in Engineering subjects, equivalent to Inter B.Sc. London and he would have been taking the equivalent local examination had he been with us this year.

/Over

-2-

If there are any detailed questions which I could answer for your further satisfaction, I should be pleased to do so at your request.

I have the honour to remain, Sir,

Your obedient servant,

P. G. CORIN.
M.A. M.Inst.C.E.

I could size up a man in minutes, and was frequently asked my opinion on a variety of subjects. With no fears, I cultivated my own discipline, and a strict code of conduct. It was at all times, in keeping with the job in hand.

Apart from a threat of intervention, oddly enough, by members of the I.R.A. at a dance in Strabane, in Northern Ireland, where I was wooing one of their ladies, there was little of consequence in my attachment to the 1st Bn KOYLI. Cass had a fetish for thirty-mile route marches, and always on a Friday. It cooled the boys for the weekend, and he never personally took part in them.

As the sole Roman Catholic officer in the unit, I was detailed to escort two trucks, loaded with troops, to Sunday Mass, at the church in nearby, Five Mile Town. Arriving in good time, we occupied three rows on the left of the centre isle, and quite near the back of the church.

Our 'gaff' became glaringly obvious as the local congregation arrived. There was segregation; ladies to the left, and men to the right. Being stuck on the left, there was no point in our moving. However, on departing the church, and mounting the transports, it was as though leaving the frozen North. There was not one single movement, and in the absolute silence, unspoken enmity showered from every corner. Parishioners simply stood and watched as we returned to camp. This was my final church parade. And now, as the sole Roman Catholic officer, I had further reason to pondering on the normal Regimental recruiting policy.

The next perplexing dilemma was to become one of my real gems, and there was no avoidance of this one. On a cold morning in early November 1941, my three months stay with Cass terminated. Nine juniors, all Emergency Commissioned Officers, were paraded before the detestable sod. We could have been cattle, so far as Cass was concerned. He actually addressed us directly, for the very first time, and this, only as a group. Twirling the end of his moustache, he was as curt, and brief as usual, it was as though it hurt the man to speak to us;

"Gentlemen; "You are leaving the battalion!" "You are being posted overseas". "The battalion you are about to join is stationed in a tropical peace station". "You will depart now, for one week

embarkation leave". "You will report to The King's Theatre, in Glasgow, on the twenty third of November"

"The Quartermaster will see to your tropical equipment needs!"

With no handshake, or wishes of goodwill, we were ushered from the office. Cass must have been in his highest heaven, at getting rid of nine ECO's, all in one bunch. He resented the very idea of 'Temporary' Commissioned Officers being accepted into his, 'regular', 1st Bn KOYLI. Posting so many ECO's, at one time, into the obscurity of a remote station in the tropics, must have given him tremendous pleasure. He reflected the attitude of so many seniors I had already met with, particularly, 'the old farts', at the regimental depot. This unfortunate malaise was endemic throughout most regimental 'old timers'.

My previous postings had been to known destinations. Now, and with no choice, I was being committed into the great unknown. I likened this experience to that previously encountered, with the dastardly Orderly Room, RE Sergeant, at Chatham. Cass was a Senior Army Commissioned Officer, and here he was replicating the damnable abhorrent conduct of the despicable, Senior Non-Commissioned Army Officer at the Chatham RE barracks.

I could not get used to the military dictum, whereby, one of lower rank had to be treated like a dog. Man to man, I knew that I could better these people, and I was on my way to proving this! It was becoming ever increasingly important to me.

I had not voluntarily joined with the British Army, to be, as I considered, insulted at every turn. To be sent overseas to some sunshine isle? That was never my wish. My training and intent was to fight against Nazi's in Europe, and, once again, with no option, I was being humiliated further, and discarded, as if of no consequence, to some undisclosed destination. My eight fellow discards were also new to the unit, each and every one of them, had an equal dislike of Cass. In the short time of our acquaintanceship, we knew little of each other personally. I realised however, that all felt as I did, and I was on my way to knowing them all, very well indeed!

Reacting to the situation, within myself, I now had a new dilemma. Did I want to stick with this unfeeling British heap, or, did I want to walk a few yards down the road, and do as I had thought at Chatham; cross the border, and join up with the Irish Republican Army, in the Irish Free State. I had a most ready and welcoming base at the homestead, in County Mayo. A number of troops had taken this route, and I was very badly torn to follow. But I didn't! This British Army was paying me eleven shillings each day, and it was more than I ever envisaged. It allowed me to make a regular contribution to my mother at home, and the living was pretty good. Life certainly compared most favourably to the dour existence, at present existing amongst my former works colleagues.

Overseas army posting was normally for a nine years stint. Maybe foolishly, having chosen this option, rather than join with the IRA, I went off on embarkation leave. The big decision was my own choice, and now, could I live with it?

Insulted and dehumanised at Chatham, discarded by Henry Wells-Cole at Cheltenham, and now the insensitive Cass episode in Ireland, left me somewhat apprehensive.

With two years service behind me, and beginning to feel, not cocky, but a little bit special, never asking a man to do anything I could not do myself. Competently and efficiently handling, weapons, mechanical and field equipment, I had stamina to spare on whatever physical tests.

Being somewhat inhibited, but not much! Having fulfilled all that mattered in my pre-war world; I had my twentieth birthday party at Blackpool, been to Chatham, London, Royal Tunbridge Wells, Essex, Northern Ireland and Scotland. Where else was there to go? In flights numbering forty to fifty, I had watched The Luftwaffe as it flew overhead, to bomb London. The sad, despondent, and prevailing memory was the awful stench of humans, when in transit through the London underground system. Untold thousands of civilians occupied platforms of the 'tube'. It was as though a permanent place of residence. The stench was vile!

At Glasgow, our 1st Battalion nine, were joined by a similar number of junior officers; they were from another KOYLI battalion. We were further joined by a similar number, from the Gloucestershire Regiment, and

Lieutenant, Watkin-Williams, of the Gloucester's was detailed; 'Officer in charge', of the combined group; now designated – 'Officer Draft Z-26'.

We were a fortunate band, having the absolute luxury of no troops under command. The circumstances allowed for great bonding, there was mutual respect all round. In the daily assembly at Glasgow's King's Theatre, there were rumours of embarkation from just about every port in England, and in Scotland. It came subsequently, and on a cold and hazy frosty morning, at the small port of Gourock, near the mouth of the River Clyde. Dismounted from transports, we stood alongside a bleak grey wall to our front. The wall towered into the misted sky, as with no end. It was the hull of P & O. ship S.S.Strathallan. The walk up the gangplank, and boarding the ship, was mind-boggling. There was splendour beyond my wildest dreams.

Strathallan had ornate staircases, ankle deep carpets, classical paintings, staff in white uniforms, including cabin stewards, and a truly scrumptious restaurant. I had the good fortune of being allocated a double bunked cabin, sharing with a Scotsman, and he was almost a stranger; William Lauder Riddell. He proved to be a tremendous colleague. He was not going to make the return journey. God Bless him!

Nurses of the Queen Alexander's Imperial Nursing Service were the last to board, and on the 4th December 1941, S.S.Strathallan set sail. As dawn broke the following morning, the mist cleared slightly, we had sight of a convoy of possibly more than seventy accompanying vessels. This was a cautious reminder that the sea, in wartime, was a very dangerous place.

William Lauder riddle
What a Friend!

34

It was confirmed, most seriously, on the second night of sailing; flames were seen coming from two ships at the tail of the convoy.

It was on the third day, Sunday, the 7th December, joy and applause rang throughout Strathallan. With no great detail, the ship's notice board announced;

"Japanese forces have attacked an American Naval base at Hawaii".

This meant that Uncle Sam had, at last, by courtesy of the Japanese, been invited to join with the British in the conflict, and the war was now a world wide affair. Reluctant as it was? America was forced into a declaration of war, and conflict with Japan. Japan was now joined with the all-conquering Axis powers, Germany, and Italy.

How ironical can it get? With not one word to Britain, Australia, or any other participating power, particularly, Churchill; Franklin Delano Roosevelt, President of the USA, had, only days beforehand, signed a three month, none-aggression pact with Japan. The pact had now blown up in his face, and he must suffer the consequences. This debacle following his earlier covert approach to Vichy France, only emphasises, and confirms, the general feelings of British distrust of USA sentiments. Roosevelt, in his isolationism, and desperation to avoid the war, was further contemplating, offering a "Lend-Lease Bill"; to China. Anything to avoid USA involvement! And now he was to join in the fun!

Thanks to the Japanese intervention, all was to change for America. They were now involuntarily committed to war! The elaborate machinery prepared to prosper them from the European war, at Britain's cost, was now, after such a long wait, a domestic matter. Having disposed of the rubbish, USA was in position to supply provisioning, and modern munitions to Britain and her Allies; already committed to the war, for a rigorous twenty-seven months!

3

CHICANERY AND MACHINATIONS OF WAR

It might, at this point, be appropriate to introduce a consolitated and potted history of the duplicity, suspicions, squabbles, signals, secrets, shocks, surprises, with downright scandles; Leading to conflict.

(Incidents unearthed in stages throughout post war years. Bits one might not know; all relevant to the 1941/42 successful Japanese assault throughout Asia).

Piecemeal turmoil – I'll start gently.

World War One; Started August 1914, ended 11th November, 1918.

(A great ending, Whoops!; Gerald Fitzpatrick was born 10th August 1919)

1874 – Winston Spencer Churchill was born; to an American heiress and a British Lord. He entered British Parliament on 15th February 1901, and died 1965.

20th April 1889 – (A date considered by many to be evil, simply because, Adolf Hitler was born that day, in Austria). His father, a customs official, changed his name from Schickelgruber.

5th January 1919 – Anton Drexler founded the German Nazi Party, in Munich.

23rd March 1919 – Benito Mussolini (El Duce); In Italy, the Fascist political movement was formed, following the founding of, the *Fasci di Combattimento Party*, one month earlier.

20th April 1929 – Mussolini led first, exclusively Fascist formed, Italian Parliament, opened by Victor Emmanuel III. Mussolini was four years ahead of Hitler in setting the scene; (28th April 1945 – Along with Claretta Petacci, his mistress, Mussolini was, later, executed by Italian partisans, and hanged, head down, in a square in Milan).

8th November 1923 – Adolf Hitler (Fuehrer); The Nazi's Beer Hall Putsch, at Munich, was the start of Hitler's rise to power. The British Government, however, was reluctant to accept that Germany was on the road towards World War–Two.

Schoolteacher, Jim Battle, himself, a WW-One veteran, whilst I was still at school, in the early 1930's, warned pupils of the possible outbreak of war, in five or six years time. He proved right, almost to the minute. Military Conscription was never a thought at that time.

31st January 1933 – Adolf Hitler became Chancellor of Germany.

15th March 1933 – Hitler made his big move into power. He proclaimed; Nazi –Third Reich, stating; "It will endure for a thousand years"

15th June 1934– Hitler and Mussolini met for the first time, in Venice. This was the formation of the Axis Powers.

30th June 1934 – German SS murdered hundreds of influential Nazis, including Hitler's rival Ernst Rohm. The treachery was dubbed; - "The Night of the long knives".

19th August 1934 – A plebiscite in Germany gave power to Adolf Hitler.

17th March 1935 – Peace Treaty of Versailles; (Made between representatives of Germany and Allied Powers, at the Palace of Versailles, on 26th June 1919, and officially ended World War One), was broken by Nazi Germany; Hitler reintroduced conscription: -
(a) French were the only other government to institute conscription
(b) German 'Youth Camps' became the envy of British counterparts.

15th September 1935– At a Nuremberg rally, Hitler made the swastika the official German flag, and issued new decrees, relegating Jews to sub-human status.

29th September 1938 – Munich Pact; signed – between GB, France, Germany, Italy; Under which the Sudetenland was surrendered to Nazi Germany; In October, Prime Minister Neville Chamberlain returned from Germany, holding the Peace Pact agreement signed by Hitler; Stating, "I believe it is peace in our time". None were in doubt of the futility of this action.

31st March 1939 – Britain/France pledge support for Poland against possible aggression from Germany.

26th April 1939 – Conscription introduced in Britain for men aged 20; The call-up began almost immediately; Conflict had been long anticipated. The dilatory action was five years too late, and within five months of the ultimate outbreak of war.

23rd August 1939 – Germany, treacherously signed, 'Pact of None Aggression' with Russia; Hitler had in mind, an assault on Poland. (Britain had failed in attempting a similar Pact, also with Russia).

1st September 1939 – Germany invaded Poland

3rd September: 1939 – Britain declared war on Germany/Italy; (Axis Powers).

October 1939 – Personal Identity Cards were issued in Britain.

17th October 1939 – Six weeks following outbreak of war; Gerald Fitzpatrick, (1882721), and workmate David Williams, (1882722), joined the British army, Sappers in the Royal Engineers,

7th December 1940 – 'Fitz' Qualified – Emergency Commissioned Officer, (ECO) into; The Kings Own Yorkshire Light Infantry

1940 – Russian/Finland War continuing, Russia was struggling with Finland, as Churchill made one of his futile supercilious speeches, soon to be retracted;

> "Many illusions about Soviet Russia have been dispelled in these last few fierce weeks of fighting in the Arctic Circle. Everyone can see how communism rots the soul of a nation, how it makes it abject and hungry in peace, and proves it base and abominable in war".

Chameleon! – "Churchill was soon to change his mind!

8th April 1940 – Germany invaded Norway and Denmark

May/June 1940 – Dunkirk evacuation; In a state of chaos, over 300,000 British military escaped from defeat in Europe, French forces surrendered.

(Churchill suppressed news of the bombing, and sinking, of SS Lancastrian, at St Nazair, at the time of the Dunkirk evacuation, with the loss of over 4,000 civilians, many of them children).

(Selectively, Churchill restricted his valorous and reflectively predacious claim, to whatever success could be drawn from the Dunkirk debacle).

14th June 1940 – Eight days following German forces entry into Paris:

22nd June 1940 – France signed the armistice with Germany. French Marshall, Petain, established Nazi occupied 'Vichy France', (mostly Southern France). Petain became the leading Nazi collaborator. French General, (later President), De Gaul, decamped to England.

Mainland Europe was occupied by overpowering German forces; England was now seen by the rest of the world, particularly USA, as a failed nation, about to be occupied by the all conquering Axis.

Colonial Territories, (British 'Sinecures'); Long established on a worldwide basis, were overseas stations, (rest homes?), for 'time expired' senior military and government dignitaries. The position holders, were usually bestowed the title of 'Governor General', or similar, and the posts were keenly sought after; - being prestigious appointments, with pay. No dignitary was of great consequence, other than to be decorative, and ostensibly; Imagined that he could speak on behalf of His Majesty's Government.

18th June 1940 – With British forces scarpering from Europe, and France collapsing before German forces, Winston Churchill made one of his, tongue in cheek pronouncements;

> *"Let us brace ourselves to our duty and so bear ourselves that if the British Commonwealth and Empire lasts a thousand years, men will still say, This was their finest hour".*

The country was in a Hell of a mess!

30th June 1940 – German forces occupied the Channel Islands. In July 2010, actor/resident, John Nettles reports, (sic),

> "The islanders lived through five years of oppression, terror, collaboration and near starvation. The terrible scar has still not healed, and there remains a lot of bitterness."
>
> "Churchill and the government almost welcomed and invited the inhuman treatment that they knew was coming, so that they could use the plight of the islanders as propaganda. They had decided that the islands were of 'no strategic importance' and were effectively, abandoning them to fend for themselves."
>
> "After the war, the Government commissioned a report on happenings during the occupation, and when the 50-year ban on publication ended; Another prohibition was slapped on it!"
>
> "Whatever makes the content of that report so super-secret?"
>
> Disgusting! Typical British reserve, and preservation of the hierarchy! The truth hurts at times. Parliament and Military become flustered and indifferent in Command. It's not that they don't want to know; They will not admit!

21st August 1940 – Blitzkrieg began in the Battle of Britain – It continued mainly, throughout August/September 1940.

23 August 1941– Heaviest blitz, worst 10 May 1942; - 1400 civilians killed by 100,000 incendiary bombs.

27th September 1940 – Japan signed a ten-year military and economic alliance, (known as, 'The Axis Alliance), with both, Nazi Germany, and Fascist Italy.

Mid 1941 Women – Conscription for women was introduced; making 33 million under orders.

June/July 1941 – Germany, having summarily renounced its two year old German/Russian Pact, attacked Russia, under operation – 'Barbarossa'; (A code secret, revealed in captured post-war documents).

This diversion proved tragic for Hitler, he errantly, deferred the anticipated invasion of England, in order to invade what he mistakenly considered, a weak Russia. German losses on the Russian front totalled more than 500,000 monthly.

Hitler's catastrophic mistake, and foolish change of plan, proved a Godsend for Churchill. In the British Prime Minister's predacious manner, he turned the truth; He gloried, in claiming Hitler's turnabout, to be a British victory, and vaingloriously, attributable to himself!

Britain and Russia – Formed a reluctant although convenient alliance. This was an essential gesture, following the previous failure by the pair to Pact.

Churchill's wife, Clementine, began fund raising for Russia, and Churchill 'the Chameleon'; altered his tune. Communism quite suddenly, stopped;

"rotting the soul".

Russian KGB officers supervised Russian ships loading at British ports.

ITIE'S – At this time, Italian Armed Forces were considered, a joke, following their 1930's military failures, in Abyssinia.

World Map – The maxim, "The sun never sets on the British Empire"; died! All was about to change. Yanks saw fit to put the 'Knife' into a failing Britain. They had for fifty years or more, been envious, and distrustful, of the widespread British Empire. Seeing Britain as a failed nation, USA sought to profit. In a timorous manner, they showed numerous, recent and denigrating, 1940 films, illustrating Britain to be in the throes of death.

USA immigrants, German, Italian and particularly, the Irish; All powerful throughout the country, and remembering the mid 1800's potato famine years, objected to USA intervention in Europe, and denied support to the Allied cause.

2nd May 1942 – HMS Edinburgh – Sunk by German aircraft in the Berents Sea with a loss of 88 British sailors. Cargo; 432 bars of Russian gold, (£45,000,000), being 'advance payment', by Russia, to USA, for wartime supplies!

No mention was made in USA of the tragic loss of so many British lives. (The full story of this tragedy was revealed, as late as October 1981. Yorkshire-man, Keith Jessop, recovered the gold).

Middle East, German forces under Rommell, crossed North Africa.

Australian Forces drastically short of provisions, including ammunition, were butchered on the island of Crete, with 9000 men lost. Australian P.M. John Curtin, wrongfully blamed General Wavell for this tragedy. Churchill readily, and equally wrongful, put the blame on Wavell, (A Russian speaking general). Dismissing Wavell, Churchill banished him to India. Ostensibly, removing him from 'active' military command, to what was considered, 'a remote Sinecure.'

June 1941 – Middle East Command passed to Auchinleck, replacing Wavell. Wavell was transferred to India.

17th September 1941 – With Germany deflected from attacking Britain, and fully committed against Russia, Churchill considered new options; – Assuming that no danger existed beyond Suez, he unwontedly, and mistakenly, ordered the diversion of ships carrying two infantry divisions/tanks/artillery/reinforcements, destined for the Far East; into the Middle East.

This catastrophic blunder was, just three months before Japan attacked the USA naval base at Pearl Harbour.

Wavell's request for Far East reinforcements was ignored, as Churchill made a further one of his recorded comments;

"Malaya and Singapore can wait, and West Africa can be fitted in, or not, as convenient". – Oh dear!

18th September 1941 – The following day! Unaware of American duplicity in their Japanese dealings, it was the ultimate case of; 'The blind leading the blind'. Churchill mollified Roosevelt on Japanese possibilities: -

"There should be no serious fighting until March 1942; Except in the Western Desert":

Once again, how very wrong was Mr Churchill?

29th September 1941 – 33,000 Russian Jews murdered in Kiev, by Nazi death squad.

November 1941 – Roosevelt deceitfully, and saying nothing of his attempted negotiations with Japan; sought further advice from Churchill, regarding possible Japanese intent; The speculative advice was given, with the usual, cocksure, Churchill conviction;

"Japan will lie quiet for a while".

"Japan was more likely to drift into war rather than plunge".

This was within days of the 7th December; Pearl Harbour catastrophe!

Roosevelt commented; *"In Japan's present mood, remonstration might have opposite effect to warning them off".* And, for once, how right he was!

In the Middle East, Churchill continued to consider forces beyond Suez, in a minor role. He caused delay in sending; 5 British infantry battalions to India.

This was followed by a manifestly greater mistake, in the next few short weeks; Churchill ordered, 'Regular', Indian and Gurkha troops, to be withdrawn from India, and sent as reinforcements, to the Middle East Cocksure, and increasingly arrogant, with no idea of Japan's burgeoning militant mood, the Indian Government was assured by Churchill;

"Delay in sending reinforcements was only a brief one"

The old British maxim continued to apply; 'Show them a man of war!

Meanwhile Churchill, having denied five infantry battalion re-inforcements to India, was supported by the Commander in Chief, British Home Fleet. The 'pair of wizards', vetoed a proposal, to deploy to Singapore, by the spring of 1942; (7 Capital ships, 1 Aircraft carrier, 10 Cruisers, 24 Destroyers). This was a catastrophic and incompetent decision, in view of the imminent activity throughout the Far East. When subsequently attempting to justify this erroneous decision, Churchill, wrote of Roosevelt; (sic)

"I was in charge of a struggling country, beset by a deadly foe. He was aloft, august, at the head of a mighty neutral power whom he

desired above all things to bring into the fight for freedom, but he could not see how to do it. Britain had to plan her own scheme of war".

Japan/China , were at war for four years in the late 1930's. News of this conflict was scant, and considered irrelevant. Far Eastern events were overshadowed by Western world concerns, and activities. Over the period of their long conflict, both oriental armies gained considerable experience in warfare.

British Intelligence, in close contact with Malaysian palm-oil farmers, and others, reported, with the warning;

"Japan had more than the war with China as an interest".

Churchill gave scant consideration to the possibilities, and commented in a manner that reflected bitter views, long held by the British public.

"If Japanese aggression drew America off the fence, I would be content to have it". "They have plundered Britain long enough".

Roosevelt Commented: -

"It would be serious to underestimate the gravity of the threat from Japan".

Little did he know; how short was the time? He also warned Churchill; *"No secret Pacts with Russia!"* And not one word of the USA underhand attempted USA pact with Japan.

Churchill, and the British people, did not trust America; USA continued, 'Sitting on the fence', they had taken no part in the first three years, of the four year long, WW-One; From September 1939, USA were, once again, 'sitting on the fence', and avoiding conflict, for 2 ¼ years.

Roosevelt's advisers were constantly, reminding him of insular and shady conduct, carried out by one of his predecessors;

19th March 1920 – Under President, Woodrow Wilson, the US Senate had rejected, for a second time, the ratification of, "The 1919, Treaty of Versailles". Hence, by so doing, preventing the USA joining the recently developed, League of Nations, fearing they would have to go to war again in the event of another member state being invaded.

A short time earlier, the same President held America back, for three years, from World War–One. He embraced the delay, until, realising that all weakened participants involved were in a state of total exhaustion. America then joined for the final year, and claimed the hollow victory.

Once again, under another very dubious President, America did not want war; until USA forces were attacked at Pearl Harbour, by a superbly equipped Japanese strike force. Throughout that long period, of bogus peace, the American sole concern appeared to be, 'profit'. USA politicians and celebrities had fun attending riotous 'Charity Parties', raising funds to send 'food parcels' to what they considered;

"The starving and vanquished British".

11th March 1941 – With Britain in financial plight, Roosevelt sought to exploit it to the full. FDR persuaded the American Congress to introduce the novel, 'Lend-Lease Bill'. This was not the charity it was made to look, and the bill was drawn; *'With no formalised account system'.*

All British Dollar assets in USA were ceased.

British were ordered to vacate all Caribbean bases.

Alastair Cooke; Official British reporter, was restricted in movement.

Churchill was warned – by Roosevelt – "No attempted agreement with Stalin"; "NO SECRET PACTS!" He saw things differently at a later date, in his Secretary of State meeting with the Japanese Ambassador.

The Lend-Lease Bill, allowed Britain to borrow millions of American Dollars, in order to buy food, arms, and essentials, in order to pursue their, 'remote' war; - so long as it remained remote. It became a heyday for prairie farmers, as they revitalised from the years of famine, to sell their products at whatever price. Yanks sat on the fence, and watched Britain suffer.

America sold Britain 51 obsolete warships; 41 of which remained unserviceable at the close of 1941.

With British money to play with, and the remote European continent in turmoil, USA developed food provisioning, and massive plants were set up on a grand scale; munitions, tanks, aircraft, and vehicles, were produced to meet 'Allied needs'.

Having got themselves out of the long years of depression, on British borrowed money, America flourished for a further nine months, before their whole world erupted.

In very short time, the whole of the, 'Lend-Lease' investment was; required to meet, USA needs. An immediate halt was called on all supplies to Britain, and production plants, paid for by Britain, diverted to meet American requirements. Britain was now, at its lowest ebb, and America expected, within a few short months, that the vanquished country would become occupied by the Axis Powers,

It was 65 years before Britain cleared, and repaid, the vindictively mighty debts, incurred throughout the manoeuvring of the ill considered, 'magnanimous Lend- Lease Bill'.

At this juncture, had the British public, and particularly, the British Armed Forces, been aware of the exploitation of them, by Roosevelt, they would, willingly, have; 'Thrown in their lot', against America.

Japanese Planning – Japan was desperate to overcome the effects of restricted sanctions on oil supplies, as applied by Britain/USA. The perils envisaged, and troubling a shaky Roosevelt, were already in an advanced stage of preparation by the Japanese Admiralty, and further developed by the Military: - In meticulous detail, Japan planned to end all embargoes imposed by foreign powers. Networks of spies and secret agents were established, to operate throughout all, 'targeted areas', of Asia.

This very special communication is sent to me by the son of a former resident of Burma, now living in England.

> "My uncle, a former Chief of the Rangoon Police, had warned the authorities, in either Rangoon or London, that the Japs were scouting the Bay of Bengal for possible landing sites as early as 1938"

He goes on to say;

> "Dorman-Smith, (British Governor of Burma), stupidity was well known. The family considered him a 'high-grade defective'.

Burmese, Thakin tribal leader; 24 year old Aung-San, (father of Aung San Suu Kyi), and his Burmese Nationalist force, were known as; "The

Thirty", and training with the Japanese. The British would consider them to be Dacoits.

The Police Chief; "Was deeply concerned about communism, of which Aung San's brother was known to be one".

U-Saw, Premier of Burma; was already incarcerated in Lisbon, Portugal; his army force, the 'Galon (Nationalist) Army', was also training with the Japanese;

World Situation; As seen by the Japanese in 1941.

1. All European colonisers of the East, as below, were held under the Axis yolk.

    British – India, Burma, Singapore, Malaya, Hong Kong, Papua New Guinea

    French – Cambodia, Thailand, Laos, Vietnam, French Indo China

    Dutch – Dutch East Indies, Indonesia

    Portuguese – Macao

With carefully planned, simultaneous insurrection, Japan targeted each one of the above European held territories;

2. Russia was committed in the war with Germany – with losses of 500,000 + men, every month; Similar casualties being suffered by Germany.
3. Britain was virtually a defunct nation;
   Ready for Nazi occupation; Once Russia was conquered.
4. American naval power was there for the taking; based at Hawaii
5. Australia and New Zealand would be easy pickings – ANZAC military forces were committed to the Western War.

THE WORLD WAS NOW, A VERY DANGEROUS PLACE

4

THE COMEDY OF LAMENTABLE COMMAND

In a quote from the opening lines of the brilliant 1939 film, 'Four Feathers',

General Herbert Kitchener, British Supremo at Khartoum, in 1898, made a plea; (sic) – "He called for aid, but no help came".

What changes? Let's see how we go from there?

Unaware of the, perverse self preservation, idiosyncrasies, and chicanery, practiced by, Parliamentarians, and those in the upper echelons of Military Command, I along with innumerable service personnel, was no more than a chattel, to be dispatched to wherever my superiors saw fit, and do as they Command. Not surprisingly; there were times when, both Parliamentary and Military Command, becoming over-faced, and flustered, showed complete disinterest, and the serviceman could never question; Morons, secure in higher echelons, are reinforced by tramp editors of certain newspapers; The Observer, (3rd June 1984), followed by Sunday Telegraph, (7th October 1984), and a succession of others, bent on sucking-up to British hierarchic tradition, unhesitatingly distorting the truth. Following them, are the scum of mendacious plagiaristic authors; mostly praising, and sucking-up to regiments, regimental associations, and campaign organisations.

Indifferent to the kerfuffle surrounding me; Commissioned, as a British, Army Officer, with pay! I was living in the lap of what I considered super luxury, and at a completely different level to that of my pre-war days. Mr Churchill, and his agent, Colonel 'Copper' Cass, were determined to keep my future, 'A Secret'. Accepting the situation, I had to make the best of it; And I did!

Little did I know that my future was to change in so short a time, and activities, about which I knew nothing, were imminently set to influence the lives of civilian and military personnel world-wide; Within the secretive and un-chartered times, diaries and activities overlapped, and interlaced; The world was on the fringe of embroilment, in the most unpredictable global turmoil.

9th November 1941; Surprisingly! Britain, with improved production of arms, and food, thanks to the efforts of ladies employed on munitions, and in the Land Army, declared itself, "less dependent on USA aid". In view of this, and completely unaware of what was to come within the space of one month, Prime Minister Churchill commented; -

"I would rather have an American declaration of war, now, and no supplies for six months, than double the supplies and no declaration".

Such rash action was completely unimaginable throughout the USA. With the rest of the world hungry for whatever supplies; America flourished. Through nefarious channels, Italian and German immigrants were provisioning their own nationals. The Irish American contingent would have no dealings with the British; *(Although many thousands of Irish men, and women, served in the British Armed Forces)*. In its resurgence, following the many years of depression, and thousands queuing at soup kitchens, America was fulfilling the dream.

War was the last thing Yanks wanted; Although Japanese planning, and intervention, was imminent, there was no such thing as a USA declaration; It was flourishing in neutrality, with two decades of hunger, and suppression behind them. Systems of supply, for cash, were developed, to whomsoever? "Be they friend or foe?" There was no such thing as loyalty, or obligation!

In late 1941, General Auchinleck, although giving the appearance of success, whilst Commanding in the Libyan Desert. He failed!

With the wave of Churchill's magic wand, 'The Auch' followed Wavell into the backwoods, 'to the back of beyond', to become Commander in

Chief, India. Having clashed with Montgomery, he became, just another; 'considered disgraced', and despatched, to the 'Sinecure' of India, only to be replaced by the more flamboyant, Bernard Montgomery.

Regimental serving officers knew nothing of the fudging, back-biting, petty jealousies, along with the downright favouritism, conducted at higher Parliamentary, or Military levels; although, it was sensed. There was a dull feeling when things were going wrong, and a better one when going right. Occasionally, activity was conducted in the most secretive, and unexpected circumstances.

Three weeks before the 7th December, Japanese bombing of Pearl Harbour, a bizarre naval encounter took place off the coast of Western Australia; A fatal conflict between two ships; Australian, HMAS SIDNEY, and the KORMORAN, a German merchantman; -. The conflict was overseen by a partly submerged Japanese submarine.

The German vessel was supply ship to the submarine, and as the SIDNEY and KORMORAN fought, each destroyed the other, both sinking into the ocean. The Japanese submarine surfaced, and rescued only the German sailors. All struggling Australians were machine-gunned; No Australian survived, and no report of the tragedy reached Australia.

In year, approximately 1998, The remarkably secret story of the HMAS SIDNEY and KORMORAN conflict, including that of the Japanese intervention, was related by a former Japanese sub-mariner, (now a naturalised Australian).

Completely unaware of the Japanese intervention, the SIDNEY loss was reported to Churchill, by Australian PM John Curtin. Both Curtin, and Churchill, chose to withhold the news from America's Roosevelt. The two Prime Ministers connived in secrecy, in order to maintain USA equilibrium, and avoid pressurising Roosevelt.

Churchill signalled to Curtin – (Memoirs Vol VII, page 232/3); (verbatim).

131 – Churchill to John Curtin London 28th Nov 1941 1-00 am.

Cablegram Winch 6

Para (3) "Accept my deepest sympathy in the feared loss of SYDNEY so close to Australian shores. 3 We also have a grievous blow this week in the loss of the BARHAM, which blew up as a result of a U-Boat torpedo, involving the death of about 700 men. This is being kept & strictly secret at present as the enemy do not seem to know and the event would only encourage Japan".

3 "The cruiser HMAS SIDNEY was lost with her entire crew off the Western Australian coast on 19th November (1941) after action with the German raider KORMORAN. The first news of her loss came when survivors from KORMORAN were picked up on 24th Nov (1941) and it was confirmed by Curtin on 30th Nov. (end of message)".

(Neither Prime Minister knew anything of the Japanese submarine covert activity.)

(Churchill Memoirs Page 238)

Signal 134 – Curtin to Churchill

Cablegram Johcu 4 sent Canbera 29 Nov 41 – 6-45pm

Received 29 Nov 1-15pm (time difference)

(The Japanese fleet was already sea-bound towards Pearl Harbour)

"I greatly appreciate your expression of sympathy in the loss of HMAS SIDNEY".

24th November 1941. Churchill advised British Foreign Secretary; (sic)

"Japan might attack Dutch possessions". "It was best leave this as a direct issue between America and Japan".

"If after a reasonable interval, the United States is incapable of decisive action, even with our immediate support, we will nevertheless, although alone, make common cause with the Dutch". "Any Japanese attack on British possessions, carries with it, war with Great Britain as a matter of course".

25th November 1941; Within less than two weeks of the imminent; 7th December, Japanese attack on Pearl Harbour; Oblivious to the microscopically detailed, and perfectly structured, oncoming Japanese onslaught, and with no word to Churchill, or to Australia's Curtin.

Roosevelt was accepting the remote, and conquered British situation as terminal. He fully anticipated the total demise of Britain, and that Axis Powers would occupy the vanquished country at will. American interest was centred upon the European theatre of war and the self-centred financial possibilities.

Within two weeks of the oncoming Japanese assault on the USA naval base, at Pearl Harbour, Roosevelt had no consideration of a possible outbreak of war in the Far East; To Americans in general, war was unthinkable.

Neutral Lisbon, in Portugal, was the nerve-centre for covert international negotiations, and a convenient place for subterfuge. It was here, with no consideration for Britain, American Secret Servicemen liaised, surreptitiously, with representatives from German controlled, Vichy France.

In Washington USA, Secretary of State, Cordell Hull, was engaged over a long period, in secret and constant negotiations, with Japanese Ambassador Nomura, and Secretary of State, Mr Kurusu; The basis of which was; -"Regarding, so much turmoil and confusion among the public in both the United States, and in Japan". In his eventual signing of the Pact, as he did with Japan, Roosevelt must have had news, from Lisbon, suggesting imminent activity, although he could not envisage it coming from the East; (See document in appendix).

Considering Britain completely impotent, Uncle Sam was set, and fully prepared, to do its treacherous business of provisioning within Nazi occupied Europe!

Knowledge of Roosevelt's underhand, and catastrophic, Presidential Pact, was not revealed for a considerable time. The deed became masked in verbosity and inane reports, to be secreted away, and conveniently overlooked.

This was high level treachery by Roosevelt; he was totally disregarding the interests of; British/Dutch/French/China/India, and Australia/New Zealand.

30th November, 1941; Whilst negotiating the signing of the secretive, USA/Japanese Pact, the Japanese 'ratted', and telegrammed to Hitler. –

"War may suddenly break out between Anglo Saxon and Japan Nations; Quicker than anyone dreams".

They were not kidding! *(The Japanese fleet was already mobilised, armed, provisioned, and under sail for Pearl Harbour).*

4th December 1941 –Gerald Fitzpatrick, a member of a draft of eighteen officers, boarded P&O ship SS Strathallan. With no regard for the sensitivity of eighteen keen young officers, the intended destination of the draft was withheld, it was guardedly announced as;

"A posting to a tropical destination".

6th December; Britain and America; although aware of Japanese fleet movements in the Pacific, failed to appreciate the imminent significance of the activity; No preparation of any form was possible, or contemplated, in readiness for the carefully planned onslaught Japan was about to launch. Japanese Prime Minister, Hideki Tojo, (Later hanged as a war criminal), congratulated and shook the hands of his Foreign Secretary, Mr Nomura, and Japanese Ambassador, Mr Kurusu. The pair had successfully hoodwinked Cordell Hull, the USA negotiator, on behalf of the President.

7th December 1941 – Message on SS Strathallan – Ship's notice board;

"Japanese aircraft have bombed American naval base at Hawaii"

Unaware of the extent of the bombing, we on board Strathallan, and still awaiting confirmation of our intended destination, rejoiced; applause rang out throughout the ship; America could, 'sit on the fence', no longer.

Additional to the massive Hawaii, Pearl Harbour assault, the devastatingly detailed, and technical Japanese attack, was launched across many fronts; With trained native corroborators guiding and assisting; Japanese armed forces, spread fan-like, throughout South East Asia, from the Malay Peninsula, to Papua New Guinea, and eventually, touching Australia. The detailed strategy, and intensive depth, of the hostile insurrection, was beyond the comprehension of Western powers.

Scandalous hypocrisy, of the highest order, was demonstrated on the evening of December 7th 1941, as two unsuspecting USA diplomats dined with Churchill, at Chequers, his country house. American Ambassador, Mr John Winant, and President Roosevelt's special envoy to Europe, Mr Averell Harriman, became caught up in a hiatus.

The two senior American civil servants would have been fully briefed, and possibly involved, on the despicable Pact, between Roosevelt and the Japanese, which was not revealed to Churchill. That they should hear, over the British, BBC wireless, of the Japanese bombing of Pearl Harbour, whilst dining with Churchill, was the ultimate in incongruities.

The two Americans had difficulty in restraining Churchill from instantly, declaring war with Japan, on the basis of a possible erratic, almost unbelievable news bulletin. Churchill was however, delighted to know that, at last; -The USA had been mercilessly drawn into the conflict, however late!

With the USA Pacific Fleet, and all planes on the Philippines destroyed, Australia and New Zealand were exposed, they had no combat troops available; All were fully committed in the Western Deserts of Africa, and mostly under British Command.

Tuesday 9th December 1941 – Whilst considering two capital ships stationed off Singapore; HMS Prince of Wales (35,000 tons), Admiral Phillips; and Battle Cruiser HMS Repulse, Captain Tennant.

Churchill was in discussion on deployment with the Commander in Chief, Home Fleet; -

(C in C begrudged warships being committed to the East).

Churchill commented, *"It's a matter of no great urgency, I'll sleep on it!"*

10th December; Japanese attacked from Saigon, 400 miles distant; 85 Japanese bombers obliterated the two warships. Admiral Phillips was killed. Captain Tennant and 40% of Repulse crew survived. 840 sailors lost their lives, 2,000 were saved.

In treating this tragedy, as with his previous adversities; other than a bland comment, no further Churchill reaction is recorded. It was left to the C in C Home Fleet to take all blame, and become 'sidelined' in Command.

Visiting the 2001 erected, National Arboretum- War Memorial, on 24th September 2011, I was somewhat sickened, to see the following disparaging comment, on the loss of both ships; The Prince of Wales, and the Repulse, attributable to Churchill: -

"In all the war I never received a more direct shock. As I turned over and twisted in bed, the full horror of the news sank into me"

The heart, now ripped out of British naval power, in the Far East. There were no Allied capital ships in the Indian or Pacific oceans.

The old maxim; 'Send in a man of war!' was never to succeed again.

Churchill showed no great remorse at the loss of the two British warships, although it was HMS Prince of Wales that had conveyed him to an earlier meeting with Roosevelt. His only reported comment is; "Poor Tom Phillips". With no mention whatsoever, of regrets for his earlier expressions of indifference; "No great urgency", and "I'll sleep on it!"

Japan controlled 8,000 miles – in all directions – 1/5th of world surface.

The vastness, speed, audacity, and sheer spunk, of Japanese activities, were astonishing. Tactics had been developed throughout several years of, what was considered a stalemate Japanese conflict, one of no consequence, against China.

11th December 1941 – Although banished, as Wavell was; and ironically, conveniently situated as the man on the spot, however curmudgeonly; he was appointed, Commander in Chief, of the Far East, including Burma.

Remote and mundane, the Far East, in its tranquillity, was considered by Churchill to be of no consequence, and little was thought of a possible extension of conflict throughout Asia. With the prospect of uprising, and turmoil, as the last thing on Churchill's mind, he gave Wavell additional responsibility; For Persia/Iraq, (PI Force).

Following his recent demoralising experiences, wherever he commanded, and the setbacks caused through Churchill's interference, Wavell had unfortunately declared, in one of his many studious edicts; "An appreciation of the situation": -

"That Burma need not be taken seriously"

With this indifferent philosophy of forethought, ingrained in the new commander, and Japan now totally committed; *"Burma was a lost cause"*, long before it became involved. This fateful sentiment and the precise words were to be pronounced by the incoming Theatre Commander, General, Harold Rupert Leofric George Alexander, the man destined to serve under Wavell. They were uttered within twenty-four hours of his arrival.

11th December 1941 – Seeking to further exploit the Pearl Harbour devastation of the USA navy, by the Japanese, Germany officially declared war on America. Oh Dear!

> *The non-aggressive USA, having sat on the fence from the outset, had carefully, and purposefully, made no declaration! Japan had dragged them into the Eastern war, and now, Germany wanted them!*
>
> *Immediate USA Embargo applied; Following the German declaration!*
>
> *(Convinced that Britain was now a defunct nation, and invasion by Germany was imminent, Roosevelt placed an embargo on all goods going from America to Britain).*

Hong Kong – 21st December 1941; Japanese assaulted;

> Churchill signalled commander, the usual claptrap!
>
> *(sic)*** "Continue vigorous fighting in inner defences, house to house if need be, maintain resistance". – "Obtain lasting honour!"*

Hong Kong fell in days. Mr Churchill was not going to, 'Obtain lasting honour'.

MOBILISATION – The Kings Own Yorkshire Light Infantry – 2nd Battalion.

Prior to the forthcoming Japanese activity, and with no hint of conflict in the Far East; Britain required the return of all Regular Army forces, to compete in Europe. From the tranquil and uncommitted existence, at the pleasant garrison town of Maymyo, in Northern Burma, the 2nd

Battalion K O Y L I were mobilised, and set to training, with the prospect of making the long sea-borne return to England

2/KOYLI Involvement; August 1941 – Completely unaware of any possibility of a Far Eastern war; the Battalion departed the comforts of Maymyo, (approximately 45 miles from Mandalay). Mobilised, they transferred to the nearby, small tableland town of Taungyi, in the Shan States of Central Burma; a temperate area, as near as possible to that of Europe.

The unit became fully committed, undertaking intense training; Preparing for European style, open warfare. They were a solid unit, with men of high quality, and experience, mostly garnished on the North West Frontier of India. They had suffered no molestation, as had Regiments returned from involvement in the Dunkirk evacuation. However, the situation was to change, rapidly, and with tragic consequences.

Reacting to reports of the rapidly developing Japanese activity, the Battalion was once again transferred. This time, and with no defined objective, it was a reversal activity, and centred upon the possibilities of immediate Asian concerns.

The allocated task was to cover the northern Salween River crossing; The China Road, the singular land-entry point into north eastern Burma.

Unfamiliar, and unpractised in jungle warfare, men of the unit spent six futile weeks, operating under an ageing World War One, Battalion Commander. The man conducted affairs in the only way that he knew; as though preparing for open European style conflict. Men were set to digging WW-One type entrenchments, a system totally inappropriate for the close contact of jungle warfare.

Rejecting an offer, 'one made on medical grounds', to withdraw the Battalion from the mosquito ridden area, Commanding Officer, Colonel Keegan, demonstrated the stubborn streak he considered patriotic. The glory-seeking decision proved to be progressively fatal within the unit. Almost 100% of troops became infested with malaria, and numerous other tropical ailments. Sickness throughout the unit was to become woefully evident, in the weeks of malarial incubation.

Late December 1941: – At a speed beyond anything of Churchill's, or the British War Office imagination, marauding Japanese forces were making towards South East Burma. In anticipation of conflict, an uncomfortable eight days of road and rail journey, was undertaken in transferring 2/KOYLI, from the Hell of the Salween River banks, to Southern Burma.

On 19th January 1942: – The highly organised, experienced, and well equipped Japanese Army, invaded Burma, to be directed by selected, and trained, Nationalist minded Burmese Guides. The whole of Asia was now in turmoil, with trained natives guiding and aiding in the dispersal and demolition of all European influence.

No western military force was trained, equipped, provisioned, or had leadership, adequate to deal with the carefully plotted, ocean-wide onslaught, as conducted by the Japanese.

February 1942; 18th British Division, whilst in transit to India, and due to operate under the Command of Wavell, was surreptitiously diverted, by Churchill, into Singapore; Unforgivably! Wavell, the Theatre Commander, was not informed, and General Percival, the Singapore Commander, was surprised, to say the least, whilst in his dogmatic manner, Churchill signalled, with his usual claptrap;

"Nothing compares in importance with fortress Singapore."

"The 18th Division has a chance to make its name in history".

"Commanders and senior officers should die with their troops".

"The honour of the British Empire and of the British Army is at stake".

"I rely on you to show no mercy or weakness in any form".

"No hostile force, can overcome the mighty Singapore defence".

Who the Hell wants to die with anybody?

The wise guidance of the Palm-oil operators, that Japanese agents were seen to be operating along the Malay coast, were ignored, in the manner renowned amongst the overbearing, and egotistic, upper-level, British officials. They were, 'always, so right'; and, "What do Palm-oil men know of military affairs?" Decreeing that;

British Officialdom, go about their menial daily tasks.

Ignoring the mighty southwards facing guns of Singapore, as all were pointing out to sea, the Japanese moved in from a completely different angle. They assaulted along the more northerly coastline of Malaya; as predicted by Palm Oil planters.

Churchill's persistent interventions did no more than scupper the hopes of many thousands of troops, and civilians. The ongoing failures, at Hong Kong, Java, and Singapore, and in other theatres, were never attributed to the unsought interventions, by Prime Minister, Winston Churchill.

Churchill was not the one dying! His diverted troops of 18th Div, had hardly occupied their Singapore barracks, and had no time to acclimatise, before being taken prisoner of war.

13th February 1942; From 2,000 miles distance, in his newly found, Java HQ, Wavell followed Churchill, in signalling Gen Percival in Singapore; (sic).

"Continued action essential!" "House to house if need be".

"It may have a vital influence on other areas".

These were great words, when spoken from that distance, particularly after his recently recorded, and damning, 'Appreciation of the situation'; "That Burma need not be taken seriously".

Sunday 15th February, at 8.30 pm; With one million civilians in danger, and under a threat of cuts in water supplies, Singapore ceased hostilities; A massive 85,000 armed forces surrendered, including the Churchill diverted 18th Div. Once again, under Wavell's command, 17,000 Australians were taken Prisoners of War.

Churchill shifted the blame once again, and demanded an explanation of failure from C in C, Percival, who was himself, within hours, a prisoner of war.

"Poor Arthur Percival"; He had been bestowed the absolutely plumb, and most favoured Sinecure of Singapore, and promoted Major General. The exalted appointment was granted in recognition, and reward, for his tyrannical 1920/22 Command, in Southern Ireland, based on the town of Cork. Commanding the Essex Regiment, he had favoured Churchill, in accommodating his brutal, and unmerciful, 'Egotistical County- Set', of British, 'Black and Tan' forces. The force consisted, mainly, of a select bunch of former Public School, 'upper-bracket hoodlums'. They showed no mercy whatsoever, against any suspect, or disliked, walking Irishman; Percival, and the B&T, accounted for between 2,000 and 4,000 killings of Irish men and women.

Churchill had good reason to favour Percival, although through his own normal face saving volition, he left his former favourite; 'To stew in his own juice'. (In ignominy, and destitute, Percival died a broken man). Churchill, a contributor to the Singapore failure, could, and should have, shared responsibility.

Quoting from the Malaysia Sunday Times, Star Magazine, 19th June 2005, we get the historical background, as seen by Malaysians of modern times. (sic): -

MENG YEW CHOONG examines how Lt-Gen Tomoyuki Yamashita, the Tiger of Malaya, defied the odds and routed an enemy three times bigger, and entrenched in a fortress, (Singapore), touted as 'impregnable':

Conventional military doctrine says an attacker needs a numerical advantage of at least 3:1 against a dug-in-foe just to have an equal chance of success as the defender.

On Feb 10, a deeply troubled General Archibald Wavell, Allied Supreme Commander for the Far East, confessed to the Governor, Sir Shenton Thomas, that; "Whatever misfortune that besieged them at the moment, shouldn't have happened", to which Thomas replied, "We lacked leaders".

On the same night, the elite Japanese Imperial Guards crossed the Johor Straits to battle the Australian 27th Brigade, at the spot between the causeway and Kranji River.

Excerpt from Lt-Gen Tomoyuki; "My attack on Singapore was a bluff – a bluff that worked. I had 30,000 men and was outnumbered more than three to one. I knew if I had to fight long for Singapore, I would be beaten. That is why the surrender had to be at once. I was frightened all the time that the British would discover our numerical weakness and lack of supplies and force me into disastrous street fighting."

Percival signed the surrender document at Bukit Timah, at 6pm, on 15th February 1942. Churchill called the surrender of Singapore, "The largest capitulation in British history"; On this, Cornelli Barnet, former keeper of Churchill archives, commented: *"Winston had a remarkable capacity for distancing himself from mistakes, and disasters that had his name over them".*

In his letters to the forum pages of The Straits Times in 1997/8, Singapore historian Dr Ong Chit Chung argued that; (sic)

"Churchill consistently underestimated the Japanese threat"; "In retrospect, the battle for Malaya was lost – even before the first shot was fired; In Downing Street!"

"Commanders in Malaya were not without fault. They were weak and indecisive. But the fact remains that Malaya and Singapore were starved of the necessary reinforcements, in particular, they were left without a fleet, and without air power".

"The commanders were expected to make bricks without straw. The main responsibility must, therefore, rest squarely on the shoulders of Churchill. It was Churchill who placed Malaya below Europe, the Middle East, and Russia, in terms of priorities and the allocation of resources. Reading Churchill's telegram (as published in his memoirs), one wonders why he was so gung-ho about defending Singapore, only at the 11th hour. It was, Too little; and Too late!"

At the faraway South Eastern end of the Japanese fan-like blitzkrieg, the first bombs were dropped on Rabaul, Papua New Guinea, on the 4th January. Once again, interference from enemy aliens, particularly German, was suspected, and with no more than primitive communications, the report of, "A full scale attack on Rabaul", did not appear in Brisbane newspapers, until nearly three weeks later; 21st January.

Reports of 15 to 20 Axis sympathiser operations were ignored, and with a frightening silence, over many stark days, communications and co-operation between Civil and Military became chaotic.

Such was the chaos, the Australian Chief of Staff reported: -

"No knowledge of happenings in New Britain from 23rd January, until 14th February". "Received from Port Moresby"

Probably the most ridiculous signal throughout the war was transmitted by an Oz Minister; *"Expect full-scale attack and landing on Rabaul"*. In attempting to mollify mainland Australians, he went on, as though the sea was some form of impregnable defence structure; *"Rabaul is 1432 miles from Brisbane".*

With the Australian Regular Army actively committed throughout all existing conflicts, Prime Minister John Curtin was rapidly becoming disenchanted with Britain's Prime Minister, Winston Churchill. The split was to come!

(See appendix; Source; "Documents on Australian Foreign Policy 1937-49.

'Selected pages' from Volume 5, pages 533/560).

16th February – With their blitzkrieg type attack, apart from Papua New Guinea, Japanese Forces were already in occupation at Bali, Makassar, and Timor.

Fully aware of a situation that he could not change, Churchill promised Wavell;

"Planes, tanks, guns, reinforcements"; "Once Libya was won?"

Libya was not won until many months later, much too late!

In Churchill's "Road to Victory 1941/45", (Page 93) Gilbert Martin. (Heinemann)

"But the war with Japan was the lesser war";

"The best that can be hoped for is that the retreat will be as slow as possible"

Churchill priorities – December 1941; Determined on board a warship, as he was bound for America –

Defence of British Isles – including – "U-Boat threat"

The Struggle in the Middle East and Mediterranean

Supplies to Russia

Resistance to Japanese assault.

Any problem in the Far East was of low priority.

A-B-D-A; (America/Britain/Dutch/Australia), Far East Command was formed, with a four headed control unit. At this point, Churchill, and other Western Commanders were completely out of their depth, totally lacking in strategies for Eastern Warfare.

With no reference to him whatsoever, Churchill readily volunteered Wavell as; "Commander in Chief, A-B-D-A", and accepted for him, by proxy; Wavell was thus designated, as though a puppet, into an appointment about which he knew nothing.

However, all was not well with others. Australian Premier, John Curtin, was livid at the arbitrarily made appointment, particularly in view of what he was experiencing; 'The never ending series, of Wavell's fatalistic failures'.

Churchill warns – whilst in USA and Canada; (sic);

"That forces to be made available would be destroyed by the Japanese onslaught", "and that he had not anticipated such widespread, and co-ordinated, action".

Tiring somewhat, Churchill was beginning to see the reality of it all, along with the folly of his interventions.

Whilst on his visit to Ottawa, Canada, in search of support to a struggling Britain, Churchill chided the Canadian/American Generals; all of whom were now very secure in their thoughts, and wholly convinced of the Vichy/Axis success against Britain.

Vehemently avowing, pro-Nazi support, the French/Canadian Military Generals responded; contemptuously to the British Prime Minister: -

"In three weeks, England will have her neck wrung like a chicken!" Churchill replied, chirpily; "Some chicken! "Some neck!"

Churchill then had a spell of hospitalisation in America; with a heart problem.

7th January 1942, A-B-D-A Command HQ; Appointed overall Commander; Wavell flew to Bandung/Batavia, on Java, and spent two hectic weeks establishing his new Headquarters. It was ridiculously sited, more than two thousand, (2,000), miles from his Operational Command. The action was taken on his receiving a policy document, drawn up by Combined Chiefs of Staff, in the comfort of London/Washington offices: -

Convinced that the 'ABDA' title, and the new-found Headquarters, might inspire more significant action, and better results, the Combined Chiefs signalled Wavell;

> "Hold the island chain, Malaya, Sumatra, Java, to Northern Australia, as essential support positions".

> "Re-establish communications with Philippines through the Netherlands East Indies, and maintain essential communications within the area generally".

Absolute balderdash! – Western politicians, and Chiefs of Staff, continued to be overtaken, outdated, and completely oblivious to the perfectly structured onslaught, and the spectacular overall success, achieved in so short a time, by Japanese forces.

Communications, within the rapidly changing field of activity, were virtually, nil, and speculative guesswork! Come what may; the Chiefs had to earn their pay!

Like a world of make belief, and 'airy-fairy land', the wishful words were defunct nonsense, and overtaken before they were written. The riotously ambitious, and all-embracing message, was outdated before the ink was dry. Japanese invaders were already in occupation of the entire line of designated islands.

Tormented and disgusted beyond measure, with uncertainty, and Churchill's numerous persistent interventions, Wavell; with a considerably higher intellect and sensitivity than Churchill, was sick at heart over the Prime Minister's constant and imperious interventions. He signalled the dynamic question, of very few words, taunting the Prime Minister, and getting right to the point;

"Am I in effective operational control?"

Crunch! — Strewth! — Sure and Begorra! The fat's in the fire! Wow! This was breaking point! Full bodied effrontery! Wavell, the seemingly obsequious servant, was, most pointedly, not applying for membership of the 'Corporal's Club'. In the normal way of things, and under no circumstances, would a General, particularly one of Wavell's intellect, ask so stupid, and ironical, a question, and for it to be submitted in this inane manner. The simple question means nothing of what it says; It is a vitriolic rebuttal, and censure of Churchill. Objecting to the Prime Minister's persistent interference into whatever task in which Wavell might be involved. The rhetorical question, with its insolence, and soft measured undertone, was clear to both; The dispatcher, and the recipient.

Significantly; There is no recorded response to the question!

The question was fully intended to irritate Churchill, Wavell's Parliamentary overlord, and to the limit of reprobation, for one so highly placed. As expected, Churchill was infuriated at what he saw as such insolence. Wavell was to feel the extent of the Prime Minister's vindictiveness, in due course of time. Unable to make early changes, Churchill stewed on the rebuttal.

19th February 1942 — Darwin, in Northern Australia was bombed by the Japanese, and in view of the devastating developments elsewhere throughout the East, invasion seemed inevitable,

Indifferent to the friction within British Commanders, and whilst losing the cream of Australian troops at every turn, particularly with Wavell in command; Australian PM, John Curtin, on 20th February, signalled to Churchill, requesting reinforcements for the defence of his own country: -

"We want Divisions not Brigades"

"Anything that is not powerful, modern, and immediate, is futile".

On the same day, 20th February; Three Australia bound ships, sailing at twenty-four hour intervals, and rounding the island of Ceylon, were arbitrarily, diverted by Churchill, towards Rangoon. Curtin was livid, and adamantly; He countermanded Churchill's ploy. Curtin required his armed forces back in Australia.

25th February 1942 – Wavell vacated his remote, and showy, A-B-D-A, HQ, on Java, (set up less than three weeks beforehand, on 7th Feb). It was never used, and was invaded by the Japanese, on 28th February. *(15,000 troops, mostly Australian, and once again, under control of Wavell, were taken prisoner).*

At the end of his tether, at seeing almost 50,000 of his good Australian troops, and numerous civilians, either killed, or captured, at Crete, Singapore, and Java, mainly under the command of Wavell, Curtin called a halt.

Expressing his disenchantment with Churchill, Curtin wrote to the Melbourne Herald. Denouncing Britain; Curtin asked the approval of the Australian people to join with the USA, as; *"Having more common interests".*

(It was much later, following a number of unsuccessful attempts, Australian Prime Minister, Sir Robert Menzies, made the break, and a final push for decimal currency in 1958. First minted on 22nd February 1965, the new currency was issued on 14th February 1966).

Demise of the proud and global British Empire, for so long distrusted by Senators and others in the USA, was now well advanced.

Government communication, embracing the above acrimony, is contained in;

"Documents on Australian Foreign Policy, 1937-49, Volume 5, pages 535-566".

5th March 1942 – With not the slightest idea of the state of affairs, and after three months journey, by road, rail, and sea; The Junior Officer draft, with G Fitzpatrick arrived at Rangoon. *(P&O shipping losses, as recorded in the three months of GF travelling; totalled 4 ships – 86,000 tons).*

5th March – General Alexander also arrived at Rangoon, by plane. He was appointed, to serve under Wavell, as Burma Commander in Chief; Within twenty-four hours, he was to abdicate, and condemn his dedicated Force.

The speed of the Japanese assault on all fronts was co-ordinated, most assiduously into Burma. Japanese forces, guided by 5th Column,

Burmese Nationalists, and others, were freely in occupation, at all strategic approach points.

Wavell made a further unnecessary comment; (sic)

"The long marvellously prepared assault of Japan"

"I could feel in anticipation the lashes which were soon to score our naked flesh".

5th March 42 – 2/KOYLI; Survivors of three weeks hazardous conflict, assembled at Llegu, a small village, approximately 20 miles to the East of Rangoon. They were joined, by the Fitzpatrick draft of 18 junior officers. The nondescript, and almost unbelievable assembly point, was a bomb crater, situated close by a rough road. With not one of the former, 'established', KOYLI Regimental officers present, this unseemly looking situation was supervised by Major Pip Moran, of the Duke of Wellington Regiment. The condition of the men, and lack of any form of organisation, was deplorable, to the point of unbelievable impossibility. One could never envisage meeting with such squalor, and believe it to be a Regiment of the British Army. It was hard to see such penury, pervading in what had been so proud a Regiment. Was this the Battalion I had been dispatched from Ireland, to join with, 'in such secrecy', and un-ceremonial a manner?

Here it was – Battalion strength; Reduced from over 500, to less than 150 men, in three strenuous weeks. Many were killed, or wounded, over the period of non-stop action. Malaria and dysentery, ingested earlier, on the futile China Road works, at the Salween River entrenchment, was greatly responsible; Having conducted ridiculous exhibitionism, undertaking an inter-company walkabout, whilst under a strong Japanese attack, Commanding Officer, Colonel Keegan was wounded, and evacuated

5th March 42 – *(There was much activity, in so short a time, a very busy day)!* Diligently using the plane in which Alexander had arrived, Wavell departed Rangoon, for Delhi. He was accompanied by three other sacked, nincompoop Generals; Hutton, McLeod, and the cowardly VC holding, Smyth; Acquiring the art of remote and ineffective control from Churchill, his master; Wavell gave the departing command; (sic)

"Hold Rangoon as long as possible;

The troops must live off the country to a much greater extent!"

Rangoon closed as Wavell left, and there was no mention of re-arming, negotiating the terrain, and feeding, throughout the 900 / 1,000 miles, to the only exit point from the country, whilst being hounded by the well led, trained, and practiced forces of Nippon.

(In three months I obtained, two pockets of peanuts, nothing more, "Off the country").

Major Moran explained the drastic situation obtaining from his modest encampment; General Smyth, VC, had, in self interest; destroyed the massive Sittang River Bridge, situated approximately fifty miles to the East of Rangoon. Cowardly Smyth, had remained on the safer West bank of the river, whilst his entire impoverished, 17th Division, was stranded on the Eastern bank, and under attack from the Japanese; Few men of all units, were competent swimmers in such formidable conditions. They were either killed, or spent the remaining war years, as POW.

Troops contained within Pip Moran's encampment, were the few survivors capable of crossing the mighty Sittang River.

It might be appropriate to mention here;

General Archibald, (later Earl) Wavell; Was recorded as; "A man willing to shoulder an unpopular burden". He was shortly to be relieved of Army service, following his recent effrontery, and his calling of Churchill's bluff. In 1943, he was virtually demoted, and removed from military command; He was appointed, Viceroy of India. We will come to, 'the un-shouldering of the burden', in due course.

Relieved of the Vice-regal post in March 1947, Wavell was succeeded as Viceroy by another man, one with Royal connections, who had arrived on similar, shaky and flaky grounds; Louis Mountbatten.

5

WHERE IS THE WAR?

Posted by the egotistical Colonel, EEE Cass, from Northern Ireland, to that undisclosed station, "in the peaceful tropics"; it was consoling to meet up with other similar sceptics, also not best pleased with the prospect. Eighteen junior officers from the KOYLI, became joined, as a group, with a similar number from the Gloucestershire Regiment; meeting at the King's Theatre in Glasgow. With a Battalion from each of the two Regiments stationed in peaceful Burma, it did not require a genius to, optimistically, determine the intended destination. In the draft of three dozen officers, no more than two or three members knew exactly where the country was geographically. It was situated in a part of the world, in which, there was not the slightest thought, or murmur, of conflict.

Great camaraderie formed within the two groups, all of whom were Emergency Commissioned Officers, and with freedom from Regimental Duties, it allowed for enterprise of expression, so denied when under the eyes of thin skinned regular senior officers. Individuals became, 'somebody's', in the free environment, and not one person flaunted himself above others. All knew that they were, with great reluctance, about to depart Britain. Speculation on the possible departure port, changed each day of the fortnight of Glasgow freedom.

After eleven or twelve days, and with a few short hours notice, we were crowded onto Army trucks, and on our way. The journey could not have been shorter. It was a few miles distant, to the port of Gourock, close by the mouth of the River Clyde.

Boarding, P & O ship, Strathallan, the cruise, was not going to be by the straight forward, jolly holiday route. The mass of shipping visible the first morning, as the mist lifted, appeared never ending. There were between sixty, and eighty vessels, forming into one large convoy. SS Strathallan was to follow a route of German 'U' Boat avoidance. It meant, crossing the North Atlantic, and somewhere between Greenland and Nova Scotia, negotiating an almighty maelstrom, with the ship appearing to be about to do a somersault. Amongst numerous others, Skipper, Captain Biggs, was reported sick for the first time in his nautical life.

Fortunately, I was unaffected by seasickness, having suffered from it, and been violently ill, some time earlier, on an Irish ferry crossing. Pleased to attend my colleagues as they succumbed to the peril; Numbers of them shared two large cabins, and with my diligent attention, I won their respect. Over ninety per cent of troops on board ship, suffered equally. My ministrations went further than the draft, when required, by a member of the Queen Alexandra Imperial Nursing Service, (QAINS). Relieving her distress, on finding her collapsed in a corridor of the ship, suffering with the dread malaise, the sweet girl became my daily comfort, for the weeks on board, until our arrival at the port of Bombay.

Known throughout the vessel, although never officially disclosed; several of the more violently sick and depressed troops, cast themselves into the sea each night. We could never envisage the present shipboard discomfort, to be so absolute a luxury, compared to the, 'dubious welcome', at journey's end.

On Christmas Day morning, in lively Freetown harbour, (21 days sailing, to avoid German 'U' boats, for a normal 4/5 day journey); on our first halt, Strathallan was surrounded by Bum-boats. Each boat was occupied by one or two occupants, and all offering every possible trinket, as souvenirs. There was no shore leave, and short stay meant departing Freetown that evening. Anchoring off Cape Town over New Year, two lovelorn couples, of shipboard romance, chose to be married by the Ship's Captain.

Hogmanay it might be, but where the hell my cabin mate, William Lauder Riddell, got the bottle of whisky from on that night, I do not know. He did however get one, and distinguished himself in the way only a dedicated Scot should do. Having had his own share of the 'golden juice', Bill carried the bottle to the top deck, and here, met with the Officer

Commanding Troops. Calling him, a 'Silly Old Bugger', he offered him a swig from the bottle.

The tragedy of this incident was, my most excellent friend was gated throughout our five days of relaxation, and enjoyment at the costal town of Durban, in which we had tremendous fun. Our party became celebrities, and particularly popular at several night clubs, as we demonstrated, 'The Hokey-Kokey' dance, to the locals. African musicians had picked up the tune from the wireless. They could not, in their wildest dreams, envisage the ridiculously choreographed dance routine; "Left arm out! Left arm in!" It was as though no other dance existed, night after night!

Each night of our stay, Bill waited at the head of the ship's gang plank to hear my exploits of the evening; (He was never to visit Durban again, as, when serving with the South Lancashire Regiment; he was tragically killed, in Burma. God Bless Him!)

Crossing the tranquil Indian Ocean, SS Strathallan departed the convoy, and sailed independently at normal speed. Apart from seeing innumerable flying fish, things were very quiet, and pleasurable, on board the delightful vessel; Docking at Bombay on the 11th January, 1942.

Tranquillity of the ocean was fine, but I was about to be presented with a most unsought after shock of my own. Having initially felt so insecure in the newness of my status as a commissioned officer, I could hardly believe what I was now hearing. To my knowledge, within the draft, there had never been a discussion on character, quality, merit, or standards of individuals, we were all as one.

I had enjoyed my afternoon 'QA Rita' moment, when Jimmy Ableson terrified me with the words; "Fitz! We've had a meeting amongst ourselves, and all agree"; "You are the man they all want beside them if we go into action".

"Bloody Hell!" I was second senior by Army Commissioned Number; (160575), but several of the draft, were older than me, and others had undertaken public school cadet courses. In the main, they all had what I considered to be, a superior education. Prophetic though it turned out, I shed that quiet tear. My peers accepting me as Number One, was obviously on the basis of my tending their needs when sick. It was a shock!

Bombay hotels were resplendent throughout, although dire conditions and squalor on the surrounds were unbelievable. As mere, 'junior officers in transit', we were obviously, considered 'Riff-Raff', by the insular sophisticates, 'the British Military and Colonial Office residents'. Denied access to the two, main classy British gentleman's clubs. However, we soon found Madam Rita's, a large palatial brothel, out north at Breach Candy, and it was here that we had our fun.

Dynamic Jimmy Ableson, was the smallest member of the draft, he spoke fluent French with Rita, and we danced with the girls. There were White, and Red Russians, Africans, and Asians. Rita had fine choice, and the girls were all good lookers. Observing the steady flow of furtive city clientele, visitors to the brothel; including senior servicemen, and, 'questionably', respectable 'posh club' members, all coming for their ten minutes of 'love', was the perfect respite for the ten or eleven days sojourn in Bombay.

Rita wanted Jimmy to remain in Bombay, to become resident, and be virtually adopted by her, but of course, that was not to be! (Jimmy was killed within twenty four hours of our arrival in Burma; God Bless Him).

Spacious and luxury train couchettes conveyed us on the steady, three day journey, from Bombay to Madras. Travelling in company with a Royal Artillery unit, we had overnight halts, and regular stoppages, for cooking, and for the boys of the Regiment to stretch their legs, and show themselves to the locals. Mangoes, the new found fruit delicacies, were heaped around the cooler; an ice block, placed in a tray in the centre of the carriage.

In Madras, Blackpool's Tim Watson was invited, and played cricket for the local Civil Servant's team. He scored a valiant seventy-two winning runs, in his first innings. The club offered him the proverbial drink, and Tim was not shy, he ordered six dozen pink gins; one for every run. They were lined up on the bar and Tim drank them, every one! (Tim served in Burma and died about two years later, in India; God Bless Him).

By mid February 1942, two months following the Japanese bombing of the American, Pearl Harbour base, with no means of communication, we of the draft had heard not one word of the rampaging Japanese military progression throughout the Far East. The silence continued as we boarded the French ship, President Doumier, for what was thought to be a final seven day sail, from Madras to Rangoon. The ship was a disgrace, infested with monster cockroaches, food inedible, and accommodation filthy. There was no communication whatsoever with the captain, or crew; all spoke, only in French. French speaking Jimmy Ableson remained 'shtoom', and kept his ears open, in order to, virtually, spy on the non-cooperating crew.

Jimmy blew his top, and I do not know the French words used in his cursing of the Doumier skipper, over his next decision. Rangoon stands about 80 to 90 miles from the Indian Ocean, up the Rangoon River. In retrospect, it is easy to know why, at the river mouth, the skipper declared his ship's engine to be inadequate to proceed to Rangoon, and that he was diverting to Calcutta; a journey of five days; He must have received information; 'on his wireless set', and been aware of the Japanese rapid advance into Burma..

Following one overnight stay in Calcutta, we were ferried back, down the River Hoogley, and boarded the 'British India' ship; SS Ellenga. This was a straight forward, no messing, small craft, with an equally no messing, English skipper. Making no bones about it; "I'll get you into Rangoon!" And that was exactly what he did, on the 5th March 1942.

SS Ellenga – Pride of Britain, last ship to leave Rangoon

73

Nearly three weeks of sailing, with both the French ship, and Ellenga, meant that our draft missed the most cruel, and critical action, carried out during the Japanese overwhelming assault, in early 1942. It was not an act carried out by the Japanese, but the destruction of the vital Sittang River Bridge; under the orders of the cowardly British Army, Divisional Commander.

The devastating act was carried out by order of the Commanding, British Major General, whose sole interest was the preservation of his own thick military skin. The man was at a loss to know what to do; he had lost control of the forces under his command. Having been bestowed with a Victoria Cross in earlier days, he considered himself, far too important to die.

Nippon forces had entered Burma on 19th January. From this point on, the doomed, and under provisioned British Force our small draft were about to join, were at the mercy of the Japanese.

Smyth's, under nourished, and virtually unarmed, 17th Division, had been in constant conflict with the enemy, on the Eastern Bank of the wide and fast flowing Sittang River. Whilst at a distance of approximately two miles from the only crossing, troops heard two very loud explosions. All were in no doubt, this meant the demolition of the massive bridge, and hearts sank. Following three weeks of unrelenting, day and night action, famished and with ammunition exhausted, they were now committed to the mercy of the enemy. The only way out, was to swim the river, and not all were competent enough to attempt the width, and flow speed of the brute. Useless rifles had bolts removed, and cast into the river.

The sister of Private; (well named on barrack room showing), "Bronk!" A top grade athlete, who died as a Prisoner of War in Rangoon Gaol, tells me that her brother simply hated water. Under no circumstances would he have attempted the swimming of a river, he had resisted bathing from childhood.

In the three months, from the commencement of our travels, the seemingly peaceful continent of Asia was in turmoil, to the extent that it affected one fifth of the earth surface. Our draft of young officers, on the way to join with Regiments, knew nothing whatsoever of this fragile situation. The speed of the marauding Japanese onslaught outpaced all existing means of communication. Cocooned in travel, the eastern world had gone from peace to global conflict, as we crossed the earth.

Ritual at Madam Rita's had provided a delightful interlude, it was comforting, after the care and attention shown by the stewards whilst on voyage. The comfortable bunks, excellent food, good 'nookie', little booze, and no responsibilities, were to change, drastically.

From the moment of arrival at Burma's Rangoon port, we were 'in action', the moment our feet touched the ground. Drama was being performed around us, as Alexander, Churchill's favourite General, arrived on the same day, 5th March. On being appointed Commander of Burma forces, Alexander had been instructed by Churchill, to get rid of what he considered, useless senior officers, Wavell, and three others; Smyth, of Sittang Bridge infamy, McCleod, and Hutton. The four departed on the plane delivering Alexander.

Ensconced incommunicado, for three months of travel, and totally unaware of the deceits, chicanery, and downright incompetence of parliamentarians, and military commanders, I was about to assume command of much disillusioned men, in the grimmest of war situations.

Battle to be joined, was in the plains, jungle, and oilfields of burma, a land I had heard of only a few short weeks beforehand. Lacking provisioning, ammunition, reinforcements, transport, and above all; leadership! It was indeed going to be grim.

There was to be no pleasure, or satisfaction for me, in this war. I was joining in a conflict, with supposedly, my having sworn avowed allegiance, to a king that I had never seen, and in a country that I had hardly heard of.

In all honesty, my service was conducted, and endured, under the same king's treacherous and indifferent commanders. The extent of the treachery, and the institutionalized perfidiousness, was revealed to me in November 2008, sixty-six long years, after the end of the war. The shattering news; resulting from a most surprising gentleman contacting me, having read my first published 2001 book; "No Mandalay, No Maymyo".

Prime Minister, Churchill, never admitted his own shortcommings; all blame was cast onto the heads of unfortunate puppets, his selected service commanders.

No individual in the British armed forces, had knowledge, or training, in the field of highly specialised warfare that I was about to enter. It was not a staff college subject. This was the ultimate challenge!

The men that I was about to command, from the group assembled in pip moran's encampment; were real men! Mostly from Yorkshire, and nothing daunted them. They were to show me guts, and humour, far beyond the call of duty. The loyalty of survivors continues, after seventy long years.

6

NOW IT'S WAR – BRITISH STYLE

Arriving at Rangoon Docks; An enthusiastic draft of reinforcement officers, about to join proud and distinguished Regiments, the Gloucestershire, and Kings Own Yorkshire Light Infantry, we were in for a rude shock. In complete ignorance of the nefarious and rascally filibustering, deceits, mishandling, and downright incompetence, conducted between national and military commanders, throughout the time of our travels, there was a rapid eye opener.

Desolation ruled, and a rapid appreciation of the stark dockside ruination, left us in no doubt of the problems ahead. With not a soul in sight, and buildings blanketed in powdered dust from devastating enemy bombing, our prospects were less than inviting.

In view of the parlous state of affairs, we were instructed by a receiving officer, to get rid of all heavy kit, and travel with no more than a bedding roll. Conveyed in a small open truck, for little more than thirty minutes, we managed a slight glimpse of the magnificent golden dome of Rangoon's Shwe Dagon pagoda, before joining with a forlorn looking trackside scene. The motley crew spread around on the ground, could only be described as, 'a rabble', and comprised of possibly, little more than fifty men. We were not to know the cause of the distressing spectacle; A damnable tragedy brought about, through a cowardly Divisional Commander.

The precious value of those twelve days of sailing, to Calcutta and return, became blatantly self evident. In that short period, the Battalion had expended ammunition, in conducting the most valiant and unrelenting resistance to the enemy. 2nd Bn KOYLI was decimated by the marauding, Japanese Army.

Replicating the earlier disastrous campaign, in Europe, wherein the super efficient German forces had rampaged throughout, including Norway. This was another far away, but similar campaign, to the European one Churchill was about to forget. In the East, Japanese forces were enjoying similar results to those of Germany. With Hong Kong, Singapore, and Java overrun, Churchill, once again, mounted his precarious, 'high handed horse'. Although he had no answer to the predicament, the man was prepared to, 'Throw out valiant words', whilst behind the scenes, his influence, and perceived machinations, were devious.

Almost unbelievable, the stark tragedy of the Battalion predicament was brought about by; The Victoria Cross holding, British General, JG Smyth VC. Was he sick, or, was he cowardly? Whatever condition he was in; It was he who ordered the destruction of the bridge. He gave the order at the break of dawn, on the morning of 23rd February, with himself and a small defence unit, remaining secure on the safer, west bank of the river. The debilitated KOYLI Battalion, along with the main body of Smyth's 17th Division, trapped on the Eastern Bank.

The bridge blowing catastrophe happened as Major, John 'Rosebud' Doyle, KOYLI, and a colleague, were about to approach Smyth, seeking instructions. In the resultant chaos, Doyle was shot in the leg, and fortunate enough to obtain a wooden stake to assist him in his crossing of the river.

From the safety of his Delhi Headquarters, Commander in Chief, General Archie Wavell, castigated Smyth over the cowardly destruction of his Command.

Smyth was; Some considerable time later;

"Subsequently disciplined by higher command, for making the wrong decision".

Wavell went further, and reported in his later studies;

"I have no doubt that the withdrawal to the West of the Sittang was bad mismanagement, by the headquarters of 17th Indian Division, and the disaster ought never to have occurred".

Brigadier J.G. Smyth VC. MC. MP. The hypocritical, lying, cowardly trollop, had the audacity to contribute a, 'Foreword', to the 1954 book; -

"OPERATION RANGOON JAIL", by Colonel KP MacKenzie, RAMC.

I quote, verbatim, from Smyth's supercilious, and patronising 'Foreword';

> Page 11 – When reporting on Far East Prisoners of War, (FEPOW); "I have been closely concerned in post war years".

> "Fortunately comparatively few of my 17th Div in Burma went 'into the bag' in the grim battle for the Sittang Bridge". (They were numerous)

> "As soon as the bridge had been blown, the frustrated Japanese division withdrew to find another crossing upstream and allowed the bulk of those who had been trapped on the far bank to swim or ferry themselves across".

> (LIES; You meet with KOYLI – FEPOW, Frank Stott, later)

> Page 22 – "A comparatively small proportion of the division was taken prisoner in this action". (As above; they were numerous)

> "On early morning 23rd February, could no longer hold the bridge, it was blown up". (Note; He doesn't say by whose orders; He gave them!)

> Page 24 – "This enabled the bulk of our troops on the far side of the river to ferry themselves or swim across, where they were re-equipped and lived to fight again". (Lies; We were neither equipped, nor provisioned, for twelve weeks!)

> Page 12 – "It is as well that the British people should remember their sufferings – and, even more important, the circumstances which brought them about – and be determined that such things should never happen again".

> (He personally, "brought them about", and we remember!)
> Signed JG Smyth
> Dolphin Square – April 1954

Nothing could be more evil, coming from the man whose cowardly actions brought about the downfall of the British Army, in 1942 Burma. He makes no mention whatsoever of the fact that he, personally, ordered the premature destruction of the Sittang River Bridge. For twelve long weeks, until virtual self deliverance by the few survivors into India, there was no re-equipment or provisioning, of food and ammunition, of Smyth's abandoned 17th Division.

The unfortunate Colonel MacKenzie, RAMC, was taken prisoner some days prior to, and remained unaware of, Smyth's misdemeanours. Formerly, he had been senior medical officer to the man, and, as a POW, he would be unaware of the foul actions to follow.

Mutilated by the action of Smyth, the debris of Burma Force, were, unapologetically, about to be discarded, by Alexander, a Churchill select, and favoured, Major General.

Within twenty-four hours; 5th or 6th March 1942, it all changed for the British Army. From being 'cajoled' to seek success, over three weeks of intense combat, under Smyth; They were to spend twelve weeks, 'castigated', and in the longest ever withdrawal of British troops.

Smyth showed his true colours; in a repeat BBC-2 T/V programme. The recording is one of a series entitled; -"The World at War", it was shown January/February 2009. Smyth is photographed, as he comments on the war in the East, and the Japanese assault throughout December 1941, and early 1942.

Glossing over the loss of Hong Kong, and making much of the dithering General Percival, and his loss of 100,000 men at Singapore, Smyth makes no mention whatsoever of his own fiasco. The cowardly man avoids mention of his own dastardly order for the destruction of the Sittang River Bridge; whereby he completely incapacitated the British Army in Burma. In avoiding any reference to his former discarded Command, Smyth's sole comment on Burma, was to say;

"The Japanese were held at the Indian border".

Recording Wavell departing Burma, accompanied by his three incompetent and dismissed Generals; I thought that I had finished with the trashing of higher ranking, Officers. I was to be proved; 'Oh so wrong!'

It was now, a matter of, 'Whom, or what, do we have in their place?' Prime Minister, Winston Churchill unearthed, what he considered; 'A jewel of a man!' He was one, kicking his heels around, on the south coast of England, and taking stock of troops, supposedly, in training? It was, Harold Rupert Leofric George Alexander, the man was later to become; 'Earl Alexander of Tunis'. He turned out to be an equally indistinctive, and comparable 'gem', to those useless Generals, recently departed.

For Alexander to have dismissed three Generals, (Hutton, McLeod, and JG Smyth VC) on the day of his arrival, he must have received disparaging information beforehand, possibly from his immediate superior; Wavell?

Alexander had previously, commanded in Italy, most probably, it would appear, by being 'carried' by his subordinates. General Tuker, a contemporary of Alexander's, and one who at an earlier date had served under him, considered; -

"That Alex' was, quite the least intelligent commander I have met in a high position".

I don't quite know why this should sound so appropriate a comment, but it proved axiomatic, in very short time. I remain impressed with Tuker's assessment.

The few strong swimmers, amongst Smyth's abandoned troops, crossed the Sittang, (width, 200/300 yards/metres). Many without boots, marched, the twenty or so miles, to the small village of Llegu. It was here that we of the officer draft, joined with them, only to be shocked to the core, to see, what looked like a rabble. To find this mishmash representing a regular battalion of the British Army was unimaginable, that this could be the appalling condition of any British Army unit, particularly one engaged on active service.

They looked a dispirited lot, but we were soon to find that this was not the case. Throughout whatever trials and tribulations facing them in the weeks to come, there was always a humorous act, or quip, from one, or other, of these men.

In the brief stay of a few hours, at Llegu, I had the good fortune to meet up with possibly the most cool and sensible of Field Officers, (Major upwards), in Major 'Pip' Moran, of the Duke of Wellington Regiment. It was a bit rare in my limited experience, to meet a good and competent senior officer. In spite of the atrocious situation in which he found himself, he had a coolness and authority to inspire. There was none of the pomp, and arrogance, that I had seen in so many of my regimental seniors. He spoke to me in a manner appropriate for the predicament, and the common ground in which we found ourselves. In spite of so brief a meeting, I found the sensitive conduct of this senior officer inspiring; I could model on the man!

With no rancour, Pip Moran expressed his annoyance at the decision, made by Smyth, in bringing about the demolition of the mighty bridge. He was in no doubt that no other one of the Divisional officers, would have attempted to subvert Smyth's pompous and domineering authority.

The officer designated senior to me on the KOYLI draft, turned out to be a lepidopterist. He was disguised in uniform; 'a dress of convenience' for the journey out, to what was thought; 'a peaceful country' for his butterfly studies. Arriving at, "That peace station in the East?" He went on his way, in the hope of pursuing his interests. With his departure, I became the instant group senior, and at Moran's 'request', I conducted a futile patrol along the nearby railway line. Here I met with a 'true blue' metal of a man, and the very best of British soldiering; Sergeant Benny Mee. Benny had nine years of service behind him, and much of that in India. He was to become my platoon Sergeant, and stalwart, throughout Burma, and later, for my more pleasurable period, in India.

Sergeant Benny Mee as Corporal, aged 24 years at 'Sale' barracks, Rangoon 1938

In the short time taken in conducting the rail line patrol, Benny Mee filled me in on all action that had gone beforehand. He did not spare his comments on the officers, particularly the duffers amongst them. Benny, a Rotherham man, had been a coal miner for a while on leaving school, but disliked the work. He wanted to see the sky above his head by day, and left pit work to join the army. Returning from my first task, Pip Moran tested me further, with one of the most demanding quests of my life, so far.

There is nothing in the Manual of Military Training, and not one word in the OCTU syllabus, of the most daunting decisions a man can make. As senior member of the draft of eighteen subalterns, and having lived with them for three months, Pip Moran appreciated that I might have first hand knowledge of each and every one's capabilities. He was required to send seven of the newly arrived officers to the North of Burma, to serve at either Brigade, or Divisional Headquarters, and retain the remaining eleven, to serve with the Battalion.

Pip delegated the onerous task of deciding this tricky one on me! The selected seven would be spread around, some of them going between approximately fifty, to four hundred miles north, away from the seemingly dross, and dereliction, of the Battalion remnants. The eleven would be required to face out the consequences of whatever might be to come, in staying with the unit. This was a very hard call, particularly in view of the obvious superiority of the approaching enemy, and the parlous situation in which we found ourselves.

I had never before been faced with a problem of this nature, and time was short. To have discussed this with others was out of the question, it would have placed considerable responsibility upon their shoulders, and that was, 'a no-no'. It would have been an easy matter of selfishness, to get myself out of the fix, and away from the morass, along with a few chums. Should I select the older ones, rather than the young? Favouritism, or assessing characteristics, as shown on the long journey out to Burma, could be no guide to the command competence of individuals.

The answer was drawn from my brief experience, when confronted by the Irish Garda, as I stood when a schoolboy, outside St Patrick's church, in Newport, County Mayo. Giving a little width, and stretching my brains

83

a little further, It revolved around what my father had often repeated, and he did not like what I might also consider; 'jumped up officers'. Remembering also the situation in which I unhappily found myself, back at Chatham Barracks, where, upon joining with the Royal Engineers, I was by one digit, senior to my friend, David Williams.

There being no more than a few weeks, or months, between all my colleagues regimental numbers, I got myself off the hook by applying a long established, first principle of army practise; The 'Battalion eleven' were retained by virtue of their seniority of commissioned service; Although it was now out of my hands, and I could not be, "by his side", I have forever reproached myself for the resultant loss of our beloved, 'Abe', (Jimmy Ableson). He was killed within twenty-four hours of my making the difficult decision.

A virtual 'bombshell' was dropped, as I was procrastinating on the selection of my colleague's. How ridiculous could this be? Unaware of the unit's total lack of weapons, and seeking to assert himself at an early date, the newly arrived Alexander, ordered; "An immediate attack, on Pegu!", a town situated 20 or 30 miles east from our location. The order was however, fortunately thwarted, when Smyth had a word with Alexander, before boarding his plane to the safety of India;

"They don't have weapons! They don't have boots! They have fought their socks off in the last three weeks! They are in no condition to attack any town!"

Smyth went further, and confided to Alexander;

The British forces in Burma are moribund. Their mere survival, in any form, will be considered success!

Within the next hour, the ridiculous Pegu order was rescinded, and we got new thinking, in order to obtain some semblance of soldiering; but it was very rough.

Simply in the hope that some relatives of my beloved colleagues might read this book, I give below, the lists of my officer selections. They go in order of seniority, starting with the Battalion.

Battalion	**Brigade/ Division**
Gerald Fitzpatrick	Allan Ibbotson
Andrew McLaren Young – (Scot)	Stuart S 'Death or Glory' Renton*
Robert 'Bob' E O Rimmer	E H 'Tim' Watson *
Leslie P Wise	Alan Whittaker
James 'Jim' Marsh	William 'Bill' McKillop – (Scot)
John A Welbourne	William Lauder Riddell * – (Scot)
V L 'Steve' Stevens	George 'Chotta' Lawrence
Douglas 'Dougie' C Haig	
Arthur E Watts	
James W 'Abe' Ableson * – (Scot)	
Douglas V Oakley	

Not to return

Looking back on my selection, I find that, had I done this on the basis of Character, Physique, Personality, Age, or simply by Random Choice, I would have come up with five or six completely different lists.

I accepted, with some grace, and thanks, a mess-tin of tea from two Privates, as they squat, busily brewing the precious liquid in a Dixie, (Metal cooker). One of them turned out to be, Danny Loben, from Bradford, and the other, 'Jacko' Jackson, from Barnsley. Our meeting, of no more than minutes, formed a friendship in service, one so deep it can not be replicated in civilian life, and in my mind, one that has lasted almost seventy years. I detail the pleasure, and my thanks, for my knowing this precious twosome, in my previously published, (2001), book.

For whatever reason, minutes seemed like hours, in the confines of the trees surrounding the men squat around the bomb crater Pip Moran had graciously adopted as his headquarters. Pip surprised me somewhat with his next requirement; -

"Fitz!" "You're to lead an advance party, and establish a reception area, at Tharrawaddy". – (A town North of Rangoon, on the Mandalay road).

Receiving no more than a few words of direction, there was no such thing as a map, and certainly no village markings. I was roughly given a location to find, and immediately given a truck full of men. My task was to establish a forward reception base, at Tharrawaddy; (about forty to fifty miles north of Rangoon). Luckily, I had Benny Mee in the party, and he knew, as rough as the information we were given, the spot for our base. It was one hell of a day for starters! I was shortly, to find out exactly why, on board ship, I had been given such exaltation by my peers.

Locating the Tharrawaddy area, we established a roadside camp. In order to facilitate cover from aircraft, it was sited close by a dense clump of trees. The nightly firefly demonstration above our heads was spectacular. This day was the one I consider; 'My start of war day'. It was as no other, and, in parting from Pip Moran, I was unaware that we were never to meet again. In so brief a meeting, I knew that I had met with the best of men.

I did not meet, nor did I know, any one of the established regular officers of the battalion I was now joined with, and certainly had no idea of their capabilities, but I was to learn of them. My short experience, and chat with Benny Mee, proved to be of inestimable value in the coming weeks.

General Alexander began to show his true colours, by attempting to 'smart-arse', with his 'cock-up', and his ordering an attack. Accepting guidance from his departing predecessors, he aborted the order.

At this point, I feel that you might not mind my deviating somewhat!

Referring to my previous book, in which, I was at a loss to accurately pin-point the identity of a doctor. He was the gentleman joined with us in the latter, jungle stages, of the withdrawal from Burma. Although I travelled with him for about two weeks, I knew nothing more than that his name was Xavier. Not only did he carry the doctor's rank of Captain, but also, a very conspicuous revolver. Prominently belted, around a rather showy bush jacket; the revolver was something of a rarity for a doctor. The man was such, that I was sceptical; Tall, young, robust, and looking far too well fed alongside our debilitated contingent. However, certain members of our, 'rank and file', had good reason to remember the man. They cynically identified him as; "The Knob Doctor, from Mandalay", and I readily accepted that; I was with expert authentication!

Endeavouring to make contact with the doctor, in order to validate the story of my first book, I approached all recognised sources, including, the British Medical Association, and the RAMC, each of which, retained no record of such a person. Not unreasonably, I had every reason to consider that I had been duped by the individual.

In order to avoid embarrassment to any family the man might have, or, to cover any impostor, I camouflaged him. I described the man as; "Pock-marked".

How fortunate I am, to be approached after sixty-six years, and, resulting from the issue of my, 'book No 1', to be fronted with the truth.

The shear delight of receiving a letter from the man's son, Patrick, was enlightenment beyond belief; My wife, and I, met with Patrick, and Annamarie, his wife, in October 2008. He very pointedly confirmed what I already knew, 'That his father, Doctor Xavier, was not, the 'Pock-marked person', as described by me. I had attempted, and failed, to disguise the fine young man, who had joined with us for so short a time. He was not emaciated, as were we. Standing well over six feet in height, he was a rotund, robust, fair haired young man, with a healthy looking, ruddy complexion.

Gerald with Patrick and Annemarie Xavier (son of doctor)

No.4003/10/A2(BA),
HQ., Burma Army, PO Mingaladon,
BURMA 12 Nov '47.

To:-
    Dr.C.M.XAVIER,
      Cherry Knowle,
        RYHOPE,
          SUNDERLAND, ENGLAND

Subject:- **PARTICULARS OF SERVICE.**

Ref your letter dated 13/10/47.

Particulars of service available in this HQ are appended below :-

20-12-41	-	Commissioned in the A.B.R.O. vide Defence Department Notification 1126/41 (with seniority as W/S.Capt. w.e.f. 1-3-42 vide B.A.O. 297/43).
29- 1-42	-	W/S.Capt. No.2 Bur Fd Ambulance.
16- 4-42) 4- 7-42)	-	W/S.Capt. M.O. 2nd Bn KOYLI.
2- 5-42) to 2- 6-42)	-	W/Capt. O.C. A.S.D. No.1 Bur Bde.
4- 7-42	-	W/S.Capt. rejoined 2 Bur Fd Amb.
15- 1-43	-	A/Maj. 2 i/c 2 Bur Fd Amb. vide B.A.O. 222/43.
2- 3-43	-	A/Maj. Relinquished 2 i/c 2 Bur Fd Amb. vide B.A.O. 222/43.
25- 3-43.	-	W/S.Capt. Posted to 77 Bur Fd Amb.
11- 7-45.	-	W/S.Capt. Joined C.M.H. AHMEDNAGA.
23- 7-46	-	Released from A/S. AHMEDNAGA

MM/ZH.
                for Asst Adjt & Quartermaster General
                      HQ., Burma Army.

> Hi Gerald,
>
> Thanks for your letter. It might be worth stating that my father qualified in Summer 1941 which would make him part of the very last intake to qualify before the Japs overran Lower Burma. Otherwise it all looks fine. (Army doctors treated VD because there was a lot of it around!) I've NO IDEA what happened to the running of the Rangoon University Medical School after that. Also, unrelated to the book, there was some attempt, by someone or other, to blame members of my family for the murder of the Burmese patriot Aung San on 19th July 1947. The facts are that the most likely candidate, my eldest uncle Dudley Xavier the sometime pre-war Rangoon Police Chief had died in Assam in 1942, and also Douglas as you now know died in '45. I don't think Douglas would ever have been involved in such horrors anyway. Dudley's major contribution to Burma was keeping the lid on in the absence of effective army leadership at the time – a fact you'll appreciate!
>
> Best wishes,
>
> *Patrick*
>
> Patrick Xavier
>
> *Patrick. Thanks!*
> *Entered – All done and dusted. Gerald*

A Letter from Patrick

It transpired; My, so called, 'Pock-marked' person, was in fact; Doctor Cedric M Xavier, a pre-war Burma resident. In 1941, (A few short months before the start of war), he qualified amongst the final intake at Rangoon University: (He completed his days, employed as a psychiatrist, at Wakefield Top Security Prison).

(Dr Xavier's Particulars of Service are shown on the previous page).

The Xavier, and Culbert families, were Burma based, and of considerably high standing in the community. They met with, and were frequently visited, by many of those in high office, as indicated in the following contribution.

It is with no embarrassment; I quote from the very revealing, and damning notes, provided by Patrick Xavier; I am sorry that so very few survivors remain, from the 1942 campaign in Burma, to hear of the alarming revelations. The dead will not have the opportunity of knowing the appalling indifferent standard of Command, and support, 'bestowed upon them', and all, supposedly, in the Military control of Churchill. I never thought, or even dreamt, that I might be in a position to publicly divulge the perfidiousness, and incompetence, of a highly regarded Army Commander. One who was prepared, so indiscreetly, to declare his surrender, abdication, and complete disinterest, within twenty-four hours of assuming Command of an Army Force, as did Alexander.

In 'book No 1', I said; "I could" have shot Alexander; I should have!

Now listen to Patrick, in his own words; (sic)

About Dolores:

Dolores Beryl Xavier, (1916-1969) nee Culbert, was my mother. Her father, Barney, was an oil man who worked in Syriam, and a Presbyterian who hailed from Silverwood, in Armagh, Ulster. Her mother Ida was of Irish, and I think Scottish descent, as well.

Dolores attended the convent of the Good Shepherd, in Rangoon (Yangon), where she was Head Girl. One day she and her 2 sisters were visited there by Mrs Fakeney, a close friend of Ida's and also, by Sir Reginald Booth-Gravelly. The latter said as a parting shot;

"If they make Dorman Smith Governor, Britain will lose Burma!"

Being highly qualified for the job, Dolores became the assistant to Mr Lloyd, at the head office of, The Imperial Bank of India, in Rangoon.

(1) On the afternoon of March 6th 1942, (within 24 hours of his arrival in Burma), a man who turned out to be General Alexander, walked into Dolores office late in the afternoon; 'To dictate his Will'. She took the dictation but not unnaturally asked; "Why a Will?"

(2) The General indicated that he'd flown in the previous day. Evidently, he had just decided to abandon his; "Projected three-week tour of the country, in order to assess, the possibility of defending Burma"; (There'd been a military disaster at the Sittang Bridge at the end of the previous month). Having made a preliminary study over 36 hours he'd decided, and stated; "Burma could not be saved!" Dolores took this appalling news back to her parents who flatly refused to accept it, but soon, Barney was engaged in pouring concrete down his oil-wells.

A really hectic twenty-four hours, for an Army Commander!

(a)– To Dictate a Will.

(b)– Abandoned His three week assessment tour.

(c)– Capitulated! Stating; "Burma could not be saved".

Lloyd offered Dolores safe passage out of Burma but she refused to leave her parents. They, and she, with the family gramophone, boarded a truck headed for Chungking, but were headed off by the Japs. They had to retrace pdq, then the petrol ran out, and so the 3 of them set out to walk over the Himalayas with other refugees. Most died on the way. Barney, notably, had never eaten; 'the food of the land', if he could help it; he'd even imported tinned apples! He boiled some rice for the first time in his life; it carried on swelling inside him, and he died of untreated intestinal obstruction. Ida, his wife, then went temporarily mad; Dolores then tossed the gramophone into a ravine.

Dolores, nursed Ida, and the pair, finally made it to Tamu, I think, but they were not welcomed into India. They and other Europeans were, somewhat reluctantly, 'allowed in'. A doctor was detailed to see them, and noticed Dolores' black teeth. She indicated that she and her mother had, on medical advice, put a crystal of potassium permanganate – no more- into each cup of drinking water, and left it for half an hour or so before use; (Others had refused this advice; they all died in the night). *"Hope yer guts are in order! NEXT!"* said the doctor. The fate of mixed race and other refugees is well documented in; -

'Through the Jungle of Death' By Stephen Brookes, Cambridge University press.

Indeed this book can be seen as a civilian parallel to; -

'No Mandalay No Maymyo 79 Survive' By Captain Gerald Fitzpatrick, I recommend it.

Importantly, refugees were told not to talk about their experiences. Further to all this, I recently learned of my Uncle, Major Douglas Norman Xavier's exploits; he'd at one stage, in 1944, been active in the Chin and Lushai/Mizo Hills, behind enemy lines. (I recall an odd-sounding family account of a jeep being used, and a colleague with an alarm clock on a thong, around his neck?) He tried to cross from Burma into India with his Anglo-Burmese wife Ma Mi, and their son George, my cousin. The authorities tried to stop his wife and son crossing, but happily failed. Douglas had cerebral malaria and died of same in 1945. He was in the 'Burma Reserve Army'.

Dorman-Smith, *(British Governor of Burma)*, was often referred to in the family as; 'that high grade mental defective'. A bit harsh!

(Another report states that, in shear desperation, the day before his hurried departure from Burma, Dorman-Smith hurled snooker balls at photographs of his predecessors, on the walls of Maymyo Gymkhana Club).

This happened.....

Never before have I heard of an Army Commander declaring his task; a failure, before assuming Command, particularly in an indiscrete utterance to an Assistant Bank Manager. Alexander's sole concern, from this day forth, was the preservation of his own precious skin, and absolving himself of all blame!

Alexander's philosophy; meant that, within 24 hours of our officer draft entry into Burma, we were virtually written off in a lost cause. The Alexander signal of defeatism; "Burma can not be saved", was sent to Churchill, confirming his disparaging appreciation of the situation. Receiving this damnable message, particularly from one of his favoured Generals, caused the struggling Prime Minister to abandon all hope in the Eastern war. The recent successive failures, at Hong Kong, Singapore, the Java HQ, and now Burma, was more than the shaky Prime Minister could tolerate.

Receiving Alexander's depressive appreciation of the Burma situation, Churchill realised he was a beaten man.

On the 6th March; (the day following both, Alexander's, and my arrival), the Japanese carried out an encircling movement, closing Rangoon off from the North. In the process, Alexander was inadvertently held in a road-block. My dear colleague, Jimmy Ableson, and his sergeant, were killed in bringing about Alexander's rescue. They was mown down by machine-guns, when making an attack on the Japanese.

For whatever reason, in his memoirs, Alexander fails to mention, this slightly embarrassing episode of entrapment; *The utter disgust of the man comes later.*

Vacating the road block, the Japanese completed the Rangoon encirclement. Alexander wasted no time in making good his escape;

heading north, to Maymyo, and ensured that; there, he was to stay, and did not move south again. The fright of his first day ambush was more than enough for; The 'Gallant?' Irish, Guardsman. He settled for Maymyo! The cool rolling hills, and soothing lakes, at almost 4,000 feet above sea level; temples, and attractive colonial style offices, and houses, along with associated services of police, and schools, made the small Garrison town, a most pleasant, and desirable habitation.

The 'E', (Evacuation) notice, announced by, Governor-General; Mr Dorman-Smith, on 6th March 1942, meant that Rangoon Town, and Port, were immediately surrendered to the enemy.

The 'E' signal signified that Burma was doomed! There was no way out of the country through the port of Rangoon, which was virtually the only exit. This meant, the residue of the Army, caught up within Burma, having to travel 900 miles, to the north, attempting entry into India; *The Government link project for road communication, between Burma, and India'*, sadly, as, so many things in this part of the world; *"Remained under consideration".* There were no identifiable tracks for three or four hundred miles of the route, and numerous steep, rugged sided hills, many of them over 4,000 feet.

Flotilla sailing on the Irrawaddy, and Chindwin River, was ruled out; they were open to Japanese air raids, and there was no railway service. Many thousands, of men and women refugees, died in attempting this formidable journey. The very restricted outlet, from the country, was by the occasional aircraft, from the northern airfield, at Myitkyina; *This speculative and uncertain route, was the one taken by regimental married families. True to perverted military Class Distinction, in the Regular British Army, (Seen as Apartheid in Africa), between Officers and Other Ranks, and their wives. Overriding priority was given to families of officers; Awaiting a flight, Major 'Dougie' Wardlesworth's wife was by Dougie's side, when she was killed by enemy aircraft fire. At the time, Dougie was, himself, recovering from an earlier wound in the arm.*

Having lost Colonel Keegan, the CO, (a man I never met), through his own stupid exhibitionism, in the conflict east of the Sittang River, a replacement arrived at my Tharrawaddy roadside base. The unfortunate gent, Major Tynte, of the Cameronian's, was killed within an hour or two of his joining. Tynte, and I, did not meet, as I was absent on patrol at the time. Tynte, apparently, walked up to a Japanese held road block, and attempted dismantling by hand, only to be badly carved by machine gun fire.

In the meantime, in dribs and drabs, a number of troops arrived at the base. The fiasco of attacking, and escaping, at Alexander's surprise entrapment, caused large numbers of men to become dispersed, far and wide, with no hope of control. Many men, seeking whatever desperate refuge, made their way back to join with families, at the Maymyo base.

The situation throughout Burma was now somewhat similar to the chaos pertaining in Britain, immediately following the Dunkirk evacuation, except that members of the Burmese irregular forces vanished completely; they went home. At the Tharrawaddy base, we remained the few identifiable remnants of a battalion, and possibly, no more than two dozen in strength, with no recognised commanding officer. The job hung around my neck for a day or two, until we were joined by Allan Chapman, a 'jumped-up', (rapid promotion), officer from the pre-war Battalion.

A villager, seen perched in a tree for some length of time, and overlooking our movements around a water point, was arrested as a possible spy. Arthur Watts, the acting Intelligence Officer, escorted him to the local police station, only to find it vacated. Following two or three further attempts, it was realised, the 'police birds had flown'. The poor sod had been staked to the ground for two or three nights, and we did not have facilities for this kind of performance. It was with Chapman's arrival, we got action. The man was taken out and disposed of. I realised, there and then; there was no point in playing around with dissidents.

On the fifth day of our sojourn, a motor cycle messenger arrived at the base, directing us to a torrid valley close by the Irrawaddy River. A testing twenty-four hours, spent in this hell-hole, with the heat, and starving, made one feel that this must be the end. It was however, almost unbelievable, as a river boat arrived, to berth alongside the small landing jetty. With alarming alacrity we joined the vessel, and I had five days of comparative luxury, mostly provided by Loben and Jacko, as we cruised northwards.

Arriving at Yenangyaung, the Central Burma oilfield, we met up with the team of Field Managers; Barney Culbert, *(father of Delores; later, the wife of Patrick Xavier. We had passed Barney's Syriam oilfield whilst arriving on board 'Ellenga', it was situated half way up the Rangoon River, and in flames); also,* W.F. Forster, Norman Kellie, and 'Smithy', a diminutive man, along with field engineers.

It was St. Patrick's Day, 17th March, and we were to support these dedicated oilmen in the destruction of oil-wells. It was essential to deny them to the advancing Japanese; The Jap's main quest was to capture the oil.

It was from this collection of civilians, we first heard of Alexander's indiscrete surrender statement. Dolores had conveyed the fatal news; "Burma can not be saved!" to her father. The story was widespread, and had been related throughout Burmese villages. As serving soldiers, and with no inkling of the Alexander revelation, we found it hard to appreciate the truth, when hearing so damnable a proclamation, coming from oilfield workers. For the reported utterance to be correct, we of the Burma Army were doomed. The recent and unexpected corroboration, (Confirmed in the above entry, by Doctor Xavier's son), simply reinforces my long held indifference, and contempt, towards many of my military superiors!

Alerted to, 'Alexander's abdication, or surrender statement,' the antagonistic and recalcitrant Burmese workforce began showing considerable hostility towards management. Understandably, they readily visualised the scorched earth policy, as the destruction of their livelihood, and refused co-operation. Our job, however, was to assist in oilfield destruction, and to protect the engineers from any aggression by these men. Days were spent dismantling central pumping stations, and dropping massive drills, and rotation cams, into the wells.

With the demolition of the Yenangyaung field completed; Commanding a small squad of men, I travelled about twenty or thirty miles north, to assist, at the smaller sized Chauk oilfield, managed by Norman Kellie. The huge swimming pool was a welcome relaxation after a days work. However, there was a surprise one evening as a huge python snake arrived. It was massive, and certainly scared the life out of me, whereas, the oilmen remained totally unconcerned. They treated the python as a friend, and on taking a fill of water, it went on its way.

On the evening of the fourth day, several bungalows along the northern edge of the oilfield became ignited, and the blaze spread rapidly. Accompanied by Ray Elsworth, Steve's batman, with him doing the driving, I mounted the jeep, carrying a Bren-gun. A small detour took us to the outer edge of the field, and here, perched on a small mound, were about sixteen or seventeen dissidents. They began gibing at the two of us, quoting Alexander's impromptu declaration, made in the Rangoon bank; Goading the pair of us, they made clear the purpose of the fires; In attracting the Japanese. It did not take me long to realise that, should one or two of the locals have guns, both Elsworth and I, could be in real trouble.

With no hesitation, I began firing two or three short bursts into the legs of the men. Not surprisingly, the speed of dispersal was incredible, as they went off, running, skipping and limping, getting to hell out of it as fast as they possibly could. Several of the individuals were scampering along the track by the Irrawaddy River-bank, which edged onto the oilfield. Whilst speeding them along with a few odd shots, I realised that these men, given the opportunity, were to become seriously hostile.

Fully aware of the inevitable danger from the hostile Burmese, (now considered a Dacoit band), and with all wells destroyed, the engineers were ready to depart. Wishing them well, and for protection, I provided an armed escort for a distance of about twenty miles north, up the Mandalay road.

I have recently had the pleasure of meeting with the daughter of Mr Norman Kellie, the Field Manager. She was a four year old at the time of our action, and confirmed how pleased her father was to have the military escort, and he mentioned it many times. Not only that, but she and her husband have visited Burma six times in the last four or five years, (now 2008). They have found the people and the country most enchanting, as it is, and want to relish it as much as possible, before it becomes; "Just another Costa".

In the end credits, I give extracts from a letter written by Norman Kellie, in which he graphically describes tragic experiences of the escaping oilmen. The most delightful couple, Anne and Bill, visited Burma once again, early in 2009. Norman's daughter says; "We find the Burmese people to be most friendly, helpful, clean and respectful". "The recent trip took us 1,000 miles up the rivers", and, "As we have now visited almost all 'permissible' areas, future trips will include some returns".

(Read Anne's glowing testimony in the appendix)

From St Patrick's Day (17-3-42), to All Fool's Day (1-4-42), remaining totally ill equipped for warfare, our time was spent patrolling, and labouring, on oilfield destruction. We were no better provisioned than when I first met up with the unit at Pip Moran's Llegu bomb site, and now, we were totally defunct as a fighting force. Probably more than eighty per cent of the men in our much depleted unit were ill, suffering one or other of the numerous tropical diseases.

It was a relief when Brigadier Bruce Scott arrived, in mid morning, to announce; -

"KOYLI! You've had enough! General Alexander is preparing to fly you out of Burma".

Depleted as we were, and with men weakening by the day, this appeared to be the only sensible way out of the moribund Battalion dilemma. Having heard, (on the jungle drums?), what sounded like good news, several malingerers returned from the regimental base at Maymyo. With those returned, we mustered a possible two hundred, mostly sick, men.

The bombshell came four hours later! Scott returned with a different story. It was never Alexander in person who passed the message! He was ensconced in a place of comparative safety, and one from which he could have easy access to escape.

The words from Scott sent a shiver down the spine;

"KOYLI; I'm sorry! I have to send you down the road once again".

"We must hold the road junction at Allanmyo in order to get a Gurkha Battalion out".

The diminished Battalion strength, of two hundred, was further reduced, as fifty-nine 'reported' men walked off, northwards, deserting to a man. They could easily have been shot as they staggered away, but what was the point? These were real sufferers, men sick, and most, hardly able to walk, many of them suffering with both, malaria and dysentery. With hundreds of miles to traverse, through rough and hostile terrain, they did not have, 'a cat in hells chance', of surviving desertion. They would have been an additional handicap, remaining with the unit.

Throughout the ten or eleven days spent helping the oilmen destroy their work-place, we were situated about forty, to fifty miles, north of Japanese lines. It would have been, a safe, and simple matter, for Alexander to visit, and inspect our unit, and, at the same time, enjoy his 'postponed' familiarisation tour. In fact, Bruce Scott was the sole visitor; and he was very brief!

This may be a Guards Officer idea of Command. We carried the proud title, 2nd Battalion, Kings Own Yorkshire Light Infantry, and Alexander assumed us to be just what it said; A complete Battalion, of 550 or so, in strength? We were, in fact, about 120 in strength, with 80% suffering serious illness, in various forms.

Alexander was feeding himself regularly, and plentifully, in the comfort of his safe Maymyo base. He failed, however, to provision what he considered to be a Battalion. He supplied adequate for no more than a Platoon, (of thirty men), in strength, and that only spasmodically. Alexander had no further interest in his Command, other than the preservation of his own precious skin!

7

CHURCHILL – 'WASHED HIS HANDS'

Serving twelve months as a Sapper in a Field Company of the Royal Engineers, followed by a further twelve months, as an out of depth, but developing, Emergency Commissioned Infantry Officer, I lacked active operational experience, having no more than witnessed the return of numerous disillusioned men from Dunkirk, and the mass of invading German aircraft. The Royal Air Force response became known as; "The Battle of Britain". It happened actively, above my head, in the summer of 1940, when housed in rail trucks, along the jetty at Folkstone Harbour.

This, "Down the road" business, as announced by Bruce Scott, was different. As an inexperienced new boy, I was about to be cast into facing a well proven, and highly successful, enemy. It was not for me to question the morality, or competence of Commanders, or of those I was about to Command. The very idea of questioning the committal instruction was inconceivable, and I was placed, 'Under Orders'; to face a successful and marauding enemy, for the first time in my life; This was not just a simple street fight, boxing match, or a game of rugby. This was to be a killing game, and the loser was not going home. Why should I know what I was about to meet, nor how on earth I was going to react?

How serious could this Bruce Scott, "Down the road again", instruction be? It is only in later life, as startling revelations come to hand, I was being; 'Dispatched on a Suicide Mission'. Alexander, my Army Commander, had already declared abdication, and signalled the verdict to his lord and master.

Supplied with one, 2000 rounds, box of ammunition; (ten rounds per man on the diminished, and mostly faltering, unit strength, of 200 men).

The paltry amount based on the Battalion strength, before the mass desertion, and carried on the back of a mule cart. The much reduced, three companies, each of which comprised of about 40 men, taking it in turns to ride; except for the muleteers; on two thirty hundredweight trucks; it was a matter of, 'ride and walk'; (ride ten miles, walk ten miles).

This move, of total commitment, was relegated into priorities, and to be implemented, only after the limited amount of transport had extricated the Royal Air Force contingent, from the nearby Magwe airfield. The 'Brylcream Boys', as they were known, given priority, were vanishing from the conflict. Somebody had got their priorities mixed, or had they? – KOYLI could wait! 'Conflict' was where they were going; RAF, flying out.

Passing the deserted Magwe airfield, on the forty-plus mile journey south, we saw nineteen or twenty plumes of smoke ascending from burning craft, all carefully dispersed around the perimeter of the air-base.

With no road signs, and no map, we arrived at the wrong road junction. It was only on hearing what turned out to be Gurkha firing, that we realised we were four or five miles short of the targeted forty-odd miles destination.

Delay in arriving at the correct point, proved to be a fortunate error, as on moving forward, we engaged a squad of Japanese. Catching them in the open, we cleaned up a large number, in very short time. Adjusting to the correct road junction, Johnny Wellbourne, was about to set up, his one anti-tank gun, and me, the three mortars. It was as though a sin to the recently appointed CO; He would have none of it. Surprisingly, he ordered the weapons, "Be left on the mule carts". Fortunately we met with no engagement, and the, 'all singing', Gurkha unit flashed past, safely, to our rear.

Perilously situated as we were, Geoffrey Chadwick demonstrated the reason he had been sidelined on mobilisation of the unit. Completing the task of covering the road junction, and with the Gurkhas departed, he showed reluctance in making any decision to move. Fully aware that Bruce Scott was not going to reappear, we, the newcomer juniors, had to help him. For those of us close by, to discern such lack of guts and chutzpah, from a Commander, was morale shattering, and, with not a word, it was noted; Chadwick was not the man to manage the battalion, already in desperate straights.

Inadequate in all respects; medical, food, ammunition, control and communications, we did not realise, nor could we have accepted, we were a lost force, and at the start of what was to become, twelve days, and nights, of almost constant conflict; Each episode of conflict occurred instantaneously, with no time for planning, discussion, or consultation. The Japanese were a small advance force, further reduced at the time of our recent engagement, but they had the advantage of being equipped, armed, fed, and not disintegrating through tropical disease. The whole of these activities doomed to take place some distance behind advanced enemy lines.

In a state of complete dereliction, and totally unaware that we were officially discarded by British Prime Minister, Winston Spencer Churchill; In exasperation; the man disgustedly, washed his hands of Burma, 'Giving up the Ghost!'

On 1st April 1942; (All Fools Day); Churchill's message to Roosevelt; (sic)

London – (via U.S. Army)
Telegram – 2106
T.O.R. – 8-32pm – 1st April – 1942
'PERSONAL and MOST SECRET'
'NO DISTRIBUTION'

"Speaking as one amateur to another, my feeling is that the wisest stroke for Japan would be to press on through Burma northwards into China and try to make a job of that. They may disturb India but I doubt its serious invasion".

(Churchill & Roosevelt – "The complete correspondence", page 438 C-62)

(Churchill Memoirs. Vol VII, page178 – 940-53)

(Churchill Papers 20/73 page 81; -as 'Personal telegram T519)

(Winston S Churchill VII (1941-45) Martin Gilbert (page 82)

Churchill was heartily sick of far eastern reverses, particularly as he, personally, contributed to each and every one of them;

It was on 9th July 2012, Nicholas Soames MP, Churchill's grandson; declared that his grandfather; "Had depression at parts of his life at Chartwell", (His country house), and objected to MP's quoting Granddad's numerous misdemeanours.

CHINA, (Chaing Kai-Shek), AUSTRALIA, (Curtin) – RUSSIA, (Stalin), and INDIA. All were denied knowledge of Churchill Psychological blips, 'The man of evil'. He felt free to contribute to disaster, as he had done on several occasions; (Crete, Hong Kong, Singapore, and whatever conflict in which Wavell was involved). The Prime Minister would not accept the word 'Defeat', particularly in any one he considered, a failed theatre; (Commanders, Auchinleck, 'Bomber' Harris, of the RAF, along with Wavell, and the First Sea Lord, followed by Mountbatten). All could shoulder the blame and shame.

With over seven weeks of unfinished business in Burma; Both, Alexander and Slim; Churchill's chosen commanders, could never know of his churlish and dismissive signal. Wartime events, and communications, do not happen by shear coincidence. Churchill's dismissive signal of renunciation was, obviously, sent as a result of his receiving Alexander's perfidious signal of abdication; the day following his arrival in Burma, three weeks earlier,

Whiskey sodden, as he must have been, to instigate action by the enemy, in such a repugnant manner, Winston Spencer Churchill distanced himself from his 'devious missile', by imposing a, 'thirty year secretive restriction', on the document. Unable to recover it, the evil words of abandonment were hidden away, until subsequently released, long after the demise of Churchill.

How drunk and disillusioned, was the disgusting man, a British Prime Minister, to send such a signal at this time? I was a very young man, serving in the British Army, in Central Burma, commanding emaciated men, in a much debilitated Battalion. We were about to face many days, and nights, of intense conflict. Ammunition was in short supply, so much so, that each man had possibly five, or at the most, ten rounds, in his magazine.

It was not until after the fall of Singapore, that Churchill saw fit to give Burma any serious consideration. Time was short, and he had plenty to occupy him elsewhere. He made priorities, and in his notes following the war, Churchill wrote; -

"To the Australians as to us, Burma was only a feature of the war".

What a lovely man? Not everybody thought so, and not everybody was suffering the predicament of Britain's humble Burma Army!

Australian PM Curtin was becoming ever more disillusioned, he did not welcome Churchill speaking on his behalf; It was under Churchill, in WW-One, Australia lost thousands of men at the Dardanelles. The blustering Prime Minister was also, recently seen as the villain, at Crete, Hong Kong, Singapore, and Java, where many more thousands of Australians were either killed, or captured.

The series of losses was incomprehensible to Churchill, and on receiving Alexander's message of abdication, he knew that Burma was sunk, every bit as were the two Capital Ships, off Singapore. As with the stoppage of pay to wives and dependants of British Prisoners of War, provisioning, and reinforcement to the Far East was terminated. Burma was now of no further consequence to the British Government.

A further missing piece of vital information, contributing to the bringing about of the Churchill treachery, was contained in the radio signal received, when, along with three or four of my colleagues, we were being dined in Smithy's bungalow; (Mr Smith, the Yenangyaung oilfield manager).

In Europe, the Germans had 'Lord Haw Haw', (Irishman, James Joyce), denigrating activities of Allied forces, from his Hamburg base.

In the Eastern War, the Japanese had 'Tokyo Rose'. This lady performed a service, one similar to Haw Haw, from Radio Saigon, possibly one thousand miles distant from Burma. The Saigon station broadcast was all that could be received in Burma, and it was in constant play to the oilmen.

It is only now, in later life, that I have been able to put together pieces of what have so far been a mystery to me; At the time that I was in Smith's bungalow, and heard the broadcast from Saigon, it would have been, almost one week before Churchill's dismissive, 1st April signal. Tokyo Rose's message was; -

"The British Army stationed in the oilfield at Yenangyaung will be annihilated": -- I was very much, a part of that British Army.

Rose's message, would equally have been received by Alexander, who, in turn, was required to forward the content to Churchill. With news of this pronouncement, coupled with Alexander's earlier debunking, Churchill realised that he was out of his depth in the Eastern theatre of war. The man turned his back, and unmercifully, ratted on his doomed troops, in sending his, 'All fools day', signal of abandonment, to Roosevelt.

For the 'missile' to be so readily received by Roosevelt, and for him to make no comment, he must have been in total agreement with Churchill.

Success of any kind, was readily acclaimed by Churchill, whilst on setbacks or reversals, he made no effort to hide his disparagement. Failed military commanders were rapidly changed, and each in turn dubbed incompetent; they were but pawns in his game. General Percival, of Singapore, although taken prisoner, was completely denigrated for the loss of the country, although Churchill's personal interference, contributed greatly to bringing about the country's collapse.

We, of the Burma Army, were from that moment onwards, unmistakably, and officially, discarded. It was interesting to hear Walter Henry Thompson, Churchill's wartime bodyguard, comment in a recently screened T/V interview. He stated that Churchill ordered raids on the French ports of St Nazaire, on 28th March 1942, and on Dieppe, 19th August 1942. Louis Mountbatten instigated, and planned both raids, and both were hopeless failures, in which thousands of Canadian troops were lost. Walter Henry Thompson chose his words very carefully, in explaining the purpose of the raids; -

Churchill with Walter Thompson (bodyguard)

"They overlooked Burma!"

The European diversions were instigated, in order to take the mind of the British public, away from the devastating Eastern conflict.

My early days of uncertainty were now well behind me. Knowing that I was stronger than most, both physically, and in command, and was determined to make it known when ready.

From the perilous situation, well behind the Japanese line of advanced troops, it meant retracing steps, over the forty or so miles that we had been ordered south, and with some discretion. Leaving the main metalled road, after more than twenty unmolested miles, and continuing on rutted cart tracks, whilst pushing mule carts throughout the night for a further four hours, we met with an outpost squad. Here, on arrival, the 'prawn' of a Major, Throckmorton, himself having ridden on the transports, was supposed to lead us to the main body of the battalion.

Surprise! Surprise! The man was lost, and went so far as to deny our exhausted walking party, a modest drink of water; Quartermaster 'Taffy' Phillips threatened to, "Shoot the bastard!" We got the water, and Throckmorton shut up! The dedicated QM would unhesitatingly have shot the man, and with no repercussions! Regretfully, 'Taffy' was to die within twenty-four hours.

Using Burmese guides, and travelling on parallel tracks, the Japanese had followed our movements throughout this blackest of nights. At daybreak they were close in, and started machine-gunning from short range. Bursts of machine-gun fire were hitting the roadside bund that I, and my mate Steve, had slept by. In desperation, the way out of the mayhem, was a speedy belly crawl. Finding ourselves in a virtual dustbowl saucer, at the junction of many cart-tracks, we were easy targets. It was a running job, with men returning sporadic rifle fire, as we scattered up the long rise of an open field, leading towards a small village.

Mortars, anti-tank gun, 2,000 rounds of ammunition, mules and carts, along with the truck, were all discarded in the mad gallop. A Mountain Battery of Indian Artillery, with horses towing guns, were hurdling mounds, and steeple-chasing fences, over to our left. The whole of the scenery was nothing, if not spectacular!

More by luck, than good judgement, it was here, at the top of a rise, laid-up in the small hill-top village we met with the remnants of the battalion. By conducting irregular movement of troops along the front, between set defence points, we were able to exaggerate numbers, in order to stall off the enemy. Reluctance of the Japanese, to put forward an attack, indicated that, although well armed, they were indeed, a small advance party. Any threat of armed conflict was far too much for us to attempt retaliation!

Regimental Sergeant Major, Alan Bootland, suffered a bullet through his jaw in the hill run, (it was considered to be a British.303). He was not a popular man; strapped onto a bullock cart he did survive a fourteen or fifteen mile journey, and eventual aid. – (Bootland's later years were spent as a Prison Officer, at Wakefield Top Security Gaol).

With men shot, and several collapsing through illness, there was no exactitude in guessing the unit strength. There were no such luxuries as pencils and paper, or time to count, and there was no chance of a wireless set for communication. Our existence was totally unrecorded, and any report, highly speculative!

In an attempt to establish contact with Command, none-rider, Arthur Watts, was mounted onto a spare Artillery horse and set forth. But not for far! Arthur fell from the animal, broke his arm, and we remained incommunicado;

Arthur proved himself, a great friend of Ninian Taylor OBE; organiser of the, 'Chinthe Women'; 'Women's Auxiliary Service Burma, (1942 / 1946)'. 250 strong, and with 56 teams, always near the front, endearing the troops, they supplied the personal touch, alongside tea and sundries, up to their disbandment date, in mid 1946).

Escaping the hill top village in the blackest of velvety black nights, with each man holding the bayonet scabbard of the man in front, it silenced any rattling. Three companies moved out independently, and at timed intervals. The target was to cross the nearby vast, and dry, sandy river bed of the Yin Chaung, a dried up feeder to the Irrawaddy River. After only a short distance, and, on hearing the rattle of mule harness, it was clear that the Japanese were ahead of us, and occupying the west side of the cutting, leading down to the Chaung.

In the darkness, and in occupation of the left side of the track, the Japs, possibly a small party, made no attempt to violate, and we moved on. Our vague rendezvous was, to arrive at any point on the far, north-side of the Chaung, and then, turning towards the East, to find the main road. Move northwards, towards Mandalay, and assemble at the first encountered ten-mile post. The small, mushroom-like milestones, remaining in situ, proved very useful. However, the instructions were nowhere near so difficult, as was the crossing.

Three quarters of the way across what was assumed to be a dried up, and sandy Chaung, we came upon a morass. This was one hell of a mess to be in, we were rapidly into mud and water, chest high, some men worse in than others. Distress cries for help, alerted the north bank defenders, who just happened to be British/Indian Troops. They were defending any possible enemy approach, coming from the southern-side of the swamp, and that was the direction from which we were coming!

As they opened fire, we recognised the familiar, steady, and regular, Da! – Da! – Da! – Da! Sound, of Bren-guns. They were firing from the base of two prominent palm trees. Easily recognising the sound of the weapons; they must be British troops, in defence situations. Tracer bullets passed just a few feet above our heads. Happily, the men firing on fixed lines, stuck to their given task. As we were approaching from the direction of the enemy, so far as the gunners were concerned, we were enemy, and must bear the consequences.

Adding to the wet and wonderful blackness of night, we began hearing the occasional gentle fluttering descent of Japanese five-inch mortar bombs. They were, fortunately, deadened in the swamp conditions. Now, along with standing chest deep in sandy water, we had the joy of receiving firing from both north and south banks of the Chaung. If ever there was chaos, this was it.

There was never time to count casualties, and there would be several. Amongst them, we suffered the tragic loss of Captain Quartermaster, 'Taffy' Phillips. He collapsed of a massive heart attack. Ironically, I had no knowledge of Taffy's demise in the absolute darkness of everything. His number two, however, the diminutive Quartermaster Sergeant 'Dogger' Riley, was close by me, and neck deep in the quagmire. He was pulled out by the scruff of his shirt by Danny Loben, with the rejoinder; "You silly old bugger, you'll forget this if ever we get out of here!"

Captain QM 'Taffy' Phillips – Brilliant, collapsed and dies in swamp

From this state of absolute chaos, and in the utter blackness of night, as our ever diminishing Company exited the Chaung on the north bank, I got a shock. Baxter, the Company Commander I was accompanying, realised that he was not up to the task, and, very surprisingly, ordered me to take over; Aware of my newness to the unit, he saw fit to add a threat, in the event of my refusal. This unusual situation was not an easy one, I accepted the challenge after, most pointedly, warning Baxter of the position that he must adopt. I had no idea of the lie of the land, although I had helped plan the rendezvous point. It was now, as turning from my fronting with Baxter, I slid down a deep crevasse, and burst a huge troublesome boil, that had developed on my arse.

Crossing stretches of the rough, undulating ground, and probing the whole way, we made to close in on the main road. Emerging from the brush, I went very close to killing two members of the Inniskilling Regiment. The two of them were sleeping under mule carts, with feet stretched under the cart. I ordered Loben and Jacko to rouse them, placing bayonets at each of their throats. They would not have survived if proved to be Japanese, or anything other than British, for that matter! Fortunately for them, they spewed out a language, one well known to soldiers, proving they were not Japs!

The pair of Inniskillings told me where I might find the Brigadier, in order to ask him to stop his British Indian troops, firing on our men, the ones remaining in the morass of the Chaung. The man turned out to be just another one of those disinterested, senior, British Army Officers. He dismissed me, and I made the mistake of not leaving a hand grenade under his cosy looking camp bed, all decked out; 'with white sheets?'

Trudging on through miles of dry powdery fields, we eventually, circumnavigated the rocks, and holes, of the derisory, and euphemistically, named Ring-Road, encircling the Yenangyaung oilfield. The very place we had departed from in such haste, on Alexander's orders, twelve days beforehand.

Following the days, and nights, of non-stop action, whilst remaining totally incommunicado; resulting from existence behind enemy lines, the unit was now in an even more degraded condition. With no chance of medical attention, many of our men nursing their struggling chums, (muckers), moved along as best they could. These were testing times, as many of the men harboured no hopes; not even the remotest chance of survival. There was reluctance in succumbing to the inevitable, as they clung, one to the other, in the company of warm and understanding 'buddies'. Oh yes! They were going to die, but not before they made sure that they would forever be enshrined in the memories of their beloved comrades.

The folly of, 'World War-One mentality', practiced by the long departed, pre-war, Battalion Commanding Officer; Digging useless trenches, in mosquito infested jungle; was now all too evident. An almost rancid condition ravished the unit's strength. The Battalion was reduced to less than one hundred and twenty men, with conditions going from bad, to worse.

Arriving at hill 512, we halted at the northern edge of Yenangyaung oilfield, alongside the even more massive, dried up Pin Chaung, another huge expanse of flat sand. To our immediate south, less than one mile distant, the Japanese were already occupying Yenangyaung town, and the oilfield. For whatever reason, they made no effort to attack our precarious base. They did, however, throughout the night, plaster the hill with steady, intermittent mortar fire, giving a fair indication that they were stretched somewhat, and possibly limited in numbers. Depleted, and virtually unarmed, as we were, there was no way that we could return the action.

It was only as a few 'strays', from other units, joined with us for cover, that we were made aware of a Japanese established road-block. With this obstacle in place, it was easy to understand the lack of haste in the Japs forcing an attack. The blockage was situated on the only road, and exit, leading northwards from the oilfield. If not moved, we of the Battalion remnants, along with all units, and civilians, locked within the oilfield, were at the mercy of the men from Japan. We were in prime position, and at the designated location, for the 'annihilation', so confidently promised, a few days earlier, by Tokyo Rose, as we dined at Smithy's bungalow.

In view of the appalling situation that Alexander, and his friends, had got me into, and of what I had seen in Chadwick's lack of temerity, along with Baxter's recent shallow threats, my antagonism, and vindictiveness over my early days in the British Army, were now well justified.

My humble Irish birth, and fighting the many years of poverty, had established within me a hard base. I knew nothing of interfering political intrigue, and had no respect whatsoever for military seniority. My new found determination was one of, self sufficiency, and a policy of, 'ME, and ME alone'. Without knowing of Churchill's evil signal, I had met with far too many totally useless seniors. My survival for the next four to five hundred miles, out of Burma, was in my hands, and my hands, alone! There was to be no mercy.

8

DEFUNCT – DISCARDED – DISINTIGRATING

British Prime Minister, Winston Spencer Churchill, had a saying, attributed to him, which went, in effect; "No war was won in retreat". For whatever reason, he failed to appreciate another saying;

"Wars, and good British troops, were lost, through lack of adequate Government planning, and provisioning, when accompanied by downright treachery!"

There is no previous historical recording, of British troops being 'ditched' into such penury, and so deliberately, by a Prime Minister, as that of the 1942 British Army in Central Burma, by Churchill. Indifference, and treachery, is further exacerbated by his selection, and appointment of Commanders: Ones he had personally favoured, but, on failure, he also saw fit to discard to the Far East.

Throughout the twelve days, and nights, spent behind the lines of Japanese advanced troops, we, the recently joined subalterns, expected competence of command. The extent of the opposite was unbelievable in the extreme, as we had the dithering, and dallying of Chadwick. The reluctantly appointed Commanding Officer was installed out of desperation, during days employed on oilfield destruction. On mobilisation of the Battalion, he was considered by Keegan, the pre-war CO, to be; "Unsuited for conflict!" As such, he had been left behind on mobilisation of the battalion, as Quartermaster, to the Maymyo garrison base, and being well fed in the process.

Desperately short of competent Senior Officers: Anything would do! In the long days of our sojourn, in what was virtually enemy territory, Chadwick had failed to make one single decision, without being prompted by one or other of our new batch of juniors. He appeared to be terrified lest we meet with conflict: Declining my earlier offer to position mortars, and Johnny Welbourne, his anti-tank gun, indicated to those of us, so new to the unit, the low calibre of the man.

With no reference to the shilly-shallying CO, and having briefly pondered on usurping the man, whilst on hill 512, I realised something had to be done, in order to retrieve ourselves from entrapment on the oilfield. Unable to raise his game to that of essential desperado, Chadwick was useless. This had to be, survival beyond his knowledge; It required the tactics I knew so well; that of being a street-fighter, where you won or lost in one straight scrap.

There was no time for thoughts of the inevitable consequent, and sentence of death, for usurping, in the event of failure. It is not possible to foresee the essential necessity, and there is no going back. Justification for such action can only be appreciated with a successful outcome.

The Japanese road-block, established close by the village of Twingon, virtually sealed off the dregs of the dwindling British force. Facing, either being killed, or remaining prisoners, Benny Mee agreed with my suggestion; That we attempt to escape the oilfield, and attack the Japanese held position. Set to alerting the squad, colleague Steve, from close by joined in: "I'm with you Fitz!"

Remaining on the oilfield, it was as though being contained within a huge animal pound, and the Japanese held the key to the door. The Pin Chaung, along the northern edge of the oilfield, was the equivalent of a fence, in that it had a shear drop of about eighteen foot, (approx 6 meters), onto a flat sandy plane. This was totally impracticable as an escape route. The only way out to the north, was by removal of the Japanese held road-block. The obstacle had to be cleared!

Thinking only of 'Me', the selfish situation I had long declared, I considered that for me to remain under Chadwick's guardianship, it would be for no more than hours, or possibly minutes, before my extermination: The man of Field Officer ranking was totally incompetent.

The debilitated condition in which he found the battalion was beyond his comprehension, and it frightened him. There was the alternative, of Japanese incarceration, and I was not there for that. With emaciated men around me, mostly suffering a multitude of diverse illnesses, it was clear that some form of action must be taken. Being herded into captivity was not an option.

Incommunicado from all superiors for almost two weeks, there was no point in awaiting orders from above. Bruce-Scott, and Army Commander, Alexander, were remote absentees, so far as we were concerned. The mute CO, Chadwick, was written off!

The dire situation of Steve and I, was unprecedented in all codes of British military experience. Other than surrender to a very aggressive enemy: There appeared to be no answer. The alternative was to abandon whatever might be considered military protocol. This was a case of sheer desperation, and, regardless of military propriety, and the possible consequences, we were now reduced to no more than a bunch of; 'Struggling desperadoes'. Contrary to all rules and regulations for warfare, particularly Churchillian ones, we were to seek survival. The Irish aggression kicked in.

Steve's, "I'm with you Fitz!" Was the start of a 'Do or Die affair', as our two almost decimated platoons, totalling nineteen very much weakened men, set forth. Moving in leap-frog fashion towards the Jap held road-block; first Steve, to the north, on the Chaung side, and then me, – oilfield side. Advancing westward, towards a small white building, close by the blockage, we made good progress over the hard undulating ground. Within about one hundred yards of the building, we faced spasmodic firing. Firing in a controlled, and very limited manner, the enemy appeared to lack machine-guns. Aware of the dire necessity to conquer, we thrust forward regardless, with my man; marksman, Corporal 'Geordie' Bareham, acting as sniper: We were winners!

Clearing the enemy from the road block, with all our men intact, we were lucky. Several dead Japanese were found, scattered around, five or six of them, lying about on the road. In view of the Japanese philosophy of, 'no surrender', some of this carnage might well have been; 'self destruct'.

Throughout the previous four months; from the December attack on Pearl Harbour, all allied action had been taken in valiant defensive opposition and attempts at planned resistance, against a formidable and clinically prepared assault on many fronts. We did not know at the time: the success in clearing the oilfield road-block was the first defeat, in the long campaign, and conquest of a Japanese held defence.

At this juncture, apparently in command, we remained a remote and isolated bunch, and wondering; "What the hell do we do now?" Standing there, with virtually nil ammunition, and a most definite target for the inevitable Japanese road-block recovery; the miracle happened.

With no more than the words; "Cover me Fitz?" Steve, shot off, departing with a few men, down a 'nullah', (crevasse), on the far side of the road. In a most dangerous manner, intending to follow the Japs, Steve was immediately out of sight, and he did not witness the God sent arrival of the Republic of China, Army Force.

Totally uncoordinated, and by the sheerest stroke of luck, a stroke I remember as one of the most magical moments of my life, a Chinese army force arrived at the north bank of Pin Chaung. Disgorging from Studebaker transports, the troops instantly swarmed across the flat sandy Chaung, towards our group.

Better than the show of my earlier days, – (witnessing numerous Luftwaffe bomber formations over Folkstone Harbour); a spectacular pageantry followed. Three Chinese commanders positioned themselves on small raised mounds, to the West of the North/South road, towards the Irrawaddy River. Each Commander accompanied by a standard bearer, and a bugler.

Calls were sounded, and men formed behind the flag, into their various companies. With no hesitation whatsoever, the contingent moved southwards, towards Yenangyaung Town. Mules were not required in this wonderful army, as no more than a few yards behind the troops, trailed camp followers, men and women. Each of whom carried provisions over the shoulder, on the traditional bamboo pole. With this inbuilt support, troops were instantly supplied with all their needs. The composition, of this wonderful force, was absolutely perfect, for the conditions in which we existed.

They passed over the heads of Steve's party, and returned safely.

With not one word to, or from, Chadwick; He had no idea where the Hell we were. Steve and I had of our own volition, done the 'Death or Glory' bit, in clearing the road-block; (The single British success action throughout the 1942 campaign; Attacking and capturing, a Japanese, defended objective). Without the intuitive, and utter desperado action, of Steve and I, all held on the oilfield were at the complete mercy of the Japs, and the gallant Chinese Forces would have been easy targets, as they crossed the huge open and flat, Pin Chaung

Manning, and possibly panicking a little, at the captured road-block, we heard an outbreak of gun-fire, coming from down the road. The intensity of fire indicated that the Chinese were meeting stiff opposition, and we were soon to witness the effects. A steady flow of young soldiers returned up the road, each with a wound to dress. Steve began tearing up captured bedding-sheets, in order to do the bandaging. Amongst friends, words are superfluous. With my tall, gaunt, quietly spoken colleague attending all needs, not one word was spoken: There is a language transcends all others, it was spoken from the eyes of the young soldiers, in expressing their gratitude for the warm attention, as they stood, twenty or thirty of them, orderly and quietly. With clean wounds, there was very little blood, and rough bedding sheets were not medically sterilised, they would however prevent being damaged by the innumerable flying objects.

With one or two of the squad, I began handing out warm rice, taken from a heated cook-pot, situated within the small captured building.

All went quiet for a short while, until the floodgates opened, once again. The gabble, the chatter, and the numbers increased, considerably. We were unaware of any British Troops being held prisoner by the Japanese. Here however, they were coming in force. A Company of Inniskilling Fusiliers, – (I believe Captain Miller?), had been captured, and held prisoner, for two or three days. Throughout their period of incarceration, and at bayonet point, the men had been used as water carriers to Jap troops. As the Chinese attacked, the Japs ignited the two-story building into which many of the prisoners had been shepherded, and we had no means of knowing the extent of any damage.

Completely unaware of their gallant rescuers identity, and with a handful of hot rice, the 'Skinns' made their way northwards: -

It was sixty years later, on meeting with Sergeant,(subsequently, Major Quartermaster), Jack McHaffey's daughter, I learnt that, not only was he taken prisoner, and successfully relieved on this occasion. He was later, taken prisoner for a second time, and held for the duration of hostilities.

(Pleased to be released, the 'Skinns' would have no idea of their saviours).

The Chinese assault around the oilfield, was unrelenting, it devastated the Japanese force, to the extent that in the time taken for the enemy to rearm, and re-equip; British units acquired a space of several days in travelling northwards. Superb action became the saviour of 17th Division, in the long withdrawal. Had the Twingon' road-block not been cleared, and the Chinese completed the destruction of the holding force at the oilfield, the complete British Army withdrawal from Burma, would have been in the hands of the ruthless enemy.

Pin Chaung – White Police/Customs Post left of lorry. Oil derrik on left. Bridge built post war

From inside the small round white building; it was either a police, or customs post, I recovered half a bed-sheet, and half an army blanket. They were obviously captured British items, and possibly belonged to me in the first place. Tucking them into a Japanese haversack, they became my bedding for the remainder of our involvement. It was, blanket to the lower end, covering my legs, and sheet to the upper, and over my head, in order to keep off mosquitoes. Of those involved in the operation, I was the only person to have adopted this most useful, and protective, bedding rig.

Steve's batman, Ray Elsworth, recovered a small, Japanese flag, thought to be a 'ground signal', – (approx 3 foot x 2 foot, – 1 mtr x 60 cms), used as an aircraft marker. Radiating from the red centre; as a sun, – the flag had the names of soldiers of the unit emblazoned. Ray used this, in the same manner as I used my bedding, it was his trophy.

At a later date, and on behalf of Ray's family, the flag was handed in to the Regimental Office, for museum display: It was immediately relegated to a remote store-room, and; Whatever happened to it then?

Robert W. Liu holding the Marker Flag

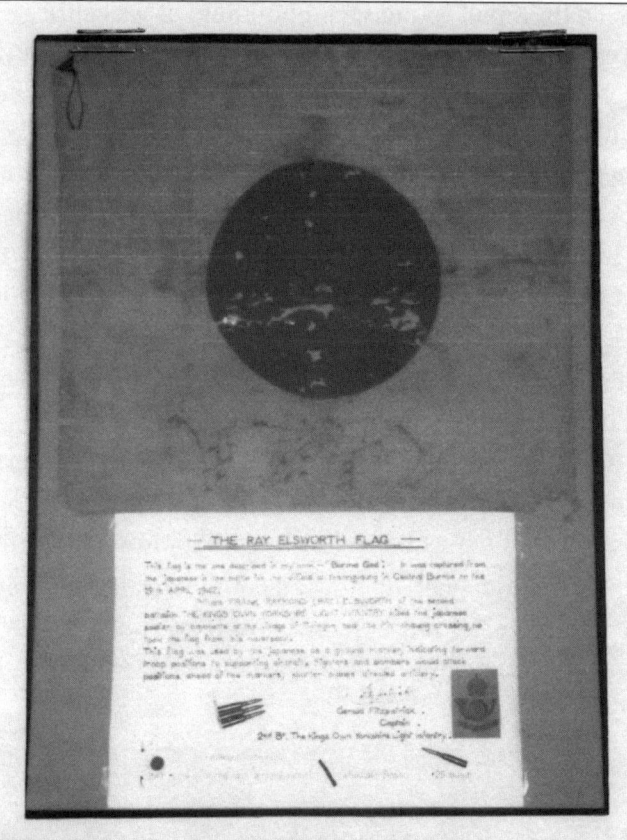

JAPANESE MARKER FLAG CAPTURED AT YENANGYAUNG, 19 APRIL 1942

---- THE RAY ELSWORTH FLAG ----
This flag is the one described in my book – "No Mandalay, No Maymyo"
It was captured from
The Japanese in the battle for the oilfield at Yenangyaung in Central Burma on the 19th April, 1942.
Private FRANK RAYMOND (RAY) ELSWORTH of the second Battalion THE KINGS OWN YORKSHIRE LIGHT INFANTRY killed the Japanese soldier by bayonet at the village of Twingon, near the Pin-chaung crossing, he took the flag from his haversack.
This flag was used by the Japanese as a ground marker, indicating forward troop positions to supporting aircraft. Fighters and bombers would attack positions ahead of the markers, spotter planes directed artillery.

Gerald Fitzpatrick
Captain
2nd Bn The Kings Own Yorkshire Light Infantry

regiment – company
to the last drop of blood   shoulder flash   .22 bullet

In order to take the flag with me, on 16th September 2012, to my meeting, in Washington DC, with a Chinese lady; -(The daughter of the Chinese Army General, Commanding the Yenangyaung assault force). The small item: Which should have had pride of place in any museum, as the, – 'Sole item of memorabilia, from the 1942 Burma campaign': The bloody thing could not be found! This is in keeping with the standard of Command throughout the 1942 war in Burma, and the British Government, Defence Secretaries, and Regimental indifference to remote activities.

For the twelve days of involvement, since being dispatched by Scott, – Alexander's envoy; we were a lost force: Defunct! Incommunicado, and totally, out of his control. As General Officer Commanding, Alexander had no idea whatsoever where we were operating, and, to emphasize the lack of control, and total indifference shown to our plight, Scott reported:

"He, (Alexander), sent a boat down the river in search of you".

But we were nowhere near the bloody river!

The irony of our twelve days of non-stop isolation, and dangerous action, was illustrated in a most unusual manner. (Two days before the Chinese Army intervention on 19th April). On the 17th April 1942:- A rare announcement featured in the London TIMES newspaper,

Note: As a security measure, actions and locations of war operational units, were strictly, not mentioned in newspapers.

The TIMES however, reported: (I give this verbatim).

NEW POSITIONS HELD ON IRRAWADDY

"MAGNIFICENT ACTION" BY THE K.O.Y.L.I.

In all honesty, we, along with the whole of 17th Division, were lost to Alexander's Command, and so out of control, this article is no more than mere conjecture, and twaddle! It is simply suggesting where his Command Headquarters, 'hoped' that we might be.

The War Office could not be blamed for the reported cock-ups. The bogus news was guesswork, and a bluffing of command, by Alexander and his staff. The Times only repeated what they were told. Any bullshit, particularly when hinting at success, suited the British Ministry of Defence!

NEW POSITIONS HELD ON IRRAWADDY

TIMES 17, APR 1942

"MAGNIFICENT ACTION" BY THE K.O.Y.L.I.

GROWING THREAT TO CHINESE FORCES

U.S. BOMBERS' SECRET BASE IN PHILIPPINES

Our forces in Burma have established new positions on the Irrawaddy after "fierce fighting" which continued throughout Wednesday. In their withdrawal from Migyaungye they were covered by The King's Own Yorkshire Light Infantry, who, according to a War Office statement, "for days have fought a magnificent action at Myingun."

The most serious Japanese pressure appears to be on the Chinese front in Burma, and the enemy's progress east of the Irrawaddy has exposed our allies' right flank and threatened the rear.

The American bombers which flew from Australia to raid the Philippines used a secret aerodrome in the islands from which to attack Japanese objectives. They brought back to Australia 44 passengers, including several senior officers from the besieged island of Corregidor.

Speculative press report – wrong – ostensible obituary for discarded army

CHINESE FLANK EXPOSED

DANGEROUS ENEMY THRUSTS

From Our Military Correspondent

Heavy fighting continues in the Irrawaddy valley. Our forces, after the evacuation of Migyaungye, have withdrawn to the neighbourhood of Minhla, covered by the K.O.Y.L.I., whose rearguard action, lasting several days, is described as magnificent. At the moment, however, matters are even more serious on the Chinese front. The Japanese have now greatly increased both the scope and the weight of their offensive against our allies.

In the first place, Japanese progress east of the Irrawaddy has exposed the Chinese right flank and even threatened the rear, according to a Chinese spokesman. It is true that the British official report records the continued occupation of the district of Taungdwingyi, between the two rivers, and states that our position there covers the Chinese right, but it seems that the Japanese must have made their way over the hills by some other route.

The enemy has himself put out a report that he has separated the British and Chinese armies. That is probably a lie, but the Chinese statement is categorical. It may be that the Japanese column referred to, moving in difficult country, is not of great strength, and it cannot be heavily equipped.

FRONTAL PRESSURE

The Japanese are certainly exercising strong frontal pressure in a northerly direction just west of the Sittang, and in the Myola region the Chinese are withdrawing slowly, fighting rearguard actions all the while. The Japanese themselves claim no more regards this part of the front than that their forces have crossed the Swa, which lies south of Myobla.

There was a further message, from: Her Majesty the Queen: Colonel in Chief, of the KOYLI Regiment. Her Regal good wishes took six months to reach the unit. Despatched in April, it did not arrive until we were well ensconced in beautiful Shillong, in Assam, in October. And that, with the Queen's hand behind it!

The Prime Minister's desperation, and utter disgust at having further reverses, was reflected in his 1st April, signal to Roosevelt. It appears that between one and the other, the Queen was brought into play. This flurry of exceptional epistles were possibly dispatched as, – 'messages of condolence'.

Our seemingly dire and terminal situation, with the hand of a disconsolate Mr Winston Churchill, preparing for the worst, we were written off: But not all of us were to die!

Totally unaware of our action in clearing the Japs, and capturing the small white building, Steve and I were eventually joined by the dithering CO, and the remainder of the Battalion; But only after we sent a runner to inform him.

Oblivious of our activities, and he didn't ask, there were no thanks from Chadwick, for the initiative shown by his, – 'questionable?' subordinates.

Moving on, and crossing the vast Pin Chaung, we found the drivers and crew of tanks, from 2/RTR, speculatively, searching for us. Finding us, they prepared a most welcoming small meal. Tanks would have been bogged down, in attempting to cross the soft sandy Chaung. Undertaking a little taxi work the tanks moved us on, to nearby Mount Popa, an extinct volcano situated in almost the centre of Burma.

In recent years, 'fly-by-night' writer, Robert Lyman, published a book, in 2004, (following my, "No Mandalay, No Maymyo"; released in 2001). Lyman, the plausible plagiarising Bastard, became cosseted by the hierarchy of, 'The Burma Star Association'; along with the gullible beguiled family of that good friend of mine, General Bill Slim. All were hoodwinked by the bullshit, and verbosity, of Lyman's offering.

Situated within the confines of Burma Army HQ, Slim, and Alexander, could have no perception of activities undertaken throughout the many days of isolation of the KOYLI, or other units suffering the same predicament. Lyman fills his book with a speculative plethora of cock and bull diatribe, and spurious activities: Endorsements by, 'whom-so-ever will', particularly 'bandwagon seeker' Mountbatten; and bogus acknowledgements, as in his patronisingly including me, as 'Mr'; along with indexes of hundreds of nonentities, places, and purely impossible, imaginative situations; all possibly offered by Smyth VC, and Alexander's cronies. Many units mentioned in the Lyman book, were shattered and disintegrated, at the cowardly Smyth debacle. Burmese Irregulars dispersed, returning to their villages. Units vanished, along with Lyman's story-tellers, in early days.

I despise the man, totally unknown to me, and whose only contact is through my book, published as 'Captain', he disingenuously refers to me as 'Mr', without the decency to approach for approval: He, erratically, saw fit to plagiarize detail contained in my book, published four years prior to his 'acclaimed' work.

Following my few hectic months in Burma, and using the experience gained, I worked for a good period, close by Slim, at; 4 Corps, Jungle Warfare and Battle School, situated at Ranchi, in central India,, (I mention this later). Slim visited the school regularly, and became a good friend to all staff, knowing and addressing all instructors by name. I agree with charlatan Lyman's assessment of Slim: But I'll swear, Slim never saw, or approved, the twaddle 'attributed to him' in the book, so readily acclaimed by, 'The Establishment', 'Slims family', and armchair historians.

Arriving at Mount Popa after nightfall, it was a tropical black night, and, as a fire was lit in the crater of the dormant volcano, a bizarre ceremony got underway. This was the only time, from my arrival in Burma, I witnessed a gathering of, let's call them; Resurrected Regimental Officers? Having been conveyed forward on the tanks, the small assembly of new faces appeared as though from nowhere, following their cosy respite at the Maymyo Garrison. Assembled, were about six established pre-war officers, and about the same number of us, the new boys. An instant split into two distinct groups, saw the established, 'old hands', monopolising the fire. We, 'the new kids', became peripheral observers.

The instant, and overriding conversation, was of deserved decorations each one of the established officers was to receive; and they were not shy. The top boy was David Martin; appearing from nowhere. Whilst he sought a Victoria Cross, none of the others were to be left out. It was as though nothing else mattered, as Steve and I sat, watching. The beauty of this cameo was that the two of us, off our own initiative, had saved the lives of the lot of them, less than twelve hours beforehand. Virtually unarmed, we had walked forward and captured a Japanese road-block, and not one of them knew anything of the most excellent, and timely, Chinese Army intervention.

In due course of time, it transpired; only days before the arrival of our draft, the present group of glory seekers were promoted, in order to meet the exigencies of the service.

Following the Sittang River crossing, not one of these established pre-war officers remained amongst the bedraggled men we joined with in the bomb crater. It appears that, apart from those wounded, they fled the conflict, and 'hot footed it', back to the security, and comfort, of the Maymyo base.

Before departing Mount Popa, CO, Chadwick emphasised the flakiness and the self-centring, of many peace-time regular officers. Having been sheltered throughout the recent weeks of trauma, he committed the cardinal sin in man management. Seeking to favour his own ambitious, and the glory seeking chums of pre-war days, he made the grave error of disregarding the ill used, debilitated, and grave condition of the majority of his men. In the darkness of night, he surreptitiously, evacuated two of the established officers; (Baxter and Green),

Both individuals were Commanding Companies, neither of them anywhere near so ill, as were large numbers of the men. Chadwick's underhand, 'dark act' was seen by the men as; Unfair favouritism of his officer friends? The two departed, were in far better medical condition than most of the struggling troops, and, in sickness, no man is better than another.

Resentment, long festering throughout the unit, went from simmering, to loathing, and open hostility. With morale so low, and aware of the manifest lack of confidence in him, the man realised that his life was in danger, and that: From his own troops?

Formal military discipline was instantly, a thing of the past: No words were spoken, or found necessary, as the mantle of control fell from officers. The situation was brought about by men recognising, and resenting, the indifference shown to them, and their bleak existence, in such appalling conditions; by a Command, ensconced far away, in remote upper echelons.

Bitterly angered over the increasing show of neglect; no food, no ammunition, no medical, and no control, the stage was set! Within the debased unit there was no ceremony, or announcement of change: Amongst doomed and discarded men, as we were, there is no such thing as hierarchal superiority, or humble subordination. Regardless of rank or military seniority, all were now on one footing, and in each seeking his individual existence, initiative became the watchword. From now on, all men had equal voice and woe-betide any man seeking to apply military discipline. Proud shoulder badges of rank had no further meaning.

Once usurped by a junior, there is no rescinding the situation, so long as the conflict continues. With the King's crown on his shoulder, Chadwick, 2nd Bn. KOYLI, titular Commanding Officer, was now, virtually, a non-entity, and the enemy of all.

It was not hard to understand; the degradation of the unit was exemplified days beforehand, when fifty-nine, possibly more, good, but very sick men, departed in mass desertion; (the number was a rapid count, within three depleted Companies). These men were soldiers of high calibre, now destitute, and undignified through incompetence of Command, and it was not to be forgotten, or forgiven, by these loyal men of the highest quality.

The remnants of what had been, a proud British Army Regiment, were now, no more than a band of increasingly weakening desperados. All ready to take their chance on escape, and accepted that they were in a state of regeneration: Although no better than the equivalent of the passing streams of skeletal civilian refugees. This was the depth into which a proud British Regiment was denigrated. The only advantage was, in being a formed group, and carrying a weapon, regardless of its uselessness.

Fully aware of the parlous situation into which he had placed himself, he acted in a manner unthinkable within a British Infantry Regiment, particularly by a Commanding Officer. As Commander in charge of a Battalion of British Infantrymen, was ensconced in what one might regard; The safest place on earth.

In fear of his life, from his own troops, the debunked CO found it necessary to appoint, 'Geordie', Bill Tighe, as 'his personal bodyguard', and to remain within ten yards of him at all times.

With almost five hundred miles to traverse, and a further five weeks inside Burma, nobody mentioned the word; 'retreat'. We were most certainly on a mission of survival, and if 'withdrawal', was the word for it, that's what we were on.

Gerald with 'Geordie' Bill Tighe – Bodyguard to Chadwick

Setting out from Mount Popa, and accompanying a mule cart, the tall elegant Corporal, 'Gigger' Lee, from Dewsbury, was walking alongside me. Having travelled a short distance, a volley of shots came in, from trees, over to our right, and 'Gigger', a pace to my front, was hit on his side. The firing stopped, and 'Gigger' was, as were we all, in no position to pursue the culprits, we went on our way.

Eventually evacuated, and returned to England, the unfortunate 'Gigger' was wrongfully reported amongst those of the unit remaining in India; "to have been killed in action in Europe"; Gigger's niece informs me recently, that his version was, that he had been, "shot in the bum". He died much later, in England. Gigger's wartime service merited his receiving a, 'Distinguished Conduct Medal'. It was presented to him by the King, at Buckingham Palace. He was a tremendous bloke! What else can I say?

(He was all that a man would want to be – a true James Bond character).

Gigger was the only man that I knew to be caught by the burst of shots. They were obviously fired by the band of former oilfield workers, the same recalcitrant mob I had recently shot up, following their arson attempt at the Chauk oilfield.

Formed as a band of Dacoits, and having missed their attempted attack on the departed British oilmen, the evil bastards were assaulting our unit. Gigger's wounding was paramount, in my rapidly, bringing about their demise.

Accepting the situation as quite normal by this time, it might be appropriate to mention the lack of facilities in the medical department. 'Gigger' Lee's flesh wound was insignificant, alongside the appalling shits, and fevers, so many were suffering. In the period of almost two months, from the time I first joined with the remnants of the Battalion, at 'Pip' Moran's Llegu base, I had not seen, or heard, of a doctor, and knew nothing of any medical aid post. Sickness meant death! A man was nursed along by his Buddy to the point of collapse.

For a Battalion to be, "Sent down the road", as we were, and be expected to survive behind enemy lines, for almost two weeks, is virtually, an impossible task. To accomplish this, starved of food, and ammunition, and to meet, and deal, with several skirmishes, whilst totally incommunicado from all Military Command, is a miracle.

9

CHINESE DELIGHT

(With a slight diversion)

It mattered not one iota where the lady was writing from, it took only seconds for me to declare: "I don't care what it costs", "I'm going to visit, and express a personal 'Thank You!' to this lady, wherever she is on this earth". Just two magic words of appreciation, for an unprecedented Chinese Army action, one that saved my life, and that of numerous wonderful colleagues: For whatever reason, the action remains unmentioned, firstly by Army Commander Alexander, and is further denied, and dismissed, by the British Hierarchy, at all levels; "Airbrushed out", in the 'covering, and overlooking', the disgusting performances of British war Commanders, and their superiors, from Churchill downwards.

Going from boy to man in four short months, and engaged in armed combat on more than a dozen occasions, I reverted to my pre-war status, as 'leader of the pack'. I had, of necessity, usurped the dithering CO whenever trouble threatened.

Puzzling over so many years, it was impossible to make known the true and vital actions: Not the distorted and imaginary ones recorded by Regimental Historians and patronising authors. Seeking to rectify events over many years, I approached numerous members of the ever rapidly changing Ministers for Defence, including King, Rifkind, Dr. Moonie, Fox, Iain Duncan Smith; A succession of Prime Ministers, Margaret Thatcher, Major, Blair, to David Cameron; and as they wore uniforms indicating possible combat ability, the Queen and her husband were invited to become involved, but all to no avail. It was as though, once recorded, and suitably received, by whatever trash, it became 'set in stone!' Why would they want to hear the blatant truth from one so intimately involved?

One can only assume that each and every one of the British hierarchy, found it necessary to, 'cover or protect', the names and reputations, of the scumbag controllers of the Burma 1942 war: The 'Cowardly' Victoria Cross holding General Smyth, and the other failed Generals, flown out of Burma on the arrival of the timorous, indifferent, abdicating Irish Guardsman, General Alexander: The Prince of Plausibility, Prime Minister Winston Spencer Churchill required extra care and protection. The man virtually declared himself 'guilty'; and found the necessity to hide away, his All Fools Day signal; "The wisest plan for Japan", sent to Roosevelt. He was exasperated, and out of his depth, in attempting control: at Hong Kong, Java, Singapore, to his disgusting explosion, and ultimate discard of Burma.

The reply I did receive was from the one person with the least reason of all to attempt to negate my approach: Asked by Defence Minister, King, to pacify and silence me; The Viscount Slim, President of the Burma Star Association, son of General William (Bill) Slim, had the plausible audacity to assume some sort of superiority over me. His ignorant, "Shut up!" letter of 1981, is shown in a later chapter.

How simple the differing letter, received 6th August 2012.

"Dear Captain Fitzpatrick,

It's a great honour and joy for me to be able to communicate with you today. First of all, let me introduce myself and explain the reasons why I am writing this letter, I am the eldest daughter of the late Chinese General Fang-Wu Liu who was the commander of 113th Regiment of the Chinese Expeditionary Force during the battle of Yanangyaung in Burma in 1942. I learned your name and background from the news of your visit to the Chinese Embassy in the UK and later from your book entitled <u>No Mandalay, No Maymyo.</u>

My father past away in 1994, and my family is preparing to write a book about him and the historic battle of Yenangyaung in Burma. Since you are one of the veterans that participated in the battle, your memories about the battle would be highly valuable to our family and to the book.

For your information, I am enclosing the following:

photo showing Mrs. Margaret Thatcher visiting General Fang-Wu Liu in USA in 1992, letter from Mr. Malcolm Rifkind, Minister of Defence, UK in 1992 and photo of my father in 1942.

I wish you all the best and look forward to hearing from you soon! Thank you.

Sincerely,

Margaret L. Sun"

It mattered not from where the letter came, and regardless of cost, I simply had to visit and say, "Thank You!" to this lady. To have done this, I could have spent as little as ten minutes with her, and been happy to turn around, and return on the same plane. The £4,000 flight cost, was as nothing, compared to the value of the name of the Republic of China Army General, Fang-Wu Liu, Margaret's father, and the most excellent force he commanded:-

The Republic of China, Army Expeditionary Force to Burma; and 113 Regiment.

With the dishevelled and desperate British forces, discarded and in complete disarray, the Chinese unit exemplified itself in the Battle of Yenangyaung: It was one action I witnessed, as though viewing from a grandstand, to be of any significance and a resounding success.

I give a detailed account of this god sent force in the book, 'No Mandalay, No Maymyo', mentioned by Margaret, only to find the indifferent twat of an Aristocratic Irish Guardsman, General Alexander, not only belittles the Chinese throughout: In his 'Memoirs', the hypocrite states; "The Chinese never once defeated the Japs".

Having travelled to Washington DC, Patricia and I decided to stay the week, and were feted beyond anything we had previously known, by Margaret, her husband Peter, and brother, Robert Wei-Ming Liu. The presentation of the rare, Republic of China, Centennial Plate by Major General Hsien-Sheng (Sampson) Lee, I found both humbling, and staggering: (The plate, the only one held in Britain, is shown on the front cover).

Above all else on the Washington visit, was the fact that I could give thanks, on behalf of my colleagues, Steve, (Victor Stevens), Sergeant Benny Mee, my batman Ted Hewitt, and so many others, long passed away. These men died knowing that all of those, in British Government, and Military Command, had failed them.

A recent British Gem – From Yorkshire Post 3rd November 2012

Arctic convoy veterans denied

Within six weeks of my receiving, (on 16th September), the precious Centennial Plate; On 3rd November 2012, the ubiquitous, anonymous, 'Foreign Office Spokesman', as reported in the Yorkshire Post, speaks on behalf of the Government; It's never Mr So-and-So, on behalf of the British Foreign Secretary, Mr William Hague MP. This important personage has to have a mask.

The Russian Government, through Mr Alexander Yakovenko, the Russian Ambassador to Britain, wants to acknowledge, and honour, the courage of the wartime British Royal Navy, Arctic Convoy Veterans, by the presentation of the prestigious Ushakov Medal: Not Mr William Hague MP, Foreign Secretary, but "The British Government Spokesman", comments:

> "The Foreign Office appreciates the Russian Government's offer, but foreign awards could only be allowed; for a specific service to a country within five years".

These valiant, long suffering men, being in their late eighties, must be delighted to hear such trash!

Immediately Post War, no government was in position to undertake minor international considerations within five years: There were more urgent domestic needs to attend to. An honour of this nature should have no time limit.

If you served in the British Armed Forces? It's your own damned fault!

*Reception at Washington D.C. Peter, Margaret, Robert and Gerald.
Fanfare – Videos – Flowers!*

*Peter, Margaret, Gerald and Robert and Riley (granddaughter)
Margaret is holding book connection 'No Mandalay, No Maymyo'.*

Robert, Patricia, Gerald, Jason C. Yuan (Taipei Economic and Cultural Representative in U.S.A.) Margaret and Peter

Robert, Major General Hsien-Sheng (Sampson) Lee, ROC Army Director General – Defence Mission, Patricia, Gerald, Margaret, and Peter

10

BRITISH HIERARCHY MEETING DIVERSITY

In the deplorable condition in which we found ourselves, and in the normal way of things, we would have had no reason whatsoever to enter a native habitation. However, there was an alert as we halted for a sparse meal, and settled close by Taungtha, a most unusual village. It was a singular habitat, contained within a stockade, constructed from teak trees, and not an inch of space between them, somewhat similarly built to those seen in old time films of far West America, and with an entrance sufficient only to accommodate a bullock cart.

The general silence was broken, as, in ones or twos, a few distraught sari clad Indian girls emerged from the narrow village entrance, each of them crying, and in turn, making a dash towards the north.

Taking Sergeant Benny Mee, and six men, I sealed the place, and on entering the village, saw the burning building, (Signal to Japanese), from which the girls were escaping. It was part of a temple or mosque, (Pungi Chung), and surrounded by a gathering of men. By dress, and bearing, the gathered group were easily recognisable as the recalcitrant oilmen; (none were wearing the traditional Burmese Lunghi). They were the ones who had harassed the European management; fired the Chauk bungalows; and chided me with the words, uttered so indiscreetly, by Alexander; Apart from this gathering, there appeared to be no others in the village.

When rounded up, the former oil-men were twenty-seven in number, and several of them, limping badly, for some reason? I wonder why?

These were now a formed band of Dacoits; the ones responsible for wounding 'Gigger' Lee, my Corporal. The same dissolute group shot by me, earlier, in the 'dust-up' at the Chauk oilfield, were to be denied any further attempt at disrupting our movements.

Arresting the lot of them, I conducted them to our base, close by a small Chaung, (dried river). When questioned, by two Burmese speaking soldiers of the battalion, they refused to answer.

Aware of the gangs increasing hostility: Being decrepit throughout, and with no means of restraint, or feeding them; releasing the oilmen was not an option. Knowing what I was about to do, the dithering weakness of Chadwick was further revealed. He cowered in his own insensitive obtuseness, and in opting out, his uncalled for comment was; "I want no part in this".

It remained with me, the apprehender of the group of men I personally knew to be actively hostile, to order their immediate extermination.

Alive to Other Ranks reluctance to be ordered, and their blatant hostility towards officers; I directed that the executions be undertaken, instantly, by the three acting Company Commanders; nine Dacoits each. (The two CC's, replacing Green and Baxter, were recently 'field promoted NCO's', and new to me. The other was another former Ex-Ranker, CSM 'Dusty' Miller).

The men were shot, and with a short distance between each executioner, three separate piles of bodies were dumped into the open Chaung.

Apart from Chadwick, each one of the executing officers, all senior to me, were aware of their own fate, in the event of their refusal, or objection. There was no such thing as the luxury of time, particularly, time taken up in squabbling. My decision, once taken, was to be carried out! There! – And Then!

The extra bonus, in dispatching the dissident oilmen, was that it denied the Japanese twenty-seven experienced operators. They were not to harass us further.

Dacoits came in many different guises, and a friend, Ian Bell, who, as an infant, was evacuated from Burma, tells me of the precarious life lived by his Teak Forest Manager father. In the Shan States, ' Sabwas', were warlords, ruling Northern borders. 'Dyaks' conducted banditry throughout the country. The whole of Burma had problems, with the spread of, 'The evil Knights of the Bushido,' making departure from the country, more expedient.

Friends of mine, recent visitors to Burma, – and there have been several. have been unable to locate the site of the stockaded village; I rather imagine that the Japanese saw the whole place as a timber yard, and shipped the precious booty back to Nippon.

At a much later date, and never hearing a word, or mention, of the 1941/42 Burma fiasco, all was centred on America, and their misdemeanours in Viet Nam. Knowing that I had dished out somewhat similar in Burma, and considering that the public ought to know, I approached 'The Observer', considered a top class publication newspaper.

In seeking publicity for my first book, I related, from start to finish, the failings of Chadwick, the clearance of a road-block, the excellent Chinese Army action, along with the rhyme and reason, for the execution of the twenty seven oilfield-worker Dacoits, to 'The Observer' editors, Donald Threlfall, and Anthony Howard.

The two vehemently, distorted, and dramatised the story as related to them. In doing so; the pair, scandalised, and attempted to criminalise me.

The heading on 'The Observer' edition, Sunday 3rd June 1984; (sic)

"WAR-TIME MASSACRE BY BRITISH TROOPS REVEALED"

"I ORDERED KILLING OF CIVILIANS IN BURMA RETREAT"

*(See appendix for full copy, also Sunday Times, and lying legal letter)

Not unreasonable, in view of the above; questions were raised in Parliament. This resulted in a demand by Prime Minister, Margaret Thatcher, for a Scotland Yard, Serious Crime Squad investigation. Senior Detective Inspector, Hardy, and a very 'thick' Sergeant Tovey, visited me on Wednesday, 24th October 1984. Tovey was so dim, he misheard, or miss-recorded everything said in the interview, and my wife had to correct him. She eventually finished up writing the corrected story, as related by me. The two Scotland Yard men also visited a number of my former colleagues, whose names I gave them: Ted Hewitt, my former batman, colleague Steve, and others, assured them of the necessity for the action: In spite of the meritorious comments made, particularly by Steve, I heard no further: Another British Governmental 'airbrush out'!

The damnable part of this despicable editorial episode, is, that I had no redress with the vile Observer incriminators of my character, and the numerous other insipid editors, world wide, copying, and following their lead.

Attempting to justify the Observer editorial staff treachery, there appeared a later contribution. It was made by a man, obviously, one 'drawing pay', as a 'Director', of the newspaper; Lord, Henry Cecil John 'Everest' Hunt; (The hill climber). Feeling the necessity of, supporting the propriety of true British uppity'; he chose to comment;

"The British Army can not be seen carrying out this kind of action!"

Can't they just?

In adversity, the British Government; Militarily and 'Lordly', have the penchant for blindness, and use of the proverbial, 'Airbrush'. Hunt makes no mention of, his two despicable employees; Threlfall, and Howard.

It was almost thirty years later, on 13th September 2012, Jack Straw, Member of Parliament, uttered the words;

"Thatcher created a culture of impunity"

The Prime Minister had set Scotland Yard to silence my revelations.

My loathing of self righteousness, pomposity, and high handedness, amongst those, all too often, priggish Seniors. The ones I encountered, during my period of almost ten years amongst them, and about whom I do not fail to comment, is beautifully illustrated in another uppity newspaper: I do go on! Jumping on the band-wagon, Press Editors can be vile.

Catherine Steven of, 'The Sunday Telegraph', violated the Sabbath, on October 7th 1984. Avoiding me completely, she was not content with following the dastardly Observer Duo's savagery: The Bitch of a Thing, explored further, in attempting to outdo, 'The Observer' pair. Seeking exclusivity, and searching for a despicable traitor, the harlot left her knickers in the office drawer. Her article is headed: -

"BURMA MASSACRE INQUIRY"

It contains the ultimate in, heinous 'put downs'. Wholly attributable to the last person in the world, from whom it should be possible to draw such venom, and one, one would least expect it to come from; Colonel CW Huxley the Regimental Colonel of my former Regiment; The Kings Own Yorkshire Light Infantry.

This hapless fool is a man that I do not know, one that I have never met with, and could not recognise. Although I served almost ten years with the Regiment, the man does not know me from Adam!

Quoting from, 'The Sunday Telegraph':

"Colonel Colin Wylde Huxley, Colonel of the KOYLI, last night could offer no explanation for the alleged massacre, and confirmed there was no record of such as (sic) incident in the regiment's records".

"I do not know Mr Fitzpatrick. He has never joined us in any events, as far as I know, and he has never dined with us".

In accepting, without question, the various newspaper diatribes, this patronising, and supercilious scum like denouncement of me, would be meant to demean, and with a touch of malice, attempt to humiliate me. The comment exemplifies the presumptive attitude of permanent superiority, and exclusivity, of 'dyed in the wool,' 'Former', Senior Regular Officers. Huxley fits the bill, in the way of so many of the obnoxious bunch. The egotistic code reverberates, and permeates, throughout the Armed Forces. Huxley's intervention and interest, was, in himself seeking prominence, at my expense. Never having met with a situation of shear desperation, as had I, it is beyond his narrow comprehension, that a subaltern should usurp a titular Commanding Officer. I find this ilk of a man, to be disagreeable, and highly offensive.

What Huxley would not know of my post war life, and I certainly know nothing of him, was that I was engaged in the hard civilian field of competitive employment. With seven kids to feed, clothe, and school, I had more to do with my money than lavish lunch on The Queen Mother, at Claridges London Hotel.

When I freely joined with the British armed forces, it was from employment responsible enough to have made me exempt from military service. Considering my allegiances to lie elsewhere, with the Irish cause, I could quite easily have decamped to join with them. With Hitler's emergence, I joined with the British, and within three days, they failed me: I was to carry the disgust and scepticism throughout my service.

The damnable part of Huxley's diatribe, is that, at the time of his blurb, I was, as was he, in regular communication with the Regimental Secretary: For God's sake! Huxley had access to me, through the same secretary.

Ironically: For many years I have organised annual reunions for veterans of, 1^{st,} and 2nd KOYLI Battalions; Huxley, 'Colonel or not?' never once attended.

Update! Aware that, on active service, the average life of an infantry officer was, one and a half days, I ignored the challenge and snatched at the idea of receiving the princely sum of eleven shillings per day pay. Taking the increase from three shillings and three pence, I took the commission.

Buggered about in England, and in Northern Ireland, I realised that I was as good, and better than most officers with whom I met, of whatever rank. However, it was when posted to some undeclared tropical station, I thought of the possible short span of life, in the event of meeting with active service.

I did not 'have' to marry when I did, but I managed to do so, on my embarkation leave. It meant that in the event of my demise, somebody was going to be provided for, with a pension, or so I thought: (We see later, it was not so).

The ironical thing is, that at my present grand old age, of ninety-three, I have received not one penny pension in all the years, owing to some shortcomings in a particular Governmental cock-up. I have recently joined with an action group; 'The Equality for Veterans Association'. We seek some form of recompense for time served, as the majority of similar ex-service personnel already do.

Churchill approved a damnable stoppage of both pay, and family support, for those unfortunate, Japanese held, Prisoners of War: (The despicable experience of Doctor Colonel MacKenzie comes later).

With the Observer, Telegraph, and numerous other world-wide publications, hammering out my plight, the British Government, and the Ministry of Defence, remained 'shtoom'. They did not want to know! Having, whilst on active service, usurped one of their prized Battalion Commanders, I had recognised, and executed, an actively hostile, band of individuals. Apart from harassing the British oilfield managers, the bastards had damaged one of my finest soldiers.

Seen to be acting contrary to all British protocol, I was, not surprisingly, 'Airbrushed', out of British history. I was now, 'of no consequence', to the King and the Country, into which Army I had, most reluctantly, enlisted.

In a letter reflecting a rare response and reaction, from a succession of Prime Ministers, and Defence Secretaries.

Reference; D/US of S/LM 1741/01/Y dated 19th APRIL 2001.

Doctor Lewis Moonie MP, – the Parliamentary, Under Secretary for State for Defence, in attempting to brush off the awkwardness, states;

"I can not accept his, (That's Me), suggestion that the forces there, (In Burma), were in any way discarded or abandoned by Winston Churchill, then the Prime Minister".

The good Doctor failed to read Churchill's signal to FDR. Suggesting; "The wisest scheme for Japan was to press on through Burma".

On 28th April 1990, under a heading in the Yorkshire Evening Post; -

"Burma massacre – officer stands easy amid row".

The article ends with; Twaddle! Hateful, Typical of British Parliamentary, Foreign Office Gobbledegook.

A Foreign Office 'spokesman', (Not named), said:

"These allegations of events nearly 50 years ago have surfaced before, the last time in 1984, and were found to be unsubstantiated. We are surprised that they should come up again". "It would be

regrettable if this turns out to be a ploy by the Burmese authorities to deflect attention from the elections to be held next month".

It avoids naming the subject; and who is this 'Spokesman'?

(These allegations are very much substantiated in the Myanmar of today).

From Churchill, to Margaret Thatcher, to present day: The British hierarchy avoids acceptance of recorded adversity, or questionable activities. (As I write this, the heads of British and American governments writhe, as a constant stream of dead are returned from a non-winnable war, in far off Afghanistan: At Christmas 2012 Prime Minister Cameron visited, and assured troops stationed in Afghanistan that they are coming home: Another 'Airbrushes out', failure). He did not mention, 5,000 were soon to be discarded.

Evasive, and ever defensive in adversity, the British Government, – 'Duck and Dive', forever avoiding the recording of unsavoury subjects in their history. Prime Minister, Margaret Thatcher, alerted two Scotland Yard dimwits, in attempting to nullify my original disclosure. The Burmese authorities are proved, very alert.

NOTE! – When arranging, by a special invitation, to visit Myanmar (Burma), a short while ago, I met with a 'stoppage signal', emanating from Burma. It was, unwittingly, sent to my travel agent by her unsuspecting researcher, based in Yangon, (Rangoon).

There is no British recognition of my action, or, offer of help against my newspaper antagonists: Using my personally recorded excerpts, I am content, and happy to be able to repeat and record this story.

A fellow historian-writer warned me, some time ago; -

"We both know that the Home Office, and Foreign Office, do <u>not</u> want the truth to come out of what went on in Burma, and they will go to any length to achieve their aims. I have written to many people who tried to help the Karen, and come out with the truth, but they have since become strangely 'silent'. Don't underestimate the opposition!"

> **To:** Mr. G. Fitzpatrick
> **Fax:**
> **Sent:** 10th Feb 2005
> **Subject:**
>
> **From:** MiMi Tin Tun Raschke
> New Horizons Travels & Tours Ltd.
> **Tel/Fax:** 020 7813 4161
> **Pages:** 1 (including Cover)
>
> Dear Mr. Fitzpatrick,
>
> Whilst preparing your itinerary for Burma a colleague of mine enquired as to whether you were the same "Second Lieutenant Gerald Fitzpatrick, who was a raw 22-year-old recruit with the King's Own Yorkshire Light Infantry when he was shipped into the hell hole that was Burma." If so you must remember well the massacre at Taungtha.
>
> He was also interested to know whether you are the author of "No Mandalay, No Maymyo".
>
> I would be grateful if could please confirm this for us.
>
> Warm regards,
>
> MiMi

Letter from Travel Agent

"I am always worried lest they suddenly 'withdraw my passport.' – there is nothing one could do about it; so I am cautious as to what I say".

Four selected men, under command of a very livewire Major David Martin, were killed in a mighty explosion, one brought about by Martin. Entering a former cinema building, now used as a storehouse, and situated close by the small town of Myingyan, the unfortunate, Martin, chose to apply a scorched earth policy, in order to prevent abandoned goods falling into enemy hands.

Using bayonets, the men punctured tins of stored Ghee, (clarified butter). Releasing the rancid butter caused the circulation of noxious fumes throughout the building, and unthinking of the gasses formed, Martin lit a flame to ignite the building; unfortunately, with him and the men inside.

Martin, and Tommy Mellia, the very popular 'Kilkenny' Irishman, were blown out of the building. The pair survived long enough to tell the tale. Wrapped in bamboo screeds we buried them both in shallow graves, and covered with heavy stones, to deter vultures, and marked with a cross.

Meeting with Tommy Mellia's brother 60 years after the war, he expressed his appreciation at hearing of Tommy's immense popularity, and the circumstances of his death.

On 2nd November 2009: By request, I forwarded a diagrammatic sketch of the burial site, to the nephew of David Martin. Remembering the layout of the village/town, the cinema, and the north-south road, I was able to virtually pinpoint the exact spot, certainly to within ten yards.

It was like wonderland as we reached the Irrawaddy River Crossing, at Sameikon, the point where the Chindwin forms the junction with the Irrawaddy.

(From this point, the two rivers become the Irrawaddy, until near Rangoon, where the Irrawaddy becomes, Rangoon River, and empties into the Indian Ocean).

There was magic, to see the small ferry boat, especially one manned by two bearded Royal Marines. It meant that we were spared the effort of eight days of marching, up river, in order to cross at the Ava Bridge, situated close by Mandalay. In the event, the bridge was destroyed days before we could have arrived, and we would, most certainly, not have survived the additional journey.

I chip in with a tit-bit, only just to hand.

As late as 20th February 2009, Patrick Xavier, informs me, although unrelated to the book; -

"There was some attempt, by someone or other, to blame members of my family for the murder of the Burmese patriot Aung San, (father of the unfortunate, and celebrated, Aung San Su Che), on 19th July 1947. The facts are that the most likely candidate, my eldest uncle, Dudley Xavier, the sometime pre-war Rangoon police chief, had died in Assam in 1942, and also Douglas, as you know, died in 1945".

It was Dudley who warned Dorman-Smith, the British Governor General of Burma, of early Japanese movements, both in south Burma, and at sea. Dudley's avowed dislike of Aung San's, communist politics, was well known by the Governor, and 'for some reason?' Dudley was transferred to another post, some distance away.

11

ENDURANCE – SWIM – SEA SNAKES

Crossing the Irrawaddy River, the long hectic days of Battalion incommunicado ended, 'for the time being'. Two, 'recently acquired', Burmese bullock cart drivers, vanished, as though ghosts in the night. Unaware, and unthinking, we were now in a different 'tribal' territory, and the discarded animals, and the carts, became our property. Versatility, amongst men in the ranks, produced drivers for the carts. Once again, caught up by Command in what might be considered safer territory, it all too rapidly changed. Within hours, we were hustled thirty miles northwards, to a riverside village, already under attack.

Very surprisingly, and hard to believe in the circumstances, we met with a company of Gurkha soldiers, pegged down by a party of Japanese. The Japs were possibly a small, Commando like squad, once again ahead of us, having been brought up river by boat, with the obvious task of disrupting our further movement. The scoundrels: Being a small boat party, and obviously misreading our impoverished condition, they considered us to be fresh reinforcements, and the firing ceased, as they vanished.

Moving up the rise from the river bank, and passing a young Gurkha, I can never forget the boy: Standing bravely, and raising his shirt, with a smile on his face, he showed the line of seven small bullet holes across his chest, as he accepted his fate.

Oh Yes! The Japanese were certainly: "Pressing on north through Burma", in the manner suggested by Churchill, weeks beforehand.

Discarded, as we obviously were, there was to be no further official provisioning throughout our final four weeks in the country. It was now a case of: forage wherever you will. The tiny man, QM, 'Dogger' Riley, certainly foraged! He found little, but somehow it managed to sustain. By this time, of course, Mr. Churchill had forgotten his failures in the Far East. He had eyes for nothing beyond Middle Eastern deserts. His world now ended at the Suez Canal!

Fuel for vehicles being considerably restricted, we were fortunate in moving on mostly flat, rough-metalled roads. The taxiing tank squadron helped, in conveying us to a safer distance, possibly thirty miles ahead of the enemy.

Long concerned over the condition of my colleague, Bob Rimmer, I was particularly pleased to see the tanks. An allergy, causing him to faint at the sight of blood, had overtaken him, and he had been totally incapacitated, 'out cold', for four days of our marching. Whilst some members thought Bob should be left to his fate: I was having none of that. The Irish childhood came into play, and, using my experience of loading mountain turf, from the bog, into creels and onto the donkeys: I roped Bob securely, each day, onto the back of a mule. With the care of his batman, Johnny Raby: himself a former jockey, from Lancashire, Bob survived: *(to become a solicitor in post-war years)*. The tanks evacuated Bob.

A little further north, we were surprised somewhat, once again, to be alerted by a most unusual lively movement amongst the accompanying column of refugees. This was the unexpected, and final, challenging attack, made by the Japanese. The small cycle patrol was spotted, and rapidly despatched by a volley of shots from our rearguard defence. It was now a case of undertaking the long road march to the decisive point of escape, where the vital decision was to be made.

Illustrating the complete indifference to our existence, and contrary to all military practice, we were invited to choose our own route for the final days of withdrawal: I call it escape. Leaving the small village of Pyingaing, we had the choice, to go west, for forty or so miles along the recognised track, towards the Chindwin River ferry-crossing point, at Kalewa. With no certainty of a ferry, and with the forty-two tanks known to be disabled, and abandoned, on this, the most favourable road route.

When it came to making a choice between the forty mile ferry route, or opting for the hundred-plus mile jungle trek: Chadwick, with pre-war experience, when asked for his opinion, performed his usual dithering act: it was left to Steve and me to decide. Realising that the main track, holding the line of tanks, and requiring the precarious ferry crossing, would almost certainly be targeted by enemy aircraft, we opted for the alternative: the long jungle trail.

At over one hundred rough miles, it was possibly three times the distance of the road and ferry route. There were no identifiable tracks to follow, and the recently acquired map gave no indication of the terrain. With two oil wells, situated at remote jungle villages, to destroy en-route, at Indaw, and Pantha, we were joined by a small detachment of Indian Sappers. Prime considerations favouring the long jungle trek, was the tree-top cover, both for shade, and from hostile aircraft. Not one man opted for the softer road route, although all were in no doubt, the jungle trip would be no picnic, particularly with so many suffering debilitating illness, and desperately short of water and food. It proved a long, arduous, and fatalistic slog.

Receiving a wireless set, a heavy and bulky square piece of equipment, in order to maintain some form of communication, we thought it might be nice to keep in touch with Alexander, our dear Army Commander. The mysticism of our very existence continued however, and we were back to normal within a few short yards of departure. In the process of ascending the first, of many 2,000 ft hills, the mule loaded with the wireless set floundered, and the set disintegrated.

A young doctor, with the name of Xavier, arrived before our departure, and said that he was to join with us for the jungle trek. He was our first contact with medical services of any form, and contact is all that it was. Tall, fair, rotund, and looking far too well fed, alongside our surviving few: which was now possibly a little over one hundred in strength. The unfortunate young man had not one single item of medical equipment. To see a man, supposedly a doctor, carrying a large revolver in so obvious a manner, and belted around a rather smart looking Bush Jacket, I questioned his credentials. I need not have bothered as, 'highly qualified affirmation', – 'authenticity personified', came from a few of the 'voracious venereal vulnerable' troops: "Sir! He's the Knob Doctor from Mandalay": "OK!" Why question further with such positive authentication.

Emaciated, and suffering debilitation, and dehydration, particularly from the Asian illness: beriberi, along with one, or more, of malaria, typhoid, and dysentery, a man would cease existence. Totally incapacitated, he would simply collapse alongside the jungle trail. Almost invariably, and with little alternative, the man's 'Mucker', being equally distressed, would remain with him. There was a beautiful, and ethereal look, on the face of each and every one departed, as they lay there, and spoke their final words: There was at all times: "Remember Me? "God Bless!"

Shortly following our departure, and with no means of aid of any kind, we would hear two distinct gunshots: They related the whole tragic story.

Acting as rearguard, I was accompanied by the doctor, of whom I knew nothing, other than his name. From the rearguard situation, we witnessed each weak and debilitated individual as they retreated, more and more, day by day. Inevitably, there came the day of surrender, as the man could no longer rise from the ground. Joined with, 'his Mucker', the two men remained behind alone, and as the doctor was in no position to dispense any form of succour, it became a matter of hearing two spaced out shots.

It was never questioned, although, whenever the doctor remained behind with the failing stragglers, there were, occasionally, two rather more rapid shots. Carrying a 0-45 inch revolver, the doctor had sympathetically obliged, and mercifully despatched the sufferers. That two small lead pellets, was the most merciful, and caring treatment a young doctor could dispense, simply reflects the appalling degenerate state of affairs into which we were sunk.

Recital of the Kohima Epitaph is truly evocative: -

When you go home
Tell them of us
And say
For your tomorrow we gave our today

For a young, recently qualified, member of the world's most trusted medical service, to be reduced to using shot from a revolver as his only comforter, denigrates the dignity of the world's proudest profession. The British public, in general, remain unconvinced that, Churchill, and

Alexander: Prime Minister, and his chosen Army Commander, would, or could, abandon, and discard, an Army Force, as we of the 1942 Burma Army found ourselves. Denied provisioning of any kind, for many weeks, we suffered numerous casualties. Dead and dying men, lay, spread along the sad jungle trail. They speak out: -The voices of judgement.

Having walked, and hacked our way, over one hundred miles of jungle, hills, and streams, for ten or eleven days, it was through such spectacular beauty, I wished to repeat the effort in more comfortable circumstances. Accompanied throughout with the 'Woogle–Woogle' call, from trees full of monkeys, and witnessing innumerable masses of butterflies covering the floors of valleys, and to hear the gentle whispering noise as they took flight, as though the sheet on a bed, being lifted from one corner. Occasionally there were the beautiful orchids, and truly spectacular scenery, viewed from hilltops: including the distinguishable stretch of the Himalayan mountain range, possibly more than four hundred miles distant.

There was a hurt in it: We did not know, and certainly had no means of recording, the numbers, or names, of those perished by the wayside. Weren't they, "just soldiers?" One I do remember, prominent, and popular, is a garrulous young boy named Fish, singer and joker, he went from busty, to skeletal, in days. Sinking to die, he wished everybody: "God Bless!"

At the end of the long trek, I remained as rearguard. The jungle hereabout, close by the Chindwin River, was ghostly, misted and damp, in an unusual way, particularly following the recent long weeks of sun and torrid temperatures. I was not aware that we had reached the river, until a runner arrived, calling for swimmers to go forward. As a young teenager, I had trained with the City of Leeds, Olympic Swimming Squad, ostensibly, for participation in the Berlin, 1936 Olympics: young, and not quite up to the mark, I did not get there. However, as a most likely competitor, I volunteered for the Chindwin swim.

My batman, Ted Hewitt, came forward with me: (Ted was a conscript, called up in the first batch, and sent out to Burma a month or two before the outbreak of hostilities. He "Hated the Bloody Army!", and never let one forget it: "War, or no Bloody War!" Cynical and sceptical, he was to stay with me throughout my tour in the East).

Arriving at the head of the column, I had my first sight of the Chindwin, it was vast, (600/700 yards/metres, possibly more, wide), and appeared to have no ending. The far western bank was but one distant shimmering line of trees, and a daunting swimming prospect, particularly in the frail and emaciated condition I knew myself to be. Hewitt took up the challenge; "You're not going to swim that Bloody thing, are you?" He knew nothing of my background, and he had no reason to think that I might not succeed. "Yes I am!" I replied, and began to strip naked, as I saw four or five men from forward parties, already swimming a short distance out in the river. That was fine, until I arrived, 'starkers', at the river bank, where I froze, and rapidly had cause to reconsidered my options.

The sight before me was terrifying: mammoth sea snakes, mostly more than twelve feet, (four meters), in length, were making their way downstream, and out to sea. The monsters were swimming pack-wise, as do a stream of elvers, only a few short feet from the river bank. No doubt, this migration is an annual ritual for the snakes, and, for some reason, they seek to escape their land locked base before the start of monsoon rains.

Within days, the monsoon season was due, and if our unit were to remain situated on the river's isolated eastern bank, all would perish. I had not come this far to end my days, stranded in the jungle, on the bank of a river, the name of which, I had never before heard. To remain there would mean certain death. Emaciated as I was, and with the loss of three stones in weight, no-matter how massive and forbidding the water obstacle looked, I had to cross. If the few swimming ahead of me were to succeed, I felt certain that I could join them. For me to remain on the remote, eastern bank of the Chindwin River was no option.

This was no altruistic gesture on my part, my main interest, was to get: Me! Gerald Fitzpatrick, across, to the safer western bank of that bloody great mass of water, as soon as possible. With no landmark to front or back when in mid river, the only guide was to hold the river flow to my right shoulder. Frightful of my debilitated condition, and obviously in a much weakened state, to swallow the water and go with the flow, was a brief thought. However: remembering the sunburnt and swollen, balloon like body, floating by, weeks earlier, as we disembarked at Rangoon, I was immediately regenerated, and continued with a steady stroke.

Arriving on the far shore, close by the small fishing village of, Yu-A, a half dozen of us swimmers pulled up eventually, with no idea of the reception we might meet with. It was magnificent! To be received with a glass, filled with the red fruity drink, it is memorable to this day.

With five or six fishing boats mustered, the villagers ferried the unit across the massive river, with the loss of but one unfortunate mule. The handler was distressed to have stumbled, and lost control of the harness.

From the first boat, I was somewhat surprised to be joined on the river bank by Dougie Wardleworth, one of the pre-war regular officers, and he was quick to claim to be first across. Wounded in the arm in early conflict, he had convalesced back in Maymyo, and joined with the unit at the start of the jungle treck. His wife had been killed by hostile aircraft fire, when by his side, and awaiting evacuation from Myitkina airfield. The basic depleted existence, and seemingly undisciplined state of the once proud battalion, was beyond Wardleswoth's comprehension. Unable to accept and adjust to the scum-like looking dishevelled lower level, he became no more than a mere supernumerary, with no accepted responsibilities.

Quite the opposite of Dougie, it was, possibly, knowing the dowdy existence of my early life that made adjustment easier for me, and, I was comfortable in command, and knew that I was respected. This was my introduction to man management. It was to carry me into the future: Army wise, and civilian.

Ted Hewitt went so far as to offer his thanks for my crossing, as he returned my meagre clothing. Had I not been fortunate enough to arrive at the fishing village of Yu-a, and obtained cooperation of the fishermen, the Battalion remnants would surely have perished on the eastern bank of the river. With the meagre food ration long exhausted, any hope of survival meant undertaking the impossible: retracing the ten or eleven strenuous days of jungle march.

There was further to go, in following a Chindwin tributary river upstream, and through a valley of death. The rancid stench was overpowering, as for hour after hour, we passed unfortunate civilians, and escaping troops, dying in their attempting the strenuous route up the western bank of the river. Exhausted, and dehydrated, numerous refugees from southern towns had halted at their first water source. There were a few living individuals amongst them, including children, but we were in no position to help.

Giving priority to Officers, and Senior Other Ranks and their wives, in the evacuation of Burma: Wives of Privates, and Junior NCO's, were given little consideration, for their being flown out: They walked, and failed, in numbers.

I can only surmise this, on the prognosis of there being no known survivor of one particular escape attempt: It is the action taken, considering the desperately limited capabilities, of a gregarious group of participants.

Desperately ill, and emaciated, with a concoction of tropical diseases, pre-war soldier, Private Thomas James Shaw, along with a group of five or six similarly afflicted, sought to escape. He was accompanied by his wife, a Burma born girl, and their two children, the eldest being a two year old. Denied knowledge of any possible departure by air, and burdened by having to carry the children, Shaw set to walking the long difficult land route. He and his wife, along with the two children died, and were possibly amongst those unfortunates: contained within, 'The Valley of Death', through which the battalion passed.

For Thomas Shaw to be buried at the village of Kohima, his body must have been found on the western bank of the Chindwin River. And for the fated family to have travelled the rough undulating and lengthy terrain, from Maymyo, and crossed the Chindwin, by ferry at Kalawa, in the frail condition Shaw was known to be in, was remarkable.

I don't think that Lord 'Everest' Hunt would like me mentioning this remarkable British soldier, particularly, as he: 'Comes from the other side of the tracks'. It's not British! He can be assured however, that not one of the sick and struggling British escapees survived the traumatic indifference to their plight.

It was not the end of our losses, as the last man to fail, within almost yards of safety, was the powerhouse rugby forward, Sergeant Ike Oldcorn. He was considerably reduced by illness, and malnutrition, almost certainly beriberi, to a skeleton of the man we knew: *(His brother, another highly respected, power-house of a man, Company Quartermaster Sergeant,*

Charles E Oldcorn, died at about the same time, a Prisoner of War, in Rangoon Jail).

Men were now feeling themselves to be a part of Burmese ecology, simply an article, to be warm by day and cold by night, and soon to be monkey food, or nutrition for the flora and fauna.

The final hill climb, out of Burma, was a long and twisting road, one carved in desperation, by Naga tribesmen, and women. It was more than a mile in length, and a drag every inch of the way. It was at the head of this tiring climb that I had my first sight of the spruced up tart: General Alexander. This was the British Army General I did not know, and who had cancelled his, "three weeks familiarisation", – (joy ride) tour, on his arrival at Rangoon.

He had gone further, in having a personal, 'Will', drawn up, and at the same time, he declared abdication of his force.

Rescued from the Japanese road-block, on his first day in the country, – *(where beloved Jimmy Ableson was killed)*, and fleeing north, Alexander never once did he venture south, in order to 'familiarise' himself with the troops under his command.

How low can a British Army Commander get?

It was my first sighting of the man. Dressed to kill, in his immaculate, 'poncy' Guardsman uniform, he was one of those Senior Officer types, I had long detested. Now, far from being the insecure subaltern, I was a proven commander. Had I shot Alexander, my men would never have revealed his sweet departure. They had learnt to respect me, for actions taken unhesitatingly, in usurping a wimp of a CO at the oilfields, destroying the band of Dacoit oilmen, and swimming the mighty Chindwin River.

Never having heard of him before, I did not know the man, dressed in battle-dress, standing close by. It was however, Bill Slim. I would have had to shoot him at the same time, and that would have been a sad loss. Slim was a real man, and featured big in my next two years.

Sadly, in my ignorance, and not being aware of the palpable shortcomings of Alexander, I had no idea of his total indifference to our very existence over the many long weeks, and I required a gesture of recognition for the nine men, constituting my platoon. I smartened myself up a bit, before buzzing the men behind me, giving the command: "March to attention: Eyes Right!" I saluted.

It required General Bill Slim, who stood nearby Alexander, to recognise the significance of our salute: In his book 'Defeat into Victory', his recorded comments are;

> "On the last day of the 900 mile retreat, I stood on a bank beside the road and watched the rearguard march into India".

> "All of them, British, Indian, and Gurkha, were gaunt and ragged as scarecrows. Yet still they trudged behind their surviving officer. They still carried their arms. They might look like scarecrows, but they looked like soldiers too".

Unaware of his own value, in that remote and isolated situation, Slim had saved the life of Alexander. Within the next few minutes, and without the slightest regard for the troops he had failed so badly, the tarted-up guardsman was gone. He flew back to the safety of England, and to his cosy future.

The Bastard! Had no thought, other than the preservation of his own precious skin. There's a trail of good men, laid out in the plains, and amongst the trees of North Burma. They bear testimony to this loathsome man!

Alexander fits the pattern of many disgusting British Military Commanders. He thought so little of the 1942 Burma Campaign: -In his curriculum vitae, contained in Collins Concise English Dictionary, he omits the mention of Burma completely. There is no mention of his cowardly failed months, of Burma Command.

Tabulated as 'Earl Alexander of Tunis', 1891- 1969, it simply states:

> "British field marshal in World War 11, who commanded in North Africa (1943), and Sicily and Italy (1944-1945); governor general of Canada (1946-52); British minister of defence (1952-54)".

In his book, 'The Alexander Memoirs', page 93, he states:

> "I took over command early in March 1942, I realise that I ought to have ordered an earlier evacuation of Burma. But at the time I was

not prepared to admit defeat before I had done everything possible. This delay resulted in the whole of our forces in the south of Burma being encircled and gave the Japanese the chance to destroy them as organised formations – and they missed their chance!"

Following six years in the Canadian 'Sinecure', as Governor General, the British Government considered Alexander, in 1952 to 1954, sufficiently qualified, to be, appointed: – MINISTER for DEFENCE

I do not know what Alexander had going for him to win such favours from Churchill, but I refer back to the comment, made by General Tuker, a senior officer who had served under the rogue': "That Alex' was quite the least intelligent commander I have met in a high position". For whatever reason, the man became favoured by Churchill following the Dunkirk hiatus, and with sly cunning, the charlatan was also thought to have shuffled the blame for the Burma 1941/42 fiasco onto Bill Slim: his second in Command.

Born into Irish aristocracy, Alexander knew how to use, and belittle people. He had the other showman, General Bernard Montgomery, dancing on a string, for the period that suited him: ("The Alexander Memoirs VII – Burma")

I do not know who wrote this twaddle for him.

Page 91

"17 Div were holding a defensive position around Pegu".

This statement is untrue! I was joined with 17 Div at nearby Hlegu. Alexander countermanded his order to attack Pegu, on the advice of the departing Smyth VC. There were no British troops near Pegu.

The remainder is pure speculation as the whole place was in constant turmoil. He carefully omits the mention of his entrapment, on his second day of his Command, as the Japanese encircled Rangoon: Jimmy Ableson, and his sergeant, were both killed in conducting his rescue.

Page 92

"I therefore ordered 17 Div to attack northwards".

Again untrue! The Division was in a state of complete and utter chaos. Men were scattered in all directions, many of them, 400 miles north, to the garrison town of Maymyo, in order to join with their families.

Page 93

"What remained of the Burma Army was eventually saved from the wreck of the campaign, more by luck than by anything else".

How little? It was certainly, not by Alexander's efforts.

Page 93

Alexander speaks disparagingly of Chinese forces – "The Chinese never won a battle against the Japs".

He knew virtually nothing of them, and never once did he see a Chinese private soldier in action, as they had been for ten years, since January 1932, when the Japanese first invaded Shanghai: (To Europeans, the word "Chinese", at that period of time, embraced almost every Asiatic).

On 19th April 1942, having cleared a Japanese held road-block I stood by the white building, aside which the road-block had been positioned, as I watched these most excellent troops, and helped them, as they won a most comprehensive battle against the Japs, at the Yenangyaung oilfield. It was here that they fought and released a Company of Inniskilling prisoners from capture: including Sergeant Mc Haffey, on his first release.

Alex does not mention the speed of his departure from Burma: Within 24 hours?

The monsoon did eventually break, on the day of our arrival at Kohima, where we were allocated a marked out square of grassland on which to sleep, in the warming rain. I was asked by Chadwick: *(now ensconced onto safer ground, in which official ranking obtained, once again)*, to count the numbers surviving with the Battalion. It amounted to no more than seventy-nine men, – of all ranks: approximately one sixth of the original number, mustered five gruelling months earlier. Meeting with pre-war friends, Wardleworth was whisked away in minutes.

The unit disintegrated in steady numbers, mainly from disease, following the earlier digging of useless slit trenches in mosquito infested jungle, close by the Salween River. The tall gaunt emaciated figure of my colleague, Steve, was but a shell of the man I knew a few short weeks beforehand. His dark beard was grown down to his chest, and his body, skeletal and fever ridden. In the intense cold of our last few nights, traversing a high plateau, I think that I saved his life: At his request, in seeking to get some cover and a little heat, Steve had shared my modest bedding,

I was not the last in the queue on the following morning, for a decent soya-link breakfast. The result of my medical check, one which was carried out throughout the unit, came as a surprise. The doctor spotted several 'jungle sores', resulting from leech attack. The sores on the backs of my legs were two inches in diameter, and I was ordered hospitalisation. Sergeant 'Busty' Taylor was so badly infested with the sores, he had walked the last hundred and fifty miles, naked from the waist down.

Debilitated, Steve was given hospital admission, and we travelled together, to the one situated at Gauhatti, where we were, once again, out on the grass for the night. This, however, was to be the parting of the ways, Steve went off to Derha Dun, an Indian hill station, and I went, 'to a heaven up the hill', Shillong, a cool town in the Khasi-Jhanti Hills, of Assam. I was not to see Steve again until, meeting with him on board ship as we were repatriated.

However, we were not the first away that morning, as we followed the useless pillock, Throckmorton! He was carrying the crown of a Field Officer on his shoulder, and now, to be recognised as a senior 'badged officer', in the free and formalised world, where rank mattered. One of those, totally incapable of command, and trusted with but one duty throughout the Burma withdrawal, he failed in that. He was 'lost', when expected to lead our marching party, to join with the unit based only yards away, and now he had bolted, on the train to Calcutta. He had run off in order to purchase: 'Pastel coloured bed sheets'?

Of the pre-war Burma based officers, in my eleven weeks action, I met with very few: Allan Chapman, (weeks 2 to 6) – Maurice Green, (5/7), – Geoffrey Baxter, (5/7) – David Martin, (7/8) – Geoffrey Chadwick, (3/11)

– Douglas Wardleworth, (9/11) – and the gem, Nicholas Throckmorton, (5/11).

It was many years later, and quite out of the blue, my wife and I called at Steve's, Potters Bar bungalow. He was out at the time, but he and his wife returned as we were in the garden at the back of the house. He did not recognise me immediately, and not unnaturally, asked, "Who are you, and what do you want?"

When, after a brief hesitation, just a slight pause, I replied, "You've slept with me!"

Steve nearly burst with pride, "It's Fitz! – It's Fitz!" You don't get better than that! Unfortunately, Steve died some years ago, but not with me nearby! Bless him! He will remain with me: forever!

I will attempt a summary!

At the age of ninety-three, I have many years of responsibility, and industrial man-management, and development, behind me. I can now, retrospectively, observe the historical turn of events surrounding my war in Burma, and later. I am in a better position to comment on the conduct, and subsequent outcome, of the fiasco that became known as: "The Forgotten Army! – Demolished by the Japanese, in Burma: December 1941 to May 1942.

The whole of the spectacular and successful campaign conducted by the Japanese was carried out following much determined and meticulous preparation. The speed of the initial assault, throughout the Eastern world, was beyond the comprehension of Western military leaders. Totally unprepared, the British floundered, as the enemy swept through Hong Kong, and Singapore. In each theatre, Prime Minister, Winston Churchill, unwarrantedly, interfered with the strategic planning of local Commanders, thus creating blunders, and insecurity.

With two regular British Infantry Battalions, based in Burma: One in the North, and one in the South, conditions were such, there was never consideration of possible conflict in this pleasant land. From languishing in the North, the Kings Own Yorkshire Light Infantry Battalion was mobilised, in late 1941. They moved from the Maymyo base, to a suitably cool training area, with an imminent view to returning to England, and joining in the war in Europe.

It was not until the, 'Impregnable Fortress of Singapore,' fell, to the Japanese onslaught, serious consideration was given, to defending Burma. In very short time, almost 100% of men of the KOYLI were to suffer malarial fever. The unit was occupied, digging useless, European type slit-trench systems, in a dangerous, and renowned, mosquito infested area.

In pre-war years, the prime function of the Battalion was simply, that of: "Assistance to the Civil Powers". There was no shortage of 'bullshit', and dandifying ceremonial events. Of course, this gentle regime required no initiative from officers, and subalterns were made to know their limitations. Seniors ensured, they held sacrosanct, any crossing of the line.

With no formal jungle warfare training, KOYLI were hustled down, to south Burma, (it took eight days), in mid-December, 1941. Their given task: "To resist the Japanese advance, into the Kra peninsula": (The long tail-like piece to the south of the country). The Battalion was dispersed over a wide area, committed to undertaking, irregular, and blundering transfers: strengthening, between two or three Indian Brigade Commands, at very short notice. Being thrust immediately into action, they learnt jungle warfare the hard way, losing numerous good men over an initial period of three weeks

From this point, to the end of, what might be called, the induction period, the conflict became a hopelessly lost cause. General Smyth, the cowardly, Divisional Commander, caused the massive, Sittang River Bridge, to be demolished: (Smyth, never once admitted, that it was He, who gave the order).   Resulting from this demolition, almost the whole of Smyth's 17th Division, was trapped, on the eastern side of the river. They were by now, virtually unarmed, and lacking provisions. The very frightened Smyth, remained reasonably secure: on the western bank

Smyth, was one of the three, sacked, British Army Generals, to be air-lifted out of Burma. He departed on the 5th March, within days of the bridge destruction. His departure was by the aircraft conveying General Alexander; the Churchill appointed GOC, into the country.

The fourth General in the departing plane was Wavell. Of convenience, and by being virtually the only senior officer in occupation of the territory, he was appointed Supreme Eastern Commander, based in the security of Delhi, in India: several hundred miles from the Burma conflict.

The extenuating cock-up of the campaign was further exemplified, with the arrival of Alexander, and in his assuming Command. His anticipated, comfortable, and ceremonious reception, to The Eastern World, had gone unceremoniously awry. Whatever update on events that he could have, were brief, and dramatically limited. Frankly! He was unceremoniously and instantly, out of his depth, and he knew it.

Like a man lost, Alexander cast around, and sought solace wherever it was to be found. Desperation overtook the man, as, fearing his own demise, he sought security for his family. There were few to whom he could turn, and in a state of panic, he realised that almost all influential individuals who could, had, for some time, evacuated Rangoon. He was fortunate, in making contact with Mr Lloyd, the Manager of The Bank of India, and Delores, his Assistant. It was to this pair, that he, casually, 'declared his hand, in the abdication of his Command'.

Before hearing one shot fired in anger, he was pompously indiscreet in declaring to the Bank Manager, and his Lady Assistant;

"Burma can not be saved!"

From that point onwards, he made sure that Burma was not saved, and the message had further reverberations of complete damnation: To our cost!

Receiving Alexander's, "Burma can not be saved" signal of abdication, following the rapid series of Eastern campaign failures: Churchill capitulated! He knew that, in the East, he was a beaten man.

Resulting from the dismissive signals, an even more damning declaration followed. It was the doom-laden, and abandonment signal, sent by Churchill, to Roosevelt, 1st April 1942:

"The wisest plan for Japan would be to press on through Burma",

In the British Prime Minister's sheer disgust, and whisky laden embarrassment: being unable to retrieve the message to Roosevelt, once sent, Churchill caused the evil document to be secreted away.

(Hidden for the next thirty years, long after his death, and with the awesome significance, at the time of dispatch, and its devastating consequences on the 'Churchill image', it was conveniently overlooked by the British Parliament, and 'airbrushed' out).

We were not: "The Forgotten Army" – we were discarded

A struggling British Prime Minister was now prescribing action to be taken by the enemy, against his own country's forces, and inviting them to walk all over British troops. How then, can an Under Secretary of State for Defence, not accept my words?

I repeat: I received a copy of a letter, Reference D/US of S/LM 1741/01/Y, written by Dr Lewis Moonie MP, the Parliamentary Under-Secretary of State for Defence,, and dated, 19th April 2001. In the letter, Moonie, in the way Parliamentarians brush off awkwardness, states;

"I can not accept his, (That's me – G Fitzpatrick), suggestion that the forces there, (In Burma), were in any way discarded or abandoned by Winston Churchill then the Prime Minister".

The Under Secretary is so typically: English Establishment crap! He was not, as I was: centrally engaged in conducting the Burma conflict.

We were: 'The discarded, and abandoned, British Army'. -

Choose whatever abusive term you wish to put to it.

Ironically, Maurice Green, the writer of the officially accepted, KOYLI Burma history, was one of the two officers dramatically, tragically, and so favourably treated, when evacuated by Chadwick, at Mount Popa: He knew nothing of further action. My ordering of the execution of the band of Dacoits incident happened following the departure of Green. Debased to the extent that there was no such thing as rank, or superiority, all were of equal status, and Outside British Military control. With a titular commander dithering, and in fear of his own life, the unwritten laws of 'desperado' applied..

Unique in British History, and as no more than a subaltern, regardless of the badge seniority of others: Following recent Dacoit hostilities, witnessed by me, I assumed juridical power, in ordering executions. Three Company Commanders were each ordered to despatch nine men: Had they not done so, they were in no doubt; I would have despatched them!

Away from the period of 'Desperation', Green obviously found it beneath him to seek the truth, particularly from Emergency Commissioned Officers: Irregulars in the Regiment:

My devoted Sergeant, Benny Mee, and numerous others, passed away, before knowing of the evil significance of Churchill's dismissive signal. Benny, in particular, was an embittered man throughout his life, at the indifference shown to former Burma forces. Ted Hewitt hated every minute of his compulsory service. Inwardly, they all knew that something had gone radically wrong, but to know that, 'the rat in the ointment', could be a British Prime Minister was unthinkable. We, the remnants of a British Infantry Battalion, were left to survive seven weeks, from the 1st April, to 23rd May, with a complete lack of any form of provisioning. So many good men did not survive long enough to appreciate my recording of these deleterious events.

Had I despatched Alexander, as I should have done, by a bullet, my men would have remained silent. I had won their confidence in conflict. They knew me as the one to act, and to speak his mind. We had all been in the swamp together, and been fired upon from two sides. They had walked with me on the 'Do or Die' capture of an enemy defended road-block, and in usurping the titular Commanding Officer. I had proved myself in action, and I was a very secure man!

The dross of Command vanished as we departed Burma: Alexander left in great haste, on the day we crossed into India. There was no apology, appreciation, thanks, or goodbyes: The man sought to be back on the London scene, as rapidly as possible. Muddled, and bemused at his complete failure in Burma, Alexander went so low as to attempt placing the blame for defeat, on Bill Slim: In due course of time, no doubt consorting with Churchill, he contributed the bestowal of the honour: "Of Burma!" to Mountbatten. It was rightfully: for Slim!

From humbler beginnings than most of the officer class, Slim was less gregarious, and pushy, than the public school cabal. He was a virtual outsider to those of the military elite, and his rather rapid promotion, could be attributed to the failure of others. Quietly spoken, he lacked the clipped and polished, tones, of his fellow Commanders. The plebeian, former engineering works clerk, met with oafish hostility, and jealousy, from General Leese, one of Bernard Montgomery's 'Queens', in India. Slim was saved by the intervention of General Auchinleck.

However, Montgomery, cocky over his European successes, and seeing Slim as a threat to his egotistical ambitions for power, along with the backing of a hostile British military establishment, made several attempts to sack Slim.

My friend Bill Slim, stayed put, and in due course, secured the appointment as Chief of the Imperial General Staff. I was fortunate in meeting with Slim, very briefly, on the occasion of my visit from Rhine Army, when handing duff material to Defence Minister, Manny Shinwell.

How the Hell Alexander managed to become; 'Alexander of Tunis', I will never understand: Subordinates must have carried him all the way, meriting the earlier comment of General Tuker, a former Commander, and one who served under Alexander in Italy, is apt: "Least intelligent". That comment, I go along with, and love to repeat! Chadwick, our useless, titular Commanding Officer, vanished from the scene instantly, in the same manner as Alexander: and did not return to the unit.

Throckmorton stayed for a while, and reverted to type. Having obtained his pastel coloured bed-sheets from Calcutta, he was now securely ensconced in a virtual peacetime situation. This was a complete change, from the precarious situation he had occupied a few weeks earlier. It was irony gone mad, when, regardless of competence, the badge of seniority meant that, for a junior to question the useless pillock's actions, it would be regarded as; insubordination.

The recently tested and proven initiative, of juniors, was history, in so far as the batch, of post campaign installed Company Commanders was concerned. Lacking interest, and knowledge, of the struggles within Burma, and the absolute incompetence of their host, the new boys partied with Throckmorton. Junior officers, particularly Emergency Commissioned ones, were precluded from such gaiety.

Many years later, and meeting by sheer chance, it was me, face to face with Chadwick, in the busy town of Harrogate. Standing no more than two paces apart, we each looked the other, face to face. I recognised him, and he certainly recognised me. It was left to him to speak first, as might be his privilege. Not one word was exchanged, as we went our separate ways.

Cynical, bitter, and condemning, as I am with many senior Commanders, I feel well justified in my reasoning. I now have the satisfaction of knowing, from one of my final 'military operations', that the, 'absolute pinnacle, of British Parliamentary Authority', can be hoodwinked, and made to look a fool: I managed it!

Captain Gerald Fitzpatrick

General Liu Fang-Wu

A British Veteran, Captain Gerald Fitzpatrick, witnessed the Yenangyaung Battle in 1942

I personally witnessed the vital part the Chinese army played in the Battle at Yenangyaung in Burma on April 19th 1942. I saw the arrival of Studebaker trucks each carrying 50 or 60 Chinese equipped troops. Systematically, as men dismounted, they streamed across the huge flat sandy expanse of the Pin Chaung. The timing could not have been more apt, Victor Stevens and I (second lieutenants at the time), along with 19 men from the King's Own Yorkshire Light Infantry (K.O.Y.L.I.), out of sheer desperation, cleared the pivotal Japanese held road block overlooking the vast Pin Chaung. This action facilitated the crossing by the Chinese forces of the Pin Chaung and their immediate attack upon Japanese forces occupying Yenangyaung town. This was the identical spot at which, two days earlier, the Japanese had captured a company of Inniskillings. They had crossed the Pin Chaung in the same manner as the Chinese, only to walk into a subtle trap.

From the vantage point of the stone building on the small hillock, it was a relief to witness the Chinese assault. It was spectacular, and efficient beyond belief, absolutely suited for the rough terrain of the oilfield. I had a panoramic view of the whole disposition and action as the Chinese set to the task. To Western eyes, the disciplined automation was astonishing; each of the three commanders in their distinctive uniforms adopted pre-planned positions, each was accompanied by a standard bearer carrying distinctive marker flags. Alongside each commander was a young bugler relaying calls and messages, as troops moved speedily into their respective unit and formed behind the flag. There was no delay, and the whole contingent moved in unison. It was a three-prong attack; one column went westward, towards the Irrawaddy River, one centrally, and the other, by the road to our front.

The intensity of rifle and machine-gun firing increased immediately the Chinese started their advance, indicating the strength of the build-up of the Japanese; obviously in preparation for the counterattack on our K.O.Y.L.I. position. All hell broke loose as the Chinese troops swarmed forward. The movement was like poetry, or a form of pageantry, with these highly disciplined troops.

As the noise of firing on the oilfield became more distant, there was a realization; the Japanese might be the ones in danger of "being annihilated at the oilfield in Central Burma', contrary to the threat made by Tokio Rose from Radio Saigon, eight days earlier.

As the Chinese began to suffer casualties, Victor Stevens and I set up a reception point in the stone building, and did what we could to treat and dress the wounds of soldiers, returning with holes in arms, legs and bodies. I did not speak Chinese, and the Chinese did not speak English. Victor Stevens ripped bedding sheets to bandage the wounded Chinese soldiers. Although I was only twenty-two years of age, I thought the Chinese soldiers to be very young; they had the ethereal look of good porcelain.

Major V. L. Stevens (Steve)
Never reminisced but wears the tie

The Chinese withdrew shortly after nightfall, the movement being almost the exact reverse of the approach; quietly, they crossed the Pin Chaung, and re-joined the transports. The spectacular operation lasted no more than four hours. Yet the consequences must have been devastating to the Japanese, and their prospect of annihilating the British Army were severely set back, with they themselves suffering many casualties. The Chinese losses, in an open frontal attack of this nature, must have been considerable.

The Chinese troops came in, did their job and got out. The British at the time were short on food and water, short on ammunition, short on medical supplies, and stricken with malaria, and other diseases. I was the sole British officer, along with my men, privileged to observe this rare spectacle; it was basic, primitive and functional, the perfect fighting machine for the conditions of Central Burma. Indeed, I was a privileged officer.

This salutary action was undertaken on 19th of April when the British Army in Burma was already discarded by British Prime Minister,

Winston Churchill. His recorded signal to the USA President, Franklin D. Roosevelt, on 1st April: "*I think the wisest plan for Japan would be to push through to Burma*", ceased all provisioning and reinforcements. It is only in recent years that I am advised of British Army Commander, General Alexander, abdicating his responsibilities on 6th March 1942, the day following his arrival in Burma, with the words "Burma cannot be saved." This would be relayed to Churchill. The Churchill signal was cowardly secreted away for thirty years. Ignored in British history, the damage done by the Chinese forces in this action destroyed the Japanese, to such extent that their rapid advance through Burma was halted, whilst awaiting reinforcements. Delaying the Japanese from their superbly planned advance was such that it became the single most action in allowing the remnants of the disheveled and starving British Army to escape northwards.

General Alexander in his memoirs belittles the Chinese; "The Alexander Memoirs VII – Burma" (p93) state "the Chinese never won a battle against the Japs". But that is not what I saw. I was the pivotal and sole witness, to the spectacular and dramatic pageantry of the 113th Chinese Regiment Expeditionary Forces, led by the late General Liu Fang-Wu, assault on Yenangyaung.

For the past 30 to 40 years, I have been trying to tell this story and denied by successive Prime Ministers and Ministers of Defense. It was not until this past August, I received a letter from Margaret Sun, daughter of the late General Liu Fang-Wu. Immediately after reading Margaret's letter, I told my wife, Patricia, who did not get a chance to finish reading the letter; "We have to visit this lady as soon as possible"; cost would be of no consequence! At age 93, I tend to do things quickly. We were able to make arrangements for our visit to the U.S.A. on September 16 2012. I told Margaret and her brother, Bob Liu, at the airport when we first met, that I could not wait another minute for this visit. After meeting the son and daughter of the late General Liu Fang-Wu, I can tell you I am SO satisfied with this visit! It nearly hurts to recall Yenangyaung, but recall I do.

Early Casualties

W W Dawson

W Abbott

W. Slee – "To The Very End"

Jim Major B.E.M.

J Isaacs and G Bareham

E T Hewitt    *M Mycock*

W Kibbler

Capt G Fitzpatrick
2nd Bn KOYLI
Mortar Platoon
24th Delhi Dec 1943

On Reg't Duty
Sgt B Mee
Pte W Kibbler
 " A Caine
 " A Crombie

DELHI CANTONMENT
2nd Bn MORTAR PLATOON

WALTON	DAVIES	MURRAY			
RICHARDSON	WOOD	BROWN	HOEY	WALKER	
STUBBS	CLARE		LOMAX	BURGESS ✓	JOLLY ✓	MYCOCK ✓	CLEGG
SGT ISAACS HAYES ✓	SGT BAREHAM ✓	SGT LAWRENCE	IBBOTSON	KING	PAINTER	McCULLOCK	GRAY
	HORROBIN ✓	BRADLEY	HARGREAVES	HEWITT ✓	FISHER	MAINWARING	McKENNA
			SGT PINDER	FITZPATRICK ✓	SGT BECKETT	FORD	BARR
			BOLAND	ROWE	BANNISTER	ELLIS	BAIRSTOW

ERIC. SGT McC
MASSICK
CAINE
CROMBIE

EX-BURMA 42 - ✓

12

WICKED HILL TO HEAVEN

From mobilisation on 2nd January 1942, 2nd Bn KOYLI travelled and fought for five months throughout Burma. Devastated in early speculative operations, and following the February Sittang River hiatus, they eventually struggled to the safety of India, on the 23rd May: (Marching 650 miles, Truck transport 670 miles, Irrawaddy River steamer 325 miles, Tanks 60 miles, and a personal Swim of almost One mile): Distance covered, about 1700 miles; plus the early eight day rail journey; Salween River to Bilin: (Detailed in appendices).

Throughout the tortuous journey, eighteen (18), head to head battles, or skirmishes, against the Japanese were encountered: Including one, chest deep in a swamp, in which we were under fire from both, Japanese and British. Several recalcitrant and hostile native problems were dealt with, particularly around the Central Burma oilfields.

Estimating killed, wounded, missing and sick, all has to be approximation, as, with no means of recording, also there were many individuals new to the battalion; It was chaotic, with numerous re-formations of the Battalion: Eight (8) officers, and two hundred and seventy five (275) men killed in action, or as Prisoners of War. – Four hundred (400) wounded, (almost same number evacuated sick), fifty (50) unaccountable.

At the parting of our ways, it was sad; me, with a fair 'bum fluff' beard, and Steve, with a dark beard, down to his chest. Steve was a very sick man and not a lot was said between us. Having seen so many men in the condition of Steve, I did not expect him to survive. It was enough; we both agreed, that the treatment we had received, in serving King and Country, was bloody appalling. Considering ourselves very lucky to survive, where dozens simply fell, and were left to die by the wayside, with no possibility of aid: I think it was Steve who made the point; "It doesn't seem like this, as you see them strutting around London parade grounds!" The men seen around Buckingham Palace always appear to be well fed, their perfumed clothing looks so smart, and the soles of their boots wear gently; not a bit like the rocker shaped soles on my man, Michael Mycroft's boots, worn down at both front and back.

One gets the feeling that the men in charge of the 'lovely boys', dancing around London, have some idea of what they are about: This is a myth! Do not for one moment, imagine that your Generals are all brave men, and know it all. It's when you have them on the testing ground, the truth will out. Between one and another of those individuals, ones considering themselves superiors; it is only in raw conflict, do we see, and experience, the failings of many. I met with this!

With the turmoil of reception at Ghauatti Hospital sorted, Steve was first away, to the hill station hospital at Dehra Dun. It became my turn, and I could not understand why I should be the one so readily settled, in the front seat of the bus, for the fifty or sixty mile journey, to a place of which I had never before heard.

It took very little time to realise why I had been given such select priority. Climbing at a steady pace, we were on a gentle assent up an un-metalled narrow road. The precipice over to our right became greater and greater, by the mile. The driver was not a shy man, giving regular accounts of where numerous vehicles had departed the road. It appeared to be at a rate of one vehicle, every four or five weeks. I had walked many miles, and been under gunfire recently, but found this heavenly elevation much more frightening. There was a shear drop to our right, of several hundred feet on almost the whole length of the virtually unmade road.

Being one of thirteen officers designated convalescent, nothing could have prepared me for the reception at this hilltop Heaven. It was a large, beautifully thatched bungalow, situated in the small town of Shillong, at an altitude of 4500 Ft, in the Khasi-Janti Hills, a delightfully cool plateau, in Assam.

Rough, and tattered though we were, immediate affection was shown by Gerry and Beth Small, the proud owners of La Chaumier. Gerry poured generous measures of Scotch Whisky. Beth introduced us to rooms, with beds made up with white sheets, and red blankets. Earthly comfort each night was provided in the first beds seen in three months, in this Heaven, with a capital 'H'. The quick shower, followed by the scrumptious curried chicken meal, was beyond my wildest dreams. I was long past thinking of such delights I had forgotten they existed.

Having lost weight, from over eleven stones, to less than eight, a loss of 3 ½ stones (21 Kg) ; (One third of my body weight). The only part of me with meat showing were my calves, they had exercised well. It took some little time to realise that in the last twelve weeks, sleeping on the hard ground each night, I had never once, night or day, removed my shirt, shorts, underpants, socks and boots except for the time I handed them to Hewitt, and swam the mighty Chindwin. The telling part of all the effort was the two inch sweated band of salt, around the chest of my shirt. It was black in the upper half, and khaki in the lower, and stank disgusting.

Truly remarkable, was the pristine state of my underpants. Several weeks beforehand, a mighty boil on my arse had burst in a slip down a small crevice, yet there was not the slightest trace of mucus, or any other deposit. It is possible that I had been carrying 'friendly cleaners', although not to my knowledge, as we had baked in the sun each day, and almost been frozen by night. The secret might lay in whatever creatures invaded my body each night, and in the morning I was finding deep purple blotches around my torso, but with no feeling, and never a sign of the animals.

With legs treated and bandaged by resident nurse, Connie Bowen, I settled down to a sleep, and slept for three long days, surfacing only for meals, until the afternoon of the third day, there was a rude awakening.

The rousting by Connie was a bit shattering. Giving me short shrift, she told me that it was about time that I made a move to get out of bed, and join with the others. My reply was not a very pleasant one, particularly to one giving me care at such a time, and I could not recall the unfortunate words. My callous rejoinder was uncalled for, rude, and totally out of order. As Connie tended my legs that night, I was repentant, and found it hard to find adequate words of apology. Unused to this type of apologetic situation, and so truly full of shame, my eyes filled, and the words did not come easily.

To say that I was staggered would be an understatement: With no reason to expect such warmth, Connie took me in her arms, held me, and kissed me. There had been no previous show of affection of any kind; but I liked it! With eight years of divorce time to make up, Connie knew exactly what she wanted, and how she wanted it, in her own peculiar way, with poor me, attempting to keep pace the whole time.

Doctor Brown visited, and, as my legs improved over the weeks, Connie would have them bandaged before his arrival, and the dear doctor was left in no doubt about our relationship. He would see the pair of us dancing at the exclusive Shillong Club each weekend. Connie and I became, what in modern parlance is known as, 'an item'. For some reason, the relationship between one considered in that 'Imperial Colonial Circle' to be, 'a menial nurse', like Connie, and I, caused a measure of unrest, within a section of upper bracket ladies. This resulted in the Government First Secretary's wife wanting her share. She not only asked me to call in for coffee; she demanded!

Of course, over the weeks, I began to feel most justifiably, 'swinging the lead', and malingering. It was snooker at the club each morning with Jack Higgins, and occasional visits to the nearby home of Joe Scott, from Batley. Joe owned, and operated, the perilous bus service, up and down the hill. Poor Scotty was banned from the club, his offence was, in being married to a local girl and having nine kids. As a Yorkshire man he did not give a toss for those pompous sods, considering themselves upper class, he was a genuine working man, and the, 'sweetie residents', were mostly, government funded.

On the high plateau, Shillong was perfect. There was nothing of the intense temperatures experienced on lower ground, and no mosquitoes. The scented pine woods, across the gentle rolling ground, were perfect for invigorating walks, why make change of any kind; but to Hell with it!

Enjoying, 'the life of Riley', from May, to late July 1942, everything was to change, dramatically! Connie slipped on pine needles when out walking in the woods, and was admitted to the Ganish Das Hospital, with a badly broken arm.

Accompanying Connie and me at the time was another young officer, a subaltern in the Royal Engineers, named Pringle. In due course of time he became a General, and I believe the senior in the Royal Engineers.

At the same time, high command were unapologetic in their action, they posted, the 2nd Bn Kings Own Yorkshire Light Infantry, to Shillong. With my unit taking over the former Gurkha barracks, I was left with no alternative: I had a miracle recovery from illness, and returned to regimental duties.

I don't know how a magician pulls rabbits from his hat. However, from somewhere, somehow, a completely new regime for battalion command appeared, all were what we ECO's called, 'Regulars': A fresh Commanding Officer, and four new Company Commanders. From where they came, I know not, but not one of the newly appointed Regimental seniors had seen action throughout the recent devastating Burma campaign. The new Commanding Officer was Lieutenant Colonel R.G.C. (Bob) Poole, and Company Commanders, Major Ricky Vallance, Captains Tony Hart, John Wood, and Gerald Whitworth.

With a completely new sheet, there was to be no looking back. The debased and torrid five or six month war period: earlier in the year, from January to May 1942, was of no consequence to; 'The Command of Resurgent Seniors'.

Recent combat experience, of so many of my compatriot juniors, was remorselessly subjugated by British Army regulations: Command and control in conflict, regardless of rank, was replaced by peacetime protocol, consisting of badges on shoulders. Competent, combat and command proven subordinates reverted reluctantly to junior status.

With the new command set on establishing pleasurable peace-time conditions, there was no attempt at 'raking over', or comprehension, of the recent past. Any attempt at castigating 'The British!' 'Parliament or Military'; frowned upon. To the new regime, the past was obliterated, proscribed, as though it did not exist. There was never mention of a possible inquiry, or investigation, into the failings throughout the recent Burma fiasco. Winston Spencer Churchill ensured thirty years of secrecy for his complete failure: To Command, Provision, Reinforce, Re-equip, or Succour, a succession of his military failures throughout the Far East.

British history happily records whatever success and adventure, whilst failures are suppressed, and one could only accept: With the long practised, 'Conspiracy of Silence in adversity'; The Japanese 1941/42 routing of the British Army in Burma, was virtually, 'Airbrushed Out!' Conveniently interspersed with later successes, in the 1943/45 Burma invasion, it was patronisingly, and as though one combined conflict, dishonourably termed; "The Forgotten Army".

The new 'Battalion Command' familiar only with, 'peace-time soldiering', reverted the regiment to pre-war standard, it was all the new regime recognised. Those of us, recently involved in the Burma showdown, were not supposed to notice the bland reticence, although I did, and with very good reason!

I was so lucky in retaining all nine of my men from the recent Burma action. I respected them for their loyalty, trust and friendship, and knew that in my time with them, they appreciated my having taken control in vital necessity. This kinship is marked in our monthly Regimental meetings held locally, more than seventy years since the war, and has continued, both ways.

Isolation and egotism were the hallmarks, as the newly induced cabal of superiors closed ranks. Segregation, and assumed subservience by others, ensured complete disinterest in the recent past. Experience, ability, and usurping a rubbish Commander, counted for nothing. Never once was reference made, to the recent dire period of desperation, 'and the rule of man': In which shattered temerity caused the Commander of an infantry battalion, of all things, to detail for himself, a personal bodyguard, it was either ignored, or discounted. However, the dithering Commander was long gone.

Such was the state of affairs, we might have been in some kind of junta: Organised in tiers, with an unapproachable upper level of seniors; a second level consisting of me and my colleagues from the 'draft'; the lower levels being Other Ranks. There was the Sergeants mess, the Corporals Club, and probably best of all, The Barrack Room Squaddies: *(Many highly regarded Privates refused promotion, in order to remain with their Buddies).* It was as though each layer consisted of differing, upper level and inferior species. A complete change of sociality to the one existing a few short weeks beforehand, wherein, under the most atrocious conditions, officers and men were privileged to fuse into one interdependent conglomerate of equals.

There was no questioning of orders or instruction given, and no discussion before action. There were no planning meetings, or conferences. I suppose it was really easy, once one got over the frustration, and accepted the crap. Simply keep your mouth shut!

As a toddler infant, I was paraded around by my father, as he attended a number of tribunals, at each of which he was denied a war pension. Having served in my same regiment in the army for nine years before World War-One, he went to France, as a member of 'The Contemptible Little Army'. From day one, he was involved in every major action of the conflict, and 'Mentioned in Dispatches' on two occasions. Each mention was for top honours, only for him to be denied, because of his, alleged, violence and insubordination to officers. His ex-service colleagues often reviled, the cowardly, and unnecessary actions of officers of all ranks.

Cynicism of rank was born in me, and it was a matter of, 'Get on with it!' Having the rich benefit of recent experience, and with a more hardened background than the newly appointed seniors, I think that I knew how to handle affairs.

With the unique pleasure of remaining; 'The three inch mortar specialist', I was never to come under the control of any one of the new found Company Commanders. 'Regulars', as pre-war officers were generally called, lacked manual skills, practical ability, or dexterity. Erecting a simple Bell-tent was beyond most of them. My few years of skills training in engineering practice were to stand me in good stead. There was plenty more to come, and I was about to exploit it to the full.

At the settling-in period at Shillong barracks, the Battalion strength was greatly reduced, as large numbers of sick, from the Burma campaign, remained hospitalised. Things began to move however, and we received a reinforcement draft of three hundred men, almost all were reluctant conscripts, some more-so than others. I was fortunate in having first choice from the bunch, as I required men of reasonable physique, and capable of, 'interpreting technical instructions', and I got them.

An unexpected bundle of sheer joy arrived within the next few days, as we became recipients of ninety-six mules, and seventeen chargers, (horses). These wonderful animals were to be the making of so many men. They were to learn, and appreciate, skills and responsibilities, never previously contemplated. New friendships were formed, each with their own selected animal, and they loved it.

The mules were huge fellows from the Argentine, and came with no experience of being handled by man. But we were going to change all that. No more than four or five of our older hands having previous experience of the animals, they were given new responsibilities, in demonstrating, harnessing, feeding and grooming. My childhood experience, with donkeys in Ireland, came in useful. By sitting back on the animal's haunch, I was able to demonstrate control, with no more than a short stick in hand. We did however, receive adequate harnessing, and we made it fun!

This set me off, on what I like to regard as, 'my whirligigs' throughout India. I was sent on a two weeks, 'animal management course', held at Jullundar, a town many miles across India. Apart from learning how to clean out the eyes, ears, nose, bum, and frogs of the mules, we did loading, and of course, feeding. Horse riding lessons, held within a walled compound, were an added bonus. Better still was riding out, into the desert. It was always fun, trying to locate our return point, when all that could be seen through the sanded heat haze, was the dull silhouette of low buildings.

Two unforgettable episodes of my visit to Jullundar are; when a naik (corporal) of the Indian Army, was thrown from his horse, with his foot held in the stirrup. The horse bolted around the arena, kicking at the unfortunate man until halted. The second episode was, in my attending a law court, for the first time, and being fined, twenty rupees, for riding a hired bicycle, with a friend sitting on the crossbar. Riding a bicycle, with a man on the crossbar, was an offence; In India?

Inculcating my new found skills to the men helped them become truly friendly with their charges. Mules began to follow handlers around, almost as would a dog. The best part for the troops was riding the animals out, on exercise, into the lush countryside. But it got better!

A truly rare Asian custom of propriety in the Khasi-Janti hills, was where women 'ruled the roost'. In this matriarchal society, whatever the ladies said applied. The women possessed other Asian rarities, good looks, and nice rosy cheeks, but it got even better! Taught, at the demanding; Welsh Mission School, the girls spoke embarrassingly better English than most of our men. It did not take long for the boys to 'catch on', and for the girls to appreciate lavish attention. That was not all that appealed to our boys. Exercising their rights, and if 'Tommy' was coming? The ladies dismissed the boyfriend, or husband, for the day.

On regular short sharp runs, route marches, and exercises, through the pine forest, it was not unusual to see one or two mules, contentedly feeding, and tethered, outside a neat bungalow, owned by one of the attractive young ladies. Recognising the mules, the marching troops were not shy in 'jossing' the handlers. The handlers had every excuse to be adrift, exercising their charges, and the mules enjoyed being ridden. Everybody was getting plenty of exercise, and whatever?

After six months delay, the arrival of the 'condolence message', sent by The Colonel of the Regiment, HM the Queen justified a parade. Things improved, and Commanding Officer, Bob Poole, demonstrated his man-management skills. Making good for shortages suffered in Burma, two generous casks of rum arrived, and rationing the delirious juice could have been a problem. Poole solved the problem, by declaring; "Let them have it!" The two casks were placed in the library, situated across the football pitch, away from the barrack rooms. It was a case of, 'Self help! There were very few shy boys in the Battalion!

With jugs, mess tins, or any vessel, the 'free day' applied all round, and the slurp continued. Failing to get back to barrack rooms in their drunken stupor, many flaked out on the football pitch, and others stretched out in the monsoon drains. It was a 'piss-up' all round, and not one man placed on a '252' (charge sheet). The men appreciated Bob Poole's, show of common sense, by emptying the containers.

Shillong was a paradise for both; the ones having served with me in Burma, and for the reinforcement draft, they could hardly believe their luck at joining with so relaxed a unit. It was such that Dixon, the Provost Marshall, asked me to accompany him one evening, as we left the club.

He was about to visit two or three known brothels, on his way back to barracks, and I was happy to join with him. At Mary's, (she had previously been, 'the friend', of a dentist down the hill, in Dhaka). Dixon spotted two feet sticking out from under the bed. He gave the lad a bollocking, and simply sent him on his way, with no charges.

It was all so perfect; with Bob Poole's good lady wife installed in a most delightful bungalow, far from the barracks. Poole was required to undertake the reconnaissance of a possible, defence strategy, for northern Burma. The chosen situation was some miles north of the port of Chittagong. Acknowledging my Burma experience, I was chosen by Poole to accompany him on the visit. The hill down to Dhaka, in Bengal, was not so perilous, as the one from Gauhatti, but longer. Here we met with an odd couple. I think they were a father and son, local born, and employed on intelligence service.

Travelling by car for a short distance, we changed the mode of transport to two young elephants, and our guides proved excellent handlers, as Poole and I mounted behind each of them. The ground throughout squelched, almost like quick sands, and the elephants moved at a rapid pace for possibly two hours. Arriving at a large river, we changed to a small boat, one with an engine.

The trip was fine, as we headed upstream in the centre of the fairly wide river. It was as we rounded a bend, we came upon a sight like I could never in my wildest dreams have imagined. It was ladies bathing day, and fifty or sixty, 'girls of the parish', stood waist deep in the shallows. They were of all ages, and dimensions, and not in the least bit shy. All were topless, and showing no embarrassment, the whole lot of them began gesticulating, and shaking tits. There were big tits, little tits, and tits of all description, being shaken in our direction, and Bob Poole laughed in a way that I had never seen before. Don't tell me; women don't do that in India! The return trip, the following day, was much subdued, as a few, 'men of the parish', kept themselves to themselves.

There is a saying; "That all good things come to an end", and they did, with spectacular suddenness. With no warning of what was about to come. Bob Poole ordered officers, to line the track overlooking the football pitch, which was also the parade ground. He wanted every 'man jack' of the battalion on parade; cooks, batmen, clerks, mess staffs, and all from the guard room. There was no exemption.

Having accompanied him on the reconnaissance, I thought Poole might be about to announce a move down to the area of our recent visit. This was a secret between Poole and me, as I had been instructed to say nothing of the possibilities.

Tension spread throughout the ranks, as men were not used to simply standing around for twenty or thirty minutes to hear the cause. Poole was a tall, slim man, and he approached in a steady manner, with no accompaniment. There were no preliminaries as the words poured forth with instant venom. "We're leaving, (and it began with F), (continued with a capital B), Shillong!" "We're having nine cases of VD every month, and The Foresters, who are taking over from us, are not getting that number in twelve months!"

Having spent recent months settling in and enjoying, the cosy ritual of peace time soldiering, the Command posting proved to be a rude awakening for Poole, and the newly installed Company Commanders. Poole's comfortable existence was shattered, as the idea of a transfer, 'down the hill, to the scorching plains', was never envisaged. He was an angry man. Very angry!

Throughout the long weeks of acclimatisation at Shillong, the Battalion Command situation aggravated those few of us; the Burma survivors. We were amazed at the blindness of it all, the total block-out of affairs occurring throughout the recent campaign. There was never discussion, or comment. It was obliterated, and possibly, regarded a disgrace. The whole thing was shrouded, as though it had never happened. The ultimate insult was the shabbiness of the regimentally accepted, and much later published, 'historical version', of the Burma campaign.

The history compiler was Green, one of the two Company Commanders, stealthily and favourably dispatched from Mount Popa by Chadwick, who brought the wrath of the Battalion down upon himself. Green had commanded the tail-end Company, in the crossing of the Yin Chaung, south of the Central Burma oilfields. Becoming lost, he then traversed out, along the Chaung, towards the Irrawaddy River, completely missing the treacherous swamp experience. He knew nothing whatsoever of our passing through chest deep water, whilst being fired upon by British Indian troops, and at the same time, being mortared by Japanese, from the south.

Having been lost at the time, he was never in position to mention the valiant action undertaken by Chinese troops, in their releasing the Inniskilling's from capture at the Yenangyaung oilfield. The same excellent Chinese also secured the road-block cleared by Vic Stevens and myself, to the north of the town. Stark truth is something that frightens, 'The Hierarchy', and many British Senior Officers, except where it might be 'seen' to be in their own favour:

British-ness: Preposterous, Patronising, and Pathetic.

Following my atrocious treatment by the British press in 1984, I wrote to a succession of Parliamentary Secretaries for Defence, seeking to establish vainglorious recognition of vital actions undertaken in the desperate Yenangyaung area, as they were not recorded in the official Regimental, or National History; I went further, in challenging any contentious opinions that may be held, and stated that I was prepared to face any consequences: The letters, and challenge, were ignominiously ignored.

On 11th April 1942, at Yenangyaung, Brigadier Bruce Scott visited the Battalion, to say;

"KOYLI, you've had enough, General Alexander is arranging to fly you out of Burma".

Less than four hours later, Scott returned, with instructions;

"I'm sorry! The General requires you to relieve Ghurkas, trapped at Allanmyo".

It was a forty mile, plus, move south. Already devastated as a Battalion, reduced to less than two hundred strong, and most debilitated by illness; the only provisioning was 2,000 rounds of ammunition; (10 rounds per man).

From the moment of departure, for fifteen days, we were incommunicado; completely outside control of Alexander's Command, and in the hands of a recently installed wimp CO, a Regular Major of the

Battalion, the one man left behind on mobilisation of the unit. A man considered 'Duff'.

When next meeting with Scott, after the two weeks sojourn in Command silence, he had the audacity to remark;

"General Alexander sent a boat down the river, seeking you".

We were at least one mile away from the river!

WHAT IS THERE FOR THE BRITISH, 'NOT TO WANT TO KNOW ABOUT?'

In July 1991, with John Major as Prime Minister, I wrote to Defence Secretary, Tom King MP: Beyond his comprehension, my letters were such that they overpowered the Defence Secretary The subject was the delicate one that Prime Minister Thatcher had enlisted Scotland Yard Serious Crime Squad, to pursue and squash! The days of Churchill's Burma Army discard, were 'Beyond the Pale', as far as British history is concerned.

Seeking to avoid embarrassing publicity, at what might be revealed to the world, and in an effort to silence me, King sought a more subtle way out. He farmed the letters out to; The pompous self centred prig: Colonel, 'The Viscount Slim'; President of the Burma Star Association, and privileged son of my friend; The man I, and others, mentored on the conduct of Jungle Warfare, based upon the format of the Chinese assault at Yenangyaung; General Bill Slim.

The Viscount; Son of Slim, goes so low as to call my actions to question, and attempts to impugn me: On Burma Star Association paper, I received a shabby 'put-down', patronising, condescending, and belittling letter, from 'The Viscount Slim', when seeking formal recognition of a most essential and desperate action. The extermination of identified enemy, by British soldiers, can never be seen as an offence. A vital life saving operation, undertaken by we, the dregs of the surviving few discarded British infantry, joined by the most excellent Chinese Army; So often belittled by Senior British Commanders, and disparagingly denied the truth, by Alexander, the British failure.

Although free to meet with him at any time, the Lordly libertine, (son of a true Lord), becomes a tramp by my standards. He preposterously attempts to chastise me as though some kind of nonentity.

With not the slightest notion of 1942 Burma conditions, and no interest in pursuing them, the man has the audacity to assume superiority, putting forward his spurious suggestions for a routine that was totally impossible in the circumstances existing, in the Hell Hole through which we survived. He was not present to witness proven superiority, and Command; -When, and where, it mattered!

Slim's smug missile, is unkempt, and reflective of 'Upper-level' Post War British Governmental, and complete Military indifference: The man is forgetful of those essential ingredients for Daddy's advancement; The early and vital guidance, given to Daddy by those of us; the few survivors, involved in recent conflict; the discarded soldiers 'backs', upon which his proud title was created, and upon which his, 'inherited Lordship', is based. (I choose to show Slim's pathetic and patronising diatribe).

There is no trace of comment by Slim, on Poodle Prime Minister, Blair, and his being led by the nose by the uninspiring Yank President, Bush; seeking none-existent, 'Weapons of Mass Destruction'. Committing British Troops into a totally idiotic war, where many unforgettable losses remain.

BURMA STAR ASSOCIATION
(REGISTERED UNDER THE WAR CHARITIES ACT, 1940)

PATRON:
H.R.H. THE DUKE OF EDINBURGH, KG, KT
VICE PATRON:
THE COUNTESS MOUNTBATTEN OF BURMA, CD, JP, DL
PRESIDENT:
COLONEL THE VISCOUNT SLIM, OBE
VICE PRESIDENT:
GENERAL SIR A. F. PHILIP CHRISTISON, BT, GBE, CB, DSO, MC*, DL
TRUSTEES & VICE PRESIDENTS:
REAR ADMIRAL F. B. P. BRAYNE-NICHOLLS, CB, DSC
GENERAL SIR PATRICK HOWARD-DOBSON, GCB
MARSHAL OF THE ROYAL AIR FORCE SIR JOHN GRANDY, GCB, GCVO, KBE, DSO
CHAIRMAN:
AIR VICE MARSHAL SIR BERNARD CHACKSFIELD,
KBE, CB, C.ENG, FRAES, RAF (RET)

HON. NATIONAL TREASURER:
G. W. BLACK ESQ. CA

HON. NATIONAL WELFARE OFFICER:
A. ST. PIERRE, ESQ. MBE
14 WELLWOOD ROAD
GOODMAYES, ILFORD, ESSEX IG3 8TR
TEL: 01-590-7080

8 ROWAN HOUSE,
BOURNE END, BUCKS. SL8 5TG
TEL: 062-85-20829

HON. NATIONAL SECRETARY:
REAR ADMIRAL M. N. LUCEY, CB, DSC

51 ST. GEORGE'S DRIVE
LONDON, SW1V 4DE
TELEPHONE: 01-828-1930

5 August, 1991

Dear Mr. Fitzpatrick,

I am at last able to write to you and apologise for the delay, but have been travelling abroad. Your letters to the Secretary of Defence are interesting, but in my view out of place. Your second letter was impolite to say the least, which is sad and unnecessary.

I reckon decorations for war cannot and should not be awarded in retrospect and certainly not after a fifty year gap. In the action you describe so well there appears to have been you and another officer involved. One, or both of you, should have initiated a citation for any of your men who deserved recognition and an award as soon as you could when the battalion was later pulled out of the line, or have found a moment to scribble the citations in rough and somehow get them to the Adjutant or whoever. Most of us have had to attempt this in war.

What you did sounds brave and splendid to me and your initiative and leadership obviously saved a dangerous moment in the withdrawal. However, so often as we both know such things happen in the heat and chaos of battle and go unseen and unrecognised. This is accepted in military circles and though I know you only have the NCO's and men of your platoon in mind, its no use bellyaching about it fifty years later.

Regretably, I really cannot support you in what you are trying to achieve, simply because I do not think it is right and, though fully understanding your feelings, suggest you drop it. Your letters could also be construed, though I am sure you do not intend it, that you should have a 'gong'. This is simply not done.

Those were the harshest and toughest of years and all courageous young officers like you and Victor Stevens displayed tremendous guts and leadership and, at an early age, knew only too well the isolation and loneliness of command in battle in Burma. It was because of officers like you that, as my father often said, we were all able to combine and lick the Jap in the end. He was proud of you.

Surely its better to dwell on the memories you lived through with the great Regiment and soldiers you were with. You too have so much to be proud of. That's why our comradeship in the Burma Star Association is unique and why we are both members.

My warmest wishes to you — come and have a chat with me at the Albert Hall Reunion or Cenotaph Parade next year. Good luck.

Yours sincerely

From: Mr M A WHITTLE, Corporate Memory Analysis
MINISTRY OF DEFENCE   Level 6, Zone G
MOD Main Building, London, SW1A 2HB

Telephone (Direct dial)   020 7218 9298
           (Switchboard)   020 7218 9000
           (Fax)   020 7218 0256

Mr G. Fitzpatrick

Your Reference:

Our Reference:
DGInfo-4-24-1
Date:
8 May 2008

Dear Mr Fitzgerald,

Thank you for your letter to the Prime Minister, dated 10 April 2008, on the subject of the British campaign against the Japanese during the Second World War. Your letter was passed to the Ministry of Defence and I have been asked to reply.

Your comments on British policy in the Far East during 1942, and on some of the individuals involved, are noted. However, there is little I can add to what Dr Moonie said in his previous letter to you other than to recommend that you read the Official History of the war in the Far East, to which Dr Moonie referred. This is an objective history of the campaign written from official sources and should be accessible to you through your local public library service. The full details of this publication are as follows:

   S. Woodburn Kirby (ed.), *History of the Second World War: the war against Japan*,
   (5 volumes). London, HMSO, 1957-1969.

Yours sincerely,

Martin Whittle

DIATRIBE
   What military man has heard of, the "Corporate Memory Analysis" branch, of the British Ministry of Defence? It is the outfit unapologetically responding on behalf of a succession of repulsive and blundering, Ministers of Defence, and Prime Ministers, from Thatcher. Its task entails the fobbing off awkward questions, on the rare occasion it may be considered appropriate to respond to awkward enquiries.
   Beyond hypocrisy; - this inane, repulsive response, is an attempt to belittle my approach to that of complete indifference!

Letter from M A Whittle – Ministry of Defenvce

London

23rd October 2011

Dear Gerald,

Thanks for the copy of your letter to P. M. Cameron. You would appear to be adopting a rather extreme measure in your defence, but I suppose you feel you have tried more moderate approaches to no avail. I do wish you the very best of luck.

I shall write a letter to Mr. Cameron in support of your case, emphasising the tremendous ordeals of the retreat and how your surviving men were depending on you to keep as many of them alive as possible, and that in order to do this, you could not risk leaving those 27 Burmese enemy sympathisers in your rear. You deserve praise for your stalwart and decisive leadership, not condemnation. The men under your command owed you so much. I shall try to make all of this clear to the P.M.

CEDE NULLIS

Jock (JOHN SCURR)

Letter from Jock Scurr

MINISTRY OF DEFENCE
WHITEHALL LONDON SW1A 2HB
Telephone 071-21 82111/2/3

SECRETARY OF STATE

D/S of S/104/92D

10th June 1992

Dear General Liu,

Mrs Margaret Thatcher has written to me telling me of her meeting with you in New York in April and of your actions, and those of your regiment, in helping to extricate the British 1st Burma Division from encirclement by the Japanese at Yenangyaung in Burma in April 1942.

This year saw the fiftieth anniversary of the battle, which was clearly fought under the most testing and difficult of conditions during the darkest days of the war against the Japanese. May I therefore take this opportunity to express my warmest appreciation for the support you and your Regiment gave to the British Army, despite very considerable casualties.

Sincerely,

Malcolm Rifkind

General Liu Fang-Wu

DIATRIBE
Beyond Hypocrisy! – By the BRITISH MINISTER for DEFENCE.
General Alexander (of Tunis) - C in C Burma 1942, States in his Memoirs V11:-
 "The Chinese never once attacked the Japs".
Treacherously, Prime Minister THATCHER attempted pacifying: -
She used Scotland Yard, Serious Crime Squad to kill the truth.

英國國防部長致函劉將軍感謝五十年前解救仁安羌被圍英軍

(The letter from the Secretary of State for Defence of UK presenting appreciation to General Liu for the action of rescuing British troops from encirclement at Yenangyaung 50 years ago)

Regardless of the nonsense, I was fortunate, in missing the move away from Shillong. Once again, absent on, 'Extra Regimental Duties', (ERD). My Burma experience, qualified me as a senior instructor at General Bill Slim's; 4 Corps, Jungle Warfare and Battle School, based at Ranchi, in Central India.

Take a slight diversion; So much for British Historical Recording?

In the official King's Own Yorkshire Light Infantry, 'Register of Officers 1755-1945', published by General C P Deedes, he makes blatant mistakes:

Showing two Colonels, V Henry Wells-Cole and Leslie F E Wieler, successively, as Commanding Officers of the 2nd Bn KOYLI, in 1942-1945, it is impossible. I was with the Battalion throughout the relevant period, and the named twosome, were England based.

In the 1st Bn list, Deedes shows EEE Cass commanding from 1944. He was Commanding in 1941- Ireland, and dispatched me to; "A place in the tropics!"

Errors in the Book of Remembrance, in York Minster, show Private Peter King as dying in February. I found him dead on the morning of the previous 2nd August. Private Tommy Melia, from Kilkenny, in Ireland, is wrongly shown, as being from Doncaster: Meeting with his family much later, they were happy to know that the boy was respected, addressed, and known by his real name, and not simply dubbed the ubiquitous: 'Paddy!'

13

A HARD SCHOOL

Several months spent in central India, at Ranchi, 4 Corps Jungle Warfare and Battle School, allowed a break in my stay at Shillong. Burma experience qualified me to help shape the school curriculum, and become an instructor. Officers up to the rank of major were trainees, and for sixteen days of a three week cycle, it was bloody tough going. The other five days were for rest, recuperation, and essential restocking.

This was an example of soft and hard extremes, and I was involved in both. It was; 'A Ball,' for the staff, and 'Absolute Hell', for 'clients'. There were days and nights of gruelling punishment for trainees, covering everything of what might be expected in jungle warfare, and there were no short cuts. Live ammunition was used on all exercises. The ethos of the course syllabus was based on the Chinese Forces action at Yenangyaung: Go in hard, and get out clean! Hit at vital points!

Alexander's shabby departure to the London scene, once out of Burma, left General Bill Slim, as Commander of 4 Corps. Slim knew and accepted, that there was much that he, personally, required to know, in conducting the specialised practice of jungle warfare. Such was the man, he was not averse to accepting guidance in order to acquire it, and became a frequent school visitor. He drew every possible facet of Burma experience from those of us amongst the instruction team. On the final day of each course he would make a point of updating all present on the Japanese situation.

Slim could stretch a story at times, particularly on Japanese atrocities, but his presence and readiness to talk to all and sundry was greatly appreciated. He had the good sense to make a point of having a word with as many individuals as possible, and it was done with no airs and graces. It surprised me when he made known a fact that I had no reason to know; He had been the man standing alongside Alexander, the chief that I saluted, and should have shot, on leaving Burma. Slim showed no favouritism, although with good reason, he did make a point of speaking to me.

Gurkha soldiers are renowned for their firm, and unfailing, allegiance to their own officers, all of whom are required to speak Gurkhali, and they have little to do with others. I was blessed in having a detachment of Gurkha mortar-men to 'supervise'. I cannot say 'command', as the word would upset genuine Gurkha officers.

Throughout this unusual situation, I certainly appreciated the liveliness and humour of the boys from Nepal, and because of my care for them I became a particular favourite of Slim, who was himself a Gurkha officer. The men enjoyed their attachment by being introduced to new interests. Apart from getting them competitive with mortar drill, and assembly, they exercised on the equipment.

Mule races were popular, and I was able to give them benefits, gained in my Jullundar training; riding out, and exercising, mounted on the animals haunches. Introducing my early morning road run and walk; run a little, walk a little and exercise a little, (frog hop, press-ups etc), was well received. Teaching them to drive, and a little vehicle maintenance; by going through; fuel, electrics, brakes, oil, water, tyres, and stripping down jeeps. With a few steady English lessons, the remarkable lads never wanted to stop, and there was no ending to each day.

It was not through my coddling up to Slim that won me favours; he spoke with my team of mortar-men. They let him know how much they were enjoying the school attachment. He was greatly surprised to have the glowing report, direct from Gurkha soldiers, and he did not hesitate to make known his pleasure. I explained that this was no more that what I did with my own men. From then on, to Slim I became simply, "Fitz!" He was the same with all the staff: I called him Sir!

Mortar bombs were far too dangerous a weapon to fire at trainees. For exhibition purposes, we would spread white bedding sheets over scrubland bushes, and create a mock village. Firing off several live rounds, the 'students' were somewhat amazed at the extent of the damage inflicted on the targets. We failed to tell them that it was the same sheets used repeatedly, on all occasions.

A tall young Gurkha, named Purney, was a little more advanced in speaking English, and he became my 'orderly', and accompanied me on all exercises. As the pair of us entered a small remote jungle village seeking clean water, a child was heard screaming with fear. Approaching a thatch roofed house beside the track, one with eaves at about shoulder height, there was a sudden bang on the ground to our front. It was a black snake, about three meters in length and solid in the body. In the timing it took, for the thing to rear up, facing us, Purney was in front of me, rattling the big silver biscuit tin we were to use for carrying water, and the animal scurried away. The girl went quiet.

Within yards of this brief encounter, we met with three men standing by the doorway of one of the low built houses. Saying saap, (snake), they pointed to the base of a huge tree, with roots above ground. At first sight there was nothing unusual about the tree. Slightly closer inspection showed one root to have thousands of ants moving from end to end. It was the body of a dead snake, with no head and no tail. The body was like a tree root, five meters in length, and twenty centimetres diameter. This must have been one hell of an animal, and we were playing games in the district.

Placid waters of a nearby dam proved perfect for river crossing and night attack exercises. It was a spectacular show, with four Bren guns mounted along a bund at the head of the dam. The guns, on fixed line firing, raked over the assault boats in their crossing, using one in four tracer bullets. The whole of the operational staff was comprised of officers, all picked for their specialist skills, although there was a bit of larking about at times.

Burma colleague Leslie Podmore Wise, and I, using Very-light pistols attempted to hit each other, by firing across the dam. Stuart Binnie of the Dukes, (Duke of Wellington Regiment), exploded charges in the water, as the assault boats approached the shore. Understandably, the guns and bombs being live, plus the Very-light pistol illuminations, the show caused mayhem, and it required guts to participate. An accident was inevitable, and as ever, the thing happened to the exception, the odd man out. The

Rajput Regiment received permission to submit a Non Commissioned Officer for the course, and a Havildar, (Regimental Sergeant Major), was accepted. The poor sod jumped from his boat, and was killed by a Binnie bomb. This caused ructions, and much annoyance, to the Rajput C.O.

One of the little treats for nurses from the nearby British Military Hospital was the invite, to witness the spectacular river crossing show. They particularly welcomed the visit to our small select officer's bar. Slim almost invariably attended the performance, and of course, paid for a drink or two. He smiled, but asked no questions as, one by one, the girls vanished from the bar, to make a special visit to an officer's basher, (individual straw building).

A spectacular, and show-biz style arrangement, was made for a visit to the school by Brigadier Whistler, the Corps Liaison Officer. This 'Top Brass' was accompanied by a Chinese delegation on what was supposed to be, a most secretive affair. It was rare, but in order to impress, I was detailed to do sentry duty on the approach road. The party arrived pronto, and, as the jeep approached down the narrow track, Whistler was busily, waving me to one side. I was, 'on guard duty', and having none of that! As Whistler became more and more frantic, putting the rifle to my shoulder, and operating the bolt, was of no consequence, as the safety catch was applied. The jeep however, skidded to a halt!

Challenging Whistlers antagonism, and with the man fuming, I demanded to see his credentials. It was a bit rewarding to see a Brigadier in such a state, and knowing that he could do absolutely nothing about it. The Chinese contingent, were laughing their hats off. They knew exactly what I was about, and appreciated my thanking them for the support given by Chinese troops, when rescuing men of the Inniskilling Regiment, and their back-up to our road-block clearance, back at the Burma oilfield.

Having previously disrupted the Rajput C.O. with his fatality, Binnie went a little too far. He caused me the only 'inflicted' wounds I was to suffer throughout the war. On field-work training, and comfortably ensconced in a small quarry, enjoying my daily crap, a long brown snake moving amongst rocks on the far side helped move me on a bit. It was a big fellow, and slowly vanished over the edge of the quarry. No sooner was it gone than I heard the bang behind me. Binnie had tossed in a hand grenade. Fortunately the grenade was a celluloid trainer, and my arse and back became impregnated with dozens of plastic pieces. The remainder of the day was spent, with the doctor using tweezers, removing debris from my back.

Entering Ranchi Officers Club in mid-afternoon, it was quiet and dark, there was just one person inside, and he was seated, with a drink, at one of the centre tables. Recognising him as Calvert, the 'nut case' Adjutant, from 501 Field Company R.E: The one who swam the freezing river at Tunbridge Wells. Going across to speak to him, the man was morose, never spoke, and never moved his eyes. Knowing full well who I was, it was as though he had no kind of feelings, and I shut up. Calvert went on later, to become second in Command to Orde Wingate. The two of them commanded the men we were training at the Battle School, ones who were to become known as, 'Chindits'. Wingate was a known 'homo', and Calvert's much later reported episode with boys, surreptitiously in a German wood, became a bit obscure, and as is customary with celebrities, it was 'airbrushed out', following much initial publicity.

Resulting from the fleeing Alexander's treacherous attempt, to put the blame for the 1942 Burma fiasco onto Slim, a cabal of: 'Senior, insider-uppity officers, of High Command', attempted to dislodge the more worldly Slim, from Burma Command. General Oliver Leese, a prominent member of the Montgomery clique; (he was also a friend of, Orde Wingate?), was given the top Asia appointment. Once installed, Leese immediately attempted to disgrace, and dislodge Slim, in order to install his chums.

Chief of Staff, Claud Auchinleck, was instantly alerted to the evil and sinister underhand ploy, he removed Leese, and Slim flourished: Only to be outdone in the 'Slim of Burma' title, by a very 'shifty' Mountbatten.

My return to Regimental Duties from Battle School instructing was brief, allowing only time, to meet and discuss with my sergeants. They included Mee, Bareham, and Isaacs, three of those who had served with me throughout Burma, and they knew exactly the demanding standards I required to be maintained within the platoon. The trip to the unit was so brief it was as though a courtesy visit. I was on my way once more, and beginning to enjoy the travelling, and in the splendid manner to which

I was becoming accustomed. There was something of a celebrity mantle growing with the job.

I was never made aware of it, but by some means, the respect shown to me by NCO's, and others, whilst in Burma, began to permeate, through officers, and all ranks of the newly arrived, and somehow, I didn't mind!

14

THE JOYS OF CEYLON

Rewarded for my Ranchi Battle School experience, Bill Slim selected me to visit Ceylon. My job was to assess the competence of a similar school, one based in the hills surrounding the central town of Kandy. Given approval to be accompanied by my batman, Ted Hewitt, it was, – 'business as usual'. Whatever the failings of so many things in India, the dependable railways were a model of efficiency and punctuality. They were installed and controlled by British operators. Our arrival at Calcutta was, spot on time.

Arriving at the office of the R.T.O. (Rail Transport Officer), at Howrah Station, I was just a little surprised to meet with Jim Battle, the son of one of my former schoolmasters. Hearing of my jaunt to Ceylon, he suggested that I had time to meet with the Garrison Brigadier. He required a task carrying out, and it should suit me fine.

After a spell of 'fishing around', the Brigadier got to the point. It appeared that the Bombay/Calcutta mail train had run off the line, possibly sabotaged, about fifteen miles west of Calcutta. My task was to report on the extent of the damage, thought to be the action of the India National Party, under Gupta Ramm; (a man considered to be a disciple of Mahatma Ghandi). The Brigadier placed me in charge of a random mix of troops, ones also in transit. Armed, and with a box full of sandwiches, we mounted a small hand operated, double railway bogy, and moved off to sort out the problem.

Of the emergent squad of fifteen, only Private Dicky Fozzard was from my own unit. The remainder were of a wide random selection. Not knowing the calibre of any of them, experience told me that I required being specific when giving orders, and careful that they be carried out.

The derailment site was unmistakable; the train remained upright, having run some distance off the rails. It was standing at the far end of a small village, situated to the north side of the track. There was no sign of passengers, although there was little doubt, they had been plundered. As though from nowhere, villagers appeared in numbers, filling the narrow street, they showed considerable hostility at our arrival. With this resentful reception, there was no point in messing about. Pulling the bogies back, a short distance from any possible pillage, allowed a little operating space. Making clear that we would tolerate no interference, it meant ordering fixed bayonets, and demonstrating, one round of ammunition in the barrels of all rifles.

Detailing three men to secure the bogies, 'and the bogy operators', we set forth to check the damage. Seeing nuts and bolts scattered around alongside the track, my engineering background held me in good stead. I realised that the rail fishplates had been manually removed, and the line deflected. This was clearly, a case of sabotage.

Unable to rectify the situation, and in order to demonstrate our determination, and control, the squad were spread out wide for the return to the bogy. When traversing back through the village, the ones attempting to show hostility, cleared before us. Returning to the bogies was fine, until we heard a crack, like thunder. A water chattee, (earthenware water container), crashed to the ground, it had been dropped from the roof of a two story shop premises, and grazed the rolled up sleeve of Dicky Fozzard's shirt. Now, Dicky was not a tall man, but he was almost as broad as long, and distinguished himself as a scrimmaging prop forward, in the Battalion rugby team. He was a very tough man.

The youth dropping the chattee made the mistake of looking over, and laughing at his action. He did not know just how much he had annoyed Dicky, and it was no more than seconds before Private Richard Fozzard was up the stairs, and had the youth in his grasp. There was a second crash on the ground, as Dicky hurled the foolhardy youth from the roof, for him to stay very still on the ground.

Dicky's severe activity was akin to insuring for the future, somewhat like a repeat of my elimination of the hostile Dacoit band in Burma. In this instance, wiping out the villagers would have been a little excessive.

There was however, an alternative: Aware that the influential shop-owners would be controllers of the mob, and prime instigators of the evil, it seemed appropriate to apply whatever strictures upon them. Setting fire to six or seven of the shops, all along one side of the street, and leaving them well ablaze, I made clear that should there be any further interference, we would return, and destroy the remaining shops.

Without mentioning the bouncing boy, or the reduction of shopping facilities, I reported my findings to the Brigadier, and was in good time to catch my scheduled connection to Madras.

The travelling, 'Indian food vendors' were the most welcoming treat on the long train journey south. Arriving at Madras' strikingly swish, Connemara Hotel. It was truly Irish, decorated in its green glazed frontage, and opulent inside.

With no room immediately available, I sat in the lounge for a while. Not for long! The lounge became alive at the entry of a gent. It turned out to be Tavenor of the Welsh Regiment; one of those attending the animal management course with me, some time beforehand, at Jullundar. He was not the sole centre of attention however; it was the tiny young leopard resting on his arm. The mother had, apparently, been shot that morning.

With three beds available in his room, Tavenor invited me to join him. That was fine until the cub started screaming for its mother in the night, but there was a greater danger. I had to make clear that my arse was not a comfort lump for my benefactor.

Other than passing a mass of people, almost living on the rail track, there was nothing of great interest on the journey from Madras, to boarding the Colombo ferry. The multitude of spectacular fish to be seen; in the clear water of the jetty, was a real eye opener. The numbers, size, variety, and colours, would grace any aquarium.

Instantly, on arrival at Colombo, there was an unmistakable marked difference in the characteristics of the populace. The Singhalese differed from the darker Tamils, as much as did the whites from both of them. There was a gentleness and courtesy in all manner of communications.

The big treat, was my arrival at the Queens Hotel; (a former British Army barracks), in the centre of Kandy. Situated a short distance from,

'The Temple of the Tooth', it was luxurious. The unforgettable pleasure, was night-time listening to the unique jingling of innumerable small bells in the trees of the hotel garden, they emphasised the tranquillity of the country: (Visiting the hotel, almost seven decades later, on the 10th October 2010, I find the trees and beautiful bells removed, to be ignominiously, replaced by a swimming pool).

The Training School, purpose of my visit, was situated in the pleasant surrounding hills, five or six miles from Kandy. The place, and the training undertaken, resembled the exquisite joy, and softness, of the country, when compared with the live ammunition firing, 'rough-house', of the Ranchi school. The concept, of training, consisted of taking gentle country walks amongst the hills. My encounter with the school commandant was brief, and for some reason, he resented my forthright opinion of his, 'Rest Camp'. Becoming 'well pissed' in the bar, the commandant became seriously obnoxious, and with a showy repertoire of offensive expletives, hurled derogatory remarks about my regiment, and his opinion of individuals involved in the Burma campaign. When lifted from the floor, he bade me leave the 'academy'.

The source of my next posting remains a secret to me. I never did know how it came about, although Slim must have approved. It introduced me to a most pleasant, and welcoming, sightseeing tour of Ceylon. Attachment to the 20th Punjab Regiment, stationed nearby the huge salt flats, at Elephant Pass, the northern entry point to the peninsula of Jaffna, was a joy. It required no more than the briefest tour of the place, to find it tranquil beyond measure: It was so appealing, I decided, on achieving the situation of retirement; this was to be the place for me. But, of course, it was all to change in later years.

Having, years before, been stationed in the country, particularly at Elephant Pass, I, along with my wife, on the 5th October 2010, were granted rare Governmental authority to visit the northern Jaffna peninsula. This proved to be an eye-opener, and revelation. The thirty years war, between insurgent Tamils, and the Singhalese Nationals, had ended less than two years beforehand, in 2008.

Strict control, allowed for only a single day visit, and that was granted, at the last minute, and to travel within less than twenty-four hours. It meant travelling, without deviation, out and back, along the rough, over one hundred and fifty miles long, war-torn road. The devastation throughout was every bit as bad, if not worse, than I had seen in Germany, in 1945.

Shell-like carcasses of rare solid built buildings, stood roofless, and burnt out, and never short of bullet marks. There was no such thing as a recognisable village, as all were now scorched earth. Seeing the odd few well-worn tented habitats, and an occasional corrugated roofed shack in the desolation, indicated the intensity of the long and unforgiving war.

So precarious is the peace, that every four or five hundred yards of the route, armed troops man look-out pill-box type observation posts, and the various regimental garrisons are positioned and signposted, at regular intervals. Travel credentials are checked several times on route, both in, and out.

The few roadside 'Comfort Stops', are at establishments similar to British NAAFI's, except these ones are canteens, and run by the local military for their own use, whilst at the same time, open to the travelling public. The one visited on our return trip, was constructed entirely of used ammunition boxes, including the seats, tables, counter, and steps leading into the place.

Somewhat surprisingly, observing about two dozen soldiers, clearing mines and operating less than ten feet from our vehicle, on the west side of the road, I know that my wife and I travelled through an existing war zone.

Starting from the Anuradhapurna hotel at 5-00 am, we travelled almost 200 miles out, and 200 miles back, returning at 6-30 pm, on very rough roads: (They were the most astonishing, and revealing, 13.5 hours I can remember since my war days).

Trincomalee, was the 'must place' to visit, whilst on attachment to the Punjab regiment, the name is so appealing, and the British Navy, at their enchanting base, lived up to my highest expectations. Possibly, the rum ration indulged in was recently received. (Almost seven decades later, my wife and I did better than this. On the basis of my age, of 91, and my long passed visit to the country, we became some sort of celebrities, and enjoyed special attention).

Taking dinner on the evening of the 6th October 2010, at the Trincomalee, Chaaya Blue Hotel, we were singled out by a gentleman, and his lady wife, expressing their pleasure at meeting with us. Somewhat surprised, he asked if we would like an invite from the Rear Admiral, Northern District Commander, to visit the former British Naval base China Bay; -. It was the place that I had visited so many years beforehand, and now, occupied by the Sri Lankan Navy.

Somewhat sceptical, as our own driver could not enter the Naval Yard when we attempted earlier, we accepted, on the basis that we were collected, and conveyed, to and from: Completely unexpected, but as promised, Admiral Colombage phoned my wife the following morning. He confirmed that an officer would collect us, and that we should be entertained to lunch at his bungalow, by Commodore DEC Jayakody.

Sceptical! We were not sure that we were not being japed, and waited.

We were collected at the hotel, promptly, by a cheerful Commander, Patric Virthana, and conveyed to the base. Here, we dined, after being conducted round the rare security-monitored museum, containing enterprisingly improvised and innovative weapons, all recovered from the recent war; by the expert, – Former Commodore, MAB Cooray.

The naval commander expressed particular pride in the condition and durability, of the infra-structure layout; roads, and buildings, throughout the vast 1,050 acre base. He made no secret that they were, as proudly left, seven decades earlier, by the departing British.

Having no troops under command, with nothing to do, except accompany the Punjabi unit as an observer, the Indian Army attachment became my 'conducted tour' of Ceylon. Given the tasked exercise; repelling an imaginary assault force, on the southern coastal town of Galle, an early place of call was Anuradhapurna, the ancient island capital, and the site of many impressive religious monuments. Sleeping in cocoanut groves, well clear of the possible fall of king cocoanuts, we made for the elevated, tea plantation town of Newara Eliya, but not without a catastrophe on route.

Opening a tin of bully beef, a little of the content remained stuck on Hewitt's fingers. Thinking nothing of it, Hewitt simply flicked his fingers, and, as the bully flew, it landed inside the 'V' neck of a Punjabi bearers', (batman), shirt, and the man exploded. This unfortunate and accidental flick of bully-beef, violated the lad's religion, and it was not reversible. The relieving consolation from this episode was that the bearer, worked for a Lieutenant Rae. He just happened to be the son of a certain Colonel Rae, the man who had, on the same religious grounds, denied us two young buffaloes, captured for the menu, whilst in Burma.

I'm not sure, but think that possibly, we conquered the imaginary invaders at Galle. Not wishing to spare me, whilst available in Ceylon; on returning to my hotel, a further assignment awaited. Detailed instructions bid me attend a five day course on Military Intelligence, and I realised that my inclusion was simply to make up the numbers. The course was arranged to be held in the Hotel Suisse, situated at the far end of the lake in Kandy, a most pleasurable morning walk,

Arriving promptly, having smartened myself up a bit, I felt pretty good as I passed through the entrance gate. At that point, it surprised me considerably, to meet with a stupid and irritating stunt. On the driveway were mounted two sentries; both casually dressed. They were unarmed, and approached me in a manner that I had not met with previously. The two advanced, with arms held forward, in an aggressively, inviting, and almost threatening manner. One of them made to lunge. He was not expecting retaliation, and as I cracked him a fairly meaty punch on the jaw, he fell to the ground. The second man withdrew, and ceased to show any further interest.

Entering the building, and not yet registered for the course, a young staff officer bade me, meet "The Chief?" I asked him, "What f-rude half-witted norp-headed-dolt, had come up with this halfwit guard idea?"

Surprise is hardly the word for it, I met with another one of Churchill's annoying, misfits; Mountbatten! He was a man, sickeningly, and persistently, exploiting a recent seagoing mishap to the full. A man Churchill wanted as far from under his nose as possible. Run of the mill junior officers, such as myself, had no idea of how selected individuals became placed in Higher Command. On meeting with the man, I thought at first, that he might have come out to look after the shipping, but this proved to be, not so.

Pestering and poncing, around London, Mountbatten had exploited his Royal connections to the full. Having failed the traditional Naval Commanders privilege, of going down with his ship, he constantly trumpeted his good fortune, in being rescued from the sea, and sought further glories. His precocious, egotistical, impetuous, and triphibious glory-seeking, was tested by Churchill. It resulted in him being allowed to plan, and commit, good British and Canadian troops, on totally impossible, unnecessary Commando Operations. Mountbatten planned Commando assaults, on Axis occupied French harbours, St Nazaire, and Dieppe. They failed, and resulted in the loss of thousands of good soldiers. The plans were muffled, and, under the secrecy of war-time Defence, 'airbrushed' from the Royal shoulders.

On 19th August 1942, under Mountbatten planning, Canadian and British Commandos were mutilated in an attempted raid on the French port of Dieppe.

Mountbatten had to: Go! It was now, a case of Churchill settling another 'failure' into a, 'Sinecure', and as far away as possible: He could follow Wavell, and Auchinleck. With its series of recent failures; The Far East theatre was considered suitable – Hong Kong, Java, Singapore, and Burma, all with remote Churchill touches, was considered a suitable dumping ground for the egotistical gent.

When Thompson, Churchill's Detective, was asked, on recent T/V, of the two French raids, his comment was: *"They 'covered' Burma"*.

When Mountbatten was asked the same question, also on T/V, the vile, lying, repugnant, bombastic, egotistical, charlatan, mock Imperial lump, had the audacity to claim: *"It was precursory to the 'D' Day landings"*. – Three years away?

I had no knowledge of the man, but; enter, the recently arrived; Supreme Commander, of S.E.A.C. (South East Asia Command).

In an attempt to exploit further his privileged existence, Mountbatten chose to site his Headquarters in the rather lush, Hotel Suisse, in Kandy, an attractive town in central Ceylon. At about two thousand miles distant from his active fronts, this was the equivalent of Wavell's sighting of his defunct Command HQ on Java. Both site choices were impractical, remote, and inaccessible from their zone of operation.

On entering the office, it was obvious from his questioning, that Mountbatten had witnessed the brief altercation at the guard-post, where he had obviously, enjoyed the pleasure of seeing others falter. Asking my name, which he already knew, and my regiment, he questioned further. He let me know that he was aware of my brief altercation with the Battle School Commandant, and now, clearly resented my involvement in a second incident, and that with one of his ridiculous innovations.

Assailed by the brazen, egotistical, irritating, choking burring voice of the elite, for a military man, and in his assumptive tone of supremacy, the part royal attempted to brand me, 'a brute'. It required my advising him of my pre-war boxing training, and recent instructor training sessions at the Ranchi Battle School, under Bill Slim; the man Churchill would have been the wiser to appoint; Supremo!

On mentioning that I had been involved in the long Burma withdrawal, Mountbatten's response was that sniffy, and contemptuous, snort of British Royals. In his fruity voice, and with no expletives, he virtually repeated the words of the Camp Commandant. It implied, as Churchill would have it: "We! Officers and Men! Should have died, defending Burma".

Mountbatten resented my bandying words, regarding the entrance gate turmoil, and my not giving ground. Wrangling with him to the point of insolence, and a not too polite Yorkshire retort, I was not too far from giving him a punch on the nose. The inquisition lasted longer than expected, as the man did not like being made to look an idiot, through his own tomfoolery. Fortunately, he knew that he was in the wrong, when setting up his stupid guard stunt, and realising that he could do absolutely nothing about it, he called an aide to escort me from the office.

A formal reprimand would have been inappropriate, although Mountbatten's annoyance at my forthrightness really showed. He was Hellish annoyed with me, but managed to contain himself. In return, my dislike of the man showed, and he knew it. My question to him, should have been equally accusative, as the one so readily tossed out to commanding Generals, by Churchill, at Singapore, and at Hong Kong; "Why did you not go down with your ship, 'The Kelly', when it was torpedoed?" The ship was at all times, specifically, referred to as; 'The Kelly!" (The singular episode of war, that Mountbatten lived off, was promoted, and endeared him to many, in years to come).

The sailor-boy's attempt at revolutionising the British Army, had failed at the first hurdle. The stupid assault course entry, using the gate sentries, was terminated instantly. Mountbatten and I were destined to meet again, some time later, although in very different circumstances.

At reception, on entering the rather splendid, Hotel Suisse, at Kandy, age 91, on the 9th October 2010, I mentioned that I had been there almost seven decades earlier, with Mountbatten. It was as though causing an explosion, all became centred on my wife and me.

Instant celebrities! We 'must' have the historically preserved room 204/5; The Mountbatten Suite. With this went the recognition, and acknowledgement, of every member of the delightful staff. – (We photographed every inch of the suite).

Recognising the small anti-room, I was delighted to confirm my earlier feelings, that he most certainly could have witnessed my wartime altercation, shattering his stupid experiment with the guards.

There was no escaping Ceylon without one further naughty little incident. When back at the Queens Hotel, one of the Indian officer arse-wallahs' attending the intelligence course, came seeking romance. To encounter two fisticuffs, and two arse-wallahs' on one trip, I must have been rather lovely looking, to have the two incidents on the one venture; but not for me! With no further incident, it was a return back to my unit, now comfortably settled at a new destination.

During my time away, and greatly to the chagrin of Bob Poole, the battalion had moved from his beloved Shillong, to rugged terrain, situated five miles from the Ranchi Battle School that had given me such pleasure.

Joining with the lads once again, was a little depressing. Those great morale boosters, the horses and mules, so loved at Shillong, were left behind for use by the fortunate Foresters Regiment. The incredible animals had been a wonderful therapy, and most unexpected experience, for so many. The men had found themselves ensconced in a completely different environment to anything they could ever have envisaged on joining the army.

With not a lot to do in the scrubby countryside, Scottish Doctor, Morrow, used his time experimenting in his own speciality. In order to measure the fitness of individuals, he conducted a series of exercises. Not the biggest of men, but a very surprised, Sergeant Potter, proved to be 'number one' in fitness.

How far Potter had attempted to prove himself, we did not know. Accompanied by Cec Dalby, my Quartermaster Sergeant, we were surprised to hear the plaintiff bleating of a goat; coming from within one of the tents. As a rather plump young nanny ran out from the structure, and scampered away, with what I considered a cheeky little smile on her face. It was followed by a rather embarrassed looking Potter. There's no real accounting for romance.

Many years later, long into civilian life, star soldier, Cockliff; (Former reinforcement, and later, Captain), approached me at a regimental function, and in a short conversation, told me of his brief attachment to the Coldstream Guards, whilst stationed in Malaya. When pitching tents, he had introduced a KOYLI established practice, as at Ranchi, of preparing 'a tent drainage system'. This simple, and practical task, was looked upon aghast by guards' officers, it was as though nothing must allow variance to their long established routine. The innovation had to await the visit of the Regimental Colonel, and seek his personal approval, before it could be adopted. The bland reply by Cockliff, when asked how he knew of this practice, was; "I served in a line regiment Sir!" How thick can Guards Officers be, to go to this extent before introducing a simple safeguard?

15

DELIGHTS OF DELHI – SETTLING IN

The resplendent, brick built barracks, at Delhi Cantonment, situated approximately four miles from the Capital, was a very different proposition to the "Military station in the tropics", that Colonel 'Copper' Cass dismissed me to, two years beforehand. The cosy environment proved the final mantle, for hiding and shedding, what was, increasingly, being seen as; 'The shame of the Burma Campaign'. It was as though the demise of the Battalion, a few short months beforehand, was something of a bygone age. The new draft of senior officers, now in Command, had not experienced the Burma conflict. In numerous ways, and for whatever reason, each, and every one of them, had somehow departed Burma, before the start of hostilities, and managed to be elsewhere throughout the arduous six months of conflict.

The superior, recently arrived set of individuals, appeared to view the Army as a place of formality, protocol, King's Regulations, and comfortable peacetime routine. This new regime had not experienced the drivel of excuses, ineptitude, failure, and apologetic gestures, of their counterparts, when under pressure. Neither had they experienced the woeful existence back in England, following the Dunkirk evacuation, and the relentless assault, by the German Luftwaffe on so many towns. In this comfortable, familiar, and delightful setting, all was at peace for these gentle-folk.

Cantonment Barracks had everything; individual company Barrack Blocks, complete with cook house; a guard room, and substantial HQ offices; sergeant's and corporal's messes; along with an impressive officer's mess, with accommodation in a scattering of bungalows. There was a gymnasium, football field and parade ground, along with a good sized swimming pool, and a cinema. The nearby 'extras' included two hospitals; British, and Indian, both complete with nurses, and the lovely WACI, (Women's Auxiliary Corps India, – communication services). This military station was made for peace-time soldiering, and that appeared to be the sole task in hand. If my seniors could enjoy this, then so could I! Boy – O' Boy!

Mules now departed, I sought new toys for my, 'Selected', to play with, and they duly arrived. Like all good things, they presented a new challenge. The seven, big four-wheeled personnel carriers, had proved useless in Middle Eastern deserts, and looked formidable. Of course, as ever, there had to be a new kind of problem. Only two men of the platoon could drive a motor vehicle, one of them being, my most unreliable individual.

Achieving the rank of Captain, I now operated in a dual role; as both: H.Q. Company Commander, and 3" Mortar Officer. Within the Company, I had Transport, Signals, Pioneers, and 'odds and sods', under my wing. With two ex-Burma boys, Sergeant Major, (Togo) Crossland, and Quartermaster Sergeant, (Howson), as office controllers, life went along swimmingly, both were brilliant.

Transport platoon NCO's took my boys in hand for driver training. A tremendous asset was a man of Hull, Transport Sergeant, Desforges. As I had done at the Battle School for the Gurkhas, Des' prepared diagrams for; the vehicle chassis, engine, transmission, brakes, electrics, fuel supply, and relished the additional interest of his being asked to train the squad. Each, and every dedicated one of them, became drivers, and capable of stripping down vehicles, and re-assembling. The squad relished the novelty of the new interest, it was virtually a free apprenticeship, and all on Army pay. The platoon took to the vehicles, exactly as they had taken to the mules. This was done in such a way, that with the skills practiced, they knew that it should prove useful to them on returning to civilian life.

Having a back up team of six brilliant sergeants running the platoon, along with the two top men in Company Office, CO. Bob Poole, continued to regard me as his utility officer. Things worked in such a way, that he knew that I could leave my team in charge as necessary. Having tested me, when accompanying him, on the North Burma reconnaissance, and found me not lacking in experience, he appreciated that my accepting responsibility was no problem. It was a little time before I heard of Poole's earlier success, as a boxer, and he had obviously heard of my misdemeanours. Closing the gymnasium doors, and much against military discipline, I had frequent sessions with the gloves on, with Private Parsons, a former fairground boxer. This obviously, contributed to Poole welcoming my report of the verbal duel with Louis Mountbatten, whilst in Ceylon.

There was no quick recovery from the Burma campaign. Numerous, 'time-served' soldiers, most of whom had been overseas, for the regulation period of nine years, or more, were due for repatriation. Those damaged in whatever way; wounded, malaria, dysentery, and other ailments, were hospitalised, or repatriated to England. Left with a small cadre of regular soldiers, the Battalion strength became mainly comprised of reinforcements, few of whom had warfare experience.

Not to lose sight of the main priorities, and with the inevitable possibility of a return to Burma, the Battalion was hurried into a training exercise. The Unit was transported to Rudd, a virtual 'nowhere' place, approximately 120 miles from Delhi. This heavily forested area, with a narrow single track, running alongside a shallow river, was ideal training ground. The four companies were dispersed, with two camped along each side of the track.

My bed, the groundsheet, was hung from above the ground roots of a monster tree. To lie there, and watch a relentless war conducted alongside me, was interesting. At a fixed point on a tree branch, almost above my head, the fat three centimetre long black ants, met with the slimmer, two centimetres long red ants. It was fascinating to watch, as there was never a change in the centre-point of unceasing conflict. This was serious warfare, and I feel sure the battle continues to the present time.

Poole proved his fitness by leading exercises, and runs, including a stretch down the bed of the river. The whole thing was a conditioning exercise, one to be seriously tested in making the return journey, back to Delhi. Seeing nothing of a village, or any villager, anywhere near the place throughout our stay of two weeks, there became the surprise. One 'spectacular parishioner', decided to make an appearance, and frantically enliven activities. Men were already formed into queues at field kitchens, awaiting their mid-day meals, as; 'the dear sweet thing', loomed into sight. It was a young woman, upright, and of the most striking appearance. She was tall and slim, with exceptional looks, as opposed to what might be expected in such remote surroundings. This beautiful girl was the only local person we saw throughout the visit. Or was it a dream?

Spectacular features of this sheer delight, was, that; she was, 'absolutely bollocko', from the waist upwards, and had the most delightful pair of fittings. From all quarters, at least one half of the dinner queues vanished, in erstwhile pursuit of this beauty. Desirable, and delightful, the dear thing outpaced the lot of them, as Regimental Sergeant Major Delaney tailed them all in vain, attempting to get their minds back to the job in hand.

The scant, although somewhat hectic, training period, was put to the test on the return journey. With no transport for this trip, it was designated, 'an inter-company competition', all four companies leaving at specified intervals.

Torrential monsoon rain struck, as the first company departed, and four hours later, I was on my way with Company, number two.

Monsoons don't await invitations, the sky darkens, and here comes the rain, with a considerable temperature drop. It all happened, as we broke camp, and set a hectic pace on the return to barracks. With the target of a two day finish, there was little time for rest, although managing a short nap on the roadside, at the pre-arranged feeding post.

My mother had bought me a rather nice gold wrist-watch for my twenty-first birthday, and on my being commissioned. It had been the only watch in the Battalion throughout Burma, as all others were ruined in the crossing of the Sittang River. In the hustle-bustle of the mad dash for Delhi, I did not notice the watch slip from my wrist, but somehow it managed to remain, stuck in the mud.

Of course, I was perturbed at the loss, and it appeared that I must accept, the precious thing had gone missing. The miracle happened on the following day as, Signals Corporal, Garlick, presented me with the watch. He had seen one strap sticking out of the mud. It remains unrepaired, and in my possession, seventy years later. Remarkably, to my surprise, on taking it from a safety box, I find the watch intact, dried out, and operating.

THE EDGAR BRITT JOCKEY CLUB

Within days of our return from Rudd, Bob Poole beckoned me into the office, and gave me; "a challenging job". He made clear that he knew of my closed door gymnasium boxing sessions with Parsons, and warned me against taking part in his next proposal. He gave me the relished task of escorting the Battalion boxing team, to the All India Championships, held at the Burt Institute, in Lahore. This suited me just fine, although Poole warned me that this competition was not for me, which I accepted.

With six boxers, two of whom had been previous champions, I was happy to undertake this, far from 'odious' duty: I loved it! Arriving four days beforehand, for acclimatisation, we were housed in the barracks of the Kings Liverpool Regiment. The men's accommodation was in an old style, arched barrack room, in which the walls were running with water. The place was pretty foul, but with no alternative, it had to be acceptable, and final preparations were made at the institute.

Invited to join with the 'Kings' officers, at the horse-race meeting, at the local course, I found the experience hilarious. Edgar Britt, a most humorous Australian, was top jockey. He was famed for, 'Going through the card', or winning six out of seven races, wherever he rode. He loved a joke with the troops, and endeavoured to master the 'Scoucer' language, which he found intriguing.

The beauty of Edgar was, in being so highly successful a jockey, he attracted rides on the best of mounts: Riding for the Maharajahs of Baroda, Kashmir, and Kolhapur, amongst others. Later, in England, he rode for King George VI, Queen Elizabeth II, the Aga Khan, and continued, for the Maharajah of Baroda. His amazing 1200 winners include the Irish Derby, seven English classics; two Oaks, two St. Legers, one Two Thousand Guineas, and a Thousand Guineas. He featured amongst the top half dozen in the Premier List.

Whilst in India, Britt, along with two or three other Australian jockeys, were known as; "The Jockey Brigade." He served well, earning fantastic money in the process.

Notwithstanding his renowned success, Mr. Britt did not mind sharing the entrepreneurial funding. He had a nicely developed understanding, which the 'Kings Liverpool' officers appreciated, all too well! With Edgar riding almost every winner at the meeting, or possibly six out of seven, the trick was to know, which of the races to, 'leave alone', and to avoid making a bet. With such resounding success, his mounts were invariably at short odds in betting, so, woe-betide those backing a loser. In his kindness, and love for the boys, Edgar helped them in making selections; of which mount to 'avoid', rather than, which ones to 'back'.

In the normal way of his riding to the starting gates, Britt would ride with head down. But! – When 'on the no-chance bogey horse', as he passed the rails behind which the officers were standing, his head would be raised.

How much the man made, I could have no idea, but it must have been considerable. In violating all Army discipline, the Kings' Regimental Quartermaster was gambling, using the Regimental Imprest, (pay), Account. It was many years later, long after the war, that one of my friends, fortunate to re-enlist after being wounded in Burma, was jailed for nine months. He foolishly, committed exactly the same offence; gambled with the Army pay-role. He did not have the helpful assistance provided by Edgar Britt. (I understand that in year 2008, Edgar, at the age of 94, continues to attend horse-racing functions, in Australia).

Unfortunately, our visit to the Burt Institute, proved far less successful than trips to the racecourse. With men suffering feverish colds, we had no winners on this occasion. It proved highly successful for my friends, the Gurkha Regiments.

DANCING QUEENS

With a small group of select musicians, formed from the versatile Regimental Buglers, a start was made on holding monthly dances in the gymnasium. This was fine except for the fact that, from an infantry battalion, you don't get many girls as dance partners There were, however, attempts made to introduce dancing, but, blokes dancing with, blokes, was a, 'No-No'! Ambassadors, Catterson, and myself, were dispatched to seek lady partners, from friendly female organisations; the WACI's, The British Military Hospital, for nurses; and to the Indian Military Hospital, where matron proved to be a little fussy, she set standards.

Nurses at the Indian Hospital were; because of the language problem; Indian, Anglo Indian, or India born English. Matron consented for six of her girls to attend: Providing, that a vehicle be sent, "accompanied by two Regimental Officers", in order to collect them, – (I realise later, that Matron missed a trick at this point, she ought to have said: "If my girls are good enough for your officers to dance with, they are good enough to be invited into your Officer's Mess!") The very idea of this, at the time of 'underhand apartheid', was totally unthinkable.

Not needing a lot of persuading, and most dutifully, Catterson and I, collected six attractive nurses for the ball. Inevitably! It happened, and our being; 'The official girl partner collectors', the onerous duty was rewarded, in the nicest possible way: Dolly picked on me, and Silvana picked on my colleague, – to form long and happy relationships. You bet! And it did improve!

MURREE AND NOT TOO GAY

Although not exactly a fitness fanatic; I did my own devised, daily, 6.00 am, 'road-run and walk', followed by a trip to the excellent swimming pool, and knew that I was as fit as any man in the battalion. It came as a bit of a surprise therefore, to find that I had contracted 'prickly heat', a condition whereby a band of irritating, and itching spots, spread around the lower chest cage of my body. Irritating as it was; some of the old-timers said that, in the event of it closing completely around the body, it could be fatal. It was just one of those things that come along at monsoon time. Treatment for 'prickly heat', in the steaming hot plane of Delhi, could be a long drawn out affair, if not impossible.

Saviour, Bob Poole, however, having long experience of overseas service, provided the remedy. He arranged for me to accompany a leave party to Murree, a hill station close by the North West Frontier. The simple remedy was cold air, at possibly 6,000 meters above sea level. In little more than twenty-four hours, the foul irritation vanished.

I did, however, very nearly come by another violent attack. It was, on entering the Officers Club, in early afternoon, on my second day in residence. An attractive blond, who was just about to leave the premises, turned, and followed me to the bar. Being the polite gent, I offered the standard 'G and T', which was accepted, and gratefully appreciated. In due course, seeking some rest, following my regular genital exertions at Delhi, I left the elegant lady remaining at the bar.

Later in the day, with several of the club members assembled, and enjoying a drink, I was invited to bare my back, for inspection. It transpired, the dear blonde lady, the wife of an Army Major, Transport Officer, stationed at Lahore, had a joyful habit of clawing the backs of all newly arrived officers. I didn't realise how lucky I was, although I think Poole knew when he sent me, that I needed a rest from my over frequent nefarious activities, with Dolly, back in Delhi.

The tough little mountain pony took me on jaunts each day around the hills, and villages. It was when I told the camp commandant of my previous connection with Mr Prasad Joo, of 3rd Bridge, Srinagar, in Kashmir, the merchant supplier of furs, I was offered the trip to die for. He knew of the same man, and invited me to join with him in his jeep, to visit the place. Awe inspiring, and almost terrifying, was the un-metalled hundred miles, or so of road to Kashmir. Apart from watching the rugged track, the scenery was truly spectacular, with a vastness of valleys and hills that appeared to stretch forever. I don't think that we saw more than two or three small villages, on the journey of about eight hours.

The reception by Prasad Joo was beyond belief. It was almost as though he wanted to pay us for taking the trouble of making the visit, although my only connection with him was in buying a few items; furs etc, which he forwarded to family in England. Accommodation, throughout the three day stay, was on the man's house-boat. Huge beyond measure, it had resident staff to see to all our needs, and for some silly reason, we partied each night on Scotch, (maybe?), whisky.

Following the 1947 partition of India, much has obviously changed, but the memory of the tranquil water, scenery, and warmest of welcomes to this hill kingdom paradise, will remain, unperturbed.

A SAD MOMENT

Returning from 'onerous' duties at Murree, I met with a situation that has rankled within me for more than seventy years. There was something radically wrong with the men of my mortar platoon, down at the mouth, in a way that was new to me, and there was never a word of explanation. Regardless of whatever the problem, my men were not the kind to come moaning, and tittle-tattling. This was one for me to sort out, and it was not a subject easily settled. Once again, I had to widen my perspective. I think that I made one of my; 'memory retrieving calls', back to the kindly action of the Irish Garda.

Things on the surface were looking good, and going swimmingly. Maybe, going much too smoothly for the general good. I was beginning to see a degree of perfection, with an unwelcome bit of hard professionalism, possibly beyond our considered status. The platoon were already dubbed; "The Cream of the Battalion", and here we were going beyond that, but with about fifty good men, not too happy about it.

Highly regarded, and good as we were, there had to be a clue to the problem. It came from a few terse words of command, spoken by my stalwart, Sergeant Benny Mee. He simply said; "I want pre-war standards!" Benny had nine years of pre-war service behind him, where time was of little consequence. When all that mattered was; the achievement of, Top Show Standards, and a load of Bullshit!

The bulk of men in the platoon were conscripts, all of them reluctantly enlisted for the duration of hostilities, and all were prepared to do their duty. They did not want it going over the top; Tarty-farting; in London parade fashion, as Benny was unfortunately, attempting to make it.

I wanted the men returned, to the happy and willing team made of them, from the start, and their arrival as reinforcements. This was not the 'regular' peace-time Army; It had a confident and more relaxed way of showing allegiance, and accepting discipline. Of necessity, there had to be change, I had to stand Benny down!

This action hurt not only Benny, but me also. He had been my mainstay from the moment I joined with the Battalion, and to replace him was agony.

Shocking Benny by appointing a conscripted, 'duration of the war' serviceman, Sergeant Frank Beckett, of Hull, I have, ever since, lived with a measure of regret. Had I waited a few short days longer, Benny was repatriated to England, and remained a most embittered man, for the remainder of his life.

Regardless of my remorse at the cruel action, the change of morale in the platoon, was instantaneous, and we were back, 'on an even keel', once more.

New boy Beckett showed his worth, by intervening, as I was about to release Lincolnshire farmer, 'Gabby' Richardson, from the platoon. Gabby was not 'up to speed' in all that we did, whether on mortars, or on simple arms drill, and took twice the time of others to assemble a mortar. He could turn left, on the command to turn right: "Don't sack him sir?" "He's worth his weight in gold in the barrack room". "He's the joker in the pack, he keeps them laughing from morning to night". That was good enough for me, and I thanked Beckett.

Having stopped the 6-00 am daily, 'Road Run and Walk", one of between two to five miles; following a series of moans of depression during the Benny Mee regime, there came a remarkable, and unique change of scene.

Somewhat guardedly, Beckett approached me, asking; "Can we start the runs again sir?" "The men are beginning to feel a need for them". I surprised Beckett with my next required condition, one that I feel remains unique in British Military History, wherein, a published order is compulsory. Yes, why not? "I'll start again on an optional basis" "If that's what they want, we'll have to see how keen they really are". "If they don't feel fit enough, for whatever reason, they can opt out of the run. But woe-betide any scrimshankers!" The spirit, and allegiance, was such, that I have no recollection of one man failing to parade. These men were not recognised as, 'The Cream of the Battalion', for no good reason.

This residual standard, and stature of civilian loyalty, along with the dedication of one man to another, as displayed in the ranks of conscripted wartime British Armed Forces, is beyond the comprehension of 'Dyed in the Wool, Military Brass-hats'. All action is required, by them, to be in accordance with one, or other, military manual. There is no relaxation.

Rigorous parade ground discipline slipped considerably, the day we were marching the three miles, into Delhi, about to mount guard, at the towns' splendid Red Fort. We were overtaken by a tonga, (horse drawn type rickshaw, with rear facing seat). In the tonga were seated two of America's leading film actresses, the two beauties were on a goodwill tour of American bases, and sat facing backwards. Both, Paulette Goddard, and Alexis Smith, had legs crossed; 'and showing the lot'!

How the hell can order be kept with this kind of a show? – Some show! The boys let them know that Yanks had nothing on the ribaldry of well disciplined, but very human, British troops.

THE CIRCUSES

Company Sergeant Major Crossland, although universally recognised by no other name, than 'Togo', lived in splendid married quarters, along with his wife and young family. He liked a gentle drink, and would organise for one or two, maybe three, sacks of beer; -(20 bottles in each sack), to be delivered each week-end. The company of friends attending were highly selective, and the coincidental ritual became a part of the monthly gymnasium dance.

Apart from enjoying the attentions of Dolly, we had the added interest of the rather spectacular gentleman, Louis Mountbatten. As junior ranks seldom hear of higher Command changes; when meeting with him earlier, I had no idea that he was the newly appointed, Supremo of Asia Command. I had assumed that, with his gauche mannerisms, and as a Navy man, he would be looking after shipping. He was albeit, promoted for some peculiar reason, and at the same time discarded, and sent to profit and prosper, from Slim's, Burma experience.

From the cosy comfort of Ceylon, Mountbatten was ordered, by Churchill, to show a bit of common sense, and vacate his lush base of comfort, and transfer his work-station, nearer to operations; he chose Delhi. Being so closely based, Louis attended our, 'Regimental All Ranks', dances fairly frequently. At all times he was accompanied by four or five, rather sweet looking young officer aides. He did rather fancy himself on the dance floor, and favoured the occasional nurse, whilst his boys took intimate stock of the soldiery.

Mr. Pandit Nehru, India's Prime Minister, was known to be a friend, and might well have been, 'in attendance', at Fortress Mountbatten, whilst Louis partied with the boys. It was surmised that Madam had a fancy, or possibly, an intimate relationship, with the Indian politician, and possibly others. It was hard to know, just how much, 'the fancy boy collection', were on the mans agenda.

It was not a subject on which I could approach Mountbatten, although I am sure that he remembered me, from our brief and sour altercation, in Ceylon. He must remember his ridiculous experiment with his H.Q. guards; he so wanted to revolutionise the Army. My brush with the man could possibly be the reason why, when asked, as he was on several occasions, the churlish gent declined invitations to join with us at the Officer's Mess. The man had to pass the Mess whenever attending dances. It possibly irked him to consider the necessity of inviting his wife, Edwina.

I was never sure whether Colonel Bob Poole put Mountbatten's reticence, and avoidance of the several invites, down to my previous encounter with the man.

A big day was the visit of, 'Gert and Daisy', (Elsie and Doris Waters), the entertainers, and top line comedienne's, of the era. Being the first day of their, 'troops entertainment tour', of India and Burma, everything was set for perfection. The travelling stage, and lighting, was set up on the football ground. In order to maximise attendance, invites were sent to all and sundry, within the Delhi region. The night was set for glory and success.

Although the two ladies offered their very best, the night proved a fiasco, glaring lights attracted flies of all description. It was as though all winged insects had deserted Delhi for the night, to such extent, that the dear ladies appeared as though in a fog. Biting insects showed tremendous interest in whatever flesh was available, and there was an ampleness to go at. I think that all future shows were programmed in daytime.

Noel Coward's show was a totally superior affair to that of the ill fated, 'Gert and Daisy'. His performance was staged in Vice-Regal Lodge, the home of the newly appointed Viceroy of India: Lord Archibald Wavell, and his dear wife, Lady Wavell. Wavell was moved out of military Command, as a result of his earlier rebuke, and his calling of Churchill's bluff, over his ABDA Command appointment. He was now in the world of indifference, at the time when; 'The Demand for Home Rule, in India', was seen as the triviality of the persistent Nationalists.

Coward performed on two evenings, one for the officers, and one for the troops. In these, his most magnificent of performances, he went through a repertoire of dozens of his highly popular songs. Operating from the Minstrel's Gallery, he was absolutely brilliant, with a few ribald jokes thrown in. Vice-Regal Lodge ballroom was crammed, and the temperature soared, as three or four times during the performance, Coward required to change his shirts. There can be few men who have witnessed such a performance as this one, and presented by, 'The Master!' One lovely memory is that of Lady Wavell, she made a point of circulating, and having a word with as many of the guests as possible.

Invited to take two of my men, to meet Coward, in one of the anti rooms, I pointed out that I had six of my ex-Burma boys with me. Lady Wavell was delighted to hear this, and all were invited. Coward had time for everyone, and wanted to hear of the men, and their feelings. It was incredible the way that he collared Michael Mycroft, the smallest and quietist man of the group. From a man that I recall receiving hardly a dozen words in months, Coward had him at singing pitch for well over twenty minutes. You don't get better than this!

The open air cinema was a fun thing, with all the best of black and white films on show. It attracted forces from far and wide, and Dolly came too. Nobody entered without a large bag of peanuts, and the four inch deep carpet of nut-shells was a pleasure to walk out over.

RAF CONTACT

From the Royal Air Force base, close by the attractive desert town of Jodpur, I received a steady stream of officers, and men, from the RAF Regiment; The special force, formed to undertake the defence of all Air

Force establishments. Introduced to 3" mortars; they required training, and our unit was favourably chosen. In dribs and drabs, three officers, and about two dozen men were accommodated. The men were well chosen, and relished the experience, getting on extremely well with my sergeants, and the mortar-men.

Resulting from the attachments of about one month duration for each man, I received, and appreciated, a response that I considered a tremendous compliment. At least a half of the NCO'S approached me, with a request to transfer to my platoon. There had to be some reason for these good men to seek such a change, particularly as they were possibly drawing better pay than mine.

A short time later, I realised the reason for the surprise transfer requests, as I along with three other Army officers, were nominated for a short attachment to the RAF, at Jodpur. It did not take long to appreciate the underlying problem of those requesting transfers. It was as though we were not expected, and there was no agenda for the attachment. In an off-hand way, the Officer Commanding brushed us aside, and passed all responsibility for our programme to a junior. One who had no idea; Why Army Infantry Officers should, 'want', to be attached to the RAF?

This was a case of; 'Help Yourself'. In the circumstances, we decided; 'To make do and mend!' We simply walked around, asking questions. It appeared that, the underlying gripe was that the unit did not like being saddled with obsolete Beaufighter aircraft. On taking off for flight, they were never sure whether it was for the last time. Of craft lost on exercises, and casualties, there was never a mention, but there had been more than one failure.

When asked if we could make a parachute jump, over the nearby desert, it was as though we were asking for the crown jewels. There was no expert to re-pack the 'chute'.

I did manage to express my regrets to several of my former pupils, and wished them well for the future.

THE TAJ BY MOONLIGHT

Novice driver training standards required to be put to the test and what better than the hundred and thirty miles trip to Agra? It would be criminal if we failed to discover a convenient mortar firing range on route. It was, 'all so difficult,' for me to think up a scheme, in order to test the squad; and, 'I was not daft?' Bob Poole smiled, with his OK! – As he put it to me, in that knowing manner, when granting approval.

As with most roads out of Delhi, the Agra road was rough, and carried variegated modes of transport – bullock-carts, camels, trucks, and grossly overcrowded buses. (The same road, on which I travelled recently, is now dual carriageway. It carries exactly the same selection of transport, and each road is equally congested, with no regard for lane discipline. Movement to north and south occurs on each of the two carriageways).

The surprise, in the fading light of day, was to see a porcupine cross the road a few yards to the front of my carrier. Having never before, or since, seen one, I thought of them as small animals, but I was surprised at the size of this one, the quills were erect, and its length covered almost a half the width of the road. Our attempts at following this gem of an animal into the brush was to no avail, and we continued to the Miadam (open space), in Agra, and pitched camp.

To see the Taj Mahal, in any circumstances, had been beyond my wildest dreams, but here we were, with the Taj at our mercy. The trick was, to see the whole of its splendour by moonlight, and we did exactly that. The massive wooden doors were closed, and very secure, until Sergeant Beckett gave them a rattle with the butt of his rifle; the chokidar, (watchman) arrived, and we entered. In our ignorance, and intending no harm, we violated the place by walking around wearing boots, but the awe in which a group of humble soldiers held the monument, was inspiring.

My recent visit to The Taj, in company with an art group, was very different, and much more deferential than the war-time performance. Having retained a little of the Urdu language, learnt in Army days, I used it when approaching the monument. It caused a small measure of consternation, amongst the few fussy women in the group, when I was permitted to wear my shoes. The attendant covered the offending garb with a plastic overshoe, and when asked; "Why the favouritism?" He simply replied; "Oh! He speaks the language!"

16

CHANGE OF COMMANDING OFFICER – DELHI

Returning from Agra, there was disappointment, in finding that time expired Colonel, Bob Poole, had departed, on repatriation to England. I never knew how he avoided the action in Burma, but I always felt that he would have been more impressive than those in charge at the time: Maybe? The surprise replacement for Poole was another senior, once again, one of those managing to miss the Burma conflict. It increasingly appeared, that numbers of the Battalion Regular Officers were absent from the unit, more than they served within; Particularly so to those of us who had arrived to meet with the unit in such a state of dereliction, and not one of the established officers in sight.

With Bob Poole gone, it was now time to take stock of his replacement. Poole was a tall, inspiring, raw boned motivator. The new man, Brownie Wood, was completely different in stature. He was shorter, and paunchy. Brownie had many long established contacts whilst previously Staff employed at Delhi, and fully intended continuing his pleasurable routine. Holding the exalted rank of Lieutenant Colonel, and commanding an infantry battalion in the locality, Brownie was eager to display his advancement. Immaculately turned out, and with the sweet smell of perfume, he boldly strode out, on his frequent visits to Delhi Cricket Club. What else mattered?

Regardless of our recent past, we, the Emergency Commissioned Officers, were rapidly put in our places. Wood was of the same gender as Cass, in Northern Ireland, in considering ECO's; 'beyond the pale'. To him, there was nothing to compare with, 'the cabal of regulars, recruited from traditional sources'. It was beneath Brownie to converse with upstarts. He knew absolutely 'sod all' of the gruelling actions his ECO's had been through, and did not want to know.

Pardon me, and disregarding the seeming setbacks, I don't mind carping on a bit, because it has to change, although I do feel one more will not go amiss.

Bootland, returned to the battalion, following repairs to his jaw damaged in Burma. He was the former Regimental Sergeant Major, and commissioned in haste, owing to the delay in the arrival of our draft. He was known as a most cynical and unpopular RSM, and the damage to his jaw, was considered to have been caused by a .303 bullet, one fired by one of our own men. All very regrettable!

My last sighting, of the man, had been, as I roped him onto a bullock cart, and sent him on his way, for fourteen or fifteen miles, to receive medical attention. There was not one word of thanks, or acknowledgement, from the man. He could be in no doubt about how his survival came about, but he was not going to give appreciation to junior officers, particularly ones, he considered to be, newly joined; upstarts! In a few short months, he had become; Just another, 'One of those!'

PEACOCKS IN JUNGLES

Jungle training at the Rudd site had been gentle, brief, and at the same time, enjoyably intensive, to a rather modest extent. To repeat the treatment with a similar session of commitment, so shortly afterwards, gave the impression of it being the call for a return to active service. Our required upgrade, and greater involvement, was to be made possible, following a spell of more intense jungle training. The site chosen was close by the small township of Alwar: situated approximately sixty miles west of Agra.

Camp was set in a remote area of fairly dense jungle. The whole thing had 'Brownie Wood' pleasantness about it. Officers had comfortable individual bell tents, with camp beds, and bedding, along with canvas wash basins. Compared with Burma conditions, this was a most delightful holiday camp. The RASC, (Royal Army Service Corps), excelled themselves, in their 'strenuous exercise'; ensuring that we were adequately provisioned, although the occasional, 'blue buck', (a deer about the size of a mule), supplemented rations.

Absolute delight of this place was the Muster of Peacocks. They were numerous, and centred at a point on the track leading towards the camp. It really was by pure accident that somebody shot one! I think? It was plucked, dressed, cooked and served in short time. So delicious, and differing from all other fowl, it is a most unforgettable feast.

With any excuse, and whatsoever 'accident', there was a steady flow of birds to the cookhouse. Brownie Wood did become a little concerned, in his thinking, "the Maharajah might not like us taking them so freely". The man loved them! And food was a hobby of his.

Following the porcupine into the bush earlier, when near Agra, was one thing, but 'no-way', was I going to follow the two visitors departing my tent. It was when within twenty yards distant, and about to enter, a pair of leopards walked out. Ignoring me, they walked off, strolled down the narrow trail, to vanish amongst the trees. The pair of them, both far bigger than I imagined a leopard to be, and their casual saunter, was one of complete indifference.

Compared to the rigorous, live ammunition firing, Jungle Warfare School, at Ranchi, the Alwar Training Camp proved to be, no more strenuous, than one specially prepared for Girl Guides, very young ones; with due apologies girls!

Public relations with the Alwar villagers flourished in a big way, resulting from the series of football matches, playing against three combinations of local talent; the town team; the army team, and a joint, town and army, team. Attendance was a full house on each of the three occasions, and our team won each game by a small margin.

The spectacular reaction was as we left the stadium, following each match. Our players were applauded by crowds filling the narrow streets. The local idea of goal-keeping was that of a man standing in the centre of the goalposts, and gently moving from right to left, or left to right. They had never before seen goalkeeping in which the keeper advanced, to dive at the feet of attackers, and our man, Simpson, was spectacular. Brownie Wood enjoyed the feel of this rare, and unusual ambient reception, particularly one bestowed by the local populace, equally as well as he did, the peacock feasts.

BRIBERY

Regimental Sergeant Major Wilkinson, of the Army, Special Investigation Branch, introduced himself, and, at the same time, politely introduced several 'guests'. They were to become new residents for the regimental guardroom. The senior, and central member, of the new and novel intake, was, Major EEE Dunnett, of the RIASC, (The Royal Indian Army Service Corps). He was a short man, could be considered diminutive, at a little over 5'- 0" in height. What he lacked in height, he made up for in girth. He was a little fat man!

Drawing out the reason for internment of such numbers of officers, took a little time. RSM Wilkinson was not SIB for no good reason. The revelation was done in stages, and funnily enough, nobody was greatly surprised. Dunnett had been displaying entrepreneurial skills, and profiting considerably. Having denied a generous share of his profits, to his Sikh head clerk, the Sikh gentleman was now reformed, and turning against his master, he became chief witness for the prosecution.

Dunnett was Officer in Charge, of all RIASC Regimental junior officer movements, and appointments: A job screaming for exploitation! The chubby-chappie was controller of, promotions, postings, and appointments, within the Corps. In the way of Indian practice, philosophy, and exploiting the job: Dunnett had a range of long established prices for all transactions. There was a scale of charges, according to importance; from probably one hundred pounds, to three hundred pounds. Charges applied: For promotion, from 2nd Lieutenant; to Lieut, and, to Captain: To be taken off a draft to the Middle Eastern conflict: Transfers into a more favourable unit: To be appointed, a lucrative, 'Local Purchase Officer', (particularly if daddy just happened, 'by chance', to be, the Regional Army Catering Contractor). All other moves were available, for a consideration, and at a price! It was an Indian thing!

Such was the extent of Dunnett's, 'fiddle', that, over a period of eighteen months, there was, at all times, at least six prisoners detained in the Delhi Barracks guardroom. The top rank prisoner was a Lieutenant Colonel, one reportedly married to an Indian Princess. Whenever the lady visited, she was accompanied by an entourage of beauties, and they were dressed in colours of every hue. It was as though, a walking tapestry, and we were never to know their duties.

Dunnett had an entitlement to comfort breaks. This meant, allowing him visits to his girlfriend, a young and attractive beauty. She was settled in a lush apartment, at Connaught Circus, in central Delhi. He was at all times, accompanied by an officer, from our unit, and none missed noticing, the female was much younger, and strikingly good looking. No matter how much anybody tried, and they did: There was no hope of dislodging Mr Wilkinson from his own casual, and private, 'comfort stops' with the same young beauty.

With the steady flow of culprits over the eighteen month period, throughout which the Battalion hosted the comings and goings, it would be hard to know the exact numbers. Legal costs involved, must have been prohibitive. All prisoners were defended by a senior barrister, Sir Tej Bahadur Sapru. The gentleman travelled from Bombay, to Delhi, and charged what was at the time, the exorbitant fee, £100-00, (One hundred pounds), per day.

JAPANESE P.O.W.

My rather frequent, maybe too frequent meetings, with Dolly, established me as a familiar figure amongst the Indian Military Hospital staff. Visits were usually of little consequence, except on the occasion I arrived as a skirmish was taking place near the entrance. Two new patients were causing a stir in a corridor, and on assisting in their apprehension, I was surprised to find that they were both Japanese.

Assisting in escorting the pair, I came across something that I knew absolutely nothing about. There was a surprise feature contained within two of the hospital wards, both were heavily secured with barbed wire. The wards were located at one end of the premises. It was a secret area, but entering as an escort, it gave me free access.

On subsequent visits to this high security preserve, the Indian Army guards readily accepted me. Delicacy was the watchword, and silence ruled, as some of the occupants were known to speak English. It was up to me to use my own eyes, and what I saw came as quite a surprise.

Few people had knowledge of captured Japanese prisoners of war, but here were between thirty, and forty, of them. The general tone of the place was, one of happiness, and shear joy. These men were enjoying regular meals, and with no duties to perform. There was humour, and it transpired, very few departed, once received into the hospital. The Danish doctor in charge was becoming an expert in the treatment of arm amputations, as about one third of the prisoners, had one hand missing. I was not advised of the cause of the injuries until some time later, when called out for special duties.

Because of my having been in action against the Japanese, Brownie Wood appeared to think that I had all knowledge, and that I could speak the language, which I could not. On the strength of this, I, along with Dennis Chadwick, was selected to take a company, of about 60 men, on a visit to Bikaneer; wherever that was to be found?

Little was said of our duties, except that they were to be unusual, and sure enough, they were. The small township of Bikaneer is possibly two hundred miles into the desert, on a branch railway line, shooting off north, from the main, Delhi to Bombay line. It was a single line track, with passing places. The mile after mile, of desert terrain, was a flat uninteresting plain, with sparse shrubs, and the occasional small band of nomads.

On arrival at Bikaneer, the task on hand was to assist in controlling, and monitoring, two compounds; each of them, containing a surprising number of Japanese Prisoners of War. In Delhi hospital I had met with the sick, but had no idea of this remote prison location, or the numbers involved.

Situated on the edge of the desert, there were about one hundred or more prisoners. All were contained within two barbed wire enclosures, and for added security, the prison camp was sited a short distance away from the township. The two circular compounds, one small, and one about double the size of the smaller one, were no more than one hundred meters apart. At all times, there was reported, a considerable amount of shouting between the two compounds.

It was clear to the local security force; a number of the communications resulted in men being mutilated, by the amputation of a hand. Apparently, there was fear, and an absolute silence, regarding the cause of amputations. In an escalating scale of Japanese imposed punishments, there had recently been a series of five or six executions, hence, the call for assistance, and from a British Military Regiment.

A fluent, Japanese speaking Englishman had been recruited onto the camp staff. He was, in no way, to converse with prison inmates. His task was to listen, and interpret commands, and conversation, as shouted between the two compounds. Not one Japanese officer disclosed themselves, all fronted up as being of equal rank. It became imperative that the guards identify Japanese Officers.

The object of the exercise, in so far as it affected our attachment, was to ensure a strict control of segregation, and abstract individuals where necessary. We were there to ensure smoothness in several transfers, forwards, and backwards, between the two compounds. This was in order that ones; those identified as officers, or ringleaders, could be segregated, and detained for special treatment.

With fixed bayonets, we formed two lines, about twenty meters apart, and made clear our requirements, as one by one, individuals moved between the two compounds. The Japanese speaking Englishman, simply, and quietly, announced a number. That number identified an individual, and he was taken to one side.

Unhurried, the operation continued over four days, and taking less than two hours on each occasion, there was time for other 'duties'.

Challenge football matches were played, similar to those previously, at Alwar. Three games were played against, the military (Camel Corps), the town civilians, and a joint military/town team. With marginal wins, our players were, once again, as at Alwar, applauded through the town. Goalkeeper Simpson was given 'star billing'.

The town's British doctor introduced me to dingy sailing, on the nearby reservoir. A cocktail party, given in our honour was a lavish affair, with the Prime Minister, and all top officials attending.

Reciprocating, we did our best. Not having a lot of booze, we decided that a nice punch would be appropriate, and returned the compliment, which was eagerly accepted.

Housed in the Dak Bungalow, (Post House), we were short of a bowl in which to mix the punch, but that was no problem! There was a Companion Set, comprised of coal scuttle, brush and shovel, one with a lovely brass blade. Nothing daunted, the scuttle was given a really good rinse out. The gin and mix were poured in, and all gently stirred with the brass bladed shovel. There was a miracle before our eyes, as the highly polished shovel emerged from the scuttle, the shiny brass had vanished. We had a problem!

Do we? Or do we not? Serve the metal tinged punch, with the guests already assembled. We did serve, to generous acclaim, and received a gesture beyond our wildest dreams.

Dennis Chadwick and I were called apart by the Prime Minister, in order to show us his intentions. The dear boy had a telegram, it was readily made out to General Wavell; now the Indian Viceroy. The message ran; "Imperative K.O.Y.L.I. detachment remain, and meet Maharajah!" Unfortunately, His Eminence, was absent from the State for a few days, and due to return shortly.

In normal circumstances, there could be no finer accolade, but the timing was not normal. Wavell was scheduled to present five Victoria Crosses. Such was the ceremony, it required to be a showy and dressy affair, and conducted close by the Red Fort in Delhi. The medals were going to Gurkha, and Indian troops. Wavell required a showpiece, with a background of white troops, and we were, 'the decoration!'

It was not easy to convince the Prime Minister, and to get him to withdraw the signal, but he did, very reluctantly. It was such that, had the signal been sent, Wavell would have no alternative, but to acquiesce.

The gesture did not finish at that, it continued as we boarded the train the following morning. Along came a bearer with a half dozen box of Johnny Walker Whisky. It was a gift for our services.

Given time to think further on the pleasant episode, one realised that this was an Indian State, and not, 'British India'. No doubt, this was the reason why Bikaneer Camel Corps, did not become involved in disciplining the Japanese. The Maharajah would be exceedingly well recompensed, for housing prisoners of war.

5 – VICTORIA CROSSES

On the day of the Victoria Cross presentations, it was hot, in the way that Delhi gets, almost unbearably hot. Fronting a Company, I stood no more than five meters in front of the presentation dais. In the frustrating way of these occasions, we were stood around for a good hour before Wavell appeared, he was never a fast mover, (Except when leaving Burma), and he took some time in getting to the point of what he was about. Stories were told of valour shown by medal recipients, and the young boys had proved gallant, and were well worthy of decoration.

Listening to the eulogies, I realised that each, and every one of them, referred to the new, combined British assault, the one commenced in 1943, and currently taking place, in Burma. Not one of them was for the discarded, 1942 army: unfed, unarmed, and un-provisioned in every way, in the testing withdrawal, endured by my Regiment two years previous: Wavell had, 'washed his hands' of the diabolical fiasco, Burma 1942, withdrawal, and Churchill, very conveniently, stood firmly by his maxim: "No war was won in retreat".

I regret not exploding, and reminding Wavell of his shoddy departure from his recent command, in Burma. I should have pointed out that there were at least half a dozen men standing behind me, on that parade, equally deserving of meritorious recognition. Of course, our dithering CO, whilst in Burma: was long departed, to happier times, with no more than a token decoration. Why would he think of others? There was much for him to forget.

It is in later life that one realises, and identifies, the shortcomings of individuals. Those considered, at one time, to be superior; in whatever field. Churchill was such an individual, in that he isolated himself. He gave no recognition, or consideration, to equating the relativity of actions undertaken in; Hong Kong, Singapore, and Burma. To him, they were by-passed, and overlooked. It was as though those campaigns never happened.

Perfectly fit, when setting forth on the medal soiree, it was on returning to barracks I was surprised to see the size of the calf on my right leg. Above my puttees, the leg looked to be twice its normal size. In so short a time, it had swollen to such a degree that I was immediately admitted to hospital.

With two generous cuts, to allow for an outflow of liquid, I was admitted to a six man ward, to see more magic. A fellow officer admitted to the ward, was so ill, that he was pronounced dead, on arrival. Within seconds, a doctor entered the ward, and instantly, plunged a syringe, of some kind, into the man's chest. Almost, as though nothing had happened, the man continued a conversation, so briefly interrupted by the doctor. It was as though witnessing the performance of a miracle.

BACK TO TYPE

Stationed in the splendour of Delhi Cantonment, the developing conflict in Northern Burma was remote, and army life had that peace-time feel. It was such that ability counted for little, and as it must, the shoulder badge of seniority prevailed. Whenever senior ranks returned to the unit, from whatever source, they expected instant respect of their badge, from all of junior rank. So long as Brownie Wood could visit the cricket club, he was happy, and spoke, very selectively, to chosen juniors. I was not one of his favourites, and was precluded from his, 'old school', circle of chums. I had long realised that it irked him, to have occasion to speak to me, an ECO, particularly one from humble origins. He spoke to me when required, by protocol, and I button-holed him periodically, when he simply had to speak.

One by one, my six sergeants attended the Small Arms School; 3" Mortar Course, situated at Saugar. Each in turn returned, qualified; 'D' (Distinguished). With success results of this standing, it was a requirement, that the C.O. invite the successful individual into his office, accompanied by the Platoon Officer, and to compliment the two of them. I could not help feeling that Wood resented this 'repetitive' duty, as I can not remember him having a word to say to me otherwise. He was happy enough to see me performing a dual role, in both Company, and Platoon Command, so long as 'He' obtained pleasurable accolades, from higher echelons. The succession of top results, obtained by my sergeants at the Saugar training school, indicated that I was doing something right. Resulting from this, I was never questioned on the specialisation that I had made my own.

Unspoken, and unthinking, the *modus-operandi*, or way of working, in the mortar platoon, was never questioned, or given senior rank consideration. The atmosphere erupted, and Brownie Wood stooped to attend a mortar demonstration for the first time. It happened because he had received a most gracious letter of thanks from the Chief of Air Command, India, for our care, and indulgence, in dealing with his mortar trainees.

Brownie Wood agitated me greatly, and in a manner in which only he could, when the Battalion Adjutant vacancy arose. My service, and duties, qualified me perfectly for the holding of my dual appointment; Company, and Platoon Commander. It was generally accepted that the job was mine. Wood, however, selected a fellow officer, one with considerably less experience than me. It was never said, but I suspected that; whatever token handshake he made, he did not want to be in close contact with a Roman Catholic, day by day. The officer selected, was a delightful individual, and he did the job, and conducted himself in the most admirable manner. He just happened to be one of those, from one of the classy Public Schools.

Long serving, 'Togo', Sergeant Major Crossland, recognised the deliberate snub, and reassured me, in grand manner: "He'd have a bloody job finding somebody to do your job!" Thank you Togo!

MILITARY SUBTERFUGE

When in command of men, either military or civilian, there are always the few, one or two, that stand out, for whatever reason. There are many ways individuals distinguish themselves; humour, diligence, loyalty etc., and I had several such. Private Peter King, a young man from one of Manchester's renowned boxing families, was a dedicated soldier; exuberant, and never less than bubbly, nothing daunted him, and never once did he require a prompt, or a disciplinary caution.

It was on Minden Day, 1st August 1944, the traditional day of Regimental celebration, and like many others, Peter had; 'Had the proverbial, skin-full'. This became a tragedy, and one masked in unexplained, and unfathomable, military subterfuge.

The following morning, 2nd August, when arriving at 6.00 hrs, for my squad regular, 'Road Run and Walk'; I found a body, lying at the base of the two-story barrack block. The body was close in, and actually touching the wall. It lay in such a position that it was not immediately identifiable, and, at first, I mistook it as being that of another person.

Speculation became rife, as Peter was known to have attempted to join a drinks party in an upper floor room, one occupied by a rather truculent Transport Sergeant, Ash, and he had been rejected. Once the body was identified, and all medical checks completed, I conducted Peter's burial service at the nearby cemetery.

Shortly following, after much speculation, and the general condemnation of one particular individual, a Court of Enquiry was formed; it comprised of, Major Dennis Chadwick, Chairman; Captain John Sellers; and me, Captain Gerald Fitzpatrick.

With eight or nine people to interview, and one individual highly suspect, the Enquiry entered into its second day, only to meet with a most unexpected, and extraordinary interference. The Brigadier, Garrison Commander, intervened in an unusually brusque, and overbearing, manner. He approached the desk we were using, and collected the papers, by sweeping them into a folder, and called a halt to the proceedings with the words: "We'll sort this out!" He then vanished, with no conversation as to the outcome. The motives of a Brigadier are not to be questioned!

To have questioned the pronounced outcome, of the Brigadier's declared "sort out", would have been interpreted as insubordination. This would be followed by a subtle posting, to some remote outpost. It was a situation requiring discretion! Mouths were shut! Senior Military action, in peacetime, is sacrosanct!

This is a glaring example, of a higher rank British Army Officer asserting himself, on the basis of; 'the badge on the shoulder', and the resignation of juniors, with unquestionable acquiescence to seniority. Considering the glaring disrespect, and temerity, shown by the Brigadier, and with the action seriously affecting one of his men, Brownie Wood, the submissive Battalion Commanding Officer, failed to show any further interest in the tragic loss of a good soldier.

The galling situation, obtaining in this situation, was that; One, 'Top Senior Officer', was not prepared to have the stigma of a possible manslaughter, or murder accusation, undertaken within his Command. And for a Battalion Commander, to succumb to his amoral senior, is unforgivable. Even more-so, considering, that we were in a peace station. Peter's family did not receive the traditional death announcement, and letter of condolence from the CO, in a way that is *de rigueur,* in the military.

Taking the scandal a little further: There is no mention of Peter King's death, taking place on the 1st / 2nd August 1944, on the Regimental Roll of Honour, held in the Regimental Chapel, at York Minster. The boy remains unmentioned in all Regimental documentation, although I have attempted, on more than one occasion, to ascertain what sort of story Peter's family were told. I have no idea. For them to have received no letter from Peter, following his meticulous, and weekly correspondence, must have caused anxiety.

Visiting the KOYLI Regimental Office, at Pontefract, in September 2009, and questioning further, the recording of Peter's death, on the date, 1/2 August 1944, the date that I knew that he had died, and on which I found his body, I received a shock.

The death is recorded on the wrong date. It gives no cause of death: Number 3715653, Private Peter King, is shown as, 'Died in India' on 9th February 1945. This was six months after he died. Why the Garrison Brigadier had reason to distort the date of Peter's death, I do not know. There was good reason to suspect foul play, and although I continued to search out the 'cause' of death, as conveyed to the boy's family. I failed!

Remarkable! Following my search of numerous MOD channels, it is now 7th December 2009, and today, I receive an answer from the Historical Disclosures Section, of the Army Personnel Centre, at Glasgow. The document is dated 03 December 2009, reference, D/APC/HD/ABLT/180911, and contains references to seven further Army Forms.

The Executive Officer states;

" 3715653 Private Peter King"

"I have examined the file relating to the above named and I can confirm that every note regarding his death from multiple fractures of the skull gives the date as 10th February 1945. This date is recorded on".

(He goes on to relate the seven forms mentioned above).

As his Company Commander, on Friday 28th July 1944, I paid him his final army payment.

(In the platoon group photograph, Peter King is central, two rows behind me, and immediately behind my batman, Ted Hewitt).

My contact with former erstwhile seniors, continued spasmodically, after the war. I met face to face, with Geoffrey Chadwick, the Burma Campaign ditherer, in his home town of Harrogate, and pointedly snubbed him, after giving him the opportunity to speak. Another one, was when attending the 1991 presentation of new KOYLI Regimental Colours, by the Queen Mother at Tidworth. I heard that Brownie Wood, of Delhi fame, was in attendance. Setting forth, to give him a piece of my mind, in the way that it can be done in civilian life, I was told; "That's him, down there, he's in the wheelchair". I had all the words ready to give him a full work-over, although, on seeing him, I stopped short. The man was wizened and shrunk, from being the bouncy, and fat, Battalion Commander. He was huddled over in a chair, and struck with blindness. I humbled myself, and said, "Hello!"

WHERE DID THE MONEY GO?

As Company Commander, of Headquarter Company, one of my tasks was to conduct, Friday, 'Payday'. In the normal way of things, I collected the pay; Seven bundles, of five-hundred rupees each; (approximately, three-hundred and fifty pounds). Stuffing the notes down my battle-dress top, I returned to Company Office, and, as a daily duty, went around to the cook-house, to ensure that all was well. Taking my bicycle, I went to deposit the cash in the metal chest in my bungalow.

Finding that one of the bundles had gone missing, I retraced my movements, finishing at the PRI; (President of the Regimental Institute, Office), to see fellow officer, John Sellers. All searches were to no avail, it therefore required my seeing, Brownie Wood, the CO, in order to borrow money. It was on the basis, that I would have cash sent from England. I have no doubt that Wood, considered the money had gone elsewhere, although he had no alternative but to acquiesce.

Not too long a time later, following my return to England, I had no chance to speak first, when at the Morpeth Holding Unit I was approached by Pinder, one of my star Sergeants. "Let me speak Sir? Was his unusual approach, "I know who stole your money!" Needles to say, this took me by surprise, and I was, 'all ears'. Pinder named two of the officers in my Company, saying, the two of them; (One was Transport Officer, and one Signals), had bought booze. They blurted out the truth, when drunk, shortly following my departure.

The Transport Officer became lost to me, and the other rogue, flourished as, 'a supposedly', honest solicitor? In two townships, quite near to my home.

Suffering another loss, I was in no doubt, about who stole a smaller amount of cash. It vanished when I went for my early morning swim. Again, it was a fellow officer, one newly introduced to our regiment, from another similar unit. In meeting up with former colleagues of the rogue, ones from his former Regiment, they were not surprised at my deducing, and assessment, of the man.

IT DID HAPPEN

Throughout my, 'trials and tribulations; Oh Boy!' Of Delhi, there was the comforting company of Dolly, my favourite nurse, and dance partner. We had much in common, resulting from our first date, when walking out to a copse of trees, in the centre of what turned out to be, the parade ground of the Rajput Regiment. Within seconds, we were surrounded from all sides by Sepoys, (Indian soldiers), and there was no point in arguing. The pair of us were apprehended, and secured in a guardroom cell.

It was only when I asked to see Captain Scott, a friend of mine, that we were released. It was something that I could not report to Brownie

Wood, as he would, possibly, and rightfully, see me as being the one at fault. He did not like our meeting with nurses from the Indian Hospital; Of all places! Dancing with them in the gymnasium was considered a completely different matter.

There does not appear to be much point, in detailing Dolly's visits to my bungalow, and remarking on simply how stunning she looked, stepping down from a tonga, in a sparkling white dress, and matching shoes. It was spellbinding!

Richardson, the Mess Sergeant, and former Burma boy, ensured that my, double food order, was brought to the bungalow, and the evening invariably went swimmingly along. It was always a private affair, with everybody, all two of us, leaving on most affable terms.

I think my dear friend, Mountbatten, had an eye for the girl. Whenever he attended the monthly dance, he would make a point of booking himself a dance with her. Several of us wondered, why he did not dance, with one or two of his ever accompanying boy-friends.

How on earth it happened, I do not know, but there came a time when, with four months of swelling beginning to show in the tummy, Dolly was relieved of her duties at the Indian hospital. She was housed in the British Military Hospital. It was here, they formed an opinion that she was within months of producing a little one. She had known all along that, owing to other commitments, I was in no position to do the right thing by her,

From a Madras family with ten children, Dolly was one of a mix of boys, and girls. The youngest of whom, was a boy aged nine, whom she considered a precocious little 'so and so'. With the grandiose name of Arnold George Dorsey, he was a very sprightly, and lively, youngster, one who threw himself into everything with gusto. What this young man did not know, however, that, at some time in the future, he was to become, highly distinguishable, and known internationally.

Walking Dolly out from the hospital one evening, I asked; "What will you call the child, if a boy?" Her answer took me aback somewhat, as I had never before heard the name; "Englebert Humperdink". She gave me detail of the gentleman, his history, and his writings. He had actually lived in my time.

Being parted, and posted with the unit, I maintained contact with her, at 4b, Springhaven Road, Harbour, Madras. In due course of time, she produced a son at Bangalore Hospital. There was, however, the inevitable break; Dolly's family moved house, and I was required to comply with regimental postings.

Several years later, there came along this singing phenomenon, changing his name in stages; From George Dorsey, to Gerry Dorsey, (Where did Gerry come from?); and then, with a further remarkable twist, to become; International Singing Star; Englebert Humperdink.

It became somewhat irritating to me, when the general public were led to believe, that the manager of Humperdink, had suggested adopting the ostentatious and outlandish title.

There was only one place that such exuberant frontage could have come from. How could I not believe that this 'skylark' was mine, in view of the forecast made by Dolly, at Delhi.

Many years later, when attending the Cheltenham wedding of one of Dolly's charming daughters, I met with Englebert. He turned out to be a man of great charm, but a little arrogant, and why not, with his international recognition, and a bank balance, sufficient to sustain a small nation. My son, born to Dolly, was there too, and I met with him for the first time, tragically, we did not, 'get on', in a way that should have been much more pleasant.

*Patricia with
Arnold George Dorsey
(Humperdink)*

*and with
his personalised limo*

241

17

FAREWELL TO INDIA

SULTANS BATTERY

Luxury of Delhi ceased, the time came to join in the conflict raging in Burma. This meant serious training, in order to join with those benefiting from the Ranchi Battle School training, now adopting the name; 'Chindits'. Once again, the chosen twosome, Dennis Chadwick and I, were detailed to take companies to a training camp at Betmangala; (a jungle training centre, better known as, 'Sultan's Battery'). Sparsely equipped, the camp was situated in Southern India, about sixty miles south of Bangalore,

Accommodation was less than inviting, consisting of a series of spacious barn like structures. The surrounding jungle was unpretentious, and unforgiving, with a strong thorny briar, known to us from Burma days, as 'Lengtana'. This main foliage, with animal-like thorns, was almost metallic, and on contact, inflicted severe cuts.

As a matter of urgency, and in anticipation of what might be to come, we were at panic stations. Having received a series of injections, for a multitude of tropical ailments, there was a call for one extra, Tetanus; This real killer, was known to be rife throughout the area, and required urgent attention. Activities halted for two days, as reactions to the jabs varied enormously, with individuals incapacitated, for up to two or three days. The main sufferer being Hayes, a young officer, he remained laid out, stiff as a board, for four days: *(Remaining in the Army, Hayes became a very senior officer).* He could have died, as the doctor was only programmed to visit weekly. The boy was recovered before the next visit.

Urgent competition for the camp 'swill contract' was keen, beyond both Chadwick's, and my own comprehension. The seemingly odious contract provided for the rights, to wash, and clean, the leavings of food; from soldiers mess plates, and take whatever other mealtime scrapings there may be. Within hours of our arrival, we were approached by contractor Number One. He made what we considered a high bid, of fifty rupees. The man had hardly left camp, before contractor Number Two appeared, with an instantly higher offer, of two hundred rupees. Surprise! Surprise! Number Two had hardly vanished before, in came contractor Number Three, and he made the unbelievably generous offer, of four hundred rupees.

The feeling was, that we two British Army Officers, were, somehow, 'being taken for a ride?' But what was it in the plot that we were missing? The coveted, and competitive contract, was assigned to entrepreneur number three. And we were left guessing.

Gentleman Number Three duly arrived, well before breakfast, complete with bullock cart, and a selection of containers. From a distance, he appeared to do all that was required, within his four hundred rupee; (thirty pounds, per month), contract. Nothing was seen to which exception could be taken.

Not satisfied with what I had seen conducted close by the Dining Hall, I collared Private Bill Kibbler, a man with granite like stature, to join me in a long distance surveillance of the bullock cart. In a very proper manner, the cart and driver proceeded up a long straight incline. It was when on the horizon, the cart took a left hand turn, which seemed to be perfectly innocent, except that it came to a sudden halt. The cart was halted, and the shafts lifted heavenward.

Within seconds, Kibbler and I were at the cart, to find the precious swill spilled around on the ground: Goodness gracious me!

The enterprising gent appeared to be somewhat bemused, and possibly a little sad, to see several tins of cookhouse provisions standing around in the excremental stench. There were; tins of fruit, jam, bully beef, soya sausages, and a generous mix of goodies, all from rations issued for consumption by our squad of trainees.

243

Whatever treacherous deal had been done, it was clearly, done by the shrewd old soldier, and dedicated cook, Sammy Rose, a man placed in a position of considerable trust. Unfortunately, there were no facilities with which to punish Rose, but in no way was he going to ride roughshod over my men.

Far better than putting the rogue into the comfort of a cell, it simply required for him to be made known; the perpetrator of an evil conspiracy. Once the men knew of the foul deed, it was for them to take action, and they did just that.

Ever the entrepreneur, Sammy was not finished. On demobilisation from the Army, and finding access to a goodly supply of timber, he travelled the streets of Leeds with a donkey and cart, hawking fire-wood.

TIGER TERRITORY

Bangalore, the name had such alluring appeal, we simply had to visit. Rough as the road was, it was something of a challenge, but with so resonant a name as Bangalore, and being within striking distance, it was a must. Scintillating! Spellbinding! At the sight of a lifetime, the truck in which we were travelling was halted, instantly. On the far side of the narrow river running parallel with the road, was a tiger, no more than about thirty meters distant from our halt. We were indeed privileged, to watch a full grown tiger, on the far bank of the river, as he slurped for a drink. Carrying weapons, we could easily have sought to take a trophy, but watching such a fantastically beautiful animal, with seemingly almighty power, it was unthinkable.

The big boy took his drink, and completed his ablutions, before striding off majestically, into the surrounding jungle. There was never a thought that, in pursuing our jungle training, we might meet with our pussy cat friend once again, but under different circumstances, and he might not be quite as forgiving as were we.

Apart from spectacular Colonial buildings, Bangalore was renowned for its strawberries, and they had been a very rare luxury in my early life, so I wanted some.

Overwhelming was the choice of the town's two famous restaurants, there was Big Bunny's, and there was Little Bunny's. Big Bunny's was the smaller of the two, so we chose to visit Little Bunny's, the bigger one. It was here that I made the dreadful mistake of choosing a shellfish based meal, and paid the price. Within hours, I was shivering and shaking. Suffering wracking pain, and with a high temperature. Ted Hewitt, was convinced that I was about to die. He nursed me through three nauseating days of vomiting, and diarrhoea.

I appreciated this attention, and Hewitt never forgot it. At times he remembered too much. It was long after the war, my wife and I visited him, and his delightful wife, at Bournemouth. His dear lady demonstrated her interpretation of Hewitt's related stories of our experiences. Seeing me purchase a scoop of prawns from a kiosk stall, Hewitt exploded, and reminded me of his wartime attentions, but his wife went one better than that. Totally indifferent to whomsoever might be around, and there were plenty, she made a grab for my lower regions, and appeared to be rather pleased, as she commented; "Not much up front!" I had no reason to be surprised.

KOLAR GOLD FIELD

How it happened, I do not know, although I am happy to put it down to catching myself on a dangerous Lengtana thorn bush. I developed a huge abscess on the back of my thigh. The thing proved painful, it became very swollen, and one of the attendants at the medical aid centre received pleasure in squeezing the brute. It was such that, I was denied a can of beer, in celebration of the news of V.E. Day: (Victory in Europe).

Afraid of the possibility that I might suffer the loss of my leg I was transferred to hospital, at Kolar Gold Field; (A territory between Bangalore, and Madras). This place was pristine beyond my expectations, the place virtually sparkled. Totally out of keeping with all surroundings, it was spacious, and the staff immaculately turned out. Not only that, it had a most exceptional member of staff. It's not a generality that one remembers the manner in which a person speaks, but this one was very special. The speech had tone, and articulation, remembered beyond anything I have heard since. The rhythm was so precise, and so modulated, it could be related to a melody.

The man speaking in such delightful manner was a tall, elegant, slim, doctor. His demeanour, and humbling attendance, equalled his vocal excellence, such that I recall him, as possibly, the most admirable professional I have met with in my life. I do not know of his origins, but he was as black as the ace of spades. In my brief stay, and being under his attendance, I did not have the cheek to enquire of his origins, lest he consider me, much too personal.

It was at Kolar Gold Field that I heard of the death, from a brain haemorrhage, of US President, Franklin D Roosevelt. He had died on the 12th April 1945, less than a month before the surrender of Germany. His furtive, secretive, and useless, "pact with Japan", made only days before, the Pearl Harbour, American Fleet hiatus, died with him. As with the Churchill's signal discarding Burma; The secretive, short term 'Peace Pact' with Japan was revealed, many years later, long after the death of Roosevelt.

My return to the unit was brief, as I got caught up with, 'Python'; (A scheme made possible following the conquest of Germany, whereby I qualified for one month home leave, and return to rejoin the unit),

Departing the unit, for possibly three months; travelling by troopship two ways and home for a month; was a drag on my conscience. So long an absence seemed a long time for me to be away from the team I loved working with; it was as though they were a part of me. It was a treat, however, at Bombay, to once again, meet up with my trustworthy Burma colleague, Steve, along with others of our outwards draft. Steve had spent three years commanding a transit camp; others had undertaken alternative duties.

One deck on the troopship was occupied by a group of lively African soldiers. All had missing limbs, either legs, or arms. It was as though they enjoyed the handicap, as there appeared to be no stopping their laughter. The boys were disembarked in a diversion to Mombassa, and with the ceasing of hostilities in Europe, there was no requirement to round the Cape of South Africa, and we continued through the Suez Canal. Enjoying a pleasant stop at Alexandria, for just a bit of shopping, and on through the Mediterranean Sea.

Arriving home, in Leeds, on 6th August 1945, I had hardly settled in, before the wireless news announced that America had dropped two atom bombs on Japan. Within days, the war in the East terminated.

Having enjoyed India in the time I was there, I would have loved to return, but it was all to change, so rapidly. 'Airbrushed out of British history', and mentioned only when expedient, is the appalling situation created on the departure of; 'The Last Viceroy'; Mountbatten, Lord Louis, of that ilk. He succeeded Archie Wavell.

On 20th February 1947, following the period of being 'carried' by others; Supreme Military Commander, was relieved of Command, and, as was Wavell, he was shunted into the backwaters. Succeeding Wavell, and given the 'poisoned chalice'; Mountbatten was appointed, 'Viceroy of India'.

It came as no surprise to me, after only six months of being in office, on 15 August 1947, to hear the termination of Mountbatten's Vice-Regal tenancy. The Union Flag was run down, and in all haste, the British withdrew from India.

In a state of absolute chaos, the vast 'Indian State' erupted, as it was left to sort itself out. Mountbatten vanished from India, in the same shameful manner that Alexander and others, had vanished from Burma. In the haste of departure, there was no coordinated transition. In the resultant carnage between religious sects, as the one country became two; 'India' and 'Pakistan', unknown numbers were slain, including 1,200 fleeing Muslims, massacred on a train, by Sikhs, at Amritsar, in the Punjab.

Indian Independence was brought about by Mahatma Ghandi, and the, 'All India Congress Party'.

I find no record of Mountbatten visiting Burma throughout the period in which he was designated Supreme Commander. With his complete lack of Eastern, and jungle warfare knowledge, he would require to be 'carried', by all and sundry. However, he had the cheek and audacity that went with his status, to grab the honour: "Mountbatten of Burma". That title was rightfully the property of Bill Slim! A more appropriate title would have been "Mountbatten of The Kelly". To him, it was as if no other ship had been sunk, and the irritating remote Royal self publicist, traded on the disaster for the rest of his life. It ended, aged 79, in 1979, off the coast of County Sligo, in Ireland.

EXPERIENCE

The boy, born of an Irish mother, and raised through the depression of the 1920s and 1930s, coming from a humble, and poverty ridden Leeds working class area, was returned to his family roots: Almost! By some miracle, my parents had moved, from the two bedroom cellar-kitchen, back to back terrace house, with no hot water, and a shared outside toilet. The new residence, was an end of terrace, three bedroom house, with indoor bathroom, and toilet, situated alongside a desirable park, in which mother cultivated a war-time allotment. Knowing that such a move could never be made on my father's indifferent, and irregular earnings, I realised that mother had received Divine Intervention; from her two brothers, long settled in America. One regret, I do have, is that I have never been able to contact the American family, to thank them. I do seriously thank them, for recognising my being commissioned into the British Army, when their true allegiance and affiliations, would be towards the Irish Republican Army.

I could have spent my wartime, 'glued' to a drawing board, and being controlled at whim, by conscientious objectors. But I did better than that!

I had enjoyed, the wonderful three month journey, by troopship and train, from Glasgow to Rangoon. It included, enduring a traumatic maelstrom in the North Atlantic, and observing sharks off Cape Town, followed by porpoises, dancing in the Indian Ocean. I met with the most wonderful men on earth, in my travel colleagues, and became further privileged: To become one of a dishevelled bunch of desperate men, British Soldiers, sat around a bomb crater, and there, to meet with Major Pip Moran, a Duke of Wellington Regimental Officer of the highest standing.

Desperation stakes of, 'Do or Die', arrived at various situations. There was no in-between, and no time for dithering or uncertainty. In instant, after instant, and on entirely my own initiative, I had defied an enemy, succeeded in my task, and walked away from what had seemed like, certain death:

(1) I usurped a dithering Commanding Officer, in conducting several arms encounters with the enemy, particularly following twenty-eight miles of night traverse, and pushing mule carts.

(2) I had been stuck, chest deep, in the morass of a swamp, on the blackest of nights, whilst being fired upon, by British troops from the front, and enemy, from behind.

(3) With colleague Vic Stevens, and twenty virtually unarmed men, I had led a successful attack on the Japanese held road-block, close by Twingon village north of Yenangyaung oilfield where I witnessed the Republic of China, Army Expeditionary Force attack, at Yenangyaung.

(4) They released a company of captured Inniskilling soldiers from the enemy: *(To meet with the daughter of one of them in later life, and hear of his second capture, and three further years of imprisonment, as a POW).*

(5) At Taungtha, I Commanded, the dispatch of a gang of 27 hostile recalcitrant oilmen, turned Dacoits.

(6) I had viewed the distant Himalaya Mountain Range, from a Burmese mountain top.

(7) At the end of a strenuous ten days jungle march, debilitated, and weakened by a body loss of three and a half stones, (21 Kg), I defied monster sea snakes, to swim the massive Chindwin River, and bring rescue to remnants, (Less than 100), of an isolated, starved, and Churchill discarded, British Army Battalion.

Oh yes! I'd enjoyed walking, with sporadic enemy encounters, for hundreds of miles, through unimagined beauty. Listening to multi-numerous butterflies taking off from mile long jungle valleys, as though bed-sheets being lifted. I also enjoyed a canopy of monkeys hollering from trees above.

We left a precious chain of jewels throughout Burma, 'Officers, and Other Ranks', stretch throughout the thousand miles, from the Billin River, in the South, to the Naga Hills, in the North. Only one man in every six, from the Battalion strength of over five hundred, survived with the unit, to leave the country, at the Indian border. Private Bernard Oats was the first man to die, he and his chum, Bill Dawson, were machine-gunned, near the southern, Billin River. Bill Dawson's left shoulder was shot away, and plugging with a colleague's shirt, it took him eight days to reach medical aid. One thousand miles to the North, and five months later, Sergeant Ike Oldcorn, was reduced from being a robust rugby forward, to a skeletal wreck. When he collapsed, with multiple tropical ailments, and died in the northern, Naga Hills, he was within yards of the Indian border.

Wounded, diseased, starving, Prisoners of War, or sometimes of their own volition, so many died uselessly, and with no real cause. Were they treated, or mistreated, by an indifferent Government, and inept Military Commanders? We now know that they were left to their own devices!

There were mothers, wives, sisters, brothers, friends and communities, mourning their loved ones, and wondering; How and Why? Little did they know the depths to which Britain had sunk in dealing with the missing?

Prisoner of War, 'A Blessed Man'; Colonel Mac Kenzie, of the Royal Army Medical Corps, illustrates the cloaked and devious shortcomings of Parliamentary and Military superiors, in his book; "Operation Rangoon Gaol". Immediately the Colonel was posted as 'Missing', his monthly remittance of cash to his wife was stopped, as were all banking facilities. Under the Churchill Government, the dear lady remained penniless. As you see elsewhere, she was left in penury, and required to vacate her family home. Many thousands of those discarded forces in the Far East never came back, and their families suffered the consequences.

Accepting the need for security, and deterred from making any kind of enquiry into defence matters, families were left in total ignorance of injustices done. They were unable to uncover the wartime, 'Governmental convenient masking cloak'; 'National Security'.

How could I know as I walked almost one thousand miles, with a well equipped enemy on my tail, fully intent upon claiming my skin, that British Prime Minister, Churchill, had long abandoned me? Further than that, Alexander, a Churchill selected, Army Commander, proved himself to be so cowardly, that within hours of assuming Command, he signalled the devastating news to Churchill,; "Burma can-not be saved". The lowest of the low, General Alexander, in presuming to nurture the troops under his Command, blatantly failed them.

EVER SO BRITISH – SUBJUGATION/TREACHERY

Unravelling the mystery underlying reason, and timing, of Churchill's 'washing of hands', has taken many years. The treachery is such that it coincides with Alexander's indiscretion, and his comment of capitulation to a bank manager.

Receiving Alexander's missile, and 'stewing on it', Churchill's testy patience exploded. The chagrin, shame, and humility, of having been so wrong in all that he forecast, revealing his shortcomings of Japanese knowledge and planning, was shattering. America's Roosevelt had his own secret and sorrowful misdemeanour revealed, in his 'Short term peace pact with Japan'.

Beyond his tether, and realising, but not forgetful of his numerous failures, resulted in Churchill dispatching what became his Far Eastern; Dismissive and abandonment signal, of 1st April 1942, to USA President F.D. Roosevelt:

> *"From one amateur to another; I think the wisest plan for Japan is to press on through Burma northwards into China and try to make a job of that".*

Sick to the gills, Churchill wanted no more to do with the Far East. The signal makes clear that Burma, and all therein, was discarded. Having constantly interfered and overruled Commanders, at Hong Kong, and at Singapore, with a series of fallacious interventions, so far as Churchill was concerned, Burma, and all beyond Suez, was a lost cause. Seeing no way of extricating the troops, why bother feeding them? Burma was written off! Provisioning throughout the Far East ceased, and the treacherous denial began.

John Curtin, the Australian Prime Minister, was unforgiving of Churchill's irrational conduct, and made known his annoyance in the Australian press.

Apart from being known as 'a party going man', General Percival served in Malaya from 1936, and as General Officer Commanding, at

Singapore, in April 1941. He was established, and regarded as a competent Commander. However, weakened by Churchill's constant pillorying, and overbearing interventions, which resulted in disaster following disaster, 'Percy' went to pieces. Unfairly blamed for the catastrophic defeat at Singapore, and unable to exonerate himself from the shadow of post war Churchill condemnation, Percival died a broken man.

Having repeatedly received similar treatment, and being downright reviled, in a similar manner to that of Percival, General Archie Wavell simply vanished from the scene. He was the one outstanding military personality who did not appear at Churchill's grandiose, and heavily publicised, 'Victory Parade'.

So delicate and treasured by the British is Churchill, that his blasted 'All Fools Day' signal, has never featured in, The Burma Star Association Magazine; "Dekho!"

There were no trimmings, or titivations, around Burma, in the early days of 1942. Generals were, 'sacked by the bunch', and there was no answer to the enemy onslaught. Wavell, and three other failed Generals were flown out, on the 5th March, in the plane delivering, Churchill's specially favoured Commander; Alexander.

Command within the country was chaotic. Weeks on end, were spent totally incommunicado: Food, Ammunition, Medical, all were denied. Back in the safer north of Burma, the dismissive General Alexander, having long declared himself a failure, by abdication, was ensuring his safe and imminent departure.

There were no pretences, individuals required to show their true colours. A company commander was so terrified of his responsibility, that he ordered me, a new raw officer, to assume command of his charges. But, to crown all; for a British Army, Infantry Battalion Commander, to find it necessary to appoint; 'a bodyguard, for his own personal defence', against men under his command, is the ultimate in cowardice, and sheer desperation.

For a British Army, 2nd Lieutenant, to usurp a Commander, whilst in an active war zone, is beyond all recorded British Military history. Once a Commander is usurped, there is no going back, and whilst showing him a modicum of respect, the man is, as was Geoffrey Chadwick; subject to the orders of the usurper. This was the state of affairs for the weeks, from 23rd March, to 24th May 1942, for the "2nd Bn KOYLI. CO Chadwick made not one decision throughout this period, and departed the Battalion immediately he exited Burma; with no comment.

The hiatus that was 1942 Burma had no chance of becoming *sub-judice*. It was as though it never happened, not once were questions asked, there was no discussion, or conferring. It was virtually seen to be an offence, whilst in service, to pursue the questioning of seniors. Any form of enquiry, would be seen as insubordination, and the inquisitive one, restricted in promotion, or instantly transferred elsewhere.

The London Times, 17th April 1942 issue, was a singular, and rare, obituary type of contribution, reporting on 2nd Battalion KOYLI, an actively involved unit. Similar sadness was implied, in the congratulatory message, or requiem, telegrammed from the Colonel in Chief of the Regiment, Her Majesty, The Queen, which took six months to reach the unit.

Becoming aware of Churchill's dastardly signal, hidden away for thirty years, I made approaches to open up a Burma 1942 enquiry. The treacherous 'Observer' newspaper editors, Donald Threlfall, and Anthony Howard, distorted, and dramatised my approach story, in their 3rd June 1984 issue. This was followed by, 'The Telegraph', David Graves, on 4th June, and Catherine Steven, on 7th October, and continued worldwide. As late as 1992 in Adelaide, Australia, I was told by a sceptic female cousin; "If it's in the newspaper, it must be true!" It really must! Must it?

The unexpected and dastardly act, carried out by Colin Huxley, The Colonel of the Regiment was a typically caustic and presumptive, 'Seniority put-down': "I do not know Mr Fitzpatrick he has never dined with us". The retort was made by a man I never knew, and totally unqualified to make any observation, or comment, on me, or my character. Huxley's comment featured in the Catherine Steven's, Telegraph article.

At no time, has there been any form of British Governmental enquiry into the Burma 1941/1942 fiasco. It is conveniently, 'airbrushed', out of existence. Books written in earlier days were by authors, speculating, and guessing on happenings, as they eavesdropped, or plagiarised, various reports. Knowledge of Churchill's abandonment of the force was denied them; In the shame of the man!

Never once is mentioned the ridiculous, secretive, and underhand, three month pact, made between USA President Roosevelt, and Japan, hours before the 7th December annihilation of the American fleet, at Pearl Harbour: With the Japanese fleet already mobilised at sea, and about to assault.

Quite easily! I could have missed all of this, had I sat by my desk, as a junior design draughtsman, at Henry Berry Ltd, Hydraulic Engineers, in Leeds. The place I had departed, with my red haired workmate, on the basis that we might serve together. Whilst still wearing civilian clothing, and as new recruits, serving together for only three days, we were evilly parted, at the whim of a brutal Orderly Room Sergeant.

This inhuman, and aggressive act of indifference, shaped my distrust of military seniority that was to stay with me for ever. I observed closely, and cynically interpreted, all controlling commands, and commanders. Subsequent revelations proved me right! From the callow youth, at the age of twenty, I was now aged twenty-six, a confident commander, and aggressive veteran, receiving the deepest respect from all with whom I served. None more-so than the most discerning of men, Sergeant Benny Mee, and his cynical, but dedicated friend, 'Geordie' Bareham. Men do not come, better than this, and they were proud to serve under me. I loved it!

Shortly following cessation of the war in The East: On the 18th September 1945, I was signalled, to report to the 5th Battalion, West Yorkshire Regiment Holding Unit, stationed at Porthcall, in South Wales. With virtually nil military duties, it was a special treat to attend the Sunday night concerts, and hear the singing from miner choirs, from the Welsh valleys.

A tragedy here was the loss of a young, sensitive, and highly educated, Irish Officer. For no known reason, the man walked out, onto the nearby golf course, and shot himself in one of the bunkers. His death became just another incident, to be smothered with the word, 'accident,' and with no, 'Court of Enquiry'. This omission precluded the possibility of establishing any contributory incidents. The Army was like that! I was witness to a similar action of overbearing indifference, with the truculent Brigadier, at Delhi Cantonment.

There is an element of sadness in reaching the age of ninety-three, and knowing that I had failed my men, when leaving Burma. I 'Could Have!' and 'Should Have!' Shot Alexander, rather than give him the salute. It would have been justice! I am, however, pleased to be able to disclose, the disgusting standard of the man.

In Alexander's CV, displayed in Collins dictionary, he becomes very restrictive: He claims the bits in which he had a measure of success, and with the cowardice in which I show him, he omits completely any mention of his failed Burma Command, and contributory treachery; Alexander has the belittling arrogance to announce in his 'Memoirs', "The Chinese made no attack on the Japs!"

TRUTH

The Republic of China, Army Expeditionary Force, 113 Regiment, Commanded by General Fang-Wu Liu, attacked and defeated the Japanese, in the 19th April 1942, Battle of Yenangyaung.

The Battle resulted in the releasing of a Company of Inniskilling Fusiliers from being held prisoner for three or four days.

Not only did my colleague Victor Stevens, and I, witness the whole of this action: We bandaged wounded Chinese, and supplied both Chinese and 'Skinns' with warm rice from a large cooking pot.

It was from this valiant chinese action – denied by British heirarchy – that whatever was left of Churchill and Alexander's debilitated force, 'we' were able to withdraw from burma.

I know and appreciate that, as I was one of them!

Reading my first book, "No Mandalay, No Maymyo", (out in 2001), the Republic of China, army command, realised; that to be in position to detail the precision of the 113 army regiment formation, and what I call respectfully, 'pagentry', in their successful battle at Yenangyaung, I had to be in position to witness the operation from very close range: My colleague Victor Stevens, and I, stood by the prominent White House.

Alexander, the rat of a British Army Commander, departed his Command within hours of his force withdrawal; 24th may 1942. Such was the man that under no circumstances was he going to declare his own shortcomings to Prime Minister, Churchill. The very idea of crediting the success of the damnably shabby withdrawal to a highly competent Chinese Force abhorred him.

The detestable Alexander flourished in the post-war peace. He went so far as to become British Minister for Defence, and accepted the tag; "Of Tunis"; A Con-man to the end!

2 K.O.Y.L.I. – Owston Ferry Reunion 2000

Frank   Joss   Gerald   Bill   Jim
Stott   Isaacs Fitzpatrick   Slee   Major

18

MEET FRANK STOTT – P.O.W. – RANGOON JAIL

Unremittingly, poignant stories abound, and unexpectedly, sixty-five years following World War – Two, I came across one such, long waiting to be told, however reluctantly. It has been under my nose for many years, although retained by Frank Stott, throughout his dignified reticence to recognise, or acknowledge, the evil of his Rangoon Jail perpetrators. It is now July, of the year 2011, and I am aged almost ninety- two. Frank Stott remains, four years my junior.

Our age difference, at the present date, is of little consequence, although the gap proved monumental in younger days. In the war against the Japanese in Burma, Frank and I, both served in the same Regiment: The Second Battalion, Kings Own Yorkshire Light Infantry. We were, however, not to meet together, until many years following the war.

Meeting at Military Re-unions, Frankie could be the star of the gathering, and, as we all do, Frank enjoyed a beer or two, or, maybe six. Reciting long dissertations of his self composed poetry, and singing modern songs, brilliantly enough to entertain frequently at working men's clubs. He mastered his private collection of fine musical instruments, representing those of an orchestra; from mouth-organ to base. Physically, he was like a flea; from a standing start, Frank could leap the height of a dining table. His other, phenomenal, and truly miraculous attribute, I give later.

On leaving school, at the age of fourteen, Frank saw no point in working for others, and decided that employment was not for him. Whether he liked it or not, Father stepped in, and at the age of fifteen, enlisted him into the Army. In short time, Frank was posted to Burma, and became a Band-Boy in the Regimental Band, a much coveted appointment. Stationed for a few joyful months, at Maymyo Regimental barracks, considered himself to be in heaven.

Change came about however, with the dear boy, nicely into his sixteenth year. The Japanese, having bombed the American naval base, at Hawaii, continued their successful assault on all territories throughout the Far East, rapidly coming to the sanguine and unprepared land of Burma.

In three weeks of chaotic conflict, with KOYLI being thrust between one and another inadequate Brigade, senior Commanders were out of their depth in competing with the meticulously planned Japanese assault. Short of food and ammunition, the British suffered numerous casualties, many of them, the best of men.

Cowardly destruction of the Sittang River, Bridge, ordered by Smyth, the Divisional Commander, not only knackered the Army in Burma, it led to the closure of Rangoon, the vital port of entry into the country, and virtually sealed all movement.

Frank, along with large numbers of the now debilitated battalion, remained on the fatal Eastern Bank of the Sittang River. Capable of making a successful swim across the torrent, he felt more secure in remaining with the larger numbers, only to suffer the inevitable consequences.

Along with all on the river bank, he was captured by the Japanese, and interned in Rangoon Jail; a Prisoner of War. He was held, punished, and starved, for more than three years. As with all former prisoners of the Japanese, many of whom I have worked, and contacted, there is never a word of the inhuman indignities inflicted upon them, nor how they suffered. Invariably, each and every one of them, remains silent, embarrassed to relate the punishing humiliation of their every day, by evil day, existence.

Frequent visits to his cosy sheltered accommodation bungalow, in Leeds, where he has good days, and bad days, he is now handicapped in walking. He will not say, but the inflamed swelling of his shins, is clearly attributable to the vicious kicking received during his confinement. Each of the Japanese kickers sought a punishable reaction from the recipient, and the joy of possible repercussions, justifying more vengeful kicks.

Asking Frank to provide me with a short synopsis of his Army and prison experiences, for inclusion into the annexure of this book, he, almost reluctantly, loaned me his copy of the remarkably revealing epistle: "Operation Rangoon Jail", written by the saint of a man: Colonel K. P. MacKenzie, of the Royal Army Medical Corps, (Retired). This God-given man relates all that Frank knows to be true, and is presented in words he would possibly be shamed, and humiliated, to relate in his own voice. This is Frank's way of acceding to my request, and most reluctantly, the equal of telling me himself. He knows that I respect his trust.

Clearly, unknown to Colonel MacKenzie, and to Frank, is the ultimate in hypocrisy, perpetrated by the British. A trait contained within so many, of the, 'True British, Senior Control Freaks'. Individuals considered utterly trustworthy.

The forward to Col MacKenzie's book, is written by the shamefully hypocritical individual causing Frank, and the Colonel, to be, as Smyth patronisingly terms it; "In the bag". I can hardly believe my luck in being able to further debunk the individual, and please bear with me, as I expose the evil doer, and the ever more, despicable one.

General, later, (reverting to rank), Brigadier, J G Smyth, VC. MC. MP, the very cowardly officer, bringing about the tragedy, agony, and humiliation, of both, Colonel MacKenzie, and Frank, having the audacity to contribute the forward to; 'Operation Rangoon Jail'. To find such downright hypocrisy, coming from this evil man, does not surprise me. I am in no way plagiarizing the good Colonel's book, in the following excerpts. I am relating the words that, my dear friend, has been unable, to freely, and openly voice, in more than sixty years.

The book excerpts are copied Verbatim.

With due respects, and my grateful thanks, to Colonel KP MacKenzie, RAMC.

Extracts from his book; 'Operation Rangoon Jail'

Boy soldier, Frank Stott (4691030) enlisted, 10th August 1938, aged 15 years 4 months.

Taken POW February 1942, for 3½ years. He rejoined and was promoted, Corporal serving in Maylaya.

Into Captivity

Page   Detail

I am a doctor and a professional soldier and have the natural reticence of the Scot. I set down this account from a sense of compulsion, from an overwhelming conviction that I must record what happened to me and to those men who shared with me a terrible experience, lest otherwise the barbaric cruelties that were inflicted upon brave and decent men are forgotten in the present fashionable attempt to represent the Japanese as a civilised and misunderstood people, who can conveniently be used to build up a bulwark against Communism in Asia and who, with a little re-education, can worthily take their place amongst the democratic nations in the councils of the world. What a fallacy this is! From my experience, I declare that the Japanese are capable of actions of which savages would be ashamed and I see no prospect, for many generations, of the Japanese understanding the decencies that mark the cultivated man, whatever the veneer of respectability and humility they place around themselves. I write this from no sense of bitterness, but set it down as a warning based upon a conviction, obtained through observation and experience.

Page 14

Prior to 1942, my career was not untypical of that of a regular officer in the R.A.M.C I was educated at Aberdeen. I graduated there as Master of Arts and then entered the Medical School. After I qualified M.B., Ch.B. in March, 1914 I was appointed as House Surgeon to the late Sir Henry M.W.Gray at Aberdeen Royal Infirmary.

On 4th August, 1914, moving quickly to participate in what we considered to be inevitably a short war, I joined the R.A.M.C. and served as a medical officer in France and in Greece.

I mention here two matters in which I take some pride, I was the first officer in the British Army to administer Evipan and I have the credit of being the man who recommended that pocket handkerchiefs should be issued to other ranks in the Army, as an article of kit.

Page 21

"From our first engagement with the Japanese, it was evident that we were fighting a barbaric and ruthless enemy. Our wounded who were not evacuated were bayoneted mercilessly as they lay on the ground. Fighting their way back from position to position, the Division had held on for a week to the line of the Billin river. But the main intermediate objective of the two Japanese divisions in their advance on to Rangoon was the Sittang river bridge, the most vital link in our lines of communication, the capture of which would give the Japanese a clear, and almost unopposed, approach to Rangoon, where it was still hoped that considerable reinforcements could be landed.

Page 22

"A comparatively small proportion of the division was taken prisoner in this action, or indeed in the fist Burma Campaign, which resulted in such an overwhelming victory for Japan and the complete withdrawal of British troops from Burma. On the early morning of 23rd February, when the Brigadier in charge of the bridgehead defences could no longer guarantee to hold the bridge, it was blown-up.

Taken prisoner, a day or two before Smyth's fatal order for the demolition of the Sittang River Bridge, Col MacKenzie accepted whatever distorted version of events Smyth chose to put to him. The Colonel remained unaware that Smyth had cowardly, 'passed the buck', and the responsibility for the bridge demolition, onto his unfortunate junior, a Brigade Commander.

A diversion: From a Japanese letter inviting British POW to commit Treason, (sic).

Page 63

On 13th August, 1942, the Japanese made their first effort to undermining our loyalty to the Crown. Each of us in 'solitary' was handed the following manifesto: (I reproduce it exactly as I received it.)

1. The Great Japan, since she was constructed about 3,000 years ago

2. In the war 1914-1919 (sic) Japan observed faithfully the Japanese-British-Military-Treaty and fought hard for the allied countries.

Page 64

3. When shall the present war end? That is when Britain and the United States shall surrender to Japan. Or that Britain shall be wiped out of existence.
4. All preparation in order to destroy the British and United States were arranged very secretly with sufficient care. (Great detail later!).
5. Thus at last war was declared on Britain and America and since the opening we have achieved many glorious victories.

Page 65

6. Thus the war situation is developing advantageously for Japan. We are now in the state to get freely petroleum, tin and rubber, food supplies are also plentiful.
7. The Germany Army have taken Sevastopol, dominated over the black sea, occupying Rostov and dashing into the Caucasus. In Africa, German and Italian ally armies are very near to Cairo.
8. If the U.S.S.R. had real power she could have attacked the back of Japan during her operations in the tropic zone.
9. Thus we fought and now we are surprised to see the weakness of Britain and United States.
10. So we want now to teach our real intention to the British and American people and relieve them from an unhappy end.
11. The Japanese have a different idea of war imprisonment from you. Your people seem to become war-prisoners shamelessly.

Page 66

12. You threw down your arms and took an oath to give up all resistance, but we see some among you are not yet obedient to us in their mind and dare not co-operate with us.

13. Probably you used to think that the propaganda by your enemies was always advantageous to them and did harm to your country. But Japanese propaganda is a different case.
14. So if Britain or United States are not able to comprehend the Japanese true intention and consequently remain to fight, their way is only to their grave.

We are calling for volunteers who are willing to co-operate in this holy propaganda act of Japan.

If you wish to volunteer write 'yes' and your signature, rank and prison number, if not write 'no' and the same.

* * * * *

Operations and Emergencies – (A letter requesting help). Page 128

To Brigadier General Hobson

through Captain B.N.Sudan, B.A.M.C.

Dear Sir, March 4, '44

I beg to inform you that for more than six months our sick men, with the permission of the Japanese, have been placed under the medical care of four British Medical Officers, Capts. Sudan, Pillay, Thomas and Rao, all Indian officers of the British Army. Among them Capt. B. N Sudan's services have been especially valuable to us. During this period we have not had a single death and three of our soldiers were virtually snatched away from the very jaws of death – all through the effort of that good officer. In consideration of the difficulties imposed upon by the Japanese and the regrettable lack of medical facilities at present, he has certainly done a great deal. It would indeed be ungrateful on my part not to acknowledge the very considerable services he has rendered to us. It is therefore, only just for me to bring his excellent services to the notice of the most senior British officer here and to express our appreciation and thanks thereby.

I will be ready and only too glad to bear testimony to the above statement when called upon to do so at any time after the war if I am lucky enough to survive it.

I beg to remain,

Respectfully yours,

H.C.CHI

Major Gen. Chinese.

"They also Serve"

Pages 138, 139

Soon after the officers were released from 'solitary' in September, 1942, we were paraded and were told to write a letter to our next-of-kin.

When we were writing these postcards, I remarked to some of my fellow-prisoners that I believed we should arrive home, ourselves, before the postcards did. I was quite right. I have now been home for several years but my postcard has not turned up yet!

During the whole time that I was in captivity my wife received no communication from me. She heard nothing from me in my own handwriting from my capture on 22nd February, 1942 until I walked into her Kensington flat, after breakfast, on 7th June, 1945. I have before me, as I write, two telegrams that told to her the whole story. The first is dated 28th March, 1942 and reads: 'Regret to inform you of notification from India that Colonel K.P.Mackenzie, M.B., R.A.M.C was reported missing on 22nd February, 1942 letter follows – Under Secretary State for war' The second dated 17th May, 1945, has the message, 'From the War Office London 16/1555/B OS/3861M. Pleased to state that Colonel K. P. Mackenzie, M.B. recovered from Japanese hands present address BHM Delhi letter follows – Under Secretary of State for War'.

The following record, of treachery, is the most deplorable, and despicable that a country can sink into; it was done by the British Government; Prime Minister, and the Government Minister of Defence, along with the Chief of the Imperial Defence Staff. The wretched act was hidden away under the screen of National Security. It is not an action, undertaken through the bumbling act of some junior official. The absolute top of, both, Government, and Military, are required to institute such rigorous fiscal control. As the evil strictures applied to the good Colonel, so would they have applied to families of those numbers of good men, left behind, in Hong Kong, Singapore, Burma, and Java, valiant men; as my dear friend; beloved, Jimmy Ableson.

Aware that the life expectancy, of an Army subaltern, was considered to be no more than twenty-four hours in wartime operational action, I had been hurriedly married, whilst on embarkation leave. My simple reckoning on that issue, was, that if I am so sure to die, somebody might as well benefit.

(Marrying in such a hurry; one of my aunts was heard to comment; "If she is? It's not beginning to show": Such is family scepticism).

I could, quite easily, have been caught up in a similar dilemma, to that of Doctor MacKenzie.

The good doctor continues, in his own sad words;

"Here I shall comment, without prejudice, on the experiences of my wife and children, while I was a prisoner. The telegram informing my wife that I was missing was placed in the letter box of her home with a bundle of other letters and, as soon as I was posted as 'missing', all pay and allowances to my family ceased. My wife was told that she was not eligible for a pension, as my death was not proved and she was not even permitted to draw upon my accumulated pay, because I had not signed the necessary form".

"She was first told to take her case to the Colonial Office, as I had been posted missing in Burma but was there informed that the matter was one for the India office, as I had been serving with an Indian Division."

"It all seems to have been, an unnecessary muddle, and a cruel muddle at that, for the result of red tape and procrastination was that my family had to give up their house and became homeless for the rest of the war. Is it absolutely necessary in these circumstances

that wives should have to add economic insecurity to all the emotional turmoil of learning that their husbands are victims of war and may never return?"

I can't believe that I soldiered for such scum! This was; 'Doing your duty, for King and Country?' How gently the good Colonel continues: -

Liberty – At Last
Pages 177, 178, 179, 180, 181

During that second day, I was helped by a stick that Sergeant Farrar gave me. But even then, before a halt was ordered, I had come to the end of my tether. I had to resort to the device of holding on to one of the handcarts, to enable me to keep on the move. Then a surprising thing happened, along came one of the most objectionable and bumptious of our guards, a little cock of a sergeant whom we had nicknamed 'Pompous Percy' and he ordered that I should be lifted on to one of the handcarts. I finished the day being pulled along still in a daze.

I have little recollection of what happened on the third day's march. I was on the handcart all the time. We were now being harassed by Allied planes, however, and the convoy had to take cover on several occasions. Light bombs dropped all around but nobody was injured.

At day break on 28th April, we found ourselves among a few deserted Burmese huts, sheltered among thin jungle growth. Our carts had to be left standing at the roadside. Every twenty minutes or so, our fighter-bombers flew over, flying low and making it quite impossible for us to move out into the open. There is nothing remarkable in the fact that our pilots thought we were Japanese soldiers, for it has to be remembered that we were now all dressed like our captors. As a result of this Allied activity, it was impossible for us to have any food cooked that day.

We spent the day lightening our load. I only retained my haversack on a sling and put a few pieces of juggaree in one pocket and a number of small raw onions in the other. By this time my feet, ankles and legs were very swollen and my shoes and stockings, which I had not removed since I left Rangoon, were in shreds.

At six o'clock in the evening of that day, we prepared to move again and it came as a shock to me to hear that the Japanese had given orders that the handcarts were to be abandoned. We were approaching Pegu. Several of our party were missing by now. They had, taken the opportunity to make off into the jungle. Our escort did not seem to worry unduly about the absentees.

I knew that I could not carry on for long unaided but I drew upon all my reserves of strength and determination and took my place in the line of march. Every movement was a conscious effort but I managed to keep going until we were called to a halt beyond Pegu. We proceeded along the railroad track and, on either side, we saw that demolition charges had been fixed. The mines nearer to Wau were already wired but those on the Rangoon side were unfilled.

I had lost all sensation in my feet. I kept knocking my toes against stones and against the sleepers and I found it increasingly impossible to lift my knees in a last effort to maintain my position with my comrades. When we halted, I knew it was all up. I sank to the ground and sent a message up to Hobson, telling him that I was unable to walk a step further, that my legs and feet had given way completely. I told him that I should have to be left behind.

Nothing more was said until the end of the halt. I rather expected some of my friends to come and say good-bye but nobody did so. When the order to move again was given, I just lay still, relieved to think that it was now all over and that I should not need to renew the struggle. I remember thinking that it was the irony of fate that I, who had seen so much beri-beri, should fall a victim to the results of this disease at the last lap of our adventure.

But it was not to work out that way. Just as the convoy was moving off, Squadron-Leader Duckenfield and Captain Brown of the K.O.Y.L.I. came up to me silently, placed my arms around their shoulders and struggled forward, bearing my inert body between them. Brown tried to get me across his back after a time, but this proved too much for him on the rough ground and in his weakened condition. They were not able to help me for long but, when they faltered, their places were taken by other men. We stopped every hour and at the end of each resting period, there were always two men beside me to drag me along and to speak a few words of comfort and good cheer.

For the last two hours the burden was borne by Sergeants Handsell and Martin. They did more for me, as did the others, than any man had any reasonable right to expect. They had had no food themselves for forty-eight hours and they were in a distressed condition. Most of the time I was in a state of coma. In a lucid moment I asked Handsell if I had talked a lot. He confirmed that I was in a state of delirium most of the time.

These two stalwarts were with me, when we halted about seven o'clock on the morning of 29th April at a small village on the Pegu-Wau road. Here I asked O'Hari San if I could have an interview with the Jap commandant for I had come to my decision. O'Hari asked why I wanted see the Commandant. I replied that it was a personal matter but when he announced that he was not prepared to forward my request, unless given a reason, I was too weary to argue any further. I drew upon reserves and said; "Please, O'Hari San, get the Commandant. I am finished. I cannot march any further. My legs and feet are useless and I am impeding the progress of my friends. I have disposed of my kit and, before we leave here tonight, I want the Commandant to do me a personal favour. I want him to put a bullet through my heart. I will mark the place on my shirt with a piece of paper or mark my chest with a coloured pencil, so that there will be no mistake. I cannot face being left behind to be murdered. The sooner the better, Mr. O'Hari, please, so that I may be buried before the column moves off again."

O'Hari appeared stunned and called around him a group of Japanese N.C.Os. They jabbered away amongst themselves excitedly but nobody made any move to fetch the Commandant. The next thing I knew was that Brigadier Hobson was called up to speak with the Commandant. When he went, I lay under a banyan tree – not caring much what happened now.

Within half an hour Brigadier Hobson called out to our bewildered assembly of nearly four hundred Allied prisoners: "We are free, we are free!"

I lay there unable to take in the news and was almost instantaneously surrounded by thirty or forty N.COs. and men shouting: "You've made it", "Congratulations, Sir", or "Well done, Colonel, well done".

I could not speak but I held my hand out feebly and one by one my companions ran up and shook it. It was perhaps the proudest moment of my life. It made me realise that what little I had been able to do for these splendid fellows in the way of doctoring and by being, as far as I could, their guide, philosopher and friend was deeply appreciated. What better tribute could any wish from his companions in adversity?

It soon got round that the Jap Commandant had told Hobson that he had decided that the march must be abandoned and that he had decided that he and his men must return to Rangoon. They were giving up responsibility for the prisoners and passing over command to Hobson. Within a few minutes, the Japs marched quickly away from us. We noticed that they were moving in the opposite direction to Rangoon!

The tragic and pathetic scenario illustrated by Doctor MacKenzie was repeated in North Burma many times, as we of the Battalion remnants traversed the long miles of withdrawal. Arid plains became dense jungle, with steep hills and difficult terrain, and it was committed territory. There was no turning back, and no backup of any form of communication.

The tall young doctor Xavier, the one who joined with us for the ten days of the Jungle trek, earned his spurs in this period. He assisted several of the ones failing, through a variety of illnesses. Words were never spoken, although I remain convinced, that Xavier obliged several pleas, or requests, for dispatch. The experience must have stood him in good stead, in later life, as he ended his days as the psychiatrist at Wakefield Top Security Gaol.

Postscript, by Colonel MacKenzie.

Page 189

I have now been back in this country for nine years and, if this book had been written earlier, it would have come before the public, not as the objective statement of fact I have tried to make it, but as the vehicle of the white-hot anger of a bitter and ill-used man. Now, while I make no claim for it as a literary work, I believe that it is a plain record of the history of a single prisoner in the hands of the Japanese – a record that deserves publication because I have been fortunate enough to be able to spare the time to think things over.

I have waited with impatience for an abler pen than mine to tell the story. I have read avidly anything that has been published about the thousands of British, American, Dutch, Indian and Chinese prisoners in Burmese jails but I have found nothing that seems to convey the picture in the way that I am anxious that it should be conveyed. This is a simple, straightforward effort and it comes at a time when those who did not suffer, as my companions and I were made to suffer, are inclined to take the attitude that the time has come to allow bygones to be bygones. Perhaps this work of mine will cause some to think again. If so, I shall be well satisfied.

I am now a town councillor of the Royal Burgh of Inverness and I try to be as unlike the retired Colonel of fiction as possible. Yet every day my contempt for and hatred of the Japanese continues, if it does not increase. But now, it is a controlled contempt, a reasoned hatred, for I can see things in their proper perspective.

I can hardly believe that Smyth, the failed British Army General, had the gall to write the twaddle shown in the Forward to Colonel MacKenzie's book, as presented below. Extricating himself from all blame, he does not have 'the bottle' to admit that;

He, Smyth, destroyed the British Army in Burma.

THE ULTIMATE IN HYPOCRICY – BY SMYTH (sic)
Forward – Pages 11 and 12

My friend, Colonel K.P.MacKenzie, has asked me to write a forward to this book in which he relates the terrible hardships suffered by himself and his fellow prisoners of the Japanese in the confines of the notorious Rangoon Jail. I am pleased and honoured to do so.

Several books have been written by Far Eastern Prisoners of War, in whose rehabilitation and welfare I have been closely concerned in the post-war years, but this one, written by a doctor, has, I think, a special interest and significance.

Fortunately comparatively few of my 17th Indian Division in Burma went 'into the bag' in the grim battle for the Sittang bridge, which gave direct access on to Rangoon, because as the bridge had been blown, the frustrated Japanese divisions withdrew to find another crossing upstream and allowed the bulk of those who had been trapped on the far bank to swim or ferry themselves across. But those who were taken, both in Burma and Malaya, went into captivity when the full tide of Japanese aggression was sweeping across South-East Asia and "England was far and honour a name". All the more credit therefore to our prisoners for their never-failing courage and humour in the face of the arrogance and brutality of their captors.

Sunday, 22nd February 1942, the day on which Colonel MacKenzie, my head doctor, was taken prisoner at Sittang, was one of those days that no one who lived through it in the 17th Division will ever be likely to forget. For weeks this so-called division, hastily re-formed in Burma from odd formations of British, Indian and Burmese troops, after the Japanese had already invaded the country, untrained and unequipped for jungle warfare and lacking any form of transport and pack rations, and riddled with malaria, had been fighting a succession of rearguard actions against the advancing Japanese. They were fought and marched to a standstill and never have I seen troops so tired.

On the night of 21st February my advanced Divisional H.Q. bivouacked within a few hundred yards of the field ambulance with which 'Mac' spent the night. All night long troops and transport continued to cross the Sittang bridge in a steady stream. It was deathly quiet in the early hours of the morning as I paused at the end of the bridge to have a word with 'Mac' on my way to reconnoitre defence positions on the far bank. He asked me to stop and smoke a cigarette with him, I refused as I was trying to give up the cigarette habit. I had hardly reached the other end of the bridge before pandemonium was let loose. A flanking force of Japanese cut in from the jungle and that was the last I saw of 'Mac' for the three years which he describes in his book.

After the war I endeavoured to obtain for our ex-prisoners of war some compensation for their years of suffering. The compensation actually obtained from the Japanese in the Peace Treaty was pitifully inadequate, but we did at least establish the principle that never again must the civilised world permit helpless prisoners of war to be treated as were our men in Japanese hands.

It is as well that the British people should remember their sufferings – and, even more important, the circumstances which brought them about – and be determined that such things should never happen again.

Dolphin Square – April, 1954 – "THE HYPOCRITE !!" J. G. SMYTH

After so many years, Frank Stott rightfully, and faithfully, continues to put Colonel Mackenzie on a saintly plain. Unstintingly, and never ending, he medically tended all and sundry. Never complaining at the lack of facilities, immensely happy to be referred to, as simply; "Senior Jock"!

I said earlier, that I would tell you of; "the miracle of Frank Stott". The kicking of the Japanese went further than just the shins, they also hit hard between the legs, and the boy was a good and regular target. The damage was such, that, when medically examined, following his prison release, the doctor Colonel declared him sterile: "You realise Stott, you are sterile, and will be incapable of raising a family?"

Not so Frankie! Once married, he set to, and in short time, came his number one child. Followed, in due course, by twins, and later, the unbelievable, a cosy set of triplets. Followed by another two singles! Well done boy! Of course, he could leap as high as a dining table!

Joining with three of his POW chums, there was one other Stott duty: Pulling up memorial stones, in the Hunslet, Leeds, burial ground. All very anticipatory!

Recovered from his POW experience, and seeking to make up for lost time, Frankie joined the Merchant Navy, and circumnavigated the globe a couple of times, including visits to Japan. He then rejoined the Army, was rapidly promoted Corporal, and served in the Malaysian troubles, of the 1950's. That's a boy for me; a soldier!

July 2011 – Visiting Frank Stott at his bungalow, I was accompanied by Barbara, the daughter of Private James Alfred Adams , a former colleague, and POW with Frank. For some reason, he opened up the conversation more than I had ever previously known, particularly in describing Dr MacKenzie, physically, and expressed his deepest feelings of thanks for all that the doctor had done for him, and all of those in captivity.

Standing 6ft-5ins, (almost two meters), in height, the tall, handsome, elegant, high ranking, and attentive gentleman, sported a Van-Dyke beard. Never sparing himself, he was at everybody's beck and call. Completely indifferent to the fact that he was incarcerated, he conducted himself at all times, as though a free man.

His demeanour, whilst never flaunting himself, irritated his captors, such that he became a prime target for torment. In spite of his ministering to all and sundry, he was brutalised more than all others, particularly by the bestial lower level guards. In any instance of group punishment, the good doctor stepped forward, suffered the treatment, and prevented it going further.

Frank Stott, and no doubt, all confined within Rangoon Jail, regarded Doctor, Colonel, Kenneth Pirie MacKenzie MA. MB. ChB, a Saint!

Having myself, received despicable treatment by what are considered to be leading British newspapers, the Colonel of the Regiment in which I served, and British Government, Ministers of Defence, I feel free to speak.

This good Doctor received not one sign of recognition for the brave deeds and guidance given to other internees during his imprisonment. The disgusting treatment of his dear wife, whilst he was in captivity was brushed aside. So far as The British Hierarchy was concerned; It was all in the past – Forget it!

That the two faced rat of a General, Smyth, patronisingly hides behind a Victoria Cross, and deceives this good man, is as British-Bullshit as it gets. I feel that I should form a dissenters-club.

19

MONTGOMERY'S – BRITISH ARMY OF THE RHINE

I was in for a change, and it was such that I could never have anticipated. My development over five years involved total commitment with men, from serving amongst them, to controlling, and commanding. I had never been remote, and out on my own, employed in remote administration. The challenge was about to arrive!

Granted leave back in Britain, on 'Exercise PYTHON': I would have been due to return to the battalion, in Southern India, in November 1945. The four weeks cruise, from Bombay, to Portsmouth, including a sail through the newly opened Suez Canal, was magnificent; particularly being able to join with Steve once again. For me however, there was to be no going back, thanks to the intervention of our, 'ever so reluctant', American Allies. Nonchalantly, by dropping devastating atom bombs, they closed out the Eastern war. American aircraft bombed two Japanese cities, killing and mutilating, hundreds of thousands of townspeople, and devastating innumerable properties.

This short-cut to a Japanese surrender, was brought about, two or three days before my twenty-sixth birthday, 10th August, 1945. The untimely bombing, 'put paid', to any idea of my returning to the Far East. I was posted to 38 Holding Unit, at Morpeth, in Northumberland. Following a six days stay in the holding unit, I was posted to Germany.

Throughout my poverty ridden youth, every place on the far side of the English Channel was called 'France!' It was as though no other continental place existed. It was a place for posh people, one which I could never have aspired to visit. Going overseas, to the Far East, in the company of a number of like minded souls, was one thing; arriving at the port of Harwich, to go to Germany, as a solitary individual, was a completely different matter. I had no idea where I might land up, and most certainly, nothing was going to replace my beloved: NCO's, and men, of the mortar platoon.

Just how lucky had I been? Recognition by my compatriots, for nursing them through several days of maelstrom, in the North Atlantic, caused them to declare me, 'Leader'. I was flabbergasted when Jimmy Ableson declared, "All the draft want you beside us, if we go into action!" It was a frightening commitment to honour, hearing of my peers selecting me as their chief. I was nowhere near any one of them, as four remain, sacramental sons of Britain, glorifying hot Burmese soil: Jimmy Ableson, Bill Riddle, Tim Watson, Stuart Renton.

Surviving the 1941/42, 'trouncing of the British Army in Burma', I had enjoyed the exploitation, from Srinagar, in Kashmir, in the North West of India, to Ceylon, in the South. I had travelled from North to South, from West to East, and seen such great treasures: On our arrival at Bombay, Madam Rita's emporium had been such a joyous reception centre. A quick glimpse at the splendiferous, Rangoon Swe Dagon Pagoda, followed by the Hell of serving in a discarded British Army.

Posted into Europe with no given task or appointment, had me in some kind of quandary; Particularly knowing the kind of success, and security, that I had left behind, in India. I was uneasy regarding my future. Nothing could replace the allegiance shown me, by Benny Mee, and the nucleus of men surviving the Burma conflict. The confident feeling of Commanding a distinguished specialist Platoon, and a Company of men, universally designated, "The Cream of the Battalion", was a little overwhelming.

To have survived Burma under two, completely useless titular seniors; both of them, supercilious, and indifferent, Regular Army, Field Officers, might be considered surprising. More surprising still, was the manner in which, completely out of the blue, and immediately following the Burma withdrawal, an abundance of senior regimental officers arrived. Ones' who had been nowhere near Burma throughout the time of conflict, and were now returned to undertake command of the Battalion; Of course! This was the British Army!

It was as though a mask was thrown over the British failure, from December 1941, to May 1942, against the superb Japanese assault throughout the Far East.

Regardless of controlling indifferences, Fitzpatrick soldiered on. I had my own interests, the pay, and conditions, were becoming brilliant! Nothing compared with the cynical satisfaction obtained, in having so successfully exploited successive seniors lack of knowledge on my specialist weapon. I had manoeuvred, and enjoyed, independence, and immunity, as; 'The Specialist Mortar Officer'. Having free-lanced my way around India, accompanied by my batman, Ted Hewitt, there were other memories, and considerations. Being a Catholic, of Irish stock, and with good reason to have, Irish Republican Army, sympathies, nothing could repay, or pacify me, for the evil done, at Chatham, Royal Engineers Barracks, on my third day of British Army Service.

When so evilly parted from David Williams, my friend, and former civilian works colleague, I was belittled, insulted, and threatened with arrest. Instantly, "Allegiance to King and Country", departed. My single mindedness had benefits: Through my usurping incompetent Commanders, whilst in Burma, I was held, 'a little askance, and at a distance', by the new regime of battalion Command, as they took over in India. It was through a Commander's timidity, that throughout a campaign of eleven gruelling weeks, I fired not one mortar bomb in anger, and lost all in one dawn attack. Of course, as ever, things were going to change!

My first European overnight stay, on 16th December 1945, was at the Belgian town of Ghent, and, knowing not a soul in the place, I wandered into the hotel bar for a drink. Within minutes, I thought myself to be surrounded. It was just one lady, and she seemed to be everywhere, back, front, and – both sides. She declared herself; 'an Advocate' (solicitor), and spared no time in offering, 'The English Officer,' a drink. Dialogue was one sided, and it was important that I understand; The poor lady's husband was imprisoned, somewhere, possibly in Russia, and she missed him so much; over, and over, again, and again. The tirade went on, and on, it became very tiresome, so we went to bed!

The following morning, I felt belittled somewhat, to receive only one great hand-slap across my face. With all the effort the poor girl had put in throughout the night, I thought that I merited, at least three or four really good wallops, and on both cheeks.

Rail progress through Germany was steady, and I soon realised why, on seeing the appalling state of affairs in passing through the vast rail marshalling yards, at Munster. Fully aware of the awesome damage inflicted on London, I had not actually seen the extent of it with my own eyes; here, it was all around me. Halted for a while, I could see before me the shell of what had been a proud town. There were no roofs, or windows, and it was dejected, not a soul moving around the place. Desolate though the town looked, the one abiding grotesque, and spectacular feature, remaining in my mind, is that of a single rail line. I could not visualise the power that had caused this narrow steel line of rail to lift, to corkscrew skywards, and stand, pointing to the sky, at a height that I could only speculate.

With no allocated task, I arrived at Bad Oeynhausen, the small town in which; Headquarters, British Army of the Rhine, with Bernard Montgomery as Army Commander, was based. I was joined, once again, with a Holding Unit; 600 Regiment, Royal Artillery. The Regiment was commanded by one of those rare gems of a gentleman; Lieutenant Colonel, Lord, Paddy Nugent. Paddy was another one of those rarities, a sensible senior officer, bringing all ranks, and all abilities, into conversations, and never the slightest glimmer of, 'one up-man-ship', or superiority.

The stay with Paddy Nugent's unit was brief, but interesting. The whole environment contrasted so different to the tropical life I'd enjoyed in recent years, and it was not only in the wearing of heavier clothing. I managed to play rugby, and hockey, at fairly high levels, but the memorable event happened at a motor cycle rally.

Accompanying two sergeant competitors, Stott, and Black, we met with a Russian representative team at a German zone, border rendezvous. The atmosphere was far from cordial. The Russian, officer-in-charge, looked completely debauched, well over six feet tall, red eyes, hair down to his shoulders, and a face the colour of raw liver.

As I pointed out, that as British officers we did not carry weapons, he stood there with a huge revolver, almost falling from the holster. The brutal looking face leered at me, as he made to draw the weapon. I fully expected him to be so much gone, on drugs, or drink, as to shoot me. He was however taken aback, as before his hand reached the gun, I had removed it, and discharged the bullets. There was a complete change of atmosphere, and the man looked very surprised, and smiled. My two sergeants proved successful in their competitive tasks.

A rather special occupant, of the Regimental guard-room, was the very likeable, German; General, Von Kietle. He was known throughout, as, 'The Boy'. This highly regarded General did not like Nazi activities, as witnessed in recent years. He proved eventually, to be a tremendous asset in the lead up to the Nuremburg Tribunals. Many former Nazi leaders were identified, and summarily dealt with; thanks to, 'The Boy'.

Just a little surprised, and with not one day of, Military Staff College training; on the 15th May 1946, I was selected to serve on general Montgomery's staff, as, General Staff Officer, Grade III, at Headquarters, GHQ Troops. It required ensuring, control of security, and movement, of all troops engaged within Headquarters BAOR, jurisdiction. The HQ office was based at the delightful small town, of Bad Salzuflen, situated, six or seven miles, from Monty's base.

Headquarters building was unusual, in the way it was kitted out. It had formerly been used to accommodate numerous small children. They were the blond, German, Arian, products of the Nazi regime. All facilities within the premises were adjusted to meet with their needs. Possibly two dozen miniature urinals, and an equal number of matching toilets, lined the basement area. Immediately opposite the offices was the Kurpark, its boundary fencing absolutely unique to me. The double railed fence was filled with cuttings from pine trees, and giving off a most delightful scented odour, to waft on the slightest breeze.

My boss at this prestigious headquarters, was, a serious competitor for the title; "The Most Obnoxious Bastard", of so many indifferent senior officers that I met with throughout my service. He was huge; possibly between twenty-two, and twenty-five stones; (130 kg -150 kg), in weight. Wearing a pretentious, showman type monocle, he was drenched in the stench of the most nauseating cheap perfume. The vile perfume, combined with a series of his rapid-fire raucous farts, and a ritualistic smoking of his single cigar, religiously, at 11-00 am, each day: The man was revolting, and stunk like a cheap, low level brothel. His additional showmanship went so far as signing his name in green ink. Named Humphreys, he had a penchant of scribing his detestable self; a condescending; "Humph!" The man never once, personally, addressed me. It was always through his intermediary, number two.

An early alert at the HQ, was the warning of a train arrival, it was due to halt at the nearby, Vlotho, rail station. The train was returning Polish prisoners of war, from the Bremen area, in North West Germany; their scheduled destination being Warsaw. Apart from ensuring that no passenger disembarked, in order to escape into Germany, we were 'tipped off' regarding a wanted man, and advised of his allocated seat.

Deploying an Infantry Platoon from the local defence Battalion, and with the train surrounded, the Military Police took little time in identifying, Theo Walasak, the targeted individual. He was wanted for about forty murders, all committed in the Bremen area. The man was relieved of a revolver, found in his possession, and escorted to the M.P. base at Bad Salzuflen. Proceeding through the entrance archway, which was situated opposite the Headquarters offices, and with no warning, Walasak pulled out a second revolver, one hidden about his person. He shot, both, the Military Police Sergeant, and the Corporal. The unfortunate Sergeant died, and Walasak was eventually, hanged at Dortmund Gaol.

My sceptical opinion, of General Montgomery, had been formed in earlier days when, as Commander, British Eastern Defence Force, in the Essex area, he called a meeting of, 'All Divisional Officers', at a Chelmsford cinema. With an assembly of possibly three-hundred, or thereabouts, we were to be addressed by Monty. Having waited a long hour over the scheduled time, he appeared on stage, and declared his requirements: "I'll give you ten minutes!" "I want no coughing, and there will be no smoking throughout my address".

He was to be the grand showman, and his address added up to no more than telling all present, what they already knew. It was all done, in order that he could introduce himself, and demonstrate; "The Great, I Am!"

"And don't you forget it!" Never having smoked in my 93 years, and as a 21 year old at the time, I found all others present equally diligent.

Nothing of Monty had changed in the intervening period of his acclaimed successes, in so far as I was concerned. I was all too well aware, that the likes of him, whilst on Middle Eastern warfare, had intercepted, and stolen my rations, three years earlier, whilst in Burma, all aided by the exasperated, Mr Winston Spencer Churchill.

Here the Rhine Army Chief, 'relishing and flaunting', the luxury of a captured Mercedes, open top, limousine; It was the car previously owned by, German Field Marshall, Herman Goering; Hitler's friend, and founder of the German Gestapo.

Monty demanded, that everybody acknowledge him, as 'King of the Castle!' He programmed himself, periodically, and at short notice, on local trips around Westphalian towns. Showmanship, and promotional attention, at nearby, Minden, Herford, Lemgo, Bad Salzuflen, were a requirement. And in order to 'rattle' the 'Control Commissioner for Germany'; Sir Sholto Douglas's 'cage'; at his Lubbecke base, Monty made the extra mile.

The small cavalcade consisted of three motor-cycle outriders, the Mercedes, 'with a raised seat, for better visibility', and an armoured car for escort.

The 'strain', of my involvement, was to arrange for six, or seven, casually dressed troops to parade, under Command of a Corporal, and, for them to 'stand by', at prominent cross-roads in each of the townships. The duty of the Corporal was to salute, and call the, 'supposedly casual gathering', to "Attention!" And Monty remained happy.

At the Hoff Hotel – now the Army HQ, in Bad Oeynhausen, Montgomery's, Aide de Camp, arrived daily ahead of the great man, and dutifully called all present to; "Attention!" He made no offer, of a polite; "Good morning gentlemen!" And with not one word of recognition, or a glance to right or left, he entered the hotel lift, and with no accompaniment, proceeded to his office. He might have been thinking of his Swiss boy friend, but this performance was to change, in short time. The words I seek for the man, are; 'Arrogant, Ignorant, and one other'!

The Volkswagen Beetle car allotted for my personal use was like a thing of magic. It was so beautiful to handle, and such a joy to drive, that I have always considered it ridiculous to attempt improving, or making change. (The sixty year endurance of the Morris Oxford model, in India, exemplifies this philosophy; I think!) I simply loved handling the car. It took me on wonderful jaunts, with Sir Sholto Douglas's, Personal Assistant: She was also, Regimental Sergeant Major, of the Women's Army Corps. With this most delightful Scottish lady, we dined frequently, at the restaurant situated on Minden ridge. The beautiful tune, "Hear my song – Violetta", played at our table by the dedicated violinist, created, the unfailing atmosphere for romance. The contrived, and romantic setting of the restaurant, screamed out; "Please Love Me?"

I had not for one moment anticipated the request, but once I deciphered the intent, which did not take long; the surprise plea, made by my partner, was beyond my wildest dreams. I was well aware that I had caused sufficient havoc to one family, back in India. Not surprisingly, I did not wish to repeat that churlish situation, and I was afraid of, 'sticking this wonderful lady up the duff'. It became very difficult, once I worked out the implications of the veiled Scottish requirement, and found it very hard to resist, when asked; "Fitz, let's take the long road home?" Oh No! We Didn't! I trust that she always remembered, and never forgot me; even, possibly, respected me?

It was dusk, and as Orderly Officer for the day, my duty, accompanied by an armed Sergeant was, escorting General Von Kietle to his secured accommodation. It was with discretion, we disregarded the incident happening to our front as we walked along the wide pavement, opposite the town park. A man ran out from the Russian Attache office, thirty or so yards to our front, and appeared to be making for the park.

Two or three shots were fired from the doorway, and the man collapsed. With no delay, two men emerged from the office, and dragged the man back inside the building. In the circumstances, the activity being no concern of the British, we walked on.

Strolling by the park, a few days later, I noticed movement in the bushes; it appeared, a lady was having difficulty with a heavy object. On enquiring, I found the dear girl discarding clothing from a suitcase, and sought the reason, why? The dear sweet thing assailed me with the words; "I am Turkey!" "I don't care if you're bloody Mother Goose!" "What are you up to?"

It transpired, the sweet young thing, was servant to one of my friends, Major Howard, and I knew that he was at the party I was about to attend. The girl was overloaded, and not surprising, as she was wearing three heavy coats, the property of Howard's wife, she was also, set to elope with a German driver.

This was a testing time for me, between one job, and another. I didn't know how well I was acquitting myself in these most unusual surroundings; I was feeling lost without responsibility for numbers of personnel. When controlling a body of men, the mob reaction indicates approval, or disapproval, and I respected that. It was as though I now existed in a completely different world, and with everything falling into place so easily, I began to consider my future.

In addition to having a young wife in England, I had now acquired a new born daughter, and had problems on my mind. Unquestionably, I was enjoying Army life to the full, and, from being a completely raw recruit, a very bitter one, at the outset, I now knew that I was good at the job. Somehow, the idea of returning to spend each day sitting, 8-00 am to 5-00 pm, facing a drawing board, I considered disdainful. I wanted to apply for a Regular Commission, and continue in the life that I was enjoying, but I had to consider my wife's reaction to Army life. In the end, I opted for the alternative, and applied for, a Short Service Commission. I was accepted, and extended my release time, for three years. They were to be three of the greatest years of my life!

20

30 CORPS – WITH BRIAN HORROCKS

There was no love lost in my departure from the cold, and indifferent headquarters, commanded by the putrid smelling Humphrey, and certainly, no goodbyes. I have no idea how my selection for the next appointment came about. With no formal coaching, training, or induction, I could never have anticipated the good fortune in making my next move, on 29th July 1946. Once again, I was about to meet with real men.

The move to Luneburg, in Northern Germany, was refreshing from day one. My immediate superior turned out to be, Major FW (Freddy) Coombes, formerly, of the 2nd Royal Tank Regiment. He was short, stocky in build, and bespectacled. There was a smile on his face at all times, and his warm speech had nothing of the staccato commonality of so many regular seniors. We had something in common, in that he, also, had served throughout the Burma withdrawal, at the time I was there, and had occasionally been required to carry troops, in or out of action. This man knew exactly the dire conditions under which I had served, and we got along, 'like a house on fire'.

However, I could never have envisaged the incredible chief I was to serve under. I had heard his name, and knew of his reputation, but to meet with General Brian Horrocks, Commander of 30 Corps, was beyond my wildest dreams. The indifference shown by so many of higher rank, simply vanished with this man. It was the first occasion on which one of higher rank had welcomed me with a handshake, and went so far as thanking me for joining him. It was like, I had just come home!

Apparently, it had always been so with Horrocks, 'The Boss', always wanted to know, whatever was going on. He visited our office each morning, to spend five or ten minutes, and enjoyed a chat about whatever might be happening. He appreciated the fact that each evening after dinner, we returned to the office, and remained, working late. There was never a time when things were quiet, the share out of Germany, into the four zones; British, French, American, and Russian, created many problems. Incidents along the Russian border were unending; house burning, cattle rustling, or physical attacks, particularly on women.

It was some time before I heard of Horrocks' staff recruitment criteria. His prime requirement was that, all must have been in active involvement against enemy. How ironical, that two of his lower ranks were from the remote, ill-fated, Burma Campaign, and from very different branches.

Appreciating dedication to the job, The Boss authorised a Humber staff car for our week-end use. At our request, the car would appear, spotlessly clean, and fully serviced with water, petrol, and oil. We visited the, WW-Two Surrender Memorial at nearby Luneburg Heath, and went on shooting expeditions in the eastern wilderness area of Wisden, to return with a car boot full of deer and game.

Fortnightly visits, to the forest based holiday centre, at Bad Hartsburg, became a little hilarious at times. Particularly the evening spent at a local night club, to find ourselves, maybe a little drunk, and in the company of two very attractive ladies. Although German, they spoke perfect English, and stated their profession to be sports commentators, based in Hannover. Why should we doubt them?

Sat at a table a short distance from ours, were a party of German men. Their presence was particularly noticeable in that, they had no female accompaniment. That was unusual in this establishment. For some reason that was not ours to question, the two reporter ladies made occasional visits to the men's table, and words were exchanged.

Not seeking to be disagreeable, Freddy and I accompanied the ladies to their hotel, and accepted the offer of 'coffee', to be taken in their room. With the water hardly boiled, and we surprisingly, still fully dressed; turmoil erupted in the hotel corridor. Becoming agitated, the girls suggested that we might be in trouble; I really think that they knew we were.

That warning was enough, as we knew we were in no condition to take on, a group of four or five aggressors. The never ending fifteen meter drop from the window, and our departure in the car, was a demonstration conducted by two experts in the art of withdrawal. We concluded that the two girls were either spies, or lures.

Although interested in knowing of Freddy and I, almost from birth, Brian Horrocks reserved his own background. He made no comment whatsoever of his wartime experience, and there was no such thing as naming his compatriots in war. Without the use of words, he made clear his dislike of both, Montgomery, and the Supreme Commander of the Allied Expeditionary Force, American General Dwight Eisenhower.

It was some considerable time later, long after army service, that I found how justified Horrocks was to obliterate his superiors from comment. However reluctantly, Montgomery had supported Eisenhower in his muddle headed planning of the final assault within Germany. Out of hand, the two superiors had rejected Horrocks' suggestion, for a quick British finish. It later transpired, that, had Horrocks' plan been adopted, it would have justified using his superior equipment, of 30 Armoured Corps. His simple and more direct plan of attack, would have reduced casualties; and considerably shortened the conflict.

Eisenhower, seeking glory for himself and his Yankee Dough-boys, was fully aware of the German Forces debilitated condition, brought about by the four years of, British, and Russian, conflict. Glory seeking, as 'Supreme Commander', and with sole American interest at heart, Ike sought to exploit the situation to the full. He sorely needed a victory, one he could attribute to American forces. Showing his true colours, 'Ike' degraded himself, expressing his whole consideration of the expedition as; "No more than, a clinical matter". The treachery that so deeply irked Horrocks, was the ready acceptance by Montgomery, of Eisenhower's underhand plan. Montgomery, in turn, sought plaudits for his shared wisdom; and in doing so, became a favourite with the American public!

Bankrupt, and having lost its Empire, Britain was, from this time, considered almost, 'a nonentity, or subsidiary', by successive USA Presidents. Each asserted themselves to the full, none more-so than Eisenhower, when his turn came.

BRIEFLY – 1st Corps (SMITH)

November 1946, to April 1947, was memorable for nothing, and much. Reluctantly, I began to meet with further changes, when without warning, or selection of any kind, I was posted to 1st Corps, stationed at Iserlohn, in the Ruhr. My wife and child came out to join with me, in order to sample life as the wife of a serving officer.

The 'Training Officer' appointment, I was given, had no significance whatsoever. I presumed it was adopted as a result of my time spent at Bill Slim's, Ranchi, Battle School, in India. There was no such thing as an office, or introductory reception; and no superior to report to. I simply turned up, and had a chat with whoever happened to be around.

I was known to be a competent Amateur Rugby League player, and was selected to represent Rhine Army, Rugby Union Team, against Royal Signals, the touring visitors. With a scattering of well known England and County players, the Signals were formidable opposition, and proved their worth.

Doing rather nicely in the first half, I merited selection. It was in the second half, I instinctively reverted codes of play, from Union to Rugby League, and clung to the ball when tackled. Releasing the ball in a Rugby League tackle being a cardinal sin, I held on. This resulted in the Union forwards forming a 'ruck' over me, and my coming out from beneath, with a damaged shoulder. For the next three or four weeks, with my arm supported in an abduction splint, I was the only man parading around Germany, with arm raised, and simulating the Nazi salute.

1st Corps Commander was Smith, a short Welsh man. I saw the man only once, and that was as he walked in the street. The few short weeks spent at this Headquarters proved to be a complete waste of time, except for the introduction of one jewel of a lady.

Through the offices of the Control Commission, I was allocated, Frau Victoria Mann, as a house servant. Without specified and restrictive duties, this lady undertook responsibility for everything throughout the home. Frau Mann's husband had served under General Rommel, as a tank driver in North Africa. A Commander highly respected by the British, and affectionately, known as, 'The Desert Fox'.

In the military sphere in which I moved, it was rare to see German children, and I could not envisage the shock I received when Frau Mann brought her two children to the house on the first occasion. It was hurtful to see the eleven year old boy, and the eight year old girl, as they stood before me. Both were terribly emaciated, and the colour of their skin, on face and legs, was a peculiar, and irregular, sickening shade of yellow.

Frau Mann was having a decent meal each day whilst at the house. Seeing the deplorable condition of her children, and having sufficient rations, I gave her permission to bring the children, and ensure that they also had a good meal each day.

To have Frau Mann take rations to her home, she could have been accused of theft. Alternatively, I could have been apprehended for possible 'black market' trading. The children and Frau Mann received a good meal each day, which meant that her husband enjoyed better, from the meagre civilian rationing.

The boy, Gunther, died several years ago, but we continue to receive Christmas, and Holiday cards, from his widow. Our kindness was appreciated.

Throughout my brief stay at 1 Corps, I answered to nobody, and nobody answered to me. I had never felt so, 'out on a limb'.

21

RHINE ARMY HEADQUARTERS – WITH BRIAN HORROCKS

Brian Horrocks assumed Command at Rhine Army, and my short moribund attachment to 1st Corps, came to a sudden halt. The Boss wanted his team back, supporting, in the manner to which he was accustomed.

It was one hell of a move, on the 15th April 1947, to become G.S.O. – III (Operations) Headquarters, British Army of the Rhine. Operations being senior to branches of the Adjutant General, and Quartermaster appointments, I had achieved the topmost Staff Captain appointment in the British Army. BAOR being the leading operational British Military force, I was holding the senior captaincy appointment in the British Armed Forces. I loved it!

Rejoining Freddy Coombes was a rare treat, with each of us, knowing the strengths, and possible weaknesses of the other. The third, and senior incumbent of General Staff; Colonel Hutchinson, was from the Royal Artillery. It did not take Freddy and I long to inculcate him into our routine, and discipline. Hutch proved to be a very acceptable leader.

Irritating activity: Between twenty, and twenty-four violations monthly occurred along the British/Russian Zone border, in the same manner as those perpetrated at 30 Corps. This resulted in British, Russian, French and American Commanders, analysing, and deliberating on the incidents at monthly meetings, held at Gatow, and Spandau, in Berlin. Contrasting versions of each incident were presented from both sides, and there was never agreement; it was never to be so.

In order to obtain verification of major incidents, particularly those in which a fatality was concerned, it was considered sensible to have some form of forensic expert investigation. Based upon my being the one Infantry Officer on the staff, and with the background of the scurrilous Burma Campaign behind me, Freddy Coombes designated me; 'The Expert!' It was not onerous, as with an armed sergeant, and driver, I visited numerous sites of crime.

Expertise came from doing the job, and using a little common sense. In the case of a shooting; when two or three bullets penetrated close together, in head or chest, I knew they were fired from short range, and could not be convinced that the shots were from, two or three hundred meters. Alternatively, when fired from a distance, I would expect to see some structural damage, to walls, or windows. With a hanging, of possibly, one, two, three, or more unfortunates, it was a matter of assessing the plausibility of the story.

On my return from investigations Brian Horrocks spent time, he required to obtain the utmost minutia from each episode. Equipped with such detailed information, Horrocks was ahead of his contemporaries from other zones. I was favoured as, 'The Expert', and enjoyed many jaunts, investigating incidents, wherever?

BERLIN AIRLIFT

Russian sensitivity, and suspicion, knew no bounds. At all times resenting the fact that; whoever, and whatever, Allied personnel or goods, visited Berlin, to whatever zone of the divided city, they went by road, or by rail. It meant traversing through a depth of about one hundred miles of Russian held territory, and there was no yielding, as individuals passed through carefully monitored checkpoints. Intimidation became the name of the game, and whatever attempt at disruption to the flow of traffic they could connive, either by road, or by rail, Russia tried it!

Information of movement, and activity, by Russian troops, arrived with the appearance of the rather special and somewhat mysterious man. Standing a little over 5'0" (five foot / 150 cm) tall, he had some kind of quality about him, and I had seen him only once before, when he visited 30 Corps Headquarters, at Luneberg. The unkempt looking gentleman arrived, 'out of the blue' – he had carefully guarded words with the Commander, and seldom with others. The man simply vanished into the community. For some reason, his distinctive demeanour was memorable.

Unprepossessing in appearance, clothed in the common manner of a European civilian of the time, his authority shone through. He had immediate and unquestionable access, to the senior Commander, both, at Luneburg, and here at Bad Oeynhausen. Once again, it was with Brian Horrocks that he made first contact. Having conversed he exchanged a few casual words with us subordinates, and was soon gone.

The man departed before Horrocks spoke of him. Referring to him as Popskie, a name used in a previous conflict. He was an Intelligence Officer, (spy), with the rank of Colonel in the British Army. He reputedly, spoke every European, and Slav language, and had no operational base.

There was not much fun in the catastrophic revelations made by Popskie. It resulted in the commencement of what was to become known as, 'The Cold War'. He reported that Russia was busily assembling over three hundred tanks around the area of the autobahn, close by the International Zone crossing point, at Helmstedt.

Not surprisingly, road impediments brought about the immediate closure of the ninety-plus mile, Berlin autobahn. This abrupt and unexpected blockage of physical communication, with two million Berlin residents, and the Allied occupying forces, was catastrophic in the extreme.

However, there remained the supply train, running daily, from Belgium to Berlin. Traversing through the British Zone, it crossed the Russian Zone border, and proceeded to Berlin. Times became precarious!

British forces numbers were being rapidly reduced as conscripts were released, discharging from a war footing, to less than fifty per cent in strength. The unthinkable, would have been to accept the challenge. With no chance of victory against the fully mobilised and heavily armed Russian Forces; To go into World War – Three, was unthinkable.

Demobilisation of conscripts, and increasingly adopting the passive role of, 'Assistance to Civil Powers', meant that any attempt at aggression with Russia, would have proved fatal. A land skirmish, with 'questionable', French, and American support, was out of the question.

Apart from the splitting of Germany into four occupied zones, the capital city of Berlin, itself, was also similarly divided – French, Russian, American, and British. Rationing of food had been desperate in Berlin throughout the war; in post-war, it became far worse. With a total disregard for the various Allied held sectors within Berlin, there was no mercy from Russian Forces. British, French, and American sectors were aggressively surrounded.

The remaining slender source of Berlin survival came from the Belgium train, carrying vegetables and general supplies. However, a constant irritant to the Russians, were two, so called; 'Sealed Coaches'. With a mix of a half dozen, British and Belgian Guards, the Russians were, irritatingly, denied entry into the two special coaches.

Following a series of unpleasant episodes, and subtle attempts at disruption happening almost daily, Russia solved the problem in a manner suiting their own needs. As with the autobahn closure; questionable necessity for repairs and replacement, on the vital railway line, close by the town of Magdeburg commenced. The "designer-maintenance", was sited well within Russian held territory. In dire straights, and with this devastating stoppage, Berlin was about to suffer starvation, there was no Russian sympathy.

Freddy Coombes and I, had not, for no good reason and without experience, starved in Burma, thanks to a Prime Minister. We knew the meaning of hunger, and Freddy was the man to come up with the answer; "We'll fly the bloody stuff in!"

Anticipating ready support for such a venture, the proposition was first, put to the former distinguished Royal Air Force executive; Sir Sholto Douglas, now appointed, Chief of the Control Commission for Germany. As civilian controller, he would be required to instigate a support system. In his present capacity, and as a former officer of the Royal Air Force, Sholto Douglas turned the suggestion down flat; to him it was 'dead in the water!' But not to Freddy; it was a matter far too serious, and much too urgent, to brook delays.

With Berliners, already long suffering from starvation, time was of the essence, and short. There was no time for tedious Parliamentary Debates, International Conferences, or Secretary of Defence intervention. The need was there, and desperately urgent if it was to succeed. The situation was like a touch-paper, and could have boomeranged into total catastrophe. This was no place for the chicken hearted!

With the words – "It's worth a try!" Both Colonel Hutchinson, and the Army Commander, approved Major Freddy Coombes suggestion. The short, podgy, bespectacled, former tank Commander approached the Russian Liaison Officer; Freddy stated his requirements, forthright, and detailed.

Demanding a five mile wide air corridor, from Bielefeld Airfield, and along the autobahn, to Berlin, he insisted that British, Dakota transport planes, should have free and unmolested, access to the stricken city, with immediate effect: I feel sure that he did not fail to mention, "atom bombs".

The Berlin Air Lift commenced, within almost hours of Freddy Coombes making clear 'His' demands. Operations commenced on the 24th June 1948, and continued under duress, for more than a year, and thereafter, for an essential period of readjustment. There were numerous attempts at 'dummy-strafing', and intimidation of pilots by Russian aircraft, in the early days. This harassment stopped immediately, once Freddy had a further word with his Russian counterpart.

As they eventually do, given time, America came in, and with their preserved numbers of both men and machines, virtually took over the task of delivery, at a share of approximately, 55/45% on the operation. Berlin, requiring 8,000 tons of food daily; about 700 British and Allied aircraft conducted more than a quarter million flights, conveying more than two million tons of supplies throughout the operation.

For the overall control of this operation to take place under my nose was remarkable. The large bare wall to one side of my office, contained the massive map of the whole of Germany, and I missed nothing of the detail. It was in my office that all the Top Brass assembled for operational conferences.

Unfortunate circumstances caused me to depart the Army before the termination of the Air Lift, and I was never fortunate enough to visit Berlin whilst serving, or to make a peace-time visit. It's just one of those regrets!

DOMESTICITY

The sadness, in moving from Iserlohn, to Bad Oeynhausen, was, in our leaving Frau Mann, she had become a friend, and the most assiduous of housekeepers. It was not possible to envisage her successor, at our new abode; 6 Lessing Strasse, situated, at the top end of the Kurpark. It was convenient for the Hoff Hotel Headquarters.

Remote though our hopes were for the replacement for Frau Mann, we could not have had one of such devastating contrast. With no such thing as an interview, or selection of any kind, the young woman was simply 'allocated'. Rough as the proverbial bear's arse, she was unkempt, stunk like a polecat, and lacked any form of etiquette.

Hopeful that access to decent facilities might help change the girl; they didn't! Within days, our daughter of very few months became internally upset, and in several daily visits, the good lady doctor could not identify a problem.

It was only when I questioned the girl that we got results. She simply vanished into whatever part of the jungle she came from, and the child made a rapid recovery. The attitude, and regard, the girl had for her employment, was demonstrated with the finding of items of her personal bodily filth, contained in the drawers of furniture throughout the house.

Contrast beyond measure, was the replacement maid. Hilda would be aged about forty, and possibly selected on the basis of compensating for her predecessor. She stood upright, dressed formally, as classy as any hotel receptionist, and I don't remember ever seeing a smile on her face. She was such a personality, and I simply had to invite three or four colleagues for week-end drinks.

Whatever it was, it could have been the boisterous week-ends, and in short time, Hilda simply vanished. Having taken a liking to this lady, of such contrast to her predecessor, I set to contact her at the village in which she lived. Avoiding a dog on the cobbled village street, my German driver skidded and hit a tree. Damaging my knees, I failed in my quest. It simply meant that we had to seek a further replacement. We got one!

Ullah (Ursulla) arrived, and speaking very good English, was a bonus, but 'Boy o' Boy!' what a chassis? She was tall, good looking, in her early twenties, and knew: She could 'pull' a man.

I had no idea, just how popular I was to grow amongst my colleagues, as the three or four week-end visitors for drinks, became ten or a dozen. Whatever did it, I do not know, but there really had to be a reason. Ulla dressed for the occasion, black tunic dress uniform, stopping some inches above the knee, and the small white apron; I really was a popular guy.

Not neglecting the domestic scene, we managed to bring forth a son. He was born with the most excellent care, on the 27th November 1947, at the hospital, situated at the nearby Minden Ridge.

Ulla was not a bad judge, she knew exactly what British Officers wanted, and arranged for a lady to give lessons on the speaking of German. The highly regarded professor was a lady, of considerable standing in the local community. Teutonic in appearance, she was tall, gaunt, of smart appearance, and sporting a fine beard.

Paying our way, the six or seven of us found the lessons difficult, and somewhat irrelevant, to our every day needs. The problematic situation was resolved eventually, as tentatively, the dear lady was confronted. We had asked for German language lessons, and that is what we were getting, except, it was outdated Teutonic German, and not the modern practical language.

Madam; obviously knew what she was doing, and we should have specified, exactly, our requirements.

VERY NEARLY – WORLD WAR THREE

The never ending border incidents, and general Inter-Zone movements, justified the appointment of additional staff, and I was joined in the office by a new colleague, Captain Southgate. In order to cover as many hours in the day as possible, the work-load was staggered; this meant that there were long periods spent alone in the office.

Coming from the Royal Army Service Corps, we failed to appreciate the man did not have the background of a recognised chain of Command. His newness, did not allow time for a full induction, and he was just a little headstrong. Having been appointed to the job, he assumed that he must know the answers.

It was when a very rare, and desperate, 'notification signal' arrived, sent by our friend Popskie; Southgate initiated movement. He indicated that the three hundred-plus Russian tanks, from Helmstedt, were newly positioned. They had moved south, from the autobahn, to close by the town of Brunswick.

Asserting himself, and very late in the day, Southgate assumed Command. Bye-passing both, Division and Brigade; He urgently, ordered the local force, 17/21st Lancers to; "Stand to!"

The delicate situation was tense, and instantly fraught with danger. With the possibility of an exchange of shots, between a Russian tank crew, and a British reconnaissance vehicle; 'The fat would be in the fire', and who would know the outcome? It could have been the start of: World War – Three.

The Lancer Squadron Commander, in all innocence, acted on the instruction, as given; whilst, at the same time, questioning the Divisional Commander.

The tall, General, 'Jock' Black, in total shock, travelled over-night, arriving at Army Headquarters with his kilt flying in the morning breeze, to meet with true astonishment: It came as a surprise to the big Jock, to find that the Army Commander, also, knew absolutely nothing of Southgate's overnight, 'Stand to!'

Russian troops probed every front, and their troops had little regard for discipline. The situation was like a powder-keg, and capable of explosion at any time.

As the British have at all times done, the fallacious "Stand to! Episode", was 'air-brushed' out of military history. The Lancer's accepted the near catastrophe as, 'a practice exercise'.

Southgate, my new found colleague, ceased to be employed at Headquarters, although, he went very close to usurping Churchill, and the War Cabinet, in starting the much feared; World War – Three.

YANKS PRETEND WITHDRAWAL!

There was no fuss, or fond embrace, as the change of 'Boss' was made at Army Command. Brian Horrocks had simply vanished, to be replaced by Wilkinson. A more staidly gentleman, totally lacking in bon-homie and showmanship; in the same manner as Monty, he chose to travel solo in the headquarters lift. With no hint of compatibility, Wilko's was a completely different routine to that of Horrocks. Horrocks simply ushered all and sundry into the lift, and he became last man in. Wilko's exclusivity, in so simple a form, reflected his drabness.

Much was made of the next major project. It was American, and in their requiring traverse through the British Zone, we had a measure of involvement. It was here that Freddy Coombes made no secret of my military withdrawal 'expertise'.

I was delegated to join with the Yanks, in 'pulling out' from their Headquarters, at Frankfurt, to possible departure, at Bremerhaven; situated possibly 350 miles distant, to the North West of Germany.

What expertise I had, was simply that of survival. It was a matter of; 'where you stop walking, there you die!' You could either pull your own trigger, or have your last favour done by your 'mucker'. Quartermaster, 'Taffy' Phillips, required no 'friendly attention'; He may, even to this day, lie in the swamp by the Central Burma Oil Fields. A succession of unfortunates, as singer-comedian, Private Fish, lay down in the butterfly graced jungle, but not before a day throughout which he had sung the popular, Vera Lynne song; "We'll meet again, Don't know where? Don't know when? But I know we'll meet again some sunny day". 'Power house', Sergeant Oldcorn collapsed dead, within yards of help, at the Indian border. There were varieties of ways in which to die: And you stayed there!

That was withdrawal; British style!

Witnessing American endeavour was completely different in contrivance, and to attempt comparison with the Burma withdrawal was impossible. The 'Start Off' parade inspection, had nothing to do with drill, or turnout, it was more interested in ensuring that all heavy equipment, including back packs, were loaded onto transport.

Troops mounted vehicles, and the steady procession moved out, coming to a hilarious halt in the Hannover region. It was here that the serious business began. Various sections, or platoons, had to find their allocated tent, as they were already erected, and sited, in disciplined lines.

As bugle calls sounded; "Cookhouse!" The dash started. Queues formed at the four, or five, counters, for steak, fish, chicken, or other dishes: The chef called; "How do you want it cooking?" All was contained within massive, brand spanking new, purpose built, stainless steel kitchens.

In these very trying times, I nearly cried! Joining the queue for steak, it was by request: Well done? – Medium? – Or, Rare? I could hardly believe my ears, as one squaddy ahead of me, blurted out, "I'll take it raw!"

The strenuous exercise continued northwards, with a similar halt in the Bremen area. It transpired the whole exercise was, principally, in order to test the lush stainless steel cookhouse, also its movement between two locations, and the combined efficiency of tent erection.

On my return to Rhine Army, I suggested that it would have been nice to have had them all with me on the trip. It was farcical, 'in the extreme'.

THE BELGIAN CONNECTION

Apart from my expertise in withdrawal, and the readiness to try anything, Freddy Coombes found me a further attachment. I was to join with, and spend a few days attached to a Company of Belgian troops, stationed at nearby Minden. He knew that I spoke Belgian, as fluently as I spoke Chinese, Japanese, and Urdu.

It was an easy one, as most Belgian Officers spoke very good English.

Made most welcome by my new friends, they sought to practice speaking English with me, and I think I managed to get a bit of Yorkshire accent into them. Accepting that most Belgians had suffered severe rationing for a number of years, I found one feeding practice, most unusual. Sardine sandwiches, at breakfast, were dunked in coffee, by all and sundry. I suppose that is not so unusual for a nation that eats horseflesh.

Friendship formed on this attachment, resulted in my having regular meetings with the Commandant, Kervan De Mierander, and his wife. I was particularly pleased when Kervan accepted my invitation, and became Godfather to my German born son.

22

DECISION TIME AND SKIING

Oh yes, it was, hurtful as hell? I had resolved that following the success, and pleasure of recent years, my career, and future, should be to remain within the generous British Army. Having accepted a three year short service commission, in order to give it a final trial, and with the recommendation to attend Staff College, I knew that I had potential. With the rare, and unusual, background of my service, and the nation's senior generals on my CV, I was destined for success. Having been tested and proved successful, in different branches within the service, I knew that I was bloody good at soldiering, in whatever capacity.

Having experienced the worst of it, I disliked and distrusted the Army's historical militarism, and Parliamentary aloofness. Regardless of my indifference to untrustworthy civil and military superiors, I simply loved soldiering for the sake of it. Knowing that I was so good at it, I could command, and receive respect from the men beneath me, whilst at the same time, knew that my peers, and equals, enjoyed my friendship and camaraderie.

'Knowing the ropes; as I did', and being a virtual 'loose cannon', whilst achieving success at all levels, there was no limit to my potential. I was living in the world of my dreams.

Good pay, Excellent food, A personal servant, Responsibility for men, Accepted and trusted by leaders, and with a physique to match the best, I could have gone to the very top.

Suddenly, the 'euphoric dream', became, no more than a 'pipe dream'. Tragically, and unfortunately, without spelling out the detail, my domestic side had health problems, not easily overcome. I was in an unforgiving situation, and must forget the dream, and make the most of what little Army time I had.

The prospect of returning to Hunslet, the industrial district, to the south side of Leeds, was not conducive to pleasantness, therefore; I was not a happy man. Hunslet was a world renowned engineering centre: There were Steelworks, Copper Works, Gas Works, and foul Chemical Works. Many of them provisioning Hunslet Engine Company, and Hudswell Clark, steam railway engineers. Fowlers Tractors, Kayes lockworks and oilcans, Henry Berry, hydraulics; Claytons, Kitsons, Kings, and a myriad of suppliers. The world's first industrial railway, carried coal from Middleton Broome Colliery, to Hunslet Coal Staithes, and to the Gas works, and all gave out muck. Green sludgy coloured air, coming from the chemical works, grey and black air from most of the others, and thick black smog throughout most winters.

Not one of these organisations functioned without men, men of the highest calibre, where trust and respect were the watchword. There was a dignity in holding employment, particularly throughout the most trying times of depression; the 1920's, and 1930's. Payment for working daily, 7.30 am to 6.00 pm, with one hour for lunch, a good tradesman would earn between £2.15s and £3.10s: (Two pounds fifteen shillings, and, Three pounds ten shillings; per week). This paltry payment did not allow for the purchase of a house, or motor car, except in very rare cases. Schoolteachers earned a steady four pounds weekly, but seldom did they own a car.

Substantial differences came about for select executives; with a wage of five pounds, or more, one could become both, a house and car owner. My pre-war studies, with a Higher National Certificate, and almost a certainty for university entrance, targeted a salary of £7. 10s: (seven pounds ten shillings; per week); comparative wealth.

The dread of my return to the drab, day by day existence, of civilian life, overtook reactions to my long suffered, superficial show of military diligence, and my perfunctory dedication, to the British cause. I went back to basics, shedding the mantle of falsehood, and sought to exploit whatever diversion was on offer, in the limited time available.

Having enjoyed small-boat sailing in India, why not indulge further; in a little skiing? Accommodated in charming Frau Reader's humble guest house, at the Lermoos leave centre in Austria, food was plentiful, and of the highest standard.

Inevitably, there has to be a Billy Bighead in almost any party, and the one such that we had, helped mentor and caution me for the trip, only for himself to fail. Getting himself rigged out with boots and skis, in such haste, he had to be first man out, and up to the top of the Pimple Hill slope. The poor sod, broke his leg, and returned on the train in which he had arrived.

With the Snowplough and Christiana turns, conquered on skis, I joined in novice races. It was adequate, I had skied. So pleasant was the place, I repeated the trip to Lermoos in the summer, in order to further exploit the spectacular scenery and hills.

Travelling by cable-car up the Zugspitze, Germany's highest mountain; (2963 mts / 9721 ft), it was eerie, to then enjoy the kilometre walk, through the permanently ice lined tunnel, caused by mountain mist. The tunnel runs between Austria and Germany. Refreshingly taking the mountain railway, from the summit, down to Germany's Garmisch Partenkirchen, the spectacular setting for future Winter Olympics, and who could resist the name?

Three tiring hours, spent climbing the nearby Sonnenspitz Mountain, had me sweating on arrival at the summit. The mountain enclosed the Schwarz See (Black Sea), at a height of about eight thousand feet. Stripped off, and 'starkers', I dived in, only to wish that I had not. Unlike the tropical warmth of Burma's Chindwin River, the Schwarz See water was almost freezing. Feeling the cold, and knowing the possibilities, I was out within seconds.

The local mountain guide, appearing from a nearby lodge, gave me a fair, 'dressing down', for my lunacy. Realising that I had a modicum of athletic potential, I was invited to join the gentleman on his return to the village. It was the most terrifying descent I have made in my life. Twenty minutes, operating as a mountain goat, returned me to the base of my three hour climb. The man led the way, as we plunged, from ledge to ledge, in almost sheer drops. He had the grace to shake me by the hand before departing. I realise, this return mountain route could qualify as a most testing Olympic event.

Obligatory to any good Catholic boy, travelling in this part of the world is a visit to Oberamergau, the small remote village, famed for its staging of the 'Passion Play', every ten years. This is a place of both, passion, and mystery.

Not long returned from Lermoos, a new challenge presented itself. I'd never been to Switzerland, and here was the opportunity. It entailed collecting a former German General. Knowing nothing of the man, except his name, and that he was to be collected from the town of Berne, I set forth, once more, accompanied by an armed driver, and Sergeant.

The two years limit of asylum, in Switzerland, having expired, the General was required to surrender. He had the choice of going to any one of the four occupying countries within Germany. Having no great regard for America, Russia, or France, the wise choice was made; he chose to surrender to the British.

Taking two days on the journey to Switzerland, I found myself, somewhat surreptitiously, booked in at Bernes', Drei Konigen, (Three Kings Hotel). It was here that I appeared to terrify a man identifying himself as; 'The British Air Attaché'. He was horrified, and expressed himself as though in disgust, at seeing me, all dressed-up, in a khaki uniform, and looking very much like a British Army officer, with three pips on both shoulders.

Gently reminding the dear sweet thing, that my mode of dress, as a simple officer in the British Army, was one that I had used for nine years, and that I had no other garb; he was mollified; emphasising, the Molly! The Air Attaché escorted me to meet with the purpose of my visit. He was a very tall gentleman, and expressed no rancour over his expulsion from Switzerland. I got the impression that he rather looked forward to enjoying his incarceration: By whatever means, he appeared to have excellent information on British prisoner of war conditions.

With arrangements made for collection of the General, on the following morning, the Air Attaché handed me sufficient Swiss currency for use on evening entertainment, and suggested a nearby club. Visiting the place,

I did not like the lecherous looks on members' faces. They leered at me; I must have looked a most desirable brute, garbed in military uniform; With pips! The 'poncy place' might have suited the dear sweet Attache. I vanished!

Collecting General Carl Von Reichoff; he was dressed in civilian clothing, and little was said, as we departed Switzerland. Within yards of crossing the Swiss border, and entering French Zone territory through which we had to pass, I ordered the General to dismount the vehicle. The Sergeant conducted a search of the man; and from previous experience, as seen with the Polish gentleman a little earlier, at Bad Salzuflen, I ensured, it was a most thorough search. Demonstrating, that my two escorts had ten rounds of ammunition in their magazines, with one up the breach, and with safety catches applied, the General was warned: "Any false move; made by himself, or any other person, would result in him, and any interloper, being shot". We started on our way.

Speaking excellent English, the General assured me that he had nothing untoward to answer for, and that he had commanded German forces in Norway. In the period of asylum, he had used his time in writing, and published two books. It was as we approached the town of Freiburg, he made a request. Stating that his wife, and daughter, occupied an apartment situated at the side of the road we were about to pass, he asked me to allow him a visit.

This was a difficult and speculative request, requiring careful consideration, as I was aware that the former German military hierarchy had a system of well established communications. Giving no decision, I insisted that he guide us to a stop immediately outside the premises. It was essential that I establish his first assurance, and description of the dwelling, was correct. Giving the OK, and hardening the conditions of capture, the visiting time was limited, and stipulated; "he must remain within sight of the Sergeant throughout". Brief though it was, the visit was made, to the General, and his family, appreciation.

Ungracious salutations followed, as we moved off through the busier part of Freiburg town. As French Moroccan soldiers lined the road, on both sides, all were waving balloons, almost as a guard of honour, and gesticulating, as though of joy. The balloons were inflated condoms, (rubber goods, or Frenchies to the English). This was possibly the first issue of any form of 'protective equipment', to these troops;

Departing the French Zone, we entered the American Sector, in order to enjoy a one night halt at Frankfurt. Unthinking, and uncharitable, the General was housed in the 'Town Gaol', a security premises staffed by American troops. It was nauseating the following morning, to see a diminutive Yank, Army Sergeant, leading the tall eloquent, and mannerly General, with a fixed bayonet held to the middle of his back. The squirt of a Sergeant was shouting: "Anybody, want to see my General?"

I was not sure whether the Sergeant wasn't the same ignorant man I had met with previously, on the 'withdrawal exercise', ranting: "I'll take it raw!" If it was not him, he certainly had all the grace of the man. I was a bit rude to him.

The following night spent in a home territory gaol, at Hanover, was smooth, with the Sergeant sleeping across the doorway of the General's room. We were on the way to Munster- Lager, where about eighty further German Generals were held. Through whatever system of, 'jungle drum communication', Carl Von Reichoff was expected, and made welcome. I never knew the outcome of whatever trial, or tribunal, the General faced. I wished him well!

23

'MANNY' SHINWELL – THE DREGS

Despite European hostilities having ceased for two years, careful rationing of essential commodities continued throughout Britain; shopkeepers honoured household ration allocations. Living conditions amongst the German populace continued to show no improvement, in fact, they deteriorated badly; rationing, communications, and refinements of all kinds, remained abysmally poor. A memorable, and modest indicator at attempts to mask the prevailing atrocious conditions, was the token emblem, carried by almost every German male. Seldom was one seen without a briefcase. Never seen open, the empty case was a tool, to put into, or take out of, and it was always, 'to hand'; For whatever nefarious reason; one never knew what opportunity might present itself?

Rationing for the occupying forces, were, frankly, brilliant compared to those of the Germans, and were frequently used in elicit, 'Black Market' trading, or fiddling, for watches and cameras. Additionally, troops now had the improved services of the N.A.A.F.I., (Navy, Army, and Air Force Institute). Although the greatly prized; newly introduced, and greatly desired, nylon stockings, and chocolates, were held by the Americans, at their somewhat superior, PX Stores, to which, few Brits had access.

The living was fine, until we received the 'bombshell'. With very little warning, possibly about New Years Day 1948, panic set in at Rhine Army HQ. The recently appointed, Parliamentary Defence Secretary, Mr. Emanuel Shinwell, MP, announced that he was about to visit B.A.O.R. He declared his needs;

"In view of the rapid demobilisation of the conscript army, he was to appraise the duties, and value, of the British Army of occupation. With particular attention paid to the perceived, ongoing aggressive attitude of Russian forces".

This called for, 'all hands to the wheel': Mr Shinwell was known to be something of a martinet, and rabble-rouser, one demanding the highest of standards, at all times. Rising from life's lower levels, he was a course man. He revelled in attacking the ones he considered, 'upper-class aristocracy', or similar. Ones he thought might treat him as an underling, or of a lower level.

Conscious of the vastness of the country, and spread of the numerous Military services, particular stress was placed upon the cartographers. They were to illustrate the layout of all British military facilities. Based in the lower reaches of the Headquarters offices, they became 'hell bent' on producing overlay maps, indicating all sectors of the Armed Services: Hospitals, Tanks, Medics, Signals, Engineers, Brigades, etc. It was a night and day operation, with current detail not readily available at all times. Heads of departments were required to check for accuracy, approve each map overlay, and prepare for their own personal presentation. It was hectic, day and night, with none wanting to slip-up.

The scene was set for Shinwell's arrival, with seventeen service chiefs assembled, all somewhat apprehensive, particularly in view of the vitriolic reputation of the new Minister. He was a man renowned for his unpleasant forthrightness. Manny's background, of being a working man, and progressing through the ranks of Trade Unionism, was anathematized, in the eyes of many of the, 'officer types', and Manny knew it. He, in turn, would see, and consider, senior military commanders, as 'upper bracket': 'Products of Public Schools'. He was, 'down upon them, in a belittling manner', at any opportunity.

Scheduled to visit, from, 11[th,] to 16th January 1948, (these dates were further confirmed by my visit to the House of Lords, Archives, on 2nd August 2007).

The Ministerial party duly arrived, and with not one blush, check, handshake, or moment of composure; on entering the building, the Minister's arms were thrown into the air, as though to embrace. Renowned for his thick skin and forthrightness, he lived up to the mark, and with plausible audacity, he continued with the words: "Come on! You Chaps!

– You know what you're doing!" The carefully manicured presentation was over before it began, and a cup of tea became important.

Humiliation, with this arrogant entrance, as seen by our dedicated team of organisers, was the ultimate degradation of the assembly of Senior Commanders. However, it became, 'Ever so British!' Within their stiff upper lips, the collection of military dignitaries, clearly afraid of any reaction by Shinwell; said not one word. 'Seventeen Senior, British Military Commanders', were insulted, En-masse. Not one, of the abject team, saw fit to raise a voice against the despicably loathsome individual.

A British Government, Defence Minister, having previously announced his detailed requirements, disregarded all considerations, possibilities, and information, on the existing perilous conditions, specifically requested by him. The possible threat, by the aggressive and belligerent Russian forces, appeared to be of no consequence.

Ironically, Shinwell was reportedly, and historically, the highest rated British Conscientious Objector, to World War – One. He spared no blushes, in his insulting the distinguished gathering. For so odious a character to be appointed to such a post, and for him to arrive as, His Imperial Majesties, Minister for Defence, was insult indeed!

The tiny consolation, for what it was worth, was that, Shinwell's driver got lost for a while, travelling many miles, in the wrong direction, along the autobahn.

The man of Government had other priorities, and how successful Shinwell's quest proved, I do not know, but it certainly had nothing to do with the British Armed Forces. He reportedly, sought to purchase a Volkswagen car; from the NAAFI, (Navy, Army, and Air Force Institute). With the Wolfsburg, 'Peoples Car', production line restored, VW cars became, 'On offer', at a cost of Sixty Pounds, Sterling, (£60.00). The enterprising franchise was rapidly terminated, by intervention of the Society of British Motor Manufacturers and Traders. Consequently, with VW cars introduced into Britain, the price doubled, and quadrupled within weeks, and I heard of no man successfully making a purchase, through NAAFI sources.

Exploiting his Parliamentary privilege, Shinwell went further. He made a, 'Goodwill visit', to the American Zone, including the PX,

(NAAFI equivalent). No doubting, the pig-headed indignity of the man, he exploited his Ministerial title to the full; obtaining Yankee, nylons, chocolates, and whatever else on offer.

His return to London did not mean that we were finished with the Ministerial, 'paragon of virtue'. An urgent request for figures was made, following his return to the Palace of Westminster. Having heard of the increasing requirement, to replace demobilising conscripted British troops, by former, German held, prisoners of war, Manny demanded to know the numbers involved; along with their nationality.

Arrangements for replacement of cover for the reducing British troop duties, was 'ad-hoc', and a localised activity. Military Commanders ceased responsibility for guard duties, at installations considered less strategic, in conjunction with Control Commission staff. Commanders simply indicated where replacements were required. The local German 'Town Mayor' appointed civilian squads; ones recruited from members of, the numerous, former prisoners of the German armed forces. The men were known as PWX, with nationality: PWX (Pole), (Czech), (Lith), (Rom), etc. With no centralisation, or collective documentation, enlistment figures varied daily.

The tempo changed rapidly, as Shinwell reverted to type. On the Monday, he demanded that figures be to hand, for a meeting to be held on Thursday. It was an impossible task. Goading me on in his understating manner, one I recognised all too well, Freddy Coombes suggested that I take a motor cycle, and dash around all HQ's, remarking; "Fitz! If Mr. Shinwell wants figures, he's got to have figures!"

However; following a few brief words with my counterparts at Divisional level, it transpired, there was no such thing as consolidated figures. It became a matter of: "If the wretch, visiting here to insult the Senior Commanders presentation, wants figures, he can have them!" Alive to the 'dingy mist' of Parliamentarian uncertainty, I was ready; Shinwell 'will' have his desired figures! Freddy, was most encouraging, and almost helpful, as I concocted the most impressive tabloid of guesswork figures.

Knowing exactly how the bogus figures had been concocted, Colonel Hutchinson smiled, and with not a word, he signed the document. All three of us; Headquarters, British Army of the Rhine, (Operations),

General Staff Officers; - GSO-I, GSO-II, and GSO-III, now implicated, and if caught undertaking such subterfuge, subject to facing, a Military Courts Martial.

The urgency of delivery became overtaken by shear desperation. How on earth could anyone fail Mr Shinwell? Certainly, not me! Hot foot! I was, surprisingly, and unceremoniously, despatched to the nearby, Bielefeld airfield; boarded a Dakota transport plane, and as the sole occupant of the bare, cold, rough interior; delivered to Oakham airfield, in Rutland.

Surprise! Surprise! A staff car awaited me, for the hundred, or so, mile trip to Westminster, where the very mention of Shinwell opened all doors. The man bounded forward, actually shook me by the hand, and I knew the rest: Overflowing with an exaggerated gush, and a generous, showy, "Thank you!" The phoney and dubious Minister, spouted out his usual; "You chaps know what you're doing!"

Desirous to be seen in company with common soldiery, he invited me into 'The House', for a drink: It was a whisky, just one, a single, and I loved the handshakes and salutations: 'Hypocrite?'

With a modest three pips on my shoulders, one might have thought it was Montgomery attending, as Manny's acolytes accumulated, in creepy adulation. Introducing me to each, in turn, as they arrived, Manny had to ask my name, at least three times, and on each occasion, I became, "Fitzgerald". Trumpeting his successful visit to BAOR, it was as though I had conducted the presentation of events; whereas, we had exchanged, not one word throughout his visit, and there had been no, 'Presentation'. My 'Personal' leadership, and success, in Europe, was applauded, although I had been nowhere near the European war, and I was wearing the ribbon of the Burma Star.

In less than thirty minutes, a British Minister for Defence, illustrated all that I have ever thought the Palace of Westminster to be: A proper Rat House, rather than the German, Rathaus.

Having a kindly word with the London Rail Transport Officer, he 'ensured' that I could not return to Germany, for a further three days. Nicely accommodated, in a cosy hotel, I managed a few drinks, a bit of horse racing, and 'startlingly', witnessed the most attractively, fashionable, ladies wear;- 'The New Look!' The style, the cut, and length, has never yet been surpassed! It was a knockout!

Practiced in receiving 'Parliamentary, paragons of virtue', we were not left to dwell on the recent resounding success for too long. Mr. Bellingham, the Shadow Secretary for Defence, insisted on re-tracing Shinwell's steps.

Reception drill, and map over-lays, were checked, and exercised, with exactly the same detail as for Shinwell. Thinking that Bellingham's, Parliamentary opposition inspection, might prove more intense than Shinwell's, nothing was left to chance. Without using the same words, the sentiment was exactly the same: Bellingham mirrored the visit made by Shinwell. He must have accepted, and appreciated, Manny's disclosures, on the Yank, PX situation, and could not get there fast enough. Of course we loved him: Three simple soldiering Staff Officers, had fooled the best that the British Government could offer!

At the time of scribing this tome, on the 23rd May 2009, the country is undergoing unprecedented Parliamentary turmoil. Shattering Governmental history, within the last few days, The Speaker of the House of Commons, having been caught 'fiddling', has declared that he, personally, is about to; "Stand Down!" Parliamentarians of all parties stand accused of gross misconduct, in exploiting the expense claims system, The Speaker, being one of them. The accepted custom, of claims control, has, until recently, been nebulous, and undefined, with the onus of determining, 'amount limitations', resting upon individuals. Each of the accused members, in turn, states, the excessive amount claimed, to be; "A mistake!"

The mistake was; 'Being caught out, Fiddling!'

Fallacious claims, made by Members of Parliament, and identified at the present time, include; Draining a garden moat, A floating island for ducks in a garden pond, Purchase of numerous bedding sheets, Man and wife, both, Members of parliament, claiming for two, 'second separate houses', 'Flipping', (profiting from moving, and upgrading house values), Tax claims, Claiming £80,000, on property, and selling on, at a discount, to a daughter.

The disgrace, and calamity, bringing about the 'Standing down'; of, 'A Speaker, of the House of Commons': This for the first time, in more than three hundred years. All is revealed, following a recently introduced Parliamentary, 'Rule of Transparency'. One is left to wonder: How far has the present investigation to go; and how long has this laxity existed? Not Long! As recent as May 2010, the Chief Secretary to the Treasury, of the newly installed Tory/Lib Dem Government, resigned. He is accused of 'fiddling' £20,000 on accommodation rental.

Had I had the culprits with me in Burma, Parliamentarians? Or Not! They would have gone the way of the Dacoit band of recalcitrant oilfield workers.

Re-editing this work, ten months after my ninetieth (10th August 2009) birthday, I find nothing changes, in Governmental, and Military, conduct. Throughout the decade, it is as though idiotism rules. For some reason, former Prime Minister, Anthony Blair, became obsessed, and had a fixation, that the Middle Eastern country of Iraq, possessed a quantity of, 'Weapons of Mass Destruction'. Blair consorted with another considered lunatic, the American President, Bush, and the disillusioned pair, committed their armies to war with Iraq. There were no WMD to be found, but the pair remained adamant, they wanted a war, so they had one: And lost numerous good men!

Frustrated in Iraq, the twosome turned to Afghanistan, and found reason to conduct a second conflict, in the hills of this remote and mountainous country. Losses, killed and injured, mount at an increasingly alarming rate, to the point where I personally, anticipate a devastating disaster, in the very near future.

Nauseatingly, throughout the decade, numerous changes are made, at both Government Under-Secretary, and Chief of Defence Staff levels. At times, there is inconsistency, to the point of imbecility. Regardless of competence: by rote; senior Generals take their turn, to become Chief of Defence Staff. Each of the egotistical minded Generals, compete for seniority, in order to justify pension rights. Rotating with measured regularity, each one completes a stint sufficient to qualify for enhanced pension, and then stands down.

As, day by day, the Afghanistan death toll mounts, Politicians, and Military Generals, enjoy constant security, each preserving lucrative pay, and pensions. Whilst remaining secure, and in office, seldom does one hear words of criticism, or condemnation.

Once freed of office, there is a rat-race, each one in turn, seeking immediate, media attention, and publicity. Recent incumbent, politicians, and they change within days, are, Derek Twigg, Bob Ainsworth, Kevin Jones, Bill Rammell, and Lord Guthrie. The Diaspora, of former military hierarchy, brings out words held deep throughout service life. A Colonel Kemp, idiotically forecasts, "Up to forty years of conflict, in Afghanistan". A contrary view is expressed by, the politically overlooked contender for the Chief of Defence Staff appointment, General Sir Richard Dannatt: He states, "We must succeed!" – "We will succeed!" How ludicrously speculative, and insipid, is a comment of this nature? The man knows; The British Army, will require withdrawal from the country, in the not too distant future. Success by insurgents, in this remote theatre, is known to be impossible! Recently, Russia lost almost 50,000 troops in a similar venture

Current newspaper snippets, and they are never ending, indicate tension existing, as the Afghan conflict struggles on: Muddle-headedness, mostly, by a selection of individuals; Ones, choosing to keep their mouths shut, whilst being paid, and operationally engaged in the military. Quoting from; -

Yorkshire Evening Post, 11th July 2009; "Ministers have again been accused of putting British forces in Afghanistan at risk through penny-pinching". Prime Minister Gordon Brown acknowledged; -"It was a very hard summer for the troops", but insisted, "The Government was resolved to seeing through the mission".

General Lord Guthrie, Chief of the Defence Staff from 1997 to 2001, a former head of the Armed Forces, accused the Government of; -"Putting UK forces at risk"; -"Commanders on the ground were struggling with too few troops".

YEPost, 19th August 2009; Britons warned today to expect more troop deaths in Afghanistan. Col Stuart Tootal, former commander of 3 Para, said; "It was a sad inevitability that there would be more losses in the run up to tomorrow's, (Afghan), elections". He urged the Government; "To ensure there was a coherent and properly resourced strategy".

Daily Mail – 14th June 2010 Editorial comments: -"Of Labours many failings in 13 years of government, perhaps the most egregious was its shabby treatment of the armed forces".

> *"After leading them into war in Iraq on a lie, Tony Blair, (ex PM), followed by Gordon Brown, (Ex PM) pitched them ever deeper into an open-ended campaign in Afghanistan. Our servicemen and women have performed their duties with heroic courage and professionalism".*

> *"Critical equipment shortages, and shameful lack of a clear mission statement, have opened up a serious breach of trust between them and their political masters in Whitehall".*

> *"Tory Defence Secretary, Liam Fox; (Two months in office), is launching a full strategic review to draw a line under Labour's woeful mismanagement".*

In panic, the Labour Government appointment of Air Chief Marshall, Sir Graham Eric 'Jock' Stirrup as Chief of Defence Staff, in 2006, and extended his appointment for two years. The inept appointment was made in order to deny the crucial post to the increasingly outspoken head of the Army, General Sir Richard Dannatt, a supporter of the opposition, Tory party.

Stirrup could fly aircraft, but he was out of his depth in controlling military ground forces. Whitehall senior figures identified his shortcomings, and he became the target of whispering campaigns. He was known as, "a dead man walking", with concerns about his handling of operations in Afghanistan. Ineffectual tactics, inappropriate equipment, out of hand costs: Yes! I had suffered this, many years ago, and with no redress.

In order to clear all hindrance to progress, the Ministry of Defence most senior governmental civil servant, Permanent Under-secretary, Sir Bill Jeffrey, was also released, (sacked), by Mr Liam Fox.

In June 2010, perfidiousness prevails throughout governmental control, as the 10,000 strong British military force, stationed in Afghanistan, suffer the degradation of being placed under the command of an American general. No serving man, or woman, was given the choice of this option, although unremittingly, the General Officer Commanding will favour, and claim any successes to America; and the British become a secondary consideration

USA General Eisenhower demonstrated the jealous American trait when in Germany. With Montgomery seeking glory for himself in America, he backed Ike in bringing about what he called, "a clinical conclusion to the war". Brian Horrocks, commanding the highly successful British 30 Corps, could have terminated activities one week earlier.

As the 2010 General Election became ever more imminent, numerous retiring Members of Parliament become outspoken on their careers, expectations, and disappointments, whilst serving in 'The House'. I quote from a selection of gems, as announced in the Yorkshire Evening Post: -

27/11/2004 – Standing down after more than two decades in Westminster, as MP for West Ham, Former Labour minister, Tony Banks admitted; "He found his constituents' problems boring, and got 'no satisfaction' from helping them", "it was often like being a high-powered social worker, dealing with complaints which were, tedious in the extreme".

7/08/2008 – Asked what was the most lucrative work he had ever done, former Tory MP Neil Hamilton replied; "I suppose getting elected to Parliament, it's money for old rope. I didn't have to do anything if I didn't want to".

19/02/2010 – Veteran Tory MP Sir Nicholas Winterton, hitting out at the new expenses culture at the House of Commons, stated; -"He was 'Infuriated', in that he can no longer travel first-class on trains".

19/02/2010 – In an article headed, "Madhouse awaits new MP's, says Battle". We hear from John Battle, 58, retiring MP for Leeds constituencies, including Armley, Bramley, Kirkstall and Wortley;

he is standing down after 23 years, having served as both Trade and Industry, and Foreign Office Minister, under the questionable Prime Minister, Tony Blair.

Battle says, in giving a stark warning to the new intake of MP's; "The House of Commons is a madhouse, this place is insane, it can crush politicians and drive them to drink". "How do you work in a place that is like a cross between a church, a prison, and an art gallery?"

"I have seen it crush people. I have seen them disappear into the bar. The people I have met here, generally, if you really scrape them, are in it because they want to change the lives of people". "And they are people. The non-people don't survive".

Comments are drawn from a local newspaper, in which each MP has sought competitive press coverage, over many years: With photographs, and seeking 'self publicity' on a daily basis. The total lack of general interest, and denied dedication to constituents, is reflected in their contributions.

That these people, at enormous cost, and trusted beyond measure, should be responsible for the conducting of wars, as they were, at the time of my total abandonment in Burma 1942, is beyond contempt.

24

RHINE BRIDGES – VIEWING

Parliamentarian visitors, having thoroughly disgusted all Senior Commanders within Rhine Army, the tone changed completely. It was hard, almost farcical, to apply strictness and discipline, in view of the contempt shown by both; Defence Minister, Shinwell, and his shadow Minister, Bellingham.

As organisers, co-ordinators, and witnesses, of the Parliamentarian visits, and the humiliating fiascos; GSO.I, GSO.II, and GSO.III, Colonel Hutchinson, Freddy Coombes, and I, scorned Senior Commanders. Respect was nil.

Commanders, all supposedly, men of valour and guts, did not get where they were by questioning Political, or Parliamentary, decisions. No doubt, in the event of their querying such nonsense, the outcome would be, at least a sideways move, as frequently practiced by Churchill; (examples; Wavell, Auchinleck, Mountbatten, Harris, the Airman Bomber, and others), or a posting. All had seen former colleagues, dethroned, and cast into the abyss. There was something rotten in the disgusting and underhand way that things transpired, particularly amongst those in upper reaches of command.

Sceptically, and with good reason, judging my seniors, and being on 'the countdown', to demobilisation, why should I not exploit, all possibilities to the full?

A colleague of mine, a fellow Staff Officer of the Royal Engineers, arrived at the office, carrying a list of R.E. officers, and requiring the signature of Colonel Hutchinson. General Staff approval was a necessary requirement, in order to authorise a visit into other occupied zones, particularly the French Zone. The general idea, and purpose of the expedition, was to admire the newly erected Rhine River crossing bridges. All officer's named on the list contained the suffix; 'RE'.

With a minimum of manipulation, I presented the list to the Colonel, and in short time, he commented: "Captain G.Fitzpatrick, K.O.Y.L.I.". He had in some way, noticed the odd man out. "This is you! Do you want to go?" "If so; you go as a liaison officer!" Assured that my initial Army enlistment was into the Royal Engineers, he readily approved and signed.

My Sapper Officer counterpart had done a most excellent job in reconnoitring the trip, and nothing was left to chance. The train was meticulously timed to join with the river cruiser. Berthing as close as possible, to each bridge, we were conveyed, most carefully, to the best of the nearby eateries: And wine flowed!

As a beer drinker, apart from the odd sherry, or port, I had no experience of imbibing copious quantities of wine, certainly not by the bottle, and that was how it, 'unfortunately, and happily,' came. I got the impression that the bridges, and the varieties of constructions, were in excellent order. It was so difficult to find fault with the structures: 'And the wine flowed!'

Far more discerning was in judging the quality of a variety of wines. All had to have a sufficiency, before decisions were made. Simple Rhine wine, first on the agenda, was considered commonplace. A little more sophisticated, was that of the Mosel River valley, where three wine cellars were visited, in order to ensure that; all pissed and present, arrived at a 'correctly determined' verdict.

Far the superior of wines, was that of the River Ahr. The secret of this delicacy, we were told: 'Ahr wine doesn't travel'. In this case, we were the 'fortunate travellers in residence'. It was a joy, and sadly, in due course, we had to depart. Arriving for lunch at Traben Traben, the small town at the river source, we were greatly entertained; to a meal of several courses, and loaded well, in order to ensure: 'A safe, and pleasurable, travel of the wine!'

A dream lunch, on the following day, surpasses all remembered throughout my ninety years. Entertained at Koblenz, by the French Control Commissioner, food flowed over thirteen delightful courses.

Absolutely delicious in every morsel, including the most succulent, and unforgettable, slice of wild boar, and each course accompanied by a careful selection of French wine. We imbibed, and simply, more imbibed, for four or five long hours. All very trying, but, what better can one do? Patriotically, Pissed as we were, we were diligently, upholding the *entente cordiale*, for King and Country?

With heavy regrets, at knowing that I was about to depart Army Service, I regarded this meal as my farewell party. It continued further, and pleasantly, as we boarded the train back to base; several cases of wine appeared, possibly, in order to ensure that we wasted no time in departure. 'I love inspecting river bridges!'

25

MAMA'S BOY

Everybody I know has a birthday; and, come to think of it? So does everybody I do not know. However very few of them can remember where they were before that, and none attempt returning to, from whence they came.

Cheeky childish pranks amongst school children brought revelations. Talk was often of naughty subjects, suggesting that friends had been hidden away for many months, and there were few exceptions. It became a little risqué to speculate, as dates of individual's births were announced. Disclosing a September date started a guessing game: 'What were Mammy and Daddy engaged in on the previous Christmas?' Easter, the moveable feast, proved a little more problematic.

I can't help but feel particularly special, stamping out my date of conception, Mammy and Daddy chose carefully: It is a day celebrated throughout the country, bands play, and parades are held in the streets, as thousands upon thousands of admirers join in the joyful demonstrating. Her Majesty, the Queen, brings flowers, and I feel ever so humble, as silence comes over the land.

For my Irish Mammy, to meet with 'the thing' that turned out to be, Daddy, there must have been something special in the offing: There was nothing. Daddy was dressed in the light blue suit of a hospitalised, wounded soldier, however done? A smooth talker, he had obviously, as they say; 'gone the rounds'.

Deducing back from my birth, on the 10th August 1919, for the period of gestation, it takes me back to, 11th November 1918. The fact that World War-One ended on that day, might have something to do with it. It does not stop me from regarding this as a big day, both before, and throughout my life. I must be the perfect linkage between the two great wars; World War-One, and World War-Two. The marriage of John Fitzpatrick to Eileen Elizabeth, (Liza), O'Grady, in May 1919, saved me from the bare bones of bastardly ignominy, by three months.

It was not the thing for a good, Irish Catholic girl, to have kids out of wedlock. Once wed, the die was cast, and there was no going back. It was a case of; 'You've made your bed, now lie on it!'

There was never a mention of the circumstances of my parents meeting, or romance, of any kind; No such thing as a hug, or a cuddle. The rare occasions they had time out together was, in attending family functions. Father John had his own priorities, and woe-betide anyone interfering between pub opening times, time at the bookies, and his cigarettes. One exceptional outstanding joint mission, was when the pair attended the, Point to Point, horse racing, at Bretton Park, near Wakefield; Mother returned, having won a 'pocket-full' of pound notes. Not a bad judge of horses, she had backed every winner.

John, and Liza, are unlikely to have had a great deal, of courtship, and conversation, in early days; or on the day of conception. It would not be long enough for John to tell of his previous Army service, which included a spell in Ireland. I don't think that he served in Churchill's, 'Black and Tans', but who knows?

Embittered; John contested the British Government denial of his war pension rights; He had served pre-war for nine years, as a signaller, in the 2/KOYLI, before WW-One. On the outbreak of war in August 1914, he was posted to France with, 'The Contemptible Little Army', and served throughout, with a measure of distinction. Twice, he was recommended for highest honours, and, on each occasion his case was found to be, unmerited! He was however; Twice – 'Mentioned in Dispatches'.

Becoming increasingly infuriated, at the ineptitude of military command, resulting in him losing numerous colleagues, John did not spare his words when 'bollocking' irresponsible senior officers and he used military equipment to do so. Whatever the mutilation, it happened, and his wounding was questionable? Questionable, though it was, it was never a subject of conversation. As a child, Daddy trailed me around a series of Military Tribunals, possibly seeking a sympathy vote. From those early days, until his death, we never once, on any occasion, walked side by side. There was no such thing as going on holidays. This was the deplorable fashion, and degradation, into which our family was dragged; Into, Depression, Repression, and Oppression, throughout the long years of, the 1920's, and 1930's.

Aware of no differing level of livelihood, and all within the surrounding neighbourhood existing in similar circumstances, our family was brought up, doomed, and, prepared to accept complete apathy. Bernard, my late younger brother knew the problem, and commented most unfavourably on Father John.

Eleven years younger than Liza, at the age of twenty-seven, her brother, Thomas, was shot and killed, in the doorway of the family homestead, by the irregular, and dreaded, British Army force, the 'Black and Tans'. Bound in a blanket, and carried on a donkey, the four miles along the shoreline, he was buried by night, at historic Newport's, Burrishool Abbey.

Ireland, for whatever reason, was no place for John to visit. Come to think of it? He never visited anywhere, so long as there was a selection of good public houses to keep him in Leeds. Mother was a completely changed person when on occasional visits to her former homestead, in County Mayo, in the West of Ireland. Funding, for vacations, was provided by her two brothers, Patrick and Dominic, both were thriving entrepreneurs in America.

Having never seen an embrace, or show of endearment from John, life was far from perfect between our two parents. The mundane, day to day, domestic chores were done, without a finger being raised by John. It would be obnoxious to attempt listing his numerous shortcomings.

Throughout vacations in Ireland, Liza was received, and feted, at every nook and turn, she was a personality of the highest standing. One serious measure of her ability was disclosed on a visit to her former school. Records were produced showing scholarly performances over many years, and Liza stood out, the distinguished one. Her marks, on all subjects, were outstandingly, the best ever for the school.

Overriding all the notable occasions was one brief moment; I am convinced it was the one, such as to sustain Mother throughout the remainder of her life. Returning, by foot, on the three mile walk, from Newport to the family farm, the centre of the quiet country road became as though illuminated. James Moran, the tall handsome postmaster, came out from his roadside store, to greet Mother. James took Mother in his arms, they embraced, he held her close, and it was as though he had waited throughout many years, for just that simple hug and embrace. Mother's face lit up, and her body radiated, it had a glow, the like of which I had never seen in her before. There was no kiss, and I can never think why so insignificant, and mundane an incident, should remain with me throughout so many years. I was never to see James Moran again, but he will never be forgotten.

Shattered somewhat, I simply had not previously seen Mother receive any form of endearment, particularly from John, nor, throughout the remainder of her life. That one brief show of emotion, by James Moran, must have stayed with, and sustained Liza, throughout her long life. This was the moment that I realised; Liza's emigration to wartime England had drastically changed her quality of living.

The opportunity was always there for her to move away, with brothers, Patrick and Dominic, flourishing in America. Religion was the hold! Patrick's obituary is shown alongside.

Being first born, with a brother Bernard, (He served in The Black Watch), and two younger sisters, Kathleen and Joan, I have no recollection of the number of times the bed was brought down to the sitting room, and I cycled, so often, to the Nurses Home, for maternity Nurse, Wrigglesworth: It was the way of things.

Throughout school days, education was Mother's province; John having been an army boxer, he sought all things physical, and it was all that he considered we two boys required to know: fighting, rugby, swimming. On introducing any new friend, his invariable first question being, "Can you slug him"?

At the age of twelve, I was exploited by the Catholic Mafia: 'The Catenians!' Interviewing me at school, in the headmaster's office, I was coerced into undertaking newspaper delivery for one of the ilk. The

Patrick Grady, Fisher Bros. Head, to Be Buried in Miami

President Ellwood H. Fisher and Executive Vice-President Timothy J. Conway of the Fisher Bros. Co. will represent the company at the private funeral services in Miami, Fla., for Patrick Grady, board chairman of the food store chain. Time for the services had not been set last night.

Mr. Grady died in Miami yesterday in the family home. He was stricken in Cleveland last fall, and his health had declined steadily until his death. He was 68.

He had been associated with the Fisher organization since 1908, when he came here from his native Newport, County Mayo, Ireland. He went to work as a clerk in the first store at 4623 Lorain Avenue established by the late Manning F. Fisher and Joseph Salmon.

Mr. Grady made such a favorable impression on his employers that a few weeks later he was made manager of a second store at 2626 Lorain Ave.

His advancement in the Fisher organization was rapid. He was superintendent of stores for many years before his elevation to board chairmanship in 1942.

His progress kept pace with the expansion of the organization from a relatively few thousand dollars in gross sales in its first year to $73,000,000 last year in 174 stores in five northeastern Ohio counties.

Several years ago his family established a residence in Miami. During his business visits here he resided at the Cleveland Athletic Club, of which he was a member. He had been in Miami for several years just prior to his death.

Surviving Mr. Grady are his wife Beatrice; two daughters, Mrs. Trixie Degret of Miami and Mrs. Doris Rivenbark of Jacksonville, Fla.; a son, Ivan Joseph Grady of Cleveland; a brother, Dominic Grady of Cleveland, and other brothers and sisters residing in England.

PATRICK GRADY

chore consisted of three morning rounds, totalling eight dozen papers, and an evening round, of twelve dozen papers: A total of two hundred and fifty deliveries each day, 6 days a week. With the modest reward of four shillings, and six pence, (4s -6d), weekly, I humbled myself, aware that the pitiable contribution provided three days of food for the family. There were so many weeks when daddy's contribution was nil. He smoked cigarettes non-stop, boozed to the last penny, and gambled, with whatever cash he could get his hands on.

Many times, as no more than a youth, I implored Mother to leave the man, but it was in vain. She would have been most welcome by both of her highly successful brothers, in America. It was a case of status-quo, once branded with the sacrament of marriage, no Catholic mother, particularly Irish, should part from the husband, no matter how detestable, cruel, or indifferent.

The situation was brought to a head in dramatic fashion, as Kathleen, aged fifteen, returned from a parish dance, after the set time of 10.00 pm. Penny-less, Daddy was sad, sober, and internally fuming, at the predicament in which he found himself. He always felt, the world owed him a living, and shortage of his good things of life, left him remorseful, and full of self pity.

In a flash, as Kathleen entered the door, the fury erupted, and she was felled with a blow. The assault continued as nosey neighbours began to congregate at the far side of the street. It was all so sudden, and violent. Somehow: Anticipating the foul action, I was out of bed, and dressed only in the day shirt, in which I also slept, I sped down the stairs.

Grabbing a hand axe from the coal cellar, I stood over my father, with the axe raised over his head; and shouted: "Stop! Don't move!" I was within one second of burying the axe into his skull. With eyes glazed over, he knew that, as he had taught me, I could have no mercy in conflict, and his fury turned to appeal. – (It was a considerable time later, I learnt convincingly, and now know, I should have carved him).

This single moment, of unashamed aggression, defined and delineated my attitude to the future. Nothing was to deter me from acting according to my needs, whilst, at all times, observing a propriety instilled into me, by my Mother.

It was as we sat in the General Elliott pub, opposite Leeds City Markets, both in our mid-seventies, and enjoying a few pints, brother Bernard turned to me, saying:- "Wasn't our old man a Bastard?" It was the only time, that conduct or approbation, of any kind, on our parents, had been mentioned. With, another four or five pints of Tetley's Yorkshire Mild beer down us, we went on to conduct a private inquest, into Father John's pleasurable demise. The verdict was, of course, in keeping with the protocol, and decorum, measured to a level that John might expect.

Throughout the period of the war, a special Government tax was introduced. It was required to pay for food supplies, and armaments: (Those desirable items that Churchill had failed to ship into 1942, Burma). Known as Post War Credits, the contributions were refundable as people reached retirement age, and John received his bounty, on his sixty-sixth birthday.

To be so well endowed with cash was rare for John, and in the next thirty-six hours, he celebrated the windfall to the full: Non-Stop! He was, what in every-day parlance, a common person would call; "Pissed as a newt!" The pity was, of course, that Mamma had to find him, comatose, in the toilet.

The 'Bounty of Post War Credits', was the illness that Bernard, and I, determined, was the cause of Daddy's death. The man was outstanding in every way, so, why should he not have a distinguished epitaph. He was such that, he would have cherished the rarity; "Post War Credits", a most singular cause of demise. It was what he was worth: Brother Bernard liked it.

Major experiences behind me, ones determining my life-style, and conduct, were the horrible exploitation, by the Catholic, Catenian, news vendors; in their taking two years of my young life, delivering newspapers for a pittance. This contrasted so radically, with the embracing acceptance, by the kindly Irish Garda, when outside St. Patrick's Church in Newport, County Mayo, of their acceptance of my Mother's evaluation of, 'an educational holiday' ; Along with my sporting achievements, in boxing, rugby, and being selected for the City of Leeds, 1936, Olympic Swimming Training Squad, nothing daunted me.

Suppressing the tragedy of her brother's Black and Tans execution, possibly explained Mother's absolute command of language. There was never a suggestion of foul language within the family, surprisingly, not even by my father. It was the word: "Churchill!" When spoken by my mother, that broke all bounds. Not frequently emitted, it was only whenever the name was mentioned in her hearing. In a modulated, and quiet voice, she would repeat, and utter, the single word, "Churchill!" The gentleness of her speech, embraced the senses of every known foul expletive, in a single blow! With the cool, soft spoken, Irish brogue, it was as though the house shook, from top to bottom, followed by a deafening silence. Knowing virtually nothing of the man at the time, and with no prompting; The fact that he could revile my mother to such an extent; I loathed him, and all that he represented.

Little did I know how deep my loathing of the man was to become, with the forthcoming turn of events, which were about to change the course of my life. Overtaking my early IRA aspirations, Mr Adolf Hitler of Germany intervened. His ordering of German troops, to invade Poland, changed everything. My accepting the challenge, tested me, and brought about the best years of my life.

Several readers of my book, "No Mandalay, No Maymyo", commented on how hard I had been on Churchill. However, the timely linkage with Dr, Xavier's son, from his reading, and appreciation, of the book, gives validation, and supports the accuracy, of my scathing Churchill evaluation.

Unperturbed by whatever setbacks, I was sorry to leave the British Army. From the most obscure, and humble of beginnings, I had been honoured by my peers shortly before conflict, as we crossed the Indian Ocean. In the most atrocious conditions of tropical warfare, I had successfully, with single mindedness, and absolute determination, commanded the very highest standard of men. In peacetime, I cared for those in my charge, and never lost sight of their needs. It was many years after the war, when attending a reunion function, that I received the ultimate in accolades.

A distinguished soldier, of the Regiment; one who had joined with me amongst reinforcements, as a Private in the mortar platoon, and in his continuing Army service for thirty-four years of service: He had proceeded through all ranks, to that of Captain; His words as approached me: "I hope you don't mind, Gerald, but I have to tell you this?" Of course I didn't mind: "You're the best officer I ever had!"

To continue in the role of what Regular Army Officers considered with disdain; an 'Emergency Commissioned Officer'; and hold, probably the senior Staff Captain appointment in the British Army, was awesome. To be recalled from a job at Corps level, and to be personally selected by General, Sir Brian Horrocks, to serve under him, at Army level, was beyond my wildest dreams.

Recommended for Staff College, as I was, with both, Bill Slim, and Brian Horrocks, in my background: Had I stayed in the Army, I was destined for the top!

My mother was very proud of me.

Finished – Aged Ninety Three years– 10th August 2011

GERALD FITZPATRICK

50th K.O.Y.L.I. 1st Bn Reunion – Gerald with Councillor Linda Middleton, Lord Mayor of Leeds

With Ted Hewitt – it was very late

Gerald and Patricia with sisters, Jeanne Lambert and Dorothy Wilson, of Maymyo Hotel

Gerald (dressed down!) with Patricia at York Reunion

Dignity

The aches, and pains, inflicted throughout life, can be acute, and may result in temporal physical affliction, agony, or annoyance. Hurt, is lifelong; indignities suffered persist in the mind, to be recalled at the mention of a name, or incident. Apart from the venom, I have had satisfaction and joy throughout my long life.

I give just one incident of absolute joy; It was in the terminating of my employment. I was in position to respond to, General, Sir Campbell Hardy, former Royal Marines Colonel Commandant, and recently installed as the token, 'Chairman' of a QUANGO organisation in which I was employed. The man threatened to retain me; "In order to, enforce compliance, with my contract of employment".

My reply; "I finish now, and you get no more work out of me!"

I did not tell the man that I already had other employment to go to; that is real joy!

Addendum

Major operations concluded, shortly following my Army discharge: December 1948

The Berlin Airlift – Started, (June 1948),

I was GSO III (Ops) – HQ, Rhine Army

Finished, (September 1949), defying a Russian road blockade. Supplying 8,000 tons of food and petrol daily: Totalling over two million tons airlifted into Berlin.

Costs to the Allies, nearly 700 aircraft, making more than ¼ million flights, losses of British and American aircrews throughout the operation, totalled a little more than eighty.

The Berlin Wall

The wall was erected out of pique, in 1961, by Russia, following other ineffective attempts at blockading Berlin. Germany was divided, split into East and West, with virtually no recognition, one of the other. Two almost completely differing cultures were created. The East was seen to be palpably poor, with comparative luxury developed in the West. Untold numbers of individuals were shot attempting to cross the wall, from East to West, and at other defined Zone boundaries.

The Cold War

It consisted of persistent bickering, some verbal, and some physical, between Russia, and, 'Western Powers', mainly USA. The 'War of Words' ended, with the demolition of the Berlin Wall, (demolition commenced 13th June 1989, Forty-four years following the cessation of WW-2). In that period, USA unsuccessfully contested spurious conflicts worldwide, the prime one being Viet Nam, where they were defeated, and chased out of the country.

India Independence

Tragically, as the Union Flag was run down, in Delhi, and the British departed, on 15th August 1947, Viceroy, Louis Mountbatten, urgently, wanted to get himself out of the country, he had a wife problem, and considered there was no requirement for formalised transition, and a 'transference of power'.

The envisaged acrimonious split, of Pakistan from India, caused turmoil, over many months. In establishing territorial boundaries, many hundreds of thousands died, and the distrust continues, on both sides.

Churchill's Victory Parade

Polish Forces were not invited to attend, although they fought on the front for The Allies, on land, and particularly, in the air.

Insulted over the years, and at every turn, by Churchill, Field Marshall, Archibald Wavell, former Eastern Army Commander, and Viceroy of India, (1943-47), boycotted the parade.

Wavell

History records; "Little has been recorded on the manner of his final removal from Military Command. He disappears from the pages of Churchill's memoirs. His toils with India Command are practically ignored, as though he had hardly existed".

"He became a remote figure" – "He was adversities General" –

"His path led not to the head of the supply queue":

Why would I not remember that?

Wavell's Dispatches (Page 206)

"In four years, I have directed 14 campaigns", "Some have been successful, some, have failed".

The whole bloody lot went wrong!

Praising the War Cabinet? – He should have crucified them! He was loyal to the end. Wavell had no appreciation whatsoever of the degradation of the troops under his command in the Burma war. His concern was, *'to ensure that commanders were given orders'*: How his orders were carried out, became no concern of his from there on. In all simplicity, he was satisfied to know that he had given orders.

Training, and equipping, for re-entry into Burma, was a two year job, in anybody's language. He comes out with the words – "The sword is sheathed!"

Wavell later wrote; "The staff system, and system of command, is too cumbersome, and elaborate, and needs revision. We have lost the merit of simplicity": He was in position, and the man who should have done something about it. He should have been with those troops inside Burma! Was he; "Enigmatic, cabbalistic, or simply Inept?" Did he see?

The spurious signal of 1st April 1942, from Churchill to Roosevelt:

"Speaking as one amateur to another, my feeling is that the wisest stroke for Japan would be to press on through Burma northwards into China and try to make a job of that. They may disturb India but I doubt its serious invasion". (It was secreted away for thirty years).

Read this as though a soldier, Sick and starving in mid Burma.

God Bless and Thank You!

As the man said;

The real underbelly of British Press reporting are the scum of the earth, and they destroy lives.

Gerald leading Armistice Parade

APPENDICES

Page 48   USA Secretary of State, Cordell Hull; Excerpt from record of his series of meetings with Japanese: (Eleven days before bombing of Pearl Harbour). He was securing short term Peace Plan.

256

711.94/2504

Memorandum [88] Regarding a Conversation Between the Secretary Of State, the Japanese Ambassador (Nomura), and Mr. Kurusu

[WASHINGTON,] November 26, 1941.

The Japanese Ambassador and Mr. Kurusu called by appointment at the Department. The Secretary handed each of the Japanese copies of an outline of a proposed basis of an agreement between the United States and Japan [89] and an explanatory oral statement. [90]

After the Japanese had read the documents, Mr. Kurusu asked whether this was our reply to their proposal for a *modus vivendi*. The Secretary replied that we had to treat the proposal as we did, as there was so much turmoil and confusion among the public both in the United States and in Japan. He reminded the Japanese that in the United States we have a political situation to deal with just as does the Japanese Government, and he referred to the fire-eating statements which have been recently coming out of Tokyo, which he said had been causing a natural reaction among the public in this country. He said that our proposed agreement would render possible, practical measures of financial cooperation, which, however, were not referred to in the outline for fear that this might give rise to misunderstanding. He also referred to the fact that he had earlier in the conversations acquainted the Ambassador of the ambition that had been his of settling the immigration question but that the situation had so far prevented him from realizing that ambition.

Mr. Kurusu offered various depreciatory comments in regard to the proposed agreement. He noted that in our statement of principles there was a reiteration of the Stimson doctrine. He objected to the proposal for multilateral non-aggression pacts and referred to Japan's bitter experience of international organizations, citing the case of the award against Japan by the Hague tribunal in the Perpetual Leases matter. He went on to say that the Washington Conference Treaties had given a wrong idea to China, that China had taken advantage of them to flaunt Japan's rights. He said he did not see haw his Government could consider paragraphs (3) and (4) of the proposed agreement and that if the United States should expect that Japan was to take off its hat to Chiang Kai-shek and propose to récognize him Japan could not agree. He said that if this was the idea of the American Government he did not see how any agreement was possible.

The Secretary asked whether this matter could not be worked out.

Mr. Kurusu said that when they reported our answer to their Government it would be likely to throw up its hands. He noted that this was a tentative proposal without commitment, and suggested that it might be better if they did not refer it to their Government before discussing its contents further informally here.

The Secretary suggested that they might wish to study the documents carefully before discussing them further. He repeated that we were trying to do our best to keep the public from becoming uneasy as a result of their being harangued. He explained that in the light of all that has been said in the press, our proposal was as far as we would go at this time in reference to the Japanese proposal; that there was so much confusion among the public that it was necessary to bring about some clarification; that we have reached a stage when the public has lost its perspective and that it was therefore necessary to draw up a document which would present a complete picture of our position by making provision for each essential point involved.

The Secretary then referred to the oil question. He said that public feeling was so acute on that question that he might almost be lynched if he permitted oil to go freely to Japan. He pointed out that if Japan should fill Indochina with troops our people would not know what lies ahead in the way of a menace to the countries to the south and west. He reminded the Japanese that they did not know what

Page 58   Excerpt from 'Documents on Australian Foreign Policy, 1937/49' Volume 5 – Pages 533-563 (546/7 – 554/6 – 562/3)

---

554   FEBRUARY 1942

vital centres are in immediate danger. This is the reason and the only reason for the reply we have sent to Mr. Churchill, which we now quote in full for your information:—

(Here follows cablegram to Dominions Office—No. 136.[3])

CURTIN

[AA:A3196, 1942, 0.5404]

359 Dr H. V. Evatt, Minister for External Affairs, to Mr J. M. McMillan, Third Secretary of the Legation in Washington

Cablegram [222][1]   CANBERRA, [22 February 1942, 5.05 a.m.]

TO BE DECYPHERED BY MCMILLAN ALONE AND HANDED BY HIM TO MR JUSTICE FRANKFURTER[2] ALONE

1. I take leave to address you on a matter of grave importance to our common cause. Some three days ago we affirmed the decision that the A.I.F. should return to defend their homeland here.[3] We had not suggested its return from the Middle East but we agreed to the proposal of Churchill that, for the purpose of reinforcing Singapore and thereafter reinforcing the N.E.I., two of our three divisions should come back. The object of the movement was to hold up the southern thrust of Japan.

2. We were glad that the divisions were to go to the N.E.I. not merely because those Indies would form a screen for the defence of Australia as a base but because they would consolidate goodwill between N.E.I. and Australia.

3. The decision was taken by Churchill and Wavell[4] not to reinforce the N.E.I. further: thereupon our expert military advisers thought that the divisions should at once come to the closest area from which the southern thrust of Japan might be met, i.e. Australia.

4. In all the technical strategical appreciations, the function of Australia as a base area to attack Japan has been underlined. Wavell himself has repeatedly said that it is vital to the Allies to defend Australia.

---

[3] Published as Document 357. It was repeated to Casey as no. 41. See the copy in Franklin D. Roosevelt Library: President's Secretary's file. Australia diplomatic.

[1] Material in square brackets has been inserted from the Washington copy in U.S. Library of Congress: Frankfurter Papers, container 53, 'Herbert V. Evatt'.
[2] See Document 356, note 1.
[3] See Document 345.
[4] Allied Supreme Commander of the A.B.D.A. Area.

FEBRUARY 1942

5. The position of our home defences is most unsatisfactory largely owing to our having sent land, sea and air forces to Britain, Middle East, Greece, Crete and elsewhere. We have struggled to improve these defences during our four months of office but they still fall far short of what is required. General Lavarack who is G.O.C. the A.I.F. and close to Wavell favoured a diversion of one division to Burma but only on condition that our C.G.S.[5] was satisfied with the condition of our home defences. But the C.G.S. expressed himself as very dissatisfied—a conclusion which really understates the gravity of the position here. Air strength is very small owing to the policy of our predecessors who concentrated upon training 10,000 air personnel for service in the U.K. and who tended to regard Australian home defence [as] of subsidiary importance.

6. In these circumstances it became utterly impossible for us to agree to the suggested diversion to Burma. Page[6] in London had instructions as to our view but failed to carry them out. As a result the Pacific War Council in London recommended a diversion of one division to Burma while the second was to come to Australia. But Wavell's technical appreciation did not favour this splitting up of our corps and in his last recommendation he suggested both divisions should go to Burma—or India.

7. A curious feature of the affair has been the concentrated barrage which has descended upon this Government from its own servants such as Page (acting outside his instructions). Subsequently Hopkins[7] and the President also sent messages based upon their belief that we were not to be seriously threatened by Japan—a belief that we cannot share.

8. But it is one thing to deal with arguments from other governments, it is another thing to be embarrassed by those who are the agents of the Australian Government. We are in our present plight because of what we have done abroad, and the people of this country would make short shrift of those who are obstructing the return of the flower of our army for the purpose of defending their homeland.

9. Today we heard of a proposal that an American division should come to Australia.[8] Of course we should welcome it and if the U.S.A. decision were altered because of ours the effect might be most unfortunate. I do not wish to refer to the controversy as to Pacific v. Atlantic for everybody now must see that we were right in asserting that a failure to take Japan seriously might lead to world successes of the Axis. Sending the American division to Northern Ireland has had a bad effect in

[5] Lt Gen V. A. H. Sturdee.
[6] Special Representative in the United Kingdom.
[7] Special Adviser to President Franklin D. Roosevelt.
[8] See Document 355.

this country because of Beaverbrook's[9] comment that this was the first and most important job which Churchill performed in America. We are glad that Cripps[10] is in office and hope that he will check Churchill whose attitude over this particular matter has been turbulent and peremptory.

10. I am aware that although our decision is on the highest plane of secrecy it may by treachery be allowed to leak out in London and Washington. It is vital to allied solidarity that we should have your sympathy and understanding.

11. I now draw your attention to an article four days ago by J. Harsch in 'Christian Science Monitor'. This is most defeatist and fifth columnist in character, and we have traced its origin in Australia to a Fascist, anti-Semitic group. It was deliberately intended to embroil Australia and N.E.I. In fact this Government has fulfilled every requisition made in relation to N.E.I. and our losses in defending N.E.I. have been very heavy both on land and in the air. I do not know whether Casey[11] or Bailey (his publicity man)[12] are counteracting this propaganda. Journalists like Harsch, Browne[13], Knickerbocker seem ready to injure this country whenever possible, and two of them are suspected by British Security Service.

12. Further, the A.I.F. decision may also be used by fifth columnists to cause difficulties between China and ourselves. Owing largely to Sir Frederic Eggleston's[14] brilliant work at Chungking we are on terms of the greatest friendship with the Chinese Government. China has always supported our emphasis upon the importance of the Pacific war. I hope you will try and explain to Hopkins that the President's goodwill should not be used by Churchill as if it were his own especial property. Casey has already been asked to explain to Hopkins but his advocacy does not appear to have been at all useful.

13. The whole incident of the suggested diversion of the A.I.F. to Burma has been alarming. I feel certain that Wavell himself only recommended diversion under pressure from Churchill. Wavell had always insisted upon the vital importance of Australia as a base. Finally the party political possibilities occurred to a few anti-Labor opportunists here and in London most of whom are distrusted by the Australian people. The

[9] U.K. Minister of War Production until 19 February. He then headed a U.K. supply mission to the United States. The decision to send U.S. troops to Northern Ireland was announced in Washington on 26 January.
[10] U.K. Lord Privy Seal.
[11] Minister to the United States.
[12] Director, Australian News and Information Bureau, New York.
[13] This is possibly a reference to Cecil Brown, who later in 1942 published a book entitled *Suez to Singapore*, of which Evatt was highly critical. See Evatt's cablegrams SL67 and SW102 of 27 October 1942 on External Affairs Dept file Spares, Drafts & Master Sheets—Outwards 'Special' cables.
[14] Minister to China.

FEBRUARY 1942

Mr Clement Attlee, U.K. Secretary of State for Dominion Affairs, to Mr John Curtin, Prime Minister

362

Cablegram 241 LONDON, 22 February 1942, 3 p.m.
Received 23 February 1942

MOST IMMEDIATE   MOST SECRET

Following from the Prime Minister[1] for the Prime Minister. (Begins):—

We could not contemplate that you would refuse our request and that of the President of the United States[2] for the diversion of the leading division to save the situation in Burma. We knew that if our ships proceeded on their course to Australia while we were waiting for your formal approval they would either arrive too late at Rangoon or even be without enough fuel to go there at all. We therefore decided that the convoy should be temporarily diverted to the northward. The convoy is now too far north for some of the ships in it to reach Australia without refuelling. These physical considerations give a few days for the situation to develop and for you to review the position should you wish to do so. Otherwise the leading Australian Division will be returned to Australia as quickly as possible in accordance with your wishes.   (Ends).

[AA:A816, 52/302/142]

Mr R. G. Casey, Minister to the United States, to Mr John Curtin, Prime Minister

363

Cablegram 343 WASHINGTON, 22 February 1942, 11.44 p.m.
Received 23 February 1942

MOST IMMEDIATE   MOST SECRET

President asks me to transmit following message to the Prime Minister.

Begins—Thank you for yours of February 21st.[1]

I fully understand your position in spite of the fact that I cannot wholly agree as to immediate need of first returning division in [sic] Australia. I think that the principal threat as against the main bases of

---

[1] Winston Churchill.   [2] Franklin D. Roosevelt.

[1] Document 358, which was received in Washington on 21 February.

562   FEBRUARY 1942

Australia and Burma, both of which must be held at all costs, is against Burma or the left flank, and that we can safely hold the Australian or right flank. Additional American fully equipped reinforcements are getting ready to leave for your area.

In view of all this and depending of course on developments of next few weeks I hope you will consider the possibility of diverting second returning division to some place in India or Burma to help hold that line so that it can become a fixed defence. Under any circumstances you can depend upon our fullest support. Roosevelt. Ends.

                                                                                                    CASEY

[AA : A981, WAR 33, ATTACHMENT B]

---

364   Mr S. M. Bruce, High Commissioner in the United Kingdom, to Mr John Curtin, Prime Minister

Cablegram 33A   LONDON, 23 February 1942

MOST IMMEDIATE   CLEAR THE LINE   FOR PRIME MINISTER   PERSONAL HIMSELF ONLY

Have just seen copy of telegram the Prime Minister[1] has sent to you this afternoon.[2] While Page[3] is dealing with it officially, and will no doubt have much to say to the Prime Minister with regard to it, I feel I must send you privately my reactions; [I] am appalled by it and its possible repercussions. It is arrogant and offensive and contradicts the assurances given to Page that the Convoy was not being diverted from its direct route to Australia. Any reaction on your part would be justified. None the less I urge restraint in your reply. I hold no brief for the Prime Minister and feel strongly that had he not effected the recent alterations in the structure of the War Cabinet it would have been essential that he should go and that quickly.

Nevertheless I feel that the alterations having been effected, the best instrument we have to our hand having been created and being at a desperate and possibly the determining point of the war, a crisis in the relations between Australia and the United Kingdom arising out of the action of one man must be avoided.

To check my view I have just seen Cripps[4] and fully discussed the matter with him. He also urges restraint in your reply. He stressed the fact

[1] Winston Churchill.   [2] Document 362.
[3] Special Representative in the United Kingdom.   [4] U.K. Lord Privy Seal.

FEBRUARY 1942

that at the moment the Prime Minister is so near the end of his tether owing to the strain of the war situation—the work involved in the Cabinet reconstruction and preparation for Tuesday's critical debate— that allowance must be made for the tone of his telegram.

He also urged that just when by the creation of the new Cabinet there was a chance of getting on to a direct co-operative working basis it was essential to avoid a first class row.

Reinforced with Cripps' view I urge that despite the provocation you should maintain in your reply the admirable tone and reasoned argument of your recent cables on the subject of the Burma diversion.

BRUCE

[AA:M100, FEBRUARY 1942]

365 Sir Earle Page, Special Representative in the United Kingdom, to Mr John Curtin, Prime Minister

Cablegram 1613　　　　　　　　　　　　　LONDON, 22 February 1942

MOST IMMEDIATE   MOST SECRET   HIMSELF ALONE

1. Have just received copy of Churchill's cablegram[1] some hours after its despatch.

2. The statement regarding diversion convoy Northwards and inability of some ships to reach Australia with their fuel conflicts with information regarding movement of ships conveyed to me and communicated to you in my P.47 and P.48.[2]

3. I am seeing Churchill who tonight is away from London first thing Monday morning to secure an explanation of the alteration of the previous instructions, of which alteration I was unaware.

4. Notwithstanding the natural resentment that your Government may feel in the absence of some satisfactory explanation that such a vital alteration has been made without prior reference I strongly urge that recriminations should be avoided as they can only do harm to our getting the maximum co-operative effort in the Allied cause.

PAGE

[AA:A2937, FAR EAST POSITION 1942]

[1] Document 362.
[2] Documents 347 and 351.

366 Mr John Curtin, Prime Minister, to Mr Clement Attlee, U.K. Secretary of State for Dominion Affairs

Cablegram 139   CANBERRA, 23 February 1942

MOST IMMEDIATE   MOST SECRET

Prime Minister to Prime Minister.[1]
Reference your 241.[2]

In your 233[3] it was clearly implied that the convoy was *not* proceeding to the northward. From 241 it appears that you have diverted the convoy towards Rangoon and had treated our approval to this vital diversion as merely a matter of form. By doing so you have established a physical situation which adds to the dangers of the convoy and the responsibility of the consequences of such diversion rests upon you.

2. We have already informed the President[4] of the reasons for our decision and, having regard to the terms of his communications to me[5], we are quite satisfied from his sympathetic reply that he fully understands and appreciates the reasons for our decision.

3. Wavell's message[6] considered by Pacific War Council on Saturday reveals that Java faces imminent invasion. Australia's outer defences are now quickly vanishing and our vulnerability is completely exposed.

4. With A.I.F. troops we sought to save Malaya and Singapore, falling back on Netherlands East Indies. All these northern defences are gone or going. Now you contemplate using the A.I.F. to save Burma. All this has been done as in Greece without adequate air support.

5. We feel a primary obligation to save Australia not only for itself but to preserve it as a base for the development of the war against Japan. In the circumstances it is quite impossible to reverse a decision which we made with the utmost care and which we have affirmed and re-affirmed.

6. Our Chief of General Staff[7] advises although your 241 refers to the leading division only the fact is that owing to the loading of the flights it is impossible at the present time to separate the two divisions and the destination of all the flights will be governed by that of the first flight. This fact re-inforces us in our decision.

[AA:A3196, 1942, 0.5424]

[1] Winston Churchill.   [2] Document 362.   [3] Document 352.
[4] Franklin D. Roosevelt. See Document 358.   [5] See Documents 355 and 363.
[6] The message from the Allied Supreme Commander of the A.B.D.A. Area was forwarded to the Commonwealth Govt on 18 February in U.K. Dominions Office cablegram 219 (on file AA:A816, 52/302/142).
[7] Lt Gen V. A. H. Sturdee.

Mr Clement Attlee, U.K. Secretary of State for Dominion Affairs, to Mr John Curtin, Prime Minister

367

Cablegram 249   LONDON, 23 February 1942, 9.23 p.m.
Received 24 February 1942

Your telegram 23rd February, 139.[1] Following for Prime Minister from Prime Minister.[2] Begins:

1. Your convoy is now proceeding to re-fuel at Colombo. It will then proceed to Australia in accordance with your wishes.

2. My decision to move it northward during the few hours required to receive your final answer was necessary because otherwise your help, if given, might not have arrived in time.

3. As soon as the convoy was turned north, arrangements were made to increase its escort and this increased escort will be maintained during its voyage to Colombo and on leaving Colombo again for as long as practicable.

4. Of course, I take full responsibility for my action.

[AA:A3195, 1942, I.7027]

Sir Earle Page, Special Representative in the United Kingdom, to Mr John Curtin, Prime Minister

368

Cablegram 1637   LONDON, 24 February 1942, 12.52 a.m.
Received 24 February 1942

MOST IMMEDIATE   MOST SECRET   HIMSELF ALONE

Further to my telegram 1613[1] the Prime Minister[2] has informed me that he is very sorry that I was not kept more closely informed of the movements of the convoy and is sure that I will understand how this happened in the very disturbed position of the war. As well, you will realize how involved has been the United Kingdom political situation. During these few days there has been a complete re-casting of British

---
[1] Document 366.
[2] Winston Churchill.

---
[1] Document 365.
[2] Winston Churchill.

Cabinet and Saturday particularly was a day of exceptional preoccupation for the Prime Minister and Officers most concerned.

2. The Responsible Officer has reported to the Prime Minister that when he gave me the information on Thursday which was telegraphed to you in my telegram P.48[3] that the convoy was steaming on its course to Australia, it was absolutely correct.[4] It was not till late Friday evening after despatch of the Prime Minister's cable 233[5] that he, confident of an affirmative answer to his appeal to divert the convoy, instructed the Admiralty to order the convoy to proceed northwards.

3. The Admiralty, anticipating that your reply to 233 would be received in time for the convoy either to go to Rangoon or proceed to Australia without any complication, issued the necessary instructions. Meanwhile the Admiralty had got anxious about the fuel position and telegraphed to the Commander-in-Chief Eastern Fleet[6] as to how far north the fleet could go and still have enough fuel if your reply was unfavourable. The reply received indicated that some ships had by that time *not* got enough fuel to proceed direct to Australia and on the recommendation of the Chiefs of Staff the Prime Minister despatched his telegram 241.[7]

4. I was pleased to note the restrained tone of your reply 139[8] which undoubtedly will assist future relations between our Governments. Since establishment of the new system of consultation I have been kept very fully and promptly informed of all matters of concern to Australia and am satisfied that the delay in informing you and me in this instance while most unfortunate in the circumstances was due to inadvertence.

PAGE

[AA:A3195, 1942, 1.7053]

---

[3] Document 351.
[4] See the note from Maj Gen Sir Hastings Ismay (Deputy Secretary (Military)) of the U.K. War Cabinet) to Churchill on his discussion with Page. This document was sent to Page on 23 February by Sir Edward Bridges (Permanent Secretary of the U.K. Cabinet Office). See Australian War Memorial: Page collection, Box 118A, File no. 3. Far Eastern Situation. Action since fall of Singapore 15/2/42 to 14/4/42.
[5] Document 352.
[6] Vice-Admiral Sir James Somerville.
[7] Document 362.
[8] Document 366.

Anne Pentland – Glowing testimony from daughter of Chauk Oilfield Manager, Norman Kellie.

> 4.3.05
>
> Dear Captain Fitzpatrick,
>
> I was born in Nyaunghla 1938 & left Burma 1.3.42. My father was employed at Chauk by BOC and involved in the denial of the oil field 19.4.42 and subsequent overland journey to India, which he thankfully survived.
>
> Books involving Burma are such a rarity in this country and I was delighted to discover, no Mandalay, no Maymyo in my local library. I wish to thank you, most sincerely, for the chapter Yenanyaung and Chauk and giving credit to the oilmen. It was wonderful for me as a letter my father wrote Sept 1942 praises the army for their assistance. I wonder if you ever met!
>
> I have an avid interest in the country and have been fortunate, through second hand sources, to acquire quite a library. Most of the forces accounts are tales of north to south so it was very, very interesting to read your account.
>
> I do not remember any of Burma and my husband & me decided to ignore political rhetoric and go there last year. We were most impressed with the people courteous, friendly, honest etc etc — living in a time warp almost. There is little crime, homelessness, abuse, no litter, very clean, tidy. No supermarkets or MacDonalds!
>
> We were so smitten we are returning this month to travel further. We visited the oil fields. Pin Chaung now has a bridge, also at Chauk but the country has very little evidence

345

Distorted and vindictive Press Reports – Examples

I ordered killing of civilians in Burma retreat

ROBERT LOW reports on a St George's Day incident

THE killing of 27 Burmese civilians by a British Army unit in 1942 is revealed for the first time today. They were shot by officers of a retreating infantry regiment who feared the Burmese could betray their position to the Japanese.

The officer who says he ordered the killings and carried out the first one himself, Mr Gerald Fitzpatrick, has broken a 42-year silence to speak to *The Observer*.

Other members of his battalion have confirmed that the incident happened, although they differ on details. Most are upset that Mr Fitzpatrick has now chosen to make it public.

The killings occurred during the retreat from Rangoon to India. The remnants of the British Army in Burma — the 'Forgotten Army' as it became known — had to travel 1,000 miles, much of it on foot, beset by sickness, fatigue and Japanese attacks.

Mr Fitzpatrick was then a 22-year-old second lieutenant with the second battalion of the King's Own Yorkshire Light Infantry.

He says he ordered the Burmese to be shot and their bodies thrown into a dried-up river bed. He killed the first one himself with a dagger. The other 26 were shot by three other officers. One officer has since died and the others cannot be traced.

The battalion had left the Rangoon area in early March with about 900 men. It was down to only 200 when it arrived outside a stockaded village some 300 miles further north on the afternoon of what Mr Fitzpatrick believes was 23 April—St George's Day.

'We were about to pitch camp and do the evening meal a couple of hundred yards away from the village when smoke started rising from it. That was a familiar invitation for the Japanese to attack so we sealed the place off and went in,' he said last week.

'The burning building was the school and about 15 Indian women were running out of it screaming. They had obviously been put in there before it was set alight. That was the usual pattern. We found 27 fit, active

Exclusive

men in the village. We interrogated them but they said almost nothing.'

Mr Fitzpatrick's view is that the villagers had seen the appalling state of his unit's men and equipment and would almost certainly betray them to the Japanese. 'We simply couldn't afford to leave them alive. I took the initiative and ordered them to be shot by the three company commanders.

'We wanted to survive. Nobody was going to knock my blokes out. Apart from being sick physically, from malaria and dysentery, our men were a bit sick at heart.

'While not openly disruptive, it was a simmering thing. They had no faith in the command. Churchill had deserted them. They were the Forgotten Army and it was getting through to them.

Shot in the head

'I decided I could not trust them to dispatch those people. That's why I ordered them to be shot by the company commanders.'

'The Burmese were taken to the edge of a *chaung*, a dried-up river bed, 18-20ft in depth and maybe 100 yds across. Each officer was allocated nine of them.

'As we moved the first group towards the *chaung*, the leading man drew a knife from his clothes. I hit him in the face with my rifle butt and stabbed him in the chest with his own knife.

'I left the officers to deal with the rest. They were shot in the head, one by one, and their bodies pushed over the edge of the *chaung*.'

Mr Fitzpatrick says he witnessed the execution of the first group and saw the bodies of all the victims.

'Having seen the first one dispatched, there was no resistance from the rest. They died on their knees, praying. When we had finished, we upped sticks and marched off two or three miles up the road.

'From then on there was quite a different feel about the battalion. The men knew the officers meant what they damned well said.

'It was a mucky blood job but they appreciated it had to be done. They were left in no doubt the officers were not softening and asking them to do things they would not have done themselves.'

Mr Fitzpatrick believes the village was called Taungtha, which is about 50 miles to the south-west of Mandalay. But two of his contemporaries, Dr Ralph Tanner and Mr Victor Stevens, say Taungtha was a much larger town.

Dr Tanner, a former lecturer in comparative religion at the University of London, said Taungtha was a town of some 6,000 people, with a cinema. The unit was there for four days, from 23-27 April.

'I was in a rest house when a group of Burmese was brought into the compound. I was given to understand they were looters. I remember hearing they were going to be shot and who was going to do it. I don't know that Fitzpatrick was involved. I remember the struggle going away and hearing shots. My memory is that it was more like 17 men than 27.'

Dr Tanner, a 21-year-old second lieutenant in 1942, went to Japan last year for a meeting of reconciliation with four officers from the division that was pursuing his unit. He does not share Mr Fitzpatrick's belief that the incident should have been unearthed all these years later. 'Frightened men with guns are profligate with human life,' he says. He now lives in Steeple Aston, Oxfordshire.

Mr Stevens, also a former second lieutenant, now of Great Amwell, Herts., said: 'To the best of my knowledge, this incident did happen.'

His recollection is that the village was the unit's first stop after leaving a place called Mount Popa. The village caught fire and its inhabitants fled. In the early morning some crept back, perhaps to salvage what they could, but were caught and suspected of spying on the British soldiers. The shooting then followed.

Mr Edward Hewitt, of Poole, Dorset, who was Mr Fitzpatrick's batman, said: 'The incident he mentions did happen. We did to them what they could have done to us.

Neither Mr Fitzpatrick nor,

Gerald Fitzpatrick as a young officer.

apparently, any other member of the unit ever reported the killings.

The KOYLI's own regimental history merely records: 'On the morning of April 23 the expected orders to move again arrived and the battalion was lifted in lorries to a large village called Taungtha, some 30 miles further north than where they were. That night the village was fired by Burmans which meant a change of position and two days later another move was necessary owing to an outbreak of cholera among the Burman troops.'

Why has Mr Fitzpatrick now revealed the incident? Is it because it had weighed on his conscience for 42 years? He dismisses the suggestion.

'I have never felt any remorse. I know I was right. Our preservation was paramount. The battalion was disintegrating by the day. Our sole concern was survival.

'It is a fact of British history and of British accountability that has never been recorded and should be. It is incredible what the memoirs miss.'

Now 64, he lives in Guiseley, near Leeds. After leaving the Army in 1948, he worked in the coal industry and as an area manager for the Road Transport Industry Training Board. He has spent the last few years researching the story and it is evident that he still harbours bitter memories of his ordeal in Burma.

The Observer – 3rd June 1984 Originator of malice: conveyed worldwide.

346

THE SUNDAY TELEGRAPH OCTOBER 7, 1984

Burma massacre inquiry

By CATHERINE STEVEN

DETECTIVES from Scotland Yard's serious crimes squad will tomorrow begin interviewing retired soldiers who may have witnessed the massacre of 27 Burmese civilians 42 years ago said to have been carried out by officers of the second battalion of the King's Own Yorkshire Light Infantry.

A murder inquiry into the incident, which was never recorded in the KOYLI's regimental history, has been ordered by Sir Tomas Hetherington, Director of Public Prosecutions, following a confession from an officer that eh ordered the killings on April 25, 1942.

Mr Gerald Fitzpatrick, who was then a 22-year-old second lieutenant, has said he killed the first Burmese with a dagger and that two other officers later shot the others during their retreat from Rangoon to India.

One officer who served with Mr Fitzpatrick, was Mr Victor Stevens, also a second lieutenant and who is now 70 and living in Hertfordshire. Mr Stevens said last night that he had agreed to meet a Scotland Yard detective on Tuesday but added: "One can forget an awful lot in nearly three years."

Mr Stevens said he was not aware of any conspiracy to conceal the killings and could not say why they did not come to light until this year.

The alleged massacre was brought to the attention of Mr Heseltine, Defence Minister, in a letter from Mr Tam Dalyell, Labour MP for Linlithgow, who took a personal interest in the allegations. His father's cousin was Major-Gen Orden Wingate, commander of the Special Force, India Command, better known as the Chindits.

Mr Dalyell said he was surprised that a decision had been taken to open a murder inquiry.

He said: "I wrote a letter to Mr Heseltine saying that I did not want to make trouble for the MoD about events which took place such a long time ago, but that I thought the matter should be cleared up one way or the other.

"It was because of memories and the fact that people from the Burma campaign are still alive today. However, I am still slightly stunned the matter should end up in the hands of the DPP."

Mr Heseltine passed Mr Dalyell's letter to Sir Michael Havers, the Attorney General, who also received letters of complaint about Mr Fitzpatrick's confession from members of the public. The file in turn was passed to the DPP for a decision.

Mr Fitzpatrick or other officers of the second battalion could not face a court martial because at the time of the alleged killings a rule was in force that an Army officer had to be charged within three years of an offence being committed.

This was later changed under a section of the Army Act 1955 which stated that after the three-year time limit expired the Attorney-General could be sought for permission to hold a court martial.

The Geneva Convention for the protection of war victims states under Article 3: "Persons taking active part hostilities ... shall in all circumstances be treated humanely." It says "violence to life and persons, in particular murder of all kinds, mutilation, cruel treatment and torture" are prohibited.

Colonel Colin Huxley, Colonel of the KOYLI—which became part of the Light Infantry Brigade in 1966—last night could offer no explanation for the alleged massacre and confirmed there was no record of such as incident in the regiment's records.

Col. Huxley said: "All we know of the second battalion is that they were a brave and gallant unit which ended up with less than 100 men after the Burma campaign."

"I do not know Mr Fitzpatrick. He has never joined us in any events, as far as I know, and he has never dined with us."

The Scotland Yard investigation is believe to be only the second of its kind. In 1970 Sir Norman Skelhorn, then Director of Public Prosecutions, ordered a police inquiry into the alleged massacre of 25 Crinese plantation workers in a Malayan village by men of the Scots Guards.

After receiving a police report, however, Sir Norman decided there was no justification for allowing the inquiries to continue. In his opinion there was no prospect of evidence that could lead to a successful prosecution.

Sunday Telegraph – Involved senior officer from my regiment

'Burma massacre' officer stands easy amid row

Y. Post 28/4 90

By RICHARD SADLER

THE retired British Army officer at the centre of an international row over the war-time massacre of 27 civilians, refused last night to speak about the affair.

Former Second Lieutenant Gerald Fitzpatrick, who served with the King's Own Yorkshire Light Infantry in Burma, is being sought by the Burmese Criminal Investigation Department over the civilian killings on St George's Day, April 23, 1942.

Mr Fitzpatrick gave the order to shoot villagers at Tuangtha, 50 miles southwest of Mandalay, because of fears that they might betray his unit's position to the advancing Japanese army. The Burmese — 27 fit and active men — knelt in prayer as they were shot. Their bodies were tipped into a dried-up river bed.

The Burmese government has taken up the case after nearly 50 years, citing Mr Fitzpatrick by name, in an apparent attempt to encourage claims of compensation by the victims' relatives.

When traced to his home in Leeds last night and asked to comment Mr Fitzpatrick, 70, said: "This is worth money. Go back and find how much you can pay me. I will have to be paid for this and it will have to be a great deal."

He refused to comment further.

The St George's Day killings have received limited worldwide Press coverage this week after Burmese officials arranged a trip to Tuangtha for journalists, including an Associated Press reporter, to interview a 70-year-old man claiming to be an eye witness.

The Criminal Investigation Department in Rangoon was reported earlier this week to have opened a murder investigation.

The incident was last raised in 1984 when Mr Fitzpatrick gave a detailed description of his part in the killings in his memoirs. A Scotland Yard investigation was ordered and a report sent to the Director of Public Prosecutions but in 1985 the DPP's office said no action was being taken because of insufficient evidence.

In July 1985 Mr Fitzpatrick had given a detailed account of his version of events in 1942 to the *Yorkshire Evening Post*.

He said the Tuangtha villagers would almost certainly have betrayed them to the Japanese.

"We were a couple of hundred yards from the village when the smoke started rising from it — a familiar invitation for the Japanese to attack, so we sealed the place off and went in.

"...We simply couldn't afford to leave them alive. We wanted to survive. Nobody was going to knock my blokes out."

He said he had decided to speak out because "it is a fact of British history and of British accountability that has never been recorded and should be.

"I have never felt remorse. I know I was right. Our preservation was paramount. The battalion was disintegrating by the day. Our sole concern was survival."

He said the battalion had left India for Rangoon 900 strong but only 87 of them returned to India.

A Foreign Office spokesman said: "These allegations of events nearly 50 years ago have surfaced before, the last time in 1984, and were found to be unsubstantiated. We are surprised that they should come up again.

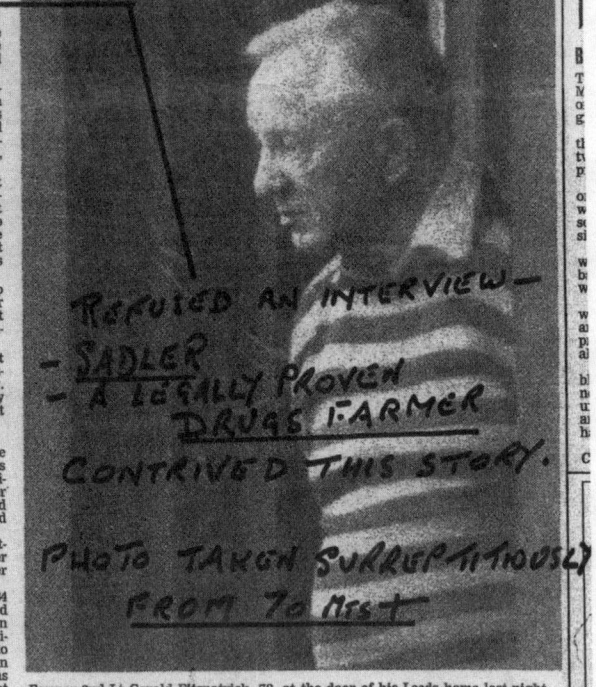

"It would be regrettable if this turns out to be a ploy by the Burmese authorities to deflect attention from the elections to be held next month."

Former 2nd Lt Gerald Fitzpatrick, 70, at the door of his Leeds home last night.

[Handwritten annotations on photo:]
REFUSED AN INTERVIEW —
— SADLER
— A LEGALLY PROVEN
DRUGS FARMER
CONTRIVED THIS STORY.

PHOTO TAKEN SURREPTITIOUSLY
FROM Yo POST

Yorkshire Post – Concocted by Legally proven Drug farmer

348

The Guardian **The Observer** **Guardian**Unlimited

Gerald Fitzpatrick

119 Farringdon Road, London EC1R 3ER
Telephone 020 7278 2332
guardian.co.uk

7 March 2005

Dear Sir,

Compensation Claim

Thank you for your letters dated 9 January and 20 February 2005 addressed to Roger Alton, editor of The Observer, which have been passed to me for a response.

I note the comments you make about your experiences when you served in Burma. I also note that you appear to be complaining about an article that you say appeared in The Observer newspaper on 3 June 1984 and that you consider that it is wholly inaccurate.

I am sure you will appreciate that as it is over 20 years since the publication of the alleged article, it has not been possible for me to investigate your complaint. We do not possess copies of the newspaper edition you refer to, and the article is not published on our website. If you had complained nearer the time, it might have been appropriate to publish a letter in response or to find some other way of resolving your complaint as appropriate. However, if we were to do so now, it would not make any sense to the reader who would be unlikely to remember the story.

In the circumstances, unfortunately, we are not able to progress this matter any further.

Yours faithfully

Jan Johannes

Jan Johannes
In-House Lawyer
jan.johannes@guardian.co.uk
Direct Phone Number 020 7713 4769
Direct Fax Number 020 7713 4481

Legal Department

Rply 8/3/05

Guardian Newspapers Limited
A member of Guardian Media Group PLC
Registered Office
164 Deansgate, Manchester M60 2RR
Telephone 0161 832 7200
Registered in England Number 908396

JJ 110304

Blatant lie by Observer Legal Department – Copy is available.

Page xx   Copy of letter from foster sisters – Dorothy Wilson and Jeanie Lambert

---

Dear Mr. Fitzpatrick,

Thank you for sending my sister, Jeanie, and myself, copies of the report in the Axholme Herald of the very touching reunion at Owston Ferry. How memories flood back, and unfortunately, not all are pleasant ones, although, we were among the fortunate ones to be looked after by the KOYLI regiment.

Our father, John Foster, made many of the K.O.Y.L.I. a warm welcome, at the hotel, and canteen, in Maymyo. He made sure there was always a good meal for all those who came, and had a building in the grounds for use at any time by 'Toc - H', (For meetings, assemblies, or quiet contemplation).

His good name was carried through to India, and the WVS in Dehra Dun approached him about taking over the running of their canteen. It was only held then in a flat, small and cramped. In a short time my father had the colonel of the regiment, stationed there, down to view the place. The outcome was a fine canteen built on the edge of a field, and named 'Auchinlek canteen', where he took over the catering, often serving 100 meals on a Saturday night.

On his post war return to Burma, I took over for some months. No simple task, but I was well guarded, and supported, by several of the officer's wives.

For his service to the army both in Burma and India father was awarded the M.B.E. He always said he had not merited this, as he had always been "A member of the British Empire", since he was born in Leeds in 1873. He did what he enjoyed, and he was an army man at heart.

Thank you for your kind thought, I am sure you must know a fund that helps to support all the work you do. I enclose a cheque for £25, a small appreciation.

Thanking you, best wishes,

Yours sincerely,

Dorothy Wilson. — Jeanie Lambert

D. Wilson (Mrs), and sister, Jeanie Lambert (Mrs)

FATHER – JOHN FOSTER – MBE.

HOTEL and CANTEEN WAS PATRONISED BY ALL RANKS – A VERY HIGH STANDARD

MINISTRY OF DEFENCE
WHITEHALL LONDON SW1A 2HB
Telephone 071-21 82111/2/3

SECRETARY OF STATE

D/S of 5/104/92D

10th June 1992

Dear General Liu,

Mrs Margaret Thatcher has written to me telling me of her meeting with you in New York in April and of your actions, and those of your regiment, in helping to extricate the British 1st Burma Division from encirclement by the Japanese at Yenangyaung in Burma in April 1942.

This year saw the fiftieth anniversary of the battle, which was clearly fought under the most testing and difficult of conditions during the darkest days of the war against the Japanese. May I therefore take this opportunity to express my warmest appreciation for the support you and your Regiment gave to the British Army, despite very considerable casualties.

Sincerely,

Malcolm Rifkind

General Liu Fang-Wu

英國國防部長致函劉將軍感謝五十年前解救仁安羌被圍英軍

MINISTRY OF NATIONAL DEFENSE
P.O. BOX 90001, TAIPEI, TAIWAN
REPUBLIC OF CHINA

May 14, 2013
Captain Gerald Fitzpatrick

Dear Capt. Fitzpatrick,

Thank you for your letter of May 3rd, 2013. Your visit was indeed precious and memorable—to us. Your courage and integrity that we felt so deeply will serve as a fine example for our young generation. Let me also say "Thank you!" for all that you have done to make known a piece of history that bears significance for all the uniformed personnel who served courageously for their countries.

The three requests from you were certainly unexpected, but well received. I will do everything I can in my capacity to help Mrs. Fitzpatrick realize your wish regarding the national flag of the Republic of China (Taiwan) and the attendance by representatives from the ROC Armed Forces. The realization, I believe, will certainly take a long while. As for the matter regarding the Martyrs' Shrine, we will leave it to the necessary consideration of responsible offices.

Thank you again for the gracious presence of you and Mrs. Fitzpatrick in Taiwan. Let me use the opportunity to offer my best wishes to you and Mrs. Fitzpatrick for the best of health and prosperity, as well as a successful quest of your due recognition from your government.

Sincerely,

Kao Hua-chu
Minister

SUPPLEMENT

"FORSEE THE FUTURE BY REVIEWING THE PAST"

(Heading to Fitzpatrick visit magazine – by ROC Army Press Unit)

Writing my 2001 published book, "No Mandalay, No Maymyo", was done with the 'Westerner' generally accepted concept, that the word, 'Chinese', was generic, embracing all. I had no idea of differing nationalities.

In her sending a simple letter, from Washington D.C. a delightful Chinese lady could not have envisaged the absolute joy it was to bestow upon me. I could not get to America soon enough to offer a simple, "Thank you!" I would have been happy to turn around, and return on the same plane, such was the impact.

For the lady to inform me that her father was General Liu Fang-Wu, Commander of the Republic of China Army Expeditionary Force, 113 Regiment, at the Central Burma, Battle of Yenangyaung on 19th April 1942, I was overwhelmed. It was the conflict I witnessed, by my own initiative driven involvement, and described the excellent formation and assault made by the Chinese force in the vital conflict.

Stranded, virtually unarmed, and having been incommunicado from British Command for several days, with a dithering emergency promoted Battalion Commander, my unit, along with many, from a variety of regiments, were virtually impounded within the vast Yenangyaung oilfield. Discarded by a whisky sodden Prime Minister, and starving through lack of provisioning; – regardless of the possible consequences, including execution, I irreversibly and dangerously usurped the weakling CO, in order to successfully conduct a death defying clearance of an enemy held road-block. The words, "I'm with you Fitz", coming from my mate, Victor Stevens, have stayed with me throughout my life. The action cleared the entrance point for the Chinese assault.

Such was the detail I covered in the book, explaining the mode, or pageantry, of the Chinese attack, along with the 'camp followers', it was clear to the Republic of China, Taiwan Government, that only a witness could record with such accuracy.

Ironically, on the basis of my factually written book being the only one to graciously acknowledge, and praise the splendour of the Chinese action, my wife and I were invited, 'as Guests of the Government', to visit Taiwan. Accepting the invite, we made the truly overwhelming visit in March 2013.

If 'proof of the pudding' was wanted, 'Beyond Hypocrisy', of British not accepting the Yenangyaung action, nothing could better illustrate, than the absolute ignorance of William Hague, the British Commonwealth and Foreign Minister. Prior to my wife and me travelling, in two letters to the man, I simply requested detail of the formal government relationship between Britain, and Taiwan. The reply was zilch! Similar lack of enthusiasm was shown to a further two letters sent on our return.

Sunday 24th March – Met at Kings Cross by our great friend, Col. Murphy Chin, and taken to Heathrow to board Taiwan's luxurious Eva Air, flight BR.O68 at 21.20 to Taoyuan Intl. Terminal. Shown to our seats and offered champagne as an appetiser. Staff could not have been more attentive, every need and wish was catered for. From the moment of reception, it was made absolutely clear that we were to be honoured in a regal way that was far beyond our comprehension. The idea of sketching, or photography, was overtaken by a never ending programme of visits, and meetings; – as shown in our copy programme.

Monday 25th March – Received at the airport by David Yu-Pin Lin, Director, International Affairs Division, DCGS and his charming wife, Josie. LTC John Chang, (our escort for the week), conducted us to the exclusive Grand Formosa Regent Hotel, to be welcomed by, Mr. Morton Johnston the General Manager, a delightful Irish-man.

With never a briefing, practice, or rehearsal, simply appropriate dress code, the formalities came naturally. It was only upon receiving photographs, were we aware of the careful background control of David Yu-Pin Lin. We were conveyed throughout our stay, by a sumptuous and well driven double flagged limousine, and escorted by Lt Col John S.C.Chang. At all times, we had the unflagging and overseeing medical follow up, and detailed attention, of Dr. Eric Lin.

Tuesday 26th March – after a little rest, we were taken by Lt Col John S.C. Chang, to visit, Minister for National Defence, Kao, Hua-chu. I presented the Minister with a copy of the book, 'Chinese Save Brits – in Burma', and a photograph taken. The Minister presented the 'Badge of Honour', and Citation. Patricia was given a hand painted silk scarf and pineapple cakes.

Returning to the hotel for lunch, and to prepare for the evening a banquet at the former home, now a restaurant, of Gen. Li-Ren Sun (Army), hosted by the ever smiling, Vice Chief of General Staff (XO), Admiral Chen Yeong-Kang. I presented him with a copy of the book and a photograph, as ever, was taken. The Admiral presented us with a most delightful Chinese Teapot, and Cups, along with a ladies rare coral brooch.

Wednesday 27th March; – A scheduled Conference, with Press and Military photographers, was followed by a prestigious 'Audience', with the Taiwan President, Ma Ying-jeou. A copy of the book was presented, and photographs taken. We were gifted; – a Taiwan WW-2 Medal, amber crystal ornament, Military Books, a watch and a Dragonfly Brooch.

Taken to the Shrine of Martyrs', and honoured by a request to lay a wreath at the magnificent memorial was overwhelming. Having seen the Taj Mahal, daytime and moonlit, as has no other person, and similar world wide monolithic tombs, this gem is up there with all of them. Doctor Student, William Wang presented a Plate picture of the shrine, and a signed picture and, once again, pineapple cakes.

Thursday 28th March – Conveyed in the comfort of High Speed Rail (HSR) to the Air Force Base, the two hundred miles were covered in one hour. The visit to the beautifully decorated memorial chapel in the heart of the base, and the hangers, I almost flew a rather snazzy fighter plane. Lunch was at 427 Wing restaurant after which we were presented with resplendent hats, mugs and coasters. On to General Sun Li-jen house, now a museum, where Patricia was given a rather nice, unusual, note book. Then it was all speed back to the train.

At the resplendent Veterans Affairs Commission, visited on our way back to the hotel, we were assured by Minister Tseng, it was not dependent upon charitable subscriptions. We were shown a video of their excellent work, and its schedule of improvements. The Minister presented me with the "Veterans" badge, a set of coasters, and a crystal paperweight. Patricia was given a rather unusual, but very pleasing necklace.

From the Veterans it was back to hotel to join the Manager, Mr Morton Johnston, for cocktails. He was most interested to know, whatever it was that brought such distinction, as our visit, to his lavish hotel.

That night, a very special dinner held in the hotel, was joined by Robert Liu, the brother of Margaret Sun. With alcohol flowing, and so much of the conversation conducted in Chinese, Maj Gen Ko was certain a good time was enjoyed by all.

7.30 am on the Friday morning, Dr William Wang, overseer at The Martyr's Shrine, visited the hotel, in order to be presented with his copy of, Chinese Save Brits in Burma.

The weather proved foul, with heavy rain and mist, for the first time in the week. This allowed us a couple of hours extra rest, and lunch in the hotel. Then, a visit to the former Prison of War Camp Memorial, situated in the centre of the island. Wet and looking dangerously slippery, I requested not to walk and Patricia was invited to lay a wreath.

Dinner that night was truly remarkable, to be joined most unexpectedly by the Minister for National Defence, Kao, Hua-chu, and heads of Military Services. With six sat around the table, Kao invited me to sing for them; – rendering the RE Sapper song, – "Good morning Mr Stevens, it's a knitty-knotty night. Hurrah for the CRE!" Incredible seriousness followed, as the Minister asked for my three expressed wishes. It was never easy to put forward the words: – In the event of my death, I requested an escort of Chinese troops at my funeral, – (they had saved me in war). There was further instant approval to my request for the Republic of China flag, but to be honoured with my being mentioned at some point on the Martyr's Shrine, had to be left in abeyance. I know that it will comfort me, and

Patricia, knowing that I was about to make those requests, bestowed her approval.

Saturday 30th March – Visited the fabulously resplendent Palace Museum, and viewed the magnificent exhibits; – one eggcup sized piece was valued at $2M, 'two million dollars'. Lunch was taken in the Palace Dining Rooms. It was on to the Stillwell Exhibition. David presented a magnificent album of photographs.

Sunday 31st March – 7.00 am we departed the hotel, seen off by friendly General Manager, Mr Morton Johnston, and travelled to the airport. Here, David presented the magnificently prepared Army News Unit magazine, containing the numerous photographs of our every movement throughout the week of glory.

There was no end to the delight, and surprise, as we were presented with photographs of the grandiose memorial monument, to the Republic of China Army It was recently erected by the family of General Liu Fang-Wu, at the site of his Burma command: – The 1942, Battle of Yenangyaung. Although unable to attend the dedication ceremony, I have the eternal pleasure of knowing that my name and words are etched in the base: -

CITATION on MEMORIAL at YENANGYAUNG

"From the vantage point of the stone building on the small hillock, it was a relief to witness the Chinese assault. It was spectacular, and efficient beyond belief, absolutely suited for the rough terrain of the oilfield. I had a panoramic view of the whole disposition and action as the Chinese set to the task. To Western eyes, the disciplined automation was astonishing.

All hell broke loose as the Chinese troops swarmed forward. The movement was like poetry, or a form of pageantry, with these highly disciplined troops.

As the noise of firing on the oilfield became more distant, there was a realization; the Japanese might be the ones in danger of; – "Being annihilated at the oilfield in Central Burma", contrary to the threat made by Tokio Rose from Radio Saigon, eight days earlier.

As the Chinese began to suffer casualties, Victor Stevens and I set up a reception point in the stone building, and did what we could to treat and dress the wounds of the soldiers, returning with holes in arms, legs and bodies. I did not speak Chinese, and the Chinese did not speak English. Victor Stevens ripped bedding sheets to bandage the wounded Chinese soldiers. Although I was only twenty-two years of age, I thought the Chinese soldiers to be very young; they had the ethereal look of good porcelain.

The Chinese troops came in, did their job and got out. The British at the time were desperately short on food and water, short on ammunition, short on medical supplies, and stricken with malaria, and other diseases. I was the sole British officer, along with my men, privileged to observe this rare spectacle; it was basic, primitive and functional, the perfect fighting machine for the conditions of Central Burma. Indeed, I was a privileged officer.

This salutary action was undertaken on 19th April. The damage done by the Chinese forces in this action destroyed the Japanese, to such extent that their rapid advance through Burma was halted, whilst awaiting reinforcements. Delaying the Japanese from their superbly planned advance was such that it became the single most action in allowing the remnants of the dishevelled and starving British Army to escape northwards.

At age 93, I tend to do things quickly. We were able to make arrangements for our visit to the U.S.A. on September 16, 2012. I told Margaret and her brother, Bob Liu, at the airport when we first met, that I could not wait another minute for this visit. After meeting the son and daughter of the late General Liu Fang-Wu, I can tell you I am SO satisfied with this visit! It nearly hurts to recall Yenangyaung, but recall I do".

Captain Gerald Fitzpatrick
Yorkshire King's Own Light Infantry GSO III (Operations) H.Q. – BAOR
Survivor of the Battle of Yenangyaung in 1942
Author of; – CHINESE SAVE BRITS – in BURMA.

BRITAINS – CORRUPT, FECKLESS, UNPRINCIPLED PARIAMENT

Possibly, Prime Minister Tony Blair, sucking up to USA President Bush, and seeking mystical 'Weapons of Mass Destruction', when there were none, in a country almost unheard of in the West, motivated the twenty-first century of Parliamentarian 'fiddlers'. None can be in doubt, when numbers are caught; and several imprisoned, or barred; – for over-claiming on expenses, false charging for accommodation, garden ornaments. Peers of the Realm, 'hawking themselves', lobbying for cash, on behalf of strange lands, and resign their seats when caught. This is the damnable country in which I live, and attempt to obtain justice for action taken in a war seventy years ago.

I met with a contrast: – To be hailed "Hero", and justifiably honoured for well proven courage, and showered with more than fifty carefully thought out gifts over the week in Taiwan, was beyond Patricia and my comprehension. There was something in the regard, and way of our reception, at every point throughout the visit, that simply does not happen in Britain. The regard continued; – On returning to Britain, our friend, Col Murphy Chin received us at the airport in order to ensure safe passage. Within two or three days following our homecoming there came three parcels, rather large square ones, containing the variety of more than fifty carefully considered gifts. They range from; military decorations, copies of relevant newspapers, to tea, books, porcelain, pictures, and more exotic Chinese sculpting.

Detailing so accurately the operation of the Chinese force, saviour of the impoverished British, in my book; – 'No Mandalay, No Maymyo', had obviously, been carefully scrutinised for detail before acceptance. Of course, I would have loved to attribute the magnificent operation to a British force, but it was not to be: – I tell it as it was!

It is not possible to adequately describe the ironical timing, for receipt of the invite to attend a meeting, in a room within the Houses of Parliament, on Monday 13th May 2013. It was so soon following my returning from Taiwan. How could I refuse?

A peacetime British Army, Second Lieutenant, was usually, one unsuited for classical employment, and joined-up, as a last resort; into the Army, or going into, 'The Church'? I knew that I was different; – roughing it through poverty, a trained boxer, worldly wise, and successful bare knuckle street fighter, meant that I was not going to be overawed, under any circumstances. Undergoing an intensive pre-war Engineering apprenticeship, with real men, along with my sporting physique, had me thinking and acting in a completely different manner to the galaxy of browbeaten, and subservient, 'Army regular' subalterns.

Virtually reneging, as was my wish, from joining with the very active Irish Republic Army; – Within six weeks of the outbreak of WW-2, I joined the British Army; reluctantly accepting subservience in the manner appropriate for a new recruit. When it became a matter of my life being at stake, there was no way that I was going to tolerate the stilted and feeble conduct of a jumped up peace-time lackey, now a dithering Commander. Usurping the man, knowing that there could be no reversal, and execution could be the outcome, I successfully took matters into my own hands.

For seventy years, the four beautiful words, "I'm with you Fitz", uttered in his soft spoken voice, by 'Steve', my trustworthy friend, Victor Stevens, have been precious to me. It is such that, throughout the recent Taiwan visit, his name and the words were repeated at every appropriate juncture.

The galling thing is to find that the British Government steadfastly refuse to acknowledge the vital battle, and its involvement of Chinese troops. I find it deplorable, having given more than nine years of my youth, serving an ungrateful nation. I am frozen out of records. A series of letters to the Queen, successive Prime Ministers, and Ministers of Defence, are ignored, as though my name might appear spurned on some device: – Possibly, a name-proscription machine?- How many servicemen have heard of the 'MOD, Corporate Memory Analysis', or the 'MOD, Asia Pacific Directorate', from whom I occasionally receive, bilge, evasive replies.

My communications are repulsed, probably because of the distorted version of my meeting with Editors, Donald Threlfall, and Anthony Howard, and published on 3rd June, 1984, by 'The Observer', a considered reputable newspaper. Oh yes! I did go further; – Commanding the execution of twenty seven recalcitrant, and hostile oilfield workers, on 23rd April, St George's Day! (His niece tells me that my Corporal, 'Gigger' Lee, was shot in the bum by them). Whilst continuing to usurp Command, (there is no going back), and only four days following the 19th April, oilfield battle; –

PM Margaret Thatcher, in 1984, set Scotland Yard, Serious Crime Squad, pursuing my guts for revealing action taken by me, in Burma, in April 1942; – This, in association with that of a Chinese force. Without revealing the Scotland Yard findings, all further reference, and my correspondence, was immediately proscribed. It was 'force meat' that got the woman, belatedly, through her Defence Minister, Malcolm Rifkind, on 10th June 1992, to mildly acknowledge the action; – see it!

I was not going to miss out, when invited to attend a meeting, – entitled, 'Steering through a sea of change', held in a dining room of the Houses of Parliament, on behalf of, 'the Taipei Office in London', on Monday, 13th May 2013. With a full house of approximately two hundred specially invited guests, and preceding the business of the meeting, I was introduced to all present, by the Chairman. It was a bit unexpected, to be referred to, as "Hero", particularly in this country, and within the, 'Parliamentary den of iniquity'. Invited to reply, I was not going to miss my opportunity.

Once again, I complimented the Republic of China, Army Expeditionary Force, in their saving of the British, and virtually all others restrained, as within the confines of a pound, at Yenangyaung, the Central Burma oilfield, on 19th April 1942. I and my small diminishing group, were the modest British contribution to the successful outcome. How could I then ignore the glaring opportunity to call attention to the insulting indifference, shown to me by Hague, the Parliamentary Minister for Commonwealth and Foreign Affairs?

Here, in front of many, and in spite of the Hague indifference, I was being hailed, – "Hero!"

Inundated by numerous representatives at the close of the meeting, I dealt with questions from diverse quarters, including an expressed and most insistent call, being virtually a demand, by Elaina Cohen, from the office of Khalid Mahmood MP, for me to meet with a number of select parliamentarians; – "in the very near future". To date, 1st June, there is no call. An acolyte in the Foreign Office, Andrew Rosindell MP, asked naively, as though in shock, "Did I mean William Hague?" I assured him, it was no other, and added a little extra, simply for the hell of it. At this juncture, as though a monkey jumping on Rosindell's shoulder, Press and Publicity man, Sandy Tanner intervened. He was to pursue the matter of his master's firm reluctance and indifference. Nothing from Tanner!

The rather shaky, Lord Lyndon Harrison, of Chester, spluttered few slurred words as possible, although making clear that he did not appreciate my, 'tone of indifference', over a Foreign Office favourite. He appeared to place any perusal of the subject onto Tanner. Nothing from Tanner, to date!

It is clear that, raising any questions regarding Churchill, particularly 'with' Hague, will be frozen out: – See enclosed the underwhelming, and reluctant, out of time, unapologetic epistle, dated 10th June 1992, to General Liu Fang-Wu, by Defence Minister, Malcolm Rifkin. In this, as appropriate and of convenience in the immediate circumstances, the man kowtows on behalf of PM Thatcher. British Commander, Alexander, in his Memoirs VII, denies action by Chinese forces, and had no interest in where I, and my long discarded unit, was operating.

In concluding this book, 1st June 2013, aged almost 94, (Ninety four), I am so proud to have had an Irish mother. It has taken many years to appreciate the vital difference, and to know that it runs through my bones. That in no way belittles the friends and colleagues, known to me over the years. Every man has a level!

COLOUR SUPPLEMENT

Foresee the Future by Reviewing the Past.
Photos of Fitzpatrick, the retired British Army Captain visiting to ROC.

費茲派翠克在高鐵車站大廳合影留念；在旅程中，費茲派翠克巧扮鬼臉，調皮地逗旁人發笑，成為列車中的開心果。

Patricia and Gerald with accompanying party

Foresee the Future by Reviewing the Past.
Photos of Fitzpatrick, the retired British Army Captain visiting to ROC.

費茲派翠克與馬總統及英國貿易文化辦事處代表胡克定（Chris Wood）、國防部長高華柱、參謀總長嚴明上將及國家安全會議諮詢委員甘逸驊等人合影留念。

Patricia and Gerald with Chinese Army Veteran,
his wife and Granddaughter.
Honoured by President, Defence Minister and Senior Militaria

贈勳表達謝意　馬總統致贈費茲派翠克紀念勳章，感謝其盡心捍衛歷史。

G. Fitzpatrick, President Ma Ying-jeou, presents a medal 'In Commemoration of Victory of the Resistance against Japanese Aggression'

鑑往知來
英退役上尉費茲派翠克訪華照片輯錄

致力宣揚國軍貢獻

馬總統在英國貿易文化辦事處代表胡克定（Chris Wood）、國防部部長高華柱、參謀總長嚴明上將及國家安全會議諮詢委員甘逸驊等人陪同下，接見長期宣揚中華民國戰史的英國退役陸軍上尉費茲派翠克；舉手投足皆展露出對我國的感謝與敬意。

G. Fitzpatrick, Audience with President Ma Ying-Jeou

致贈紀念勳章

高華柱部長致贈國防部紀念勳章、證書給費茲派翠克,肯定他對國軍的支持。

G. Fitzpatrick, Defence Minister, Chen, Kuo-Hua presents 'The Badge of Honour'

Representative Lyushun Shen Ph.D Taipei Office, UK, G. Fitzpatrick

Veterans Affairs Commission Welcome Board

*Doctor William Wang, Mrs P. Fitzpatrick, G. Fitzpatrick
depart Martyrs' Shrine*

過程中，由海軍儀隊官兵擔任的裏儀在西式儀程下，手持花圈引導費茲派翠克從山門緩步邁入大殿，費茲派翠克並以舉手禮向烈士致敬，隨後以片段「與記憶中的戰場實況完全相同」，不須透過翻譯也能馬上了解，並對忠烈祠的細心安排，與國軍重視歷史的考究留下深刻印象。

費茲派翠克伉儷，與忠烈祠英挺的儀隊官兵合影。

ROC Army Guards, Mrs P. Fitzpatrick, G. Fitzpatrick at Martyrs' Shrine

Memorial at Yenangyoung Battle site, Burma

高部長與費茲派翠克握手道別，談笑模樣好似相識多年的摯友。

Defence Minister Chen Kuo-Hua, G. Fitzpatrick

MINISTRY OF NATIONAL DEFENSE
P.O. BOX 90001, TAIPEI, TAIWAN
REPUBLIC OF CHINA

May 14, 2013

Captain Gerald Fitzpatrick

Dear Capt. Fitzpatrick,

Thank you for your letter of May 3rd, 2013. Your visit was indeed precious and memorable—to us. Your courage and integrity that we felt so deeply will serve as a fine example for our young generation. Let me also say "Thank you!" for all that you have done to make known a piece of history that bears significance for all the uniformed personnel who served courageously for their countries.

The three requests from you were certainly unexpected, but well received. I will do everything I can in my capacity to help Mrs. Fitzpatrick realize your wish regarding the national flag of the Republic of China (Taiwan) and the attendance by representatives from the ROC Armed Forces. The realization, I believe, will certainly take a long while. As for the matter regarding the Martyrs' Shrine, we will leave it to the necessary consideration of responsible offices.

Thank you again for the gracious presence of you and Mrs. Fitzpatrick in Taiwan. Let me use the opportunity to offer my best wishes to you and Mrs. Fitzpatrick for the best of health and prosperity, as well as a successful quest of your due recognition from your government.

Sincerely,

Kao Hua-chu
Minister